D1626407

# Professional and Practice-based Learning

Volume 2

For further volumes:
http://www.springer.com/series/8383

Series Editors:

Stephen Billett, Griffith University, Australia
Christian Harteis, University of Regensburg, Germany
Hans Gruber, University of Regensburg, Germany

*Professional and practice-based learning* brings together international research on the individual development of professionals and the organisation of professional life and educational experiences. It complements the Springer journal *Vocations and Learning: Studies in vocational and professional education.*

Professional learning, and the practice-based processes that often support it, are the subject of increased interest and attention in the fields of educational, psychological, sociological, and business management research, and also by governments, employer organisations and unions. This professional learning goes beyond, what is often termed professional education, as it includes learning processes and experiences outside of educational institutions in both the initial and ongoing learning for the professional practice. Changes in these workplaces requirements usually manifest themselves in the everyday work tasks, professional development provisions in educational institution decrease in their salience, and learning and development during professional activities increase in their salience.

There are a range of scientific challenges and important focuses within the field of professional learning. These include:

- understanding and making explicit the complex and massive knowledge that is required for professional practice and identifying ways in which this knowledge can best be initially learnt and developed further throughout professional life.
- analytical explications of those processes that support learning at an individual and an organisational level.
- understanding how learning experiences and educational processes might best be aligned or integrated to support professional learning.

The series integrates research from different disciplines: education, sociology, psychology, amongst others. The series is comprehensive in scope as it not only focusses on professional learning of teachers and those in schools, colleges and universities, but all professional development within organisations.

Ann Webster-Wright

# Authentic Professional Learning

Making a Difference Through Learning
at Work

 Springer

Dr. Ann Webster-Wright
University of Queensland
Teaching & Educational
    Development Institute
4072 Brisbane Queensland
Australia
a.websterwright@uq.edu.au

ISBN 978-90-481-3946-0          e-ISBN 978-90-481-3947-7
DOI 10.1007/978-90-481-3947-7
Springer Dordrecht Heidelberg London New York

Library of Congress Control Number: 2010931444

Printed on acid-free paper

Springer is part of Springer Science+Business Media (www.springer.com)

# Series Editors' Foreword

There is considerable and growing interest in professionals learning across their working lives. The growth in this interest is likely premised upon the increasing percentage of those who are being employed under the designation as professionals or para-professional workers in advanced industrial economies. Part of being designated in this way is a requirement to be able to work autonomously and in a relatively self-regulated manner. Of course, many other kinds of employment also demand such behaviours. However, there is particular attention being given to the ongoing development of workers who are seen to make crucial decisions and take actions about health, legal and financial matters. Part of this attention derives from expectations within the community that those who are granted relative autonomy and are often paid handsomely should be current and informed in their decision-making. Then, like all other workers, professionals are required to maintain their competence in the face of changing requirements for work. Consequently, a volume that seeks to inform how best this ongoing learning can be understood, supported and assisted is most timely and welcomed.

This volume seeks to elaborate professional learning through a consideration of the concept of authentic professional learning. What is proposed here is that, in contrast to programmatic approaches towards professional development, the process of continuing professional learning is a personal, complex and diverse process that does not lend itself to easy prescription or the realisation of others' intents. Instead, a phenomenological approach is adopted here that emphasises the importance of personal experience and intentionality as the key premise for professionals' ongoing learning. The author makes the point that, while seeking to capture this learning through advancing the concept of authentic professional learning, it is important to understand it as a personal phenomenon and not to lose its unique diversity and complexity for each individual.

Not surprisingly, the methodological orientation adopted here is one of phenomenology (i.e. the study of experience). Consistent with this orientation is a strong focus on learning, rather than the provision of courses and developmental strategies. Instead, the pedagogic emphasis is on professional learning as a self-directed activity and not only in terms of activity-directed towards achieving what others wish to be achieved. The emphasis here is on what each individual wishes to achieve, hence, the interest in intentionality. Such an orientation is argued for throughout this book. The emphasis is on respecting the diversity of meaning and highlights agency and capability in self-directed approaches to learning. Consequently, here pedagogic qualities are those enacted and directed by the learner. Epistemology, here, focuses strongly on the set of beliefs and interests which individuals exercise in their learning. The theorising draws upon seminal contributions from phenomenology, yet these contributions are supported and augmented by those from a range of other disciplines.

Consistent with the key orientation, however, and throughout, the author emphasises that professional learning cannot be mandated, coerced and controlled by others, but can be effectively supported, assisted and guided. This orientation is supported by empirical work, which concluded that professionals learn in situations that are important for them. These situations are usually areas they care enough about to engage with effortfully and with intentionality, yet, at the same time, experience uncertainty and doubt. The author proposes that learning in such situations involves complex interconnections with previous experiences, of themselves and others, and leads through transitions involving novel features to a change in professional understanding. Such learning follows a circuitous trajectory, being open to many possibilities in the path that is taken, so that it is not easily amenable to outside control.

It is proposed in this book that there is a need to understand professional learning from the perspective of the professionals themselves and through a consideration of the context of everyday professional practice in which they think, act and learn. Moreover, by using such a theoretical framework to conceptualise professional learning as being something that is personally constructed and becomes embedded within the lived experience of being a practising professional, this book does more than merely challenge the traditional way of conceptualising professional development. It also offers bases for reshaping efforts to secure all ongoing professional learning in ways centred on the learners themselves.

Brisbane, Australia                                              Stephen Billett
Regensburg, Germany                                               Hans Gruber
Regensburg, Germany                                         Christian Harteis
January 2010

# Preface

Professional learning has been eclipsed for many years by the rise of mandatory continuing education. As part of a discourse of justification and audit, many professions have instituted systematic programmes for registration or awarding continuing status for their members. These systems, that typically involve the collection of credit points or hours, have dominated discussion of professionals learning. In the process they have taken a complex process, over-simplified it and packaged it as a consumer product. While this may be effective in managing accountability and in exposing some less-committed members of the professions to current knowledge and practice, it is not necessarily good at promoting responsible continuing professional learning that will enhance the quality of practice.

One of the reasons for this is that there has been a rollout of programmes and measures without concomitant research that helps us understand how professionals learn independently of the goading of continuing professional education systems. A deep appreciation of how professionals view their continuing development and what they do when they learn professionally is needed if practice is to be improved.

Ann Webster-Wright is one of a small number of researchers seeking this understanding and conducting research that illuminates the development of professional practice after registration. This excellent book portrays the professional learning that a group of practitioners undertakes for themselves. It attends in a vivid way to what they do and what is important for them in their daily professional practices and through this explores implications for continuing professional development.

It uses a phenomenology of the experience of a group of professionals learning in their current working context to argue for a paradigmatic shift in the conceptualisation of continuing professional learning. The study has major implications for how professional education is regarded and how it needs to move beyond the assumption that learning can be equated with participation in certain kinds of programs.

The author takes the phenomenology as an empirical grounding for a thoughtful discussion of both practical considerations and philosophical issues. These range from the dissonance between the reality of professionals' experiences of learning and the rhetoric of stakeholders expectations of professional development to the question of what 'being a professional' means. She argues for a paradigm shift in professional education, sketches a framework of what she terms 'authentic professional learning' and discusses how it might be supported.

This book is a pioneering example of the kind of studies that are needed to further understanding of professional practice and how it can be improved. It focuses on what practitioners can do to act together for themselves. It applies the notion of being professional to the core of practice: learning from what one does.

Professor of Adult Education                                                      David Boud
University of Technology, Sydney, Australia
January, 2010

# Acknowledgements

There are many people who have supported me in different ways through the undertaking of this research and writing of this book. I am grateful to the professionals who shared their experiences with me, openly acknowledging the dilemmas and delights of their professional practices. I am particularly indebted to Gloria Dall'Alba and Merrilyn Goos, at the University of Queensland, without whose encouragement and support this book, and the original research that informs it, may not have occurred. I deeply value the influence of multiple colleagues, too numerous to mention individually, whose ideas and experiences, shared through conversations and read in books, shaped and continue to inspire my learning and my life. Finally, but not least, I am eternally thankful for the ongoing love and support of my partner and children.

# Contents

# List of Figure & Tables

## Figure

## Tables

# Part I
# Introduction

How do professionals keep learning through their working lives? This book draws on learning experiences from practicing professionals to understand more about the realities of such learning. Phenomenological analysis of data from diverse experiences of learning revealed commonalities that have been developed into a framework of "Authentic Professional Learning". Drawing on this framework, an argument is made in this book for reframing professional development: shifting from a focus on delivery of content, to support for professionals as they inquire into and adapt their practices in the contemporary workplace.

This book is structured into five parts and nine chapters. A single page introduces each part, describing the content of chapters within. Part I, "Introduction", consists of one chapter, "Professional Learning at Work," where the complexity and diversity of professional learning, need for re-conceptualisation of professional development and value of researching the experience of professionals as they learn at work are introduced. Part II, "Exploration", consists of three chapters that review literature relevant to professional development and learning, introduces key concepts used within this phenomenological perspective and outlines the research methodology. Part III, "Understanding", contains the book's pivotal chapter "Authentic Professional Learning", describing the commonality and variability across diverse learning experiences and the phenomenological "structure" of learning, with descriptions of practice and ways of being a professional. In Part IV, "Integration", three chapters integrate the empirical findings in the light of phenomenological philosophy and other empirical research, to examine dissonance and authenticity in professional life and implications for stakeholders in supporting learning. Part V, "Conclusion", consists of the final chapter, summarising the research and future possibilities for "Making a Difference" to professional learning. The potential impact of such changes on problems in contemporary society is discussed.

The book is structured with all parts interlinked, yet readers with differing needs can focus on particular parts. Thus those new to the area and method of research could pay particular attention to Part II. Workplace educators or those with a particular focus on the experiences of learning may focus on Part III. Educational philosophers, researchers and policy makers may find Part IV of particular interest. Although the focus of the research is on the learning of health professionals, the book draws on research from a range of other professions. This book aims to contribute to an ongoing dialogue about how professionals can be supported in ways that are sustaining for them as individuals as well as lead to worthwhile and sustainable outcomes for society.

# Chapter 1
# Professional Learning at Work

Okay you might laugh at this one but I'll tell you anyway. I didn't used to know how to chew gum, and I've just learnt. On my lunch break one day, I was sitting at my desk and I had some gum in my mouth. One of my clients who lives here happened to be wandering around and I said, "Hey come in and sit down," and he sat down by my desk. He uses one or two words, so you can have a conversation with him. So I'm reading and talking to him and was also trying to chew gum at the time. I went to blow a bubble, and it fell out of my mouth. I just glanced up at him because I was really embarrassed, and he burst out laughing and laughed so much that tears started pouring down his face. This is a client who laughs a lot when other people are laughing but you can tell it's just a "Heh heh I'm laughing 'cause everyone's laughing, I don't know what's funny". Whereas this was a genuine "that was really funny" and it was a real, shared experience. I saw him and his abilities in a different way after that (Nerida).

I went to a course and they mentioned about the advantages of a technique, and I thought who would I try it on in therapy? My supervisor wanted me to present my results at a seminar, but when the time came I didn't have any real results. I had tried it on a nine year old who was very unco-operative. It was terribly difficult and frustrating as I had no response at all. I could only talk about what not to do rather than what to do, and I felt I couldn't present that. So I changed my attack. I decided that as I couldn't give a presentation on my results I would do a literature review instead. I find that's a good way to learn, when you've actually got to present it, because you've got to be very clear and logical. You have to really know it. Doing the literature review helped me change my direction. Since then I've had some good results with other clients, because I'd studied the information in a bit more detail and had to present it in a logical way. When I next went back to the same boy I could put all of this together, so I had a different approach which worked (Sally).

As this book is based on research into real-life experiences, it opens with the voices of professionals describing situations where they have learnt. The first description was given by a young therapist, Nerida[1] who works full time at a residential setting for adults with intellectual disability. Nerida commented that she often learns as a professional in seemingly incidental situations, with such incidents building upon each other. From the "gum" incident, she described not only learning more about her client but also learning more about communicating with adults with intellectual disability. The second description is from Sally, an experienced therapist, who works part time in a rural community-based setting with children with multiple disabilities. Sally commented that she loves learning but is anxious about never knowing enough. In the situation described she was worried about presenting a technique to her colleagues. She described how she learnt from her preparation for the seminar as well as from applying what she learnt to clients at work.

In both situations, Nerida and Sally describe having learnt as professionals, but these descriptions differ in many ways beyond their being planned or incidental in nature. The reasons for such differences are complex, related to the professionals themselves, their past experiences, how they understand learning and the varied situations in which they practice every day. To give a glimpse of one such working context, the following vignette describes an average morning at work for two other professionals who lent their voices to this book.

## 1.1  A Morning at Work

Gina and Paula are therapists who work with children with disabilities, as part of a community-based multidisciplinary team. I am watching as preparations are made for the day ahead. The two rooms where the therapists work are spacious, open and light, with a variety of colourful toys and equipment set out. The rooms look similar. The programme in each is similar, beginning with group time and moving to individual activities. These activities are designed to engage the children in play whilst facilitating therapeutic goals that are carefully planned by the team. It is not until the children arrive that a significant difference is noted between the rooms.

In Gina's room there is a flurry of activity. All four staff, teachers and therapists, are relaxed yet focused. They talk amongst themselves as they prepare, with several conversation threads going at once. *Remember last time we tried . . . it didn't work as well. Why don't we do . . . ? What do you think if we . . . ? I'll set up the video today to get some of the action . . . what position will we use for that? His mum said . . . last time. Why don't we try . . . ?*[2]

At 9.30 the children straggle in with siblings and parents. As they come, each is warmly greeted with a discussion about significant events in that family's life over the past week. After the group activity each child is directed towards some particular game or task. The atmosphere is busy but not rushed. Gina spends considerable time

---

[1] Names are pseudonyms, with details about the professional practice altered if these contain potentially identifiable information.

[2] Words in italics are those spoken by participants of the research. Quotes from other sources are in normal text enclosed by quotation marks.

watching different children; moving to alter a pillow slightly or address a comment to a child, parent or staff member. People come and go: a father goes outside to smoke, one therapist leaves to measure equipment and a teacher aide comes in to borrow a digital camera for a birthday in the other room. Gina continues to watch and react. She quietly verbalises aloud as if to herself: *I don't know whether to let him try that or not. I wonder if I should do. . ..* She seems to be thinking through and weighing up options, often discussing these with others, then noting the impact of any changes she introduces.

In Paula's room there are fewer adults as there are no parents present. The children are slightly older, but the same types of activities are in place. There is limited talking between staff, little questioning about what to do and what works and few verbal exchanges overall. Paula is the only adult talking as she quietly engages with a child. Children are interacting with activities but there is an apparent disengagement on the part of the staff from each other and from what they are doing. There is a sense in their actions and expressions of "I wish I wasn't here". It's as if they are acting out of habit: just getting through the morning.

There is a distinctly different atmosphere between the two rooms. The physical environments and planned programmes are almost identical, but the "energy" in the rooms is in stark contrast. The difference in these two working contexts seems related to the human interactions rather than to anything physical, yet the result has a physical overtone to it. It is quieter in the second room. The air seems more still and heavy. There seems to be less happening. Both Gina and Paula had told me in earlier interviews that they learn at work. As I write up my observations about the morning, I am aware that the differences I noticed would impact on the professional learning of the two therapists, but in what way?

When I later talk to Gina and Paula separately about their mornings, I'm struck by the different nature of our conversations. Gina is still engaged. She talks brightly about *how much she learns from the children.* Her curiosity and imagination effervesce through our discussion on learning. She says she *loves this work,* that it's *always changing* and that she *loves exploring new ideas.* Paula, on the other hand, answers my questions in a matter-of-fact manner. She says the morning was *a bit depressing* but she doesn't know what to do about it. She wonders if she should attend some professional development activity as she's *run out of ideas* about this area and knows she should *keep more up-to-date* with *what's new* to help inject some enthusiasm. Later interviews and analyses revealed further differences in the way that Gina and Paula experienced learning, but at the time of collecting these data, differences were already tangible yet elusive.

## 1.2 Intent of This Book

In the beginning of this book I introduce the notion of continuing professional learning (PL) as complex and diverse. As can be seen from the experiences described so far, even when professionals work at the same workplace, their experiences of PL differ. Amongst the professionals described through this book, learning is experienced in varying ways. A key question directing this book is: How can widely varying experiences of PL be investigated and understood in a way that does not remove the experiences from their context, nor strip them of their diversity and complexity? More crucially, why is this important? In what way can a better understanding of continuing PL help support professionals in their learning and enhance professional practice?

Learning as a practicing professional can be viewed as both straightforward and complex. It is straightforward in the sense that all practitioners keep learning in some way. Professionals talk about how they learn from their clients, from what works and what doesn't, from watching and working with their colleagues and often from broader experiences in their non-working lives. Most professionals working in the "caring" professions, and this includes health, education and social services, want to continue to grow as people and professionals because of their commitment to "making a difference" to the lives of those they care for, whether they be patients, students or clients. Yet the strong focus on continuing professional development (PD) in today's practice, on keeping up to date and accruing PD points by attending workshops, often seems out of touch with the complexities of the everyday reality of learning at work; the uncertainty and doubt, breakthroughs and satisfactions, of working together to make a difference to people's lives.

This book listens to the voices of practitioners, drawing on vignettes of learning garnered from working practice. These descriptions form the basis of empirical phenomenological research that attempts to understand PL as a living experience. I use the term "authentic" PL to refer to PL as it is lived, in and through practice, with others over time. My research found a troubling dissonance between what really happens as professionals learn at work and the customary rhetoric from workplaces, professional associations and universities about PD. In clarifying such dissonance, this book builds on research into professionals' experiences to propose realistic strategies for enhancing support for professionals to continue learning in ways that make sense to them as individuals, whilst contributing to an enhancement of their shared practice. Using phenomenology (the study of experience), as both a rigorous methodology and coherent theoretical framework, philosophical insights from epistemology (the study of knowledge), ontology (the study of reality) and axiology (the study of values) are drawn upon to address issues of professional practice – to do with who professionals are and what they value, what they know and how they act and how they learn and find meaning through their work.

Research into the learning of professionals has become a truly interdisciplinary enterprise that can profitably draw on the literature from a number of related research areas, such as professional education (undergraduate and continuing education), workplace learning (informal learning, communities of practice), adult and community education (transformative and emancipatory learning) and organisational learning (human resource management and training and development). In addition, there is value in research that examines the learning of different professional groups, comparing commonalities and differences, although little currently exists (see Daley, 2001; Eraut, 2007). This book draws on research from various professional groups across a wide range of educational inquiry that is relevant to PL.

In my first study, a cohort of 16 allied health professionals (occupational therapists, physiotherapists and speech pathologists) was investigated. They worked in different organisations and workplaces, but all worked in community settings with children or adults with a chronic illness or disability. This original research has been validated and extended with other professionals in varying contexts, predominantly those in the caring or human services professions. An argument could be made that all professionals "care" about the service they provide and that all such services ultimately affect human beings. This book also draws on research into learning from other professions, such as engineering or law. Current research is continuing into the learning of academics and other mixed professional cohorts with a focus on frameworks of support. Although both the original and extended research are referred to in this book, vignettes of practice focus on the original cohort. Qualitative research findings are not generalisable, being context bound. Because phenomeno-logical research highlights features that are common across diverse experiences of the same phenomenon (in this case continuing PL), the research findings may have applicability beyond the original context.

Because the continuing learning of professionals is of vital interest to multiple stakeholders, research in this area is growing. This book offers a fresh perspective on continuing PL as an alternative way of conceptualising PD. Through understanding authentic PL and developing congruent support strategies, the intent of this book is to challenge conceptualisations underlying the *delivery* of traditional PD activities to professionals, arguing for a shift in focus towards *supporting* them as they engage in self-directed PL. As an approach that focuses on the perspective of professionals and takes account of real-life experiences in their multifarious and entangled partic-ularity, the nuances of working life can be explored in relation to learning. Concrete issues such as time schedules and workloads, the way that a workplace supports collaboration or stifles difference, tensions or doubt related to change and the need to interact with messy issues of humanity whilst producing tangible, measurable outcomes of practice can all be examined.

This book will be of interest to a range of stakeholders in PL, such as educa-tional researchers, academic teachers, workplace learning facilitators and human resource managers. As a book that explicates the realities and uncertainties of professional practice and continuing learning, it could be useful for professional undergraduates. The book also highlights the value of a phenomenological approach to understanding lived experience for researchers investigating PL and practice across a range of professions. Doctoral students and early career researchers will find details about methodological choices, sometimes glossed over in phe-nomenological research. Similarly, some practice implications of phenomenological philosophy, often difficult to locate amongst dense texts, are described for those new to phenomenology.

## 1.3  Research Basis

The genesis of this research came from my experiences, over a number of decades, as an allied health practitioner, professional supervisor, workplace learning facilitator, academic educator and educational researcher. I became increasingly aware of changes in the workplace; in particular, altered and varying expectations about professional practice with an increasing focus on evidence, standards and outcomes. There was also a generally held perception by professionals that their work had intensified, with increasing and competing pressures on their time. Together, these changes in working life seemed to raise problems about continuing learning for the health professionals with whom I worked. The professionals were acutely aware of their responsibility to continue learning and assiduous in their intent but were grappling with issues about what was important to learn and how to fit learning into personal and professional lives that were already full.

I was also aware that, despite increased focus on the necessity of continuing learning following graduation, there appeared to be a disparity between research findings and practice in this area. An evidence-based consensus had developed amongst educational researchers that effective PL was active, social, situated, continuing and related to authentic practice issues (Garet, Porter, Desimone, Birman, & Yoon, 2001; Penuel, Fishman, Yamaguchi, & Gallagher, 2007; Putnam & Borko, 2000). Seminal research from the past 30 years had effectively challenged assumptions underpinning traditional PD; that knowledge could be transferred into the minds of professionals that would then be translated into practice. This "container" notion of learning was debunked in recent history by Jean Lave (1993), but even two and a half thousand years ago, Confucius had noted that the educated person was not an empty vessel (Cheang, 2000). Despite significant research into PL and resulting interest in innovative ways of supporting professionals through collaborative networks or action research, there appeared to be little change in PD in most professions with traditional, didactic practices continuing essentially unabated.

In exploring the reasons for such lack of change, I looked to the experiences of the professionals concerned, and in seeking a research approach that took a comprehensive approach to experience, turned to phenomenology. All research is based on underlying philosophical assumptions about how reality and knowledge are understood and can be investigated, although these often remain implicit. The way that research is conceptualised informs and directs that research in powerful ways. It determines the design, data collection and analysis, interpretations of findings and conclusions drawn. Conceptual frameworks also act to exclude other ways of looking at an issue so that all research has limitations. Thus I do not claim that the phenomenological framework outlined in this book is the only, or even the best, way to research the continuing learning of professionals. What I do claim is that through disrupting conventional notions in this area of research, a different understanding of and support for PL may emerge.

Phenomenology is the study of phenomena (e.g. parental love, being disabled, being a teacher or continuing PL) as experienced by people in everyday life. The notion that people are *already* part of the world as they experience life is integral to understanding experiences through phenomenology, with the person and their world being inextricably intertwined through lived experience. Phenomenology explicitly rejects a dualist ontology that considers the subject (professional) and object (workplace situation) as separable. It also rejects an objectivist epistemology that views professional knowledge as a commodity that can be transferred, or analysed separately from the professional and working contexts. In drawing explicitly on a phenomenological research approach, PL can be conceptualised and investigated as embedded and enacted through the lived experience of being a professional in practice. Through a focus on the experience of everyday practice (which is not confined to the mundane but also includes the exceptional), individual professionals and their sociocultural and professional contexts are viewed as always and irrevocably intertwined, unable to be meaningfully separated in research.

Phenomenology offers a distinctive means of exploration. In practical terms, phenomenology occupies a space between the close inspection of learning activities or focus on individual professionals' learning narratives and broader research that scans contextual or organisational situations and discourses with respect to learning. Such an approach shares commonalities with other practice-based, sociocultural perspectives, but has unique features enabling different insights into continuing PL with relevance for practice. Phenomenology looks across a diversity of individuals' experiences, highlighting commonalities whilst accounting for differences. In its examination of professional life, phenomenology also seeks to reveal and foreground features that are so embedded in that life that they are taken for granted. Professionals often practice within habitual patterns of behaviour (as do researchers). Through disclosure of implicit aspects of professionals' experiences, a phenomenological approach aims to open fresh perspectives on PL.

In keeping with my intention to focus on professional experience, the empirical phenomenological methodology of Amedeo Giorgi (1997, 2005, 2009) was chosen as appropriate, because of his focus on gaining rich, detailed descriptions from participants that are grounded in concrete, real-life situations. I collected descriptions of learning during semi-structured interviews, where participants detailed situations where they had learnt as professionals. The research was designed to maximise the possibility of gathering diverse descriptions of PL experiences. Data were collected using a variety of sources in addition to interviews, such as observation of participants at work and during PD activities, and documentation and artefacts related to learning. Phenomenological analyses of data revealed commonalities. These commonalities account for what was essential for the participants to identify experiences as PL experiences. In phenomenological terms, these interlinked commonalities are described in the form of a complex "structure" of APL that seeks to reveal essential features of that phenomenon.

As a stakeholder who has been involved with PL in a number of professional capacities, I take a reflexive position throughout the research and this book. The primary purpose of this reflexivity was to raise and critique assumptions about PL I brought to this study from previous experiences. I was a health professional who had worked in community contexts and had experiences of learning similar to those of my participants. In addition, as an educator I have stood in other stakeholder positions, as an academic lecturer, a convenor in a professional association and a workplace professional supervisor. The impact, both positive and negative, of these multiple stances on my approach to this research is discussed in the book. I mention reflexivity here to highlight that this research is a co-construction with the professionals who participated and is written in a manner that reflects this approach to research.

Another aspect of this book's style refers to the need to communicate across disciplines. Despite the fact that most professional practice is interdisciplinary and rhetoric from governments and universities supports interdisciplinary collaboration, there are significant difficulties with interdisciplinary research. Not least of these is the use of differing jargon, discourses and theoretical frameworks. In the literature from different disciplines that I draw upon there are differences in terminologies, meanings of concepts and underlying theoretical assumptions. I am acutely aware of different expectations and understandings when addressing academic audiences from health, education or other professional bodies. I therefore place particular emphasis on explicitly clarifying the perspective this research takes, the meaning of the terms and concepts used and the underlying philosophical assumptions.

I use the term authentic PL to describe learning as experienced by practising professionals. It is the participants in this research, rather than myself, who delimit authentic PL by describing situations where they consider they have learnt. One advantage of using this term is to differentiate between such lived experiences and the rhetoric and varying definitions of terms such as professional development (PD), continuing education (CE), staff training, informal, workplace or lifelong learning. The term authentic PL is inclusive of situations, both formal and informal, that are discussed under the umbrella of these other terms. It is the learning of professionals that does (or does not) occur through PD, CE or any other activities that is the focus of this research rather than specific activities. Use of the term authentic PL also avoids the dichotomy between formal courses and everyday professional growth, which are often considered separately in research and practice. Dichotomies related to PL abound in the literature, between individual and collective learning, theoretical and practical learning and professional and personal learning. Other educational researchers have also objected to the tenuous nature of sharply drawn dichotomies (Colley, Hodkinson, & Malcolm, 2002; P. Hodkinson, Biesta, & James, 2008; Usher & Edwards, 2007). For convenience, I use the acronym APL to refer to authentic PL in the remainder of this book, noting that in the United Kingdom, APL also refers to accreditation of prior learning.

## 1.4 Understanding Professional Learning

The importance of and need for continuing PL is well established as both an implicit professional responsibility and an explicit registration requirement (Freidson, 2001; Friedman, Durkin, Phillips, & Davis, 2000). To address this need for continuing PL, significant resources are expended on PD programmes, amongst increasing evidence that many fail to result in sustainable changes in PL or enhanced practice (Borko, 2004; Cervero, 2001; Fullan, 2007; Knight, Tait, & Yorke, 2006). The argument against this traditional "training" model, focused on delivering content rather than supporting learning, is compelling, with research highlighting that professional knowledge is not confined to the mind of an individual but is constructed through engagement in practice with others (Kemmis, 2005; Schwandt, 2005). Despite evidence that effective PL takes into account diversity in professional identity and context, whilst engaging professionals in working with others on practice-based issues (Beijaard, Meijer, Morine-Dershimer, & Tillema, 2005; Eraut, 2007; Glazer & Hannafin, 2006; Groundwater-Smith & Mockler, 2009; McCormack, Gore, & Thomas, 2006), many PD programmes remain as episodic information updates "delivered" to "deficient" professionals in a didactic manner (McWilliam, 2002). Critique of PD across professional boundaries is increasing with calls for re-evaluation of PD theory and practice (Dall'Alba & Sandberg, 2006; Evans, 2008; Gravani, 2007; H. Hodkinson & Hodkinson, 2005; Luke & McArdle, 2009; Rodrigues, 2005).

Despite a continuing prevalence of traditional PD, innovative strategies for supporting PL have emerged, such as mentoring (Brockbank & McGill, 2006), communities of practice (Stoll, Bolam, McMahon, Wallace, & Thomas, 2006) and action learning (O'Neil & Marsick, 2007). Although valuable, there are pitfalls in the naive use of such strategies if philosophical assumptions about PL are not re-conceptualised, so that the strategy still "delivers" PL with a focus on content and outcomes rather than on respecting and supporting professionals' agency in making meaning through their learning. Unfortunately, assumptions underpinning the delivery of PD activities to professionals, no matter how well designed, flexible or practical are not examined in many cases. Judith Sandholtz and Samantha Scribner (2006) report on a significant PD activity for teachers in a school district in the United States where innovative, collaborative models of support were engaged, but a failure of key stakeholders to examine assumptions, accompanied by constraints of bureaucratic context, stymied the anticipated outcomes. Stakeholder rhetoric surrounding PD generally focuses on the need for quality assurance and maintenance of professional standards, with a measurable change in professional performance towards an agreed best practice. Tension sometimes exists in workplaces between PD for accountability and performativity requirements and PL that is driven by the agendas of professionals and their needs. The balance of ensuing benefits for the organisation and individual professionals may be contestable (Ball, 2003; Davies, 2005). Frank Coffield's (2007) critique of such pressures in the post-compulsory education and skills sector, as "running ever faster down the wrong road", resonates with the research reported in this book.

Findings from the phenomenological research described in this book demonstrate that PL is essentially a self-directed activity, as much about ontology and professional identity as epistemology and professional knowing, yet traditional PD focuses on the latter. The key argument outlined in the following chapters is for a change in focus, from PD involving the delivery of content in a didactic manner to deficient professionals, to support for PL that respects diversity of meaning and highlights agency and capability in self-directed PL (Walker, 2006). To find practical ways of support that are sustaining for the individual professional as well as sustainable from an organisational perspective, there is a need for research that listens to the experiences of practice and seeks to further understand PL as it is lived. This book aims to contribute to that understanding.

As detailed later in the book, commonalities across diverse experiences of APL were identified in terms of 13 sub-constituents, grouped under 4 main interlinked constituents: understanding, engagement, interconnection and openness. These constituents formed the basis of an APL structure that can be used to understand and support PL. My research found that professionals learn in situations that matter to them. These are usually areas they care about enough to *engage* with, but feel uncertain about. Learning in such situations involves complex *interconnections* with previous experiences, of themselves and others, and leads through transitions involving novel features to a change in professional *understanding*. Such learning follows a circuitous trajectory, being *open* to many possibilities in the path that is taken, so that it is not easily amenable to outside control.

The research identified tensions in continuing to learn at work between professional agency and the need for accountability, particularly where participants felt their learning (and indeed their "being") were primarily valued in terms of their contribution to organisational efficiency and productivity. Such tensions contributed to the feeling of dissonance and apparent disconnection between reality and rhetoric described so far. Discussions about dissonance were mainly shared between colleagues working in supportive and trusting environments. Similarly, admitting to "not knowing" was often limited to such environments. However, uncertainty and not knowing were identified as essential to the structure of APL. Different ways of dealing with dissonance are described by participants in terms of their differing "professional ways of being" (Dall'Alba, 2004).

The implication of the research reported in this book is that PL cannot be mandated, coerced or controlled, but can be supported, facilitated and shaped. I argue for a move from a deficit model of delivering PD to a strengths model of support for capability in PL, from a focus on control and standardisation to appreciation and celebration of diversity, and from a primary concern with the measurement of outcomes of PD to an understanding of meaning-making in PL. Change in professional understanding is the crux of APL and such change is related to what "matters" to the professional. What matters varies but a common thread in the case of my participants – as reflected in the title of this book – is making a difference to the lives of their clients.

There are situations when provision of traditional PD programmes is an effective way to share information quickly or widely. Similarly, the provision of essential information for new staff is necessary as part of induction. Care must be taken, however, not to assume that information provision, through written means or workshops, is synonymous with engaged learning that results in changed practice. As examples of novice therapists in this book indicate, even with support, learning does not always proceed according to plan. If we accept the inherent openness of APL and our inability to control the outcomes of professionals' learning, then how do we deal with situations where we are supporting professionals to learn to change, where assumptions about the nature of practice and ways of being a professional are shifting and professionals may be resistant to such changes? Such problematic concerns are raised in this book. A supportive approach need not negate questioning and challenging. Indeed I argue that starting from what matters to professionals whilst supporting their sense of agency forms a better basis for challenging and supporting changes in practice than traditional PD. Strategies and guidelines are discussed towards the end of the book that aim to support learning and change that is sustainable as well as authentic. By sustainable I mean that strategies contribute to long-term changes that enhance practice outcomes, use existing resources where possible and support the organisation's strategic direction as well as the well-being of professionals. By authentic I mean that strategies reflect the reality and meaning of professional life, engage with authentic problems that matter to professionals and society and support professional growth and integrity.

Whereas authenticity is alluded to initially in this book by using the term APL to distinguish the experience of PL from rhetoric surrounding PD, in later chapters this notion is extended beyond its reference to lived reality by drawing on phenomenological philosophy. In particular, I refer to Martin Heidegger's (1927/1962) phenomenological analysis of what it is to be human, to explore the empirical material, considering what it means to work and learn as a professional in a contemporary workplace. The possibility of authenticity in professional life is raised in describing how learning not only affords quality practice but also is implicated in the making of meaning at work. Authenticity in professional life does not merely refer to an individual quality, but is described in this book as a social as well as personal construct, within a reflective and ethical awareness. It is related to a professional capability for inquiry into practice, which questions assumptions underpinning that practice, in the light of what is valued by professionals and society.

To reiterate, there is a need to understand APL from the perspective of the professionals involved, within the context of everyday professional practice with its implicit workplace issues. By using a theoretical framework that conceptualises PL as constructed and embedded within the lived experience of being a practising professional, this research challenges the traditional way of conceptualising PD. The ultimate aim of understanding more about APL is to enhance support for professionals in this vital aspect of their practice in a way that is congruent with their experience whilst cognizant of workplace expectations. Whilst organisationally inconvenient, the realisation that no professional can be made to learn opens opportunities for exploring innovative ways to support and shape learning that are authentic and sustainable, and allow for agency as well as provide for accountability.

In summarising this chapter, as well as introducing the professionals, the research and the book, I argue that support of APL is important for the well-being of clients, growth and satisfaction of individual professionals, enhancement of practice within a profession and ultimately the capacity of organisations who employ them to deliver sustainable outcomes. It is only through questioning assumptions underlying taken-for-granted practices in PD that we, as researchers, can engage in constructive debates to make a difference in this important area of research. I invite readers to re-examine their own assumptions about PD and PL whilst reading this book, through reflecting on their own learning as they continue working as academics, educators, managers or in any other type of professional practice.

# References

Ball, S. J. (2003). The teacher's soul and the terrors of performativity. *Journal of Education Policy, 18*(2), 215–228.

Beijaard, D., Meijer, P., Morine-Dershimer, G., & Tillema, H. (Eds.). (2005). *Teacher professional development in changing conditions*. Dordrecht: Springer.

Borko, H. (2004). Professional development and teacher learning: Mapping the terrain. *Educational Researcher, 33*(8), 3–15.

Brockbank, A., & McGill, I. (2006). *Facilitating reflective learning through mentoring and coaching*. London, PA: Kogan Page.

Cervero, R. M. (2001). Continuing professional education in transition, 1981–2000. *International Journal of Lifelong Education, 20*(1–2), 16–30.

Cheang, A. W. (2000). The master's voice: On reading, translating and interpreting the analects of Confucius. *The Review of Politics, 62*(3), 563–581.

Coffield, F. (2007). *Running ever faster down the wrong road: An alternative future for education and skills*. London: Institute of Education, University of London.

Colley, H., Hodkinson, P., & Malcolm, J. (2002). *Non-formal learning: Mapping the conceptual terrain. A consultation report*. Leeds: University of Leeds Lifelong Learning Institute.

Daley, B. J. (2001). Learning and professional practice: A study of four professions. *Adult Education Quarterly, 52*(1), 39–54.

Dall'Alba, G. (2004). Understanding professional practice: Investigations before and after an educational programme. *Studies in Higher Education, 29*(6), 679–692.

Dall'Alba, G., & Sandberg, J. (2006). Unveiling professional development: A critical review of stage models. *Review of Educational Research, 76*(3), 383–412.

Davies, B. (2005). The (im)possibility of intellectual work in neoliberal regimes. *Discourse: Studies in the Cultural Politics of Education, 26*(1), 1–14.

Eraut, M. (2007). Learning from other people in the workplace. *Oxford Review of Education, 33*(4), 403–442.

Evans, L. (2008). Professionalim, professionality and the development of education professionals. *British Journal of Educational Studies, 56*(1), 20–38.

Freidson, E. (2001). *Professionalism: The third logic*. Chicago: University of Chicago Press.

Friedman, A., Durkin, C., Phillips, M., & Davis, K. (2000). *Continuing professional development in the UK: Policies and programmes*. Bristol: Professional Associations Research Network.

Fullan, M. (2007). *The new meaning of educational change* (4th ed.). New York: Teachers College Press.

Garet, M., Porter, A., Desimone, L., Birman, B., & Yoon, K. S. (2001). What makes professional development effective? Results from a national sample of teachers. *American Educational Research Journal, 38*(4), 915–945.

Giorgi, A. (1997). The theory, practice and evaluation of the phenomenological method as a qualitative research procedure. *Journal of Phenomenological Psychology, 28*, 235–260.

Giorgi, A. (2005). The phenomenological movement and research in the human sciences. *Nursing Science Quarterly, 18*(1), 75–82.

Giorgi, A. (2009). *The descriptive phenomenological method in psychology: A modified Husserlian approach*. Pittsburgh, PA: Duquesne University Press.

Glazer, E. M., & Hannafin, M. J. (2006). The collaborative apprenticeship model: Situated professional development within school settings. *Teaching and Teacher Education, 22*(2), 179–193.

Gravani, M. (2007). Unveiling professional learning: Shifting from the delivery of courses to an understanding of the processes. *Teaching and Teacher Education, 23*(5), 688–704.

Groundwater-Smith, S., & Mockler, N. (2009). *Teacher professional learning in an age of compliance: Mind the gap*. Dordrecht: Springer.

Heidegger, M. (1927/1962). *Being and time* (J. Macquarrie & E. Robinson, Trans., 1st English ed.). London: SCM Press.

Hodkinson, P., Biesta, G., & James, D. (2008). Understanding learning culturally: Overcoming the dualism between social and individual views of learning. *Vocations and Learning, 1,* 27–47.

Hodkinson, H., & Hodkinson, P. (2005). Improving schoolteachers' workplace learning. *Research Papers in Education, 20*(2), 109–131.

Kemmis, S. (2005). Knowing practice: Searching for saliences. *Pedagogy, Culture and Society, 13*(3), 391–426.

Knight, P., Tait, J., & Yorke, M. (2006). The professional learning of teachers in higher education. *Studies in Higher Education, 31*(3), 319–339.

Lave, J. (1993). The practice of learning. In S. Chaiklin & J. Lave (Eds.), *Understanding practice: Perspectives on activity and context* (pp. 3–31). Cambridge: Cambridge University Press.

Luke, A., & McArdle, F. (2009). A model for research-based state professional development policy. *Asia-Pacific Journal of Teacher Education, 37*(3), 231–251.

McCormack, A., Gore, J., & Thomas, K. (2006). Early career teacher professional learning. *Asia-Pacific Journal of Teacher Education, 34*(1), 95–113.

McWilliam, E. (2002). Against professional development. *Educational Philosophy and Theory, 34*(3), 289–299.

O'Neil, J., & Marsick, V. J. (2007). *Understanding action learning.* New York: American Management Association.

Penuel, W. R., Fishman, B. J., Yamaguchi, R., & Gallagher, L. P. (2007). What makes professional development effective? Strategies that foster curriculum implementation. *American Educational Research Journal, 44*(4), 921–958.

Putnam, R., & Borko, H. (2000). What do new views of knowledge and thinking have to say about research on teacher learning? *Educational Researcher, 29*(1), 4–15.

Rodrigues, S. (Ed.). (2005). *International perspectives on teacher professional development: Changes influenced by politics, pedagogy and innovation.* New York: Nova Science.

Sandholtz, J. H., & Scribner, S. P. (2006). The paradox of administrative control in fostering teacher professional development. *Teaching and Teacher Education, 22,* 1104–1117.

Schwandt, T. A. (2005). On modeling our understanding of the practice fields. *Pedagogy, Culture and Society, 13*(3), 313–332.

Stoll, L., Bolam, R., McMahon, A., Wallace, M., & Thomas, S. (2006). Professional learning communities: A review of the literature. *Journal of Educational Change, 7,* 221–258.

Usher, R., & Edwards, R. (2007). *Lifelong learning: Signs, discourses, practices.* Dordrecht, Netherlands: Springer.

Walker, M. (2006). *Higher education pedagogies: A capabilities approach.* England: Open University Press.

# Part II
# Exploration

Part I argued for re-evaluation of professional development (PD) practices, based on a clearer understanding of how professionals continue to learn within their current working context. The notion of Authentic Professional Learning (APL) was introduced as a complex, lived phenomenon that is experienced in a variety of ways.

The three chapters in Part II are linked by their purpose: to detail the conceptualisation, design and execution of the research underpinning this book. In these chapters I explore literature relevant to PD in delineating the focus of the research (Chapter 2), expound the theoretical perspective used and its philosophical assumptions (Chapter 3) and describe the adaptation of the methodological approach (Chapter 4). Metaphors of exploration are used in these chapters. In undertaking this research I navigated considerable distance across disciplinary boundaries to locate and refine the issues raised about PD, as described in Chapter 2, "Mapping the Research Terrain". Throughout the study I have used the "lens" of phenomenology in framing the search, as described in Chapter 3, "A Phenomenological Perspective". Empirical phenomenological approaches were adapted to devise specific processes for data gathering and analysis, as described in Chapter 4, "Delving into Methodology".

Chapter 2 traces the history of PD across fields of professional practice and integrates, problematises and builds on a range of literature relevant to PD from professional education, workplace learning, adult education and organisational learning. Chapter 3 introduces essential concepts underlying phenomenological investigation as both a philosophical, theoretical approach and empirical research method. Phenomenology encapsulates a broad field of inquiry. The specific perspective taken in this research is presented, referring to the work of Heidegger, Merleau-Ponty and Gadamer, with respect to ontology, embodied experience and understanding. Chapter 4 details how Giorgi's rigorous, empirical phenomenological methodology was adapted in this research with reference to the evocative textuality of van Manen's work and the reflexive meta-methodology of Alvesson.

There is always a disparity between the process of research and its product as text. Particularly in qualitative research the process can be circular and iterative. Yet this research is reported as a linear, logical text. This belies the fact that when seeking to understand the experiences of others, there is no clear-cut pathway. The messiness of this exploration is partly hidden by its neat presentation in book form.

# Chapter 2
# Mapping the Research Terrain

A wide diversity of literature exists that is relevant to examining PD and understanding PL, making such investigation an interdisciplinary area of inquiry. This inquiry is located at the intersection of a number of areas of research and of policy. Research into the continuing learning of professionals can be informed by the literature from higher education and continuing professional education, workplace and informal learning, adult and community education and organisational learning and human resource management. Until recently, research from these areas was rarely integrated, let alone focused towards the particular concerns of the continuing learning of working professionals. Nevertheless, seminal research from these diverse areas over the past 40 years has significant implications for how we currently understand PL and practice PD. Similarly, policy concerns influencing the practice and development of working professionals sit somewhat awkwardly within the post-secondary "Learning Society" (Coffield, 2007), between the higher education sector, the technical and vocational education and training sector, the community or further education sector and the work-related or organisational learning sector. Demarcations of research areas and education sectors vary in differing countries. The terminology I use refers to mainly the American, Australian and British contexts.

Scanning of this broad literature terrain could be undertaken in a number of constructive ways, with two possibilities being spatial or temporal reviews (see Easterby-Smith, Crossan, & Nicolini, 2000). In related research, I took a spatial perspective, reviewing literature across fields of inquiry mentioned above to examine what we know about how professionals learn (Webster-Wright, 2009). In that review, analysis of a representative "snapshot" of current PD literature from across different professions, published over a 1-year period, demonstrated that a substantial proportion (three-quarters) focused on traditional delivery of content rather than innovative support for learning, essentially overlooking important research findings about how professionals learn. In this chapter I review relevant literature from a temporal perspective, looking back to examine changes in the focus of research and of practice in PD that have occurred over the past 40 years, and how they inform current practice. I also describe and delimit what I mean by the terms "learning" and "professional", whilst comparing "traditional PD" with more innovative forms of support for PL that have emerged.

A. Webster-Wright, *Authentic Professional Learning*, Professional and Practice-based Learning 2, DOI 10.1007/978-90-481-3947-7_2, © Springer Science+Business Media B.V. 2010

## 2.1 Exploring Professional Learning and Development

Drawing on decades of research into work-related learning, Frank Coffield (2000a) bemoans the lack of clarity about what is meant by learning and the absence of coherent research-based theories of learning underpinning much policy about continuing education and lifelong learning. Certainly, in any research into learning the theories in use and their assumptions should be clearly articulated. This section briefly summarises the assumptions about learning that underpin this book, details of which are illustrated through this chapter.

### *2.1.1 Learning Theories*

"Learning" is a word in such common usage that multiple interpretations abound. All learning is dependent on who is learning, what is learnt and under what conditions it is learnt. As with any complex concept, theories have evolved to explain the sometimes paradoxical results of empirical research. The difference between these theories is largely determined by underlying assumptions about the nature of knowledge, of people as learners and of the process of learning. Common to most theories is that learning involves change, but whether this change involves knowledge, behaviour or practice varies.

Currently, several learning theories coexist, which influence research and drive practice involving PL in different ways. Etienne Wenger (1998, p. 14) describes theories of learning along four different axes, but the most common axis along which theories can be placed is one between the learning processes of the individual, as opposed to the sociocultural context of the learning. At one extreme of this continuum is a neuropsychological perspective that describes cognitive processes and equates learning with individual rational thinking. At the other end is a critical social perspective, where learning is seen as largely determined by cultural perspectives and social structures, strongly influenced by power relationships. Two theories within this range, commonly used in research into PL, take a sociocultural perspective on learning involving "social constructivism" (Biggs, 2003; Higgs, Richardson, & Abrandt Dahlgren, 2004) and "social constructionism" (Gherardi & Nicolini, 2006; Sandberg & Dall'Alba, 2006). Although each term encompasses a range of slightly different perspectives, and are sometimes used interchangeably, differences in the origin and assumptions of both approaches have been distinguished (Crotty, 1998, p. 57; Schwandt, 2000, p. 187).

Constructivism views knowledge as actively constructed by the learner, whilst being influenced by past experience and present interactions with the social learning context. Although the influence of sociocultural interaction is stressed, social constructivism tends to foreground the individual in the making of meaning and construction of knowledge with others. Proponents of this perspective vary in their explanation of the influence of sociocultural interactions (Engeström, 1999; Vygotsky, 1978). The social constructionist perspective describes learning through the inter-subjective construction of meaning. It emphasises that reality and knowledge are socially constituted, so that the learner and the world are irrevocably interrelated through lived experience. Again proponents of this perspective vary in attention paid to differing aspects of social interaction, from a focus on practice to a focus on language (Bourdieu, 1990; Gergen, 2001).

Both these approaches view knowledge as constructed and are attentive to individual and social aspects of learning, but social constructivism has been described as having a more individual emphasis on the construction of meaning, whereas social constructionism emphasises the inter-subjective nature of this construction. Although similar, different perspectives on learning may lead to quite different research traditions and researchers being drawn upon (Rowland, 2000, p. 6). Social constructionism has influenced my framing of this research. Peter Berger and Thomas Luckmann's (1966/1981) phenomenological analysis of reality and knowledge offers a detailed example of a social constructionist perspective on learning.

## 2.1.2  Conceptions of Professional Knowing and Learning

Different conceptions of professional knowledge underpin the way that PL is understood. Professional knowledge has commonly been viewed in terms of interrelated domains, such as propositional knowledge of facts, professional craft knowledge of practice and personal experiential knowledge, that are drawn on in various ways in practice (Higgs & Titchen, 2001). Significant research has been undertaken to understand the complexities of knowledge as it is used in practice. Much of the recent research poses more questions than are resolved, but generally challenges an objectivist epistemology, where knowledge is seen as a commodity to be transferred and managed. Increasingly, research supports the notion that professional knowledge is embodied through practice. Certainly in a study into the experience of learning, knowledge cannot be separated from the knower, as John Dewey (1929/1960) maintained in arguing against a "spectator" theory of knowledge. Research drawn upon in this book conceives of knowing as involving the whole professional as a social being, rather than as just his or her mind. A shift from knowledge to knowing entails a shift from an epistemology of "possession" to one of "practice" (Cook & Brown, 1999; Schön, 1995).

Different conceptualisations of PL at work coexist in the literature, varying with the intent and assumptions of the research (Fenwick, 2008b; Sawchuk, 2008). They often examine different aspects of the phenomenon of PL. Assumptions about learning can be usefully expressed in terms of metaphors. Instead of being conceived in terms of acquisition of a commodity, learning at work is increasingly viewed as a process of construction (Hager, 2004). More ephemeral metaphors have also been used. Workplace learning has been conceived of as participating in a mystery to be explored rather than purely a problem to be solved (Gherardi & Nicolini, 2006). In an article on becoming a researcher, Robyn Barnacle (2005) maintains that knowledge is "inherently partial" in nature, and knowing and learning involve an inquiry towards the unknown.

From a social constructionist perspective, knowing and learning are conceived as being constructed and embedded within the professional's embodied social practices.

Research reviewed in this chapter supports the notion that professionals learn from experience and accepts that learning is context dependent. One of the primary distinctions made in research with respect to PL has been the differentiation between formal, informal and incidental learning (Marsick & Watkins, 1990). Michael Eraut (2004) developed a further typology of informal learning as implicit, reactive and deliberative. Paul Hager and John Halliday (2006) highlight the value of informal learning, at work and through life, and its contribution to the ability to make nuanced judgements. An extensive review of research into non-formal learning considered dimensions of formality and informality as part of a continuum rather than absolute qualities (Colley, Hodkinson, & Malcolm, 2002). The relationship between formal and informal learning for the continuing learning of professionals remains indeterminate.

In the research underpinning this book, the focus question is asked: *How do professionals experience continuing learning within the current working context?* Description of experiences as formal or informal, education or training, theoretical or practical, collaborative or individual is left to the participants who described experiences that, for them, entailed learning.

### 2.1.3  Traditional and Innovative Professional Development

In Chapter 1, the notion of "traditional" PD was raised and critiqued. The main criteria of traditional PD, as originally critiqued by Cyril Houle (1980), were the didactic nature of delivery by an expert, in a transient event with a predetermined beginning and end. I do not dispute the value of expertise or guidance, but question the assumption that it is the only or best way to learn as a professional in practice. As this chapter will demonstrate, this assumption has been challenged by evidence from research into more innovative ways of supporting PL, particularly from research into the teaching profession.

Extensive empirical research demonstrated innovative approaches to be more effective in producing sustainable reforms and changes in practice than traditional PD (Garet, Porter, Desimone, Birman, & Yoon, 2001; Penuel, Fishman, Yamaguchi, & Gallagher, 2007; Putnam & Borko, 2000). Compared to traditional PD, innovative approaches involved more active, in-depth engagement than possible in standard workshops, mentoring or coaching, involvement in networks or learning communities or participation in action learning or research. To be effective, PD needs to be interactive, long term and related to practice, with multiple opportunities for cycles of engagement and reflection, involving collaborative participation that creates trusting relationships and "investigative cultures" (Penuel et al., 2007, p. 929). Coherence was also stressed as important, referring to alignment between PD activities and teachers' beliefs about what matters for them in relation to their own and their students' learning.

From this research, William Penuel and colleagues (2007, p. 928) argue that instead of focusing on the type of PD, for example, mentoring versus workshops, it is important to focus on the design of activities, with a particular need for "proximity to practice". They maintained that a mentoring relationship may be more like traditional PD, whereas a workshop could be designed to be innovative with active engagement related to ongoing practice. Similarly, if assumptions about the nature of PL are not examined, mentoring could still focus on expert delivery of content rather than on supporting professionals to make sense of changes in practice through active involvement. Innovative approaches build on research that has challenged epistemological assumptions that implicitly underpin traditional PD: assumptions that learning is primarily cognitive, and knowledge is a commodity that can be delivered into the mind of a professional. But how did assumptions underlying traditional PD come to be taken for granted?

## 2.2  The Development of Professions

In seeking, in vain, the origin of the term "professional development" I came upon the "Engineers Council for Professional Development"[1] established in 1932 in America. Upon closer inspection however, I saw that its primary focus was the development of the relatively new profession of engineering, rather than a reference to PD in the sense we currently use. Thus the folly of assuming that language-fixed meaning over time was revealed yet again. The development of the idea and practice of PD is certainly linked to the development of professions: a development that is contingent upon the sociocultural, economic and political twists and turns of the history of the twentieth century.

Understanding the way that different professions have evolved over time can shed light on the way that particular practices of PD have been formed. It is only when looking back over a substantial stretch of time that threads, weaves, patterns (and holes) in the fabric of any human endeavour can be recognised. In taking a temporal view of these developments, my aim is to frame an understanding of how taken-for-granted features of PD, as it is currently practiced, came to be assumed. Assumptions, for example, that provision of information will lead to changes in practice and that learning requires teaching or expert facilitation underlie traditional PD. In following the trajectory of mainstream ideas and noting the traces of alternative views, I am guided by the intent, rather than method, of Michel Foucault's (1984) genealogical analysis, that is, I am not interested in the "history of the past in terms of the present", but in the "history of the present" and how it came to be. Through this review, features of the landscape that constitute trends in research and practice, relevant to PD and PL, will be examined. This view of the literature is necessarily partial, yet purposeful, locating the inquiry that underpins this book in the overall research terrain.

---

[1] Accreditation Board for Engineering and Technology http://www.abet.org/history.shtml

Three sources of evidence will be woven together. Historical and sociological literature about the development of professions and of PD ideas is located in time, juxtaposed against seminal research findings about how professionals learn. These two threads are linked through the prism of my own experience in different professional positions, over the past four decades. My decision to draw on experience was influenced by David Boud's (2006) review of student-focused learning in higher education, where he examined changes in the focus of teaching and learning, illustrated through his professional experience. My experience of being a professional began in the late 1960s, at a time when there were significant changes occurring in professional practice and higher education.

The focus of my research, and of this book, is on professions, although many occupations and vocations share qualities of professionalism, have similar issues relating to their continuing learning in contemporary workplaces and may find research in this book relevant. Whilst agreeing that there may be limited value in separating professions from other occupations and vocations, and that demarcation is highly variable and contestable, I wish to draw attention to specific influences at play in the practice of these professionals. Although present to some degree in most occupations, in the traditional professions, tensions in working practice and continuing learning, between responsibility and accountability on the one hand and autonomy and agency on the other, are honed to a particular sharpness.

Whilst focusing on the development of professions, I hasten to add the proviso that such notions of profession and professional are not "unitary" constructs. Although we refer to a doctor in the profession of medicine or an auditor in the profession of accounting, the individuals involved may have more in common with each other than with the assumed "average" practitioner of their profession. Both may, for example, share a fervent interest in using their professional skills in the advancement of human rights. Nevertheless, the professional body to which the practitioner belongs is worth examining, as it arguably shapes the individual's identity, learning and practice in powerful ways.

Many of these forces are explicit, such as legal registration requirements and compulsory PD; others are more subtle. A process of professional socialisation takes place continuously, moulded by implicit discourses. By discourses, I refer to more than language. It is not only the accepted jargon (including ubiquitous acronyms only insiders recognise), but also ways of thinking and acting that privilege or constrain particular people, ideas and action. James Gee (1990, p. 142) describes such social discourses as "ways of being in the world [and] displaying (through words, actions, values and beliefs) *membership*[2] in a particular social group." Different professions and organisations have their own discourses as evidenced by shared behaviour, practices and expectations (Mishler, 1984). Dewey (1933) referred to the development of such "habits of mind" that reinforce taken-for-granted practices.

---

[2]In this book, all quotes from another author maintain the original punctuation and emphases. Any additions are in [square brackets].

A fabric of implicit discourse covers the literature about practices in professions. Only broad contours in the development of professions and practices over time are mapped below.

## 2.3 Pathways to Professionalism

Historical accounts, typically focused on the development of one profession, are fairly uniform in tone in their discussion about the growth in importance and value of their profession. The sociological analyses of professions are more nuanced and critical. In this review I refer to books reviewing the past, from the professional fields of engineering (Perrucci & Gerstl, 1969), law (Felstiner, 2005), social work (Leighninger, 2000), therapies (Bentley & Dunstan, 2006; Germov, 2009), medicine (Burnham, 1998; Gabe & Calnan, 2009; Tallis, 2005), accounting (Linn, 1996), information technology (Bennett, Broomham, Murton, Pearcy, & Rutledge, 1994), teaching (Fullan, 2007; Goodson & Hargreaves, 1996) and academia (DeZure & Marchese, 2000; Lee, Manathunga, & Kandlbinder, 2008). This spread of professions mirrors the range reviewed in my spatial snapshot of current PD literature (Webster-Wright, 2009).

In the latter half of the twentieth century, the development of professions emerged as a central feature of western societies (Cervero, 2001; Cheetham & Chivers, 2005; Larson, 1977). New professions are continually emerging, currently for example, in environmental, technological and human services areas. Of course, historical and sociological analyses of the professions do not necessarily tell a coherent story, being hotly contested (Brint, 1993). Nevertheless, one way of viewing the development of professions over the past century is to consider the development of professionalism through a process of professionalisation of occupations (Freidson, 1986, 2001; Larson, 1977). These two terms are related though distinct, with the latter focusing on an explicit process of education and development, the former focusing on a way of thinking or being. The review begins with consideration of the widely assumed "characteristics" of a profession, before mapping the development of professions and changes in the understanding of PD and PL across decades since the middle of the twentieth century. The phrase "Pathways to Professionalism" was inspired by Phillip Bentley and David Dunstan's (2006) book recounting the development of the physiotherapy profession in Australia. I draw on physiotherapy in places through this review, as one particular example of a relatively new profession.

### 2.3.1 Characteristics of a Profession

The traditional trinity of medicine, law and theology boasts of an educational pedigree and professional prestige dating back centuries. Emerging professions often referred to these established "ideal" professions in their claims for professional status (Freidson, 2001). For example, when social work emerged as a new professional field in 1910 in North America, discussion focused on the establishment of a shared knowledge base for practitioners, similar to that of doctors and lawyers

(Leighninger, 2000). Even in accounts of the engineering profession, the doctor was described as "the apotheosis of the professional model" (Perrucci & Gerstl, 1969, p. 10). The proviso was added, however, that "white coats do not make a professional", as prestige accrues to those occupations embodying professional ideals and characteristics.

The notion of particular characteristics defining professions developed in the middle of the past century is simplistic, yet is still reported in a remarkably uniform manner by different professions, as a largely unexamined presumption. Drawing from multiple, current sources, these characteristics can be summarised as follows:

1. **Knowledge:** A specialised body of knowledge with defined and regulated means of professional education involving clear and specific entry, registration (or certification) and regulation requirements.
2. **Obligation:** A responsibility to the public that is scrutinised by a regulatory body (or bodies) and is legally enforceable, with the possibility of litigation against professional malpractice.
3. **Autonomy:** A form of peer regulation that defines standards and quality of practice, with acceptance that professionals are independently responsible for their own judgements and that shortcomings will be dealt with by elected peers.
4. **Commitment:** A commitment to a code of ethics, guided by a service orientation, with professionals entrusted to act for the common public good, linked to an assumed ideology focused more on the value of work than on monetary return.

Professional knowledge, involving theoretical, practical and attitudinal components, was and still is seen to be specialised, requiring specific and lengthy periods of education, controlled by universities, professional associations and governments. It is guarded by delineated, and sometimes contested, professional boundaries (Germov, 2009). Professional knowledge has been parodied as neither "too general and vague" nor "too narrow and specific" than is necessary to maintain a "fog of mystique" around professional practice (Freidson, 2001, p. 13; Perrucci & Gerstl, 1969, p. 11). This knowledge was seen as so specialised that sometimes care needed to be undertaken in devolving it to others, particularly the general public. In a history of the physiotherapy profession, for example, ethical guidelines from 1955 cautioned against "usurp[ing] the functions of a doctor or a nurse", teaching others their practice "indiscriminately" and "impart[ing] professional information to a lay audience without specific permission" (Bentley & Dunstan, 2006, p. 203).

Acceptance of professional authority by the public was seen to be tempered by the professionals' assumed ethical commitments, social responsibility and legal obligations. This sense of uninformed public trust that infuses descriptions of professions from the middle of the last century stands in contrast to the knowledgeable consumer of our current decade. Professionals were, and still are, trusted to make daily judgements: some with life and death implications. These judgements are not only about their own practice but also concern the limits of their autonomy, such as when to seek assistance from or refer to other practitioners. Professional autonomy was, and is, a contested notion, especially in our current working climate of increasingly regulated education and practice. The notion of the teacher or psychologist practicing behind closed doors has mixed connotations of freedom on the one hand and isolation on the other. It is curious that professionals today are still entrusted with relative autonomy in their daily judgements, yet increasingly are not entrusted to direct their own learning, including when to seek further information and support.

## 2.3.2 *Developing Authoritative Experts*

It was the post-war boom of the 1950s and the 1960s decades that ushered in substantial expansion and growth in the professionalisation of the workforce, especially in "occupational" professions such as engineering or paramedical areas. Post-war growth led to the development of large-scale building and technological projects, increasing demand for a range of professionals. This era is described as the "golden" age of professionals, in terms of status, trust and autonomy, where they were viewed as authoritative experts (Cervero, 2001; Freidson, 2001; Perrucci & Gerstl, 1969). It is from this era that common assumptions about professional characteristics are drawn.

In response to the need for professionals, there was an increasing focus by western governments on the education necessary to produce skilled and knowledgeable practitioners. For example in Australia, government inquiries were held into the role of higher education in this growth (Lee et al., 2008). The higher education sector expanded to support the education of groups previously considered to be semi-professional occupations, such as teaching (Etzioni, 1969). Many of the newer professions originated in craft-based or community-based activities, for example physiotherapy in massage and hydrotherapy (Bentley & Dunstan, 2006), or social work in community care (Leighninger, 2000). Often, skills and abilities had previously been developed through forms of work-based apprenticeships with substantial practice experience (e.g. journalists and nurses). Shifts to university education implicitly assumed a body of knowledge that was so specialised it could not be taught by immersion in practice.

These newer professions strove towards evidence of worth using scientific criteria to validate their practices and establish their boundaries. By the mid-1960s, use of the term "profession" had become explicitly linked to involvement with higher education and an increasingly well-defined sequence of qualifications focusing on a specialised body of knowledge (Burnham, 1998, p. 105). This sequence is largely unchanged 40 years later, although increasing content has been added. In most professional courses today specialised theory is taught first, gradually integrated into supervised practice, with professional ethics introduced before graduation. Researchers have argued against the adequacy of this sequenced model (Barnett & Coate, 2005; Dall'Alba, 2004) and changes are being made towards work-based integration of learning and practice (e.g. Boud & Solomon, 2001), but this sequence and focus on specialised knowledge remain the norm.

There was little reference to continuing education through this period. At the time, teaching was largely considered to be the transmission of knowledge as a disembodied commodity. Learning was essentially conceptualised as a psychological process. Exciting developments in understanding the social nature of learning were developing in the mid-1960s. These included insight into the social construction of reality and knowledge (Berger & Luckmann, 1966) and understanding the sociocultural basis of the mind and of learning (Vygotsky, 1962). These theories did not have an impact on professional education at this stage, with awareness of them not even permeating social research until the 1970s.

But the times, they were changing. The late 1960s witnessed widespread unrest with challenges to the established status quo in many areas of society. In 1968, a year when significant movements for social change swept across the world, there were student protests, beginning in Paris, questioning the purpose, means and equity of higher education. After conservative decades of stability following depression and war of the 1930s and the 1940s, a wave of changes gathered momentum, in areas from civil rights to gender equality. According to sociologists of the professions, the "unmasking of a previously taken-for-granted benign reality" was under way (Gabe & Calnan, 2009, p. 3).

At that time, I was an undergraduate student at university in Australia, in the relatively new profession of physiotherapy. It was a reasonably traditional didactic course, with little questioning or debate about what we were given to learn. Whilst enthusiastically devouring course lectures, knowing I was entering a profession where we felt we could make a difference, I also read philosophers such as Jean-Paul Sartre and Simone de Bouvoir in awe, without really understanding them. One reflection about those heady times concerns the grey-belted uniforms with starched white collars that we wore in hospital practicums, akin to our previous school uniforms. I remember changing from the uniform into jeans to attend protest marches, with no thought about the contrast between these activities, embodied through wearing these outfits. The two worlds of my professional practice and involvement in social change remained separated in my mind.

### 2.3.3 Defining Boundaries and Uniform Standards

Houle (1980) mapped professional growth and education through the 1970s, presenting his research, undertaken across 17 different professions, in his influential book. This book is recognised as the first widely accepted monograph highlighting continuing education for professionals. Although there was some use of the term "continuing professional development", the usual term at that time was "continuing professional education". Houle accurately predicted the rise in importance of continuing education in the professions until it rivalled undergraduate preparatory education in importance, and he foreshadowed mandatory continuing PD and the development of professional standards.

With the impact of the late 1960s' activism reverberating, criticism of the power monopoly of professions and the need for more accountability to the public were raised (Freidson, 1970; Gabe & Calnan, 2009). Ivan Illich (1971, 1975) also questioned the growing institutionalisation of professions in society, such as education and medicine. He criticised the medicalisation of experiences of human life, where treatment often did more harm than good, introducing the notion of "iatrogenic" disease caused by treatment. Several scandals of professional practice were exposed. Houle (1980, p. 6) described a "shadow" over professions that had "spread and darkened since 1960", sowing seeds of mistrust as reputations were tarnished by incompetent and disreputable professionals. In focusing on continuing education, Houle stressed the need for "control and incentive systems" that could "reward excellence and punish deficiency" in professional practice (p. x). Although he discussed all professions, his examples of misconduct were mainly restricted to doctors and lawyers. Indeed most of the sociological critique of this era was concerned with the "older" professions. The newer professions were still establishing themselves.

With the move to higher education largely established for many professions, the focus was on ensuring a universally high standard of education. Within specific professions, uniform registration procedures, including means of evaluating qualifications obtained in different countries, were established. Education, qualifications, registration and continuing education were overseen by professional associations, a situation that is continued to some degree today, at least in Australia. Peer review committees were established to maintain "heightened vigilance" and devise continuing education programs for practitioners about practice issues, such as "relationships with other health professionals and maintaining comprehensive health records" (Bentley & Dunstan, 2006, p. 205). The 1970s were marked by battles to delineate and defend boundaries of professional territory, with new professions jostling for recognition (Williams, 2009). In the case of allied health professions, for example, they were described as emerging from under the "shadow" of medicine (Boyce, 2006). Defining an identity as a specific profession was considered important at this stage, and in uniformity, strength was sought.

A prescient insight of Houle's (1980) book is the value placed on research across professions in investigating continuing learning. He argues, as do I, that although each profession has its own knowledge base and perspective and guards these boundaries diligently, they use remarkably similar approaches and practices in the area of continuing education and learning. Yet despite this, in "implicit acceptance of uniqueness", each profession "goes its own way alone, winning its victories, making its mistakes, and maturing in its own conceptions" (p. 15). Even now when inter-professional education is widely stressed (Barr, Koppel, Reeves, Hammick, & Freeth, 2005), limited collaboration between professions occurs in the area of continuing learning. Yet most work involves professionals working together in practice.

Looking in retrospect, Houle (1980) advances innovative ideas. His research found that many of the activities constituting "traditional" PD (e.g. lectures, journals, conferences) failed to result in changes in practice, noting comments that they may be as useful in supporting learning as "shouting out of the window" (p. 266). He stresses self-directed learning rather than purely formal education, critiquing the term "continuing education" as it focuses on instruction. Houle highlights the need for a diversity of approaches, drawing on his typology of three modes of learning: inquiry, instruction and performance (p. 31). His assumptions about learning, similar to those of his colleagues at the time, are betrayed when he describes such diversity, however. He suggests that leaders in the profession use inquiry to develop new methods, which are then "disseminated" by instruction to practitioners, who practice their performance to incorporate them into practice (p. 33). Such hierarchical statements are at odds with his espoused focus on the need for self-directed learning (p. 13). In hindsight, Houle recognised problems in using an instructional model to support continued PL. At that time, however, research into and theories about learning, that could explain and suggest means of support aligned with his research into practice, were not widely disseminated.

Arguably, the landmark research of relevance to PD from the 1970s was the work of Malcolm Knowles (1973) on andragogy. His principles of adult learning helped shape the fields of adult education, staff training and human resource management. Although education of adults was considered a separate field from the 1950s and the term "andragogy" had been in use in Europe even earlier (Knowles, Holton, & Swanson, 2005, p. 59), the clear differentiation of adult learning from compulsory schooling of children effectively defined and conceptualised the field. Andragogy has had a significant impact on present-day practice of PD, with its focus on the learner, on flexible delivery that takes prior experience into account and its orientation towards inquiry into problems. However, even 30 years later, in the sixth (posthumous) 2005 edition of his book, the focus remains on "training", on learning as a managed event, with agreed objectives and outcomes, and on the trainer as facilitator of this event, albeit in negotiation with the learner.

Simultaneously, interesting developments were occurring in the new field of organisational learning and practice-based research methodologies. Chris Arygris and Donald Schön (1974, 1978) developed an "action science" to inquire into how problems were solved in practice. Their work drew from the field of cybernetics in ways that anticipated the systems approach to organisational problems. They developed a distinction between "single and double loop" learning. In single-loop learning, problems are investigated and solved within the usual frame of understanding of the person or a group, whereas in double-loop learning implicit assumptions are illuminated and questioned through a process of change, where usual ways of understanding may be transformed. The value of foregrounding and challenging assumptions in learning raised by this research was further highlighted in the 1980s and the 1990s with increasing emphasis placed on the value of critical reflection in PL.

Although in practice an understanding of learning as primarily psychological and cognitive was still enacted, changes were occurring. Research had expanded what was known about interactions between the human body, mind, culture and society, with significant ramifications for education, but little of this was drawn upon with respect to continuing professional education in the 1970s. The experience of learning, rather than the process of learning, was beginning to be explored. William Perry (1970) described ways of thinking in students in higher education, from reliance on authority as the source of knowledge, through awareness of multiple perspectives, to construction of their own version of knowledge. Ference Marton and Roger Säljö (1976) described qualitatively different experiences of students from a surface to deep approach to learning. Facilitation of a deep approach to learning, with the intention of understanding rather than reproducing knowledge, was introduced into the higher education lexicon by the late 1990s, influencing changes in curriculum design and teaching strategies.

The frontiers of research method and social inquiry of relevance to education were beginning to shift, from reliance on quantitative positivism towards glimpses of the value of interpretive research and critical theory. Research methods involving ethnography and phenomenology were used in exploring human experience (e.g. Giorgi, 1970; Spradley, 1979). In Europe, the 1970s saw a burgeoning of philosophical and critical social theory that extended and challenged understanding in the human sciences, in ways that positivistic scientific research could not (Bourdieu, 1977; Foucault, 1980; Gadamer, 1965; Habermas, 1973). In particular, these changes introduced new ways of theorising practice (See Schatzki, Knorr-Cetina, & von Savigny, 2001).

As a professional, new to practice, I recall the enthusiasm and dedication of my professional peers during that period, as we were striving for legitimacy. There was limited orientation at work, with most learning occurring from watching and talking to colleagues. I also became a novice academic in the mid-1970s, with orientation involving attending a lecture about giving a lecture. Nuances of tutorial and clinical teaching were acquired through trial and error. In research, the importance of statistics for validity was stressed, with Fortran computer language and card punching involved. In the relatively new area of chronic pain research I was involved in, we sought numerical scales to "objectively" capture what was essentially a subjective experience. When working in England in the late 1970s, exploring alternative pain treatments, I was aware of the emerging women's and human potential movements and the potential for explanations beyond the accepted standards. I kept a low profile about these interests in my professional life, however.

## 2.3.4 Seeking Scientific Rigour and Evidence

During the 1980s, scientific research expanded to inquire more into the practice of professionals, seeking rigorous evidence to develop guidelines for "good" practice. Although professional journals had been produced for years, it was not until now that research-based articles became the norm for newer professions. In Australia and elsewhere, postgraduate qualifications in specific professions (such as pharmacy, dentistry and physiotherapy) and peer recognition of expertise followed the long-term example of the medical profession to establish colleges of fellows, who were specialists in their field (Bentley & Dunstan, 2006, p. 199).

Tensions existed then, and still do, about what "counts" as scientific research in a profession (Stenhouse, 1981). With the introduction of large-scale clinical trials in medicine, evidence other than expert opinion could increasingly be relied upon in recommending interventions, marking the beginnings of evidence-based medicine (Tallis, 2005). Whereas standardised clinical trials could be developed for dosages of aspirin, professional practices such as counselling or teaching were not so amenable. In health, differences developed between medically orthodox ways of understanding illness and newer notions of "wellness" and preventative health. Increasing community interest in alternative approaches to health highlighted emotional and spiritual dimensions of illness, previously considered to be purely physical. According to the scientifically based health professions, these alternative views lacked scientific evidence. During the 1980s, however, evidence began to accumulate for approaches that were previously dismissed, for example, in the new field of psychoneuro-immunology or acupuncture for pain. The notion that the type of research inquiry determined the outcome confronted previous certainty about the empirico-analytical scientific paradigm.

To keep up to date with new evidence from research in professions, increasing emphasis was placed on the need for continuing education. By now the notion of PD, as a means of updating knowledge and improving practice, was an increasing focus of associations. Support was offered through newsletters, monthly update lectures and occasional practical workshops under the tutelage of an expert in a particular field. Examination of what it meant to be an expert led to the development of the stage theory of development (Benner, 1984; Dreyfus & Dreyfus, 1986). Indeed the perceived purpose of much PD was, and still is, to support the progression of professionals along the continuum from novice to expert. It has been argued more recently, however, that expertise is not simply linear, being a more complex construct (Dall'Alba & Sandberg, 2006).

During the 1980s there was an explosion of research about the learning of professionals and other adults with particular relevance for PD. This research was not integrated into the practice of PD at that time; indeed, it can be argued that much of this research still informs only innovative PD practices. Paradoxically, in this era of emphasis on scientific rigour in professional research, the breakthroughs in educational research highlighted the value of experience and reflection, both areas difficult to investigate in a quantitative manner. Much of this research owed some debt to renewed interest in Dewey, the American educational philosopher. Richard Rorty (1982) brought Dewey's (e.g. 1933) theories of learning, as reflective inquiry into experience, to a new generation of educational researchers, as Schön also did to researchers into professional practice.

This paradox, between rational, scientific evidence and evidence gained through reflection on practice experience, formed the crux of Schön's (1983) influential research into the "messy swamp" of practice problems. He contrasted the relevance of this "low ground" of everyday practice with the rigour of the "high ground" of scientific research. According to him, the latter addressed problems in admirable detail in areas that often lacked relevance for practitioners. He recognised not only Dewey's influence but also that of Michael Polanyi's (1967) exploration of the tacit nature of much specialised knowledge. Schön argued that conceptions of professional knowledge as primarily propositional acquisition of facts didn't capture the complexity of knowing in practice, nor explain professional judgement in solving problems in the midst of practice. He argued against a division between theory and practice, stressing in his epistemology of practice the importance of recognising and framing problems, and the artistic, intuitive features of such reflection in action.

Although his work has been criticised (Eraut, 1994; Usher, Bryant, & Johnston, 1997), it was groundbreaking in its impact on professional education (Schön, 1987). Despite lack of attention to social and embodied features of learning, his critique of "technical rationality" as an unsuitable framework for examining professional practice is still as relevant today, especially with respect to continuing PD.

In research still reverberating today, Jean Lave's (1988) inquiry into mathematical reasoning in everyday life cogently critiqued the established concept of cognition as located within the mind and separate from social context. Her work extended into other explorations of situated learning with Wenger (Lave & Wenger, 1991) where they described how practitioners learn at work through participation in communities of practice. Thus the social and situated nature of learning, and the value of learning in authentic contexts rather than removed from practice (e.g. J. S. Brown, 1989), was highlighted in ways that are still having an impact on how we understand PL. Current questions about the adequacy of considering professional knowledge as a commodity, that can be transferred through PD into the minds of professionals to top up their knowledge, draws on the research of Schön and Lave in the 1980s.

Interest in frameworks to support learning in authentic contexts on real problems of practice turned to the processes of action learning and action research. Although both these processes can be traced back to the pre-war period, increasing interest in their use occurred through the 1980s. Both are cyclic, iterative processes involving planning, action, evaluation and reflection. Although there is ambiguity surrounding these terms and the meaning attributed to them varies in different contexts, distinctions can be drawn (e.g. Greenwood & Levin, 2007; O'Neil & Marsick, 2007). Action learning is often traced to the work of Englishman, Reg Revans (1965), on problem solving in workplaces. Although interest remains in organisational development, action learning has also been drawn upon in teaching and learning in higher education contexts. The outcome of learning, and making improvements to practice based on this experience, is a particular focus. Action research is often linked to the American, Kurt Lewin's (1951/1997), sociological field theory. The outcome of social or cultural change, with improvements contributing to public knowledge, is a particular focus. It is now an established participatory research methodology in education and organisational management as well as in community development.

Both these approaches have relevance for considering how professionals learn from experience, alone or in a collaborative group, in an incidental manner or as part of a planned cyclic intervention. Boud and colleagues (1985) considered reflection to be the key that enabled learning from experience. The experiential learning cycle of David Kolb (1984) is often used to explain this process and has been adapted into continuing spirals of action learning (Cowan, 2006) or collaborative action research (Kemmis & McTaggart, 1988), as used in higher education and workplace learning contexts. In highlighting and theorising the role of informal and incidental learning at work, Victoria Marsick and Karen Watkins (1990, p. 245) were prescient in proposing action learning as a potential model for innovative PD. Since then many variations on action learning and research models have emerged. Common to most is the linking of experience and reflection, highlighting the value of collaborative inquiry and questioning of assumptions, such as David Tripp's (1998) "action inquiry" in supporting teachers to learn from critical incidents in practice. Although not always recognised, Dewey's legacy of linking active experience with reflective inquiry is apparent through this body of research.

The impact of critical theorist Jürgen Habermas (1973) influenced the rising interest in critical reflection in PL by the end of the 1980s, with Jack Mezirow, Max van Manen and others acknowledging his influence. In examining the philosophical basis of knowing and practice, van Manen (1977, p. 226) described three levels of reflection, with the "highest" level being critical. His article is referred to in much teacher theorising about reflection, without acknowledgement of the epistemological paradigms (instrumental, interpretive and critical) underpinning these levels and how different paradigms shape the form of any reflective activity. Within the critical paradigm, for example, ideological assumptions underlying social conditions, power, authority, equality and justice are questioned. This critical approach to reflective inquiry was particularly advanced in adult education (Brookfield, 1987; Mezirow, 1991). Having worked in community development, Mezirow (1963) stressed the transformative potential of critical reflection, for learning leading to social change.

Through the 1980s, the role of qualitative research in understanding human experiences, such as learning, increasingly gained legitimacy in the social sciences, although many professions viewed the value of such research with scepticism. Mary Field Belenkey and colleagues' (Belenky, Clinchy, Goldberger, & Tarule, 1986) descriptions of *Women's Ways of Knowing* highlighted the role of emotions and identity in learning. Other work about the importance of emotions in learning and at work (e.g. Hochschild, 1983) eventually found "scientific" validation in the work of neuroscientist Antonio Damasio's (1994) studies of emotions in reasoning. Qualitative research into PL, such as life history inquiry (Marsick & Watkins, 1990, p. 101), found resonance with Belenkey's research, as evidenced in the collection of *Professionals' Ways of Knowing* (Baskett & Marsick, 1992).

I had moved to working in the relatively new field of community-based practice, working in multidisciplinary teams in health and education. We had to rethink our practice assumptions and certainties, through listening to the needs of families. We often found that clients' perspectives and involvement were more useful in planning action than our standardised assessment tools. As a part-time academic, and a contributor to a professional association, I was also involved in running courses for professionals despite having a limited understanding of the new field of adult learning. Whilst keeping up to date with new scientific research about my profession, I was increasingly aware that such research was not answering all my questions about learning and practice.

### 2.3.5  Progressing Relentlessly Towards Excellence

During the 1990s, the world appeared to grow smaller, yet faster, with the pace of change accelerating. Global concerns stretched beyond national borders to international networks of exchange and competition: of people, goods and services, including education (Kanter, 1995). Changes in access to information and communication, with the development of personal computers and the World Wide Web, had a profound affect on the work and education of professionals (OECD, 1996). Lifelong learning appeared centre stage (OECD, 1998b). Visions of learning, as a pathway to justice and emancipation (Freire, 1996), and a means of developing human potential espoused as "Learning to Be" (Delors, 1996), were seen as coming closer to fruition. Unfortunately, these visions are not widely realised with lifelong learning seen as an ambiguous, overused concept, which is, according to Coffield (2000a, p. 4), "under-researched, under-theorised, unencumbered by doubt and unmoved by criticism."

Despite such ambiguity about continuing learning, the use of knowledge by employees became an important concern for organisations in what was increasingly described as a "knowledge economy" (Drucker, 1992). Organisational learning discourse drew on human capital and systems theory (Streumer, 2006). The notion of "human capital" gained prominence, where employees are considered as essential resources whose "capacity" could be developed for competitive purposes (OECD, 1998a). Systems theory became a sophisticated framework for supporting organisational change and learning. For example, Peter Senge (1990) described a dynamic systems framework for understanding interrelationships in the workplace and "harnessing" collective aspirations. People and their sense-making processes in organisations were sometimes referred to as "soft systems" (Checkland & Scholes, 1990). Debates in organisational learning arose, concerned with: the relative needs of the organisation, the work group or the individual; whether the change in learning was about knowledge or behaviour; the relative value of action and outcomes compared to theoretical frameworks; and the evaluation of training to ensure effectiveness and efficiency (Easterby-Smith et al., 2000; Rowden, 1996). The latter focus, reflecting the economic rationalism of the era, grew in importance.

Governments as well as organisations were focusing more on the continued learning of professionals, with their specific skills seen as an increasingly important component of labour market regulation. Staff training in skills necessary for organisational life became linked to notions of continuing education and PD. Introduction to information technology was often the first experience of workplace training for many professionals who had previously had their PD needs supported by professional associations. They found the structured seminars a useful way to develop these skills; implementing them into their practice was not so straightforward, however (Bennett et al., 1994). Continuing education being provided by employers, whether government or private organisations, raised issues about the purpose of such learning, its evaluation and whether it should be mandatory or voluntary. In the health sector in the United Kingdom, researchers found that continuing education, conceived of as an opportunity by those in charge, could be perceived as a threat by professionals involved (Hewison, Dowswell, & Millar, 2000, p. 193). It was not that the professionals lacked motivation to learn, but that opportunities were too regulated and inflexible, and failed to take into account their busy lives and complex practices. In a recent study examining conceptions of continuing PD across a range of professions, a similar mismatch was found between stakeholder ideals and those of practitioners (Friedman & Phillips, 2004). Questions have been raised about whether continuing professional education can be considered as a "panacea, placebo or poison" (Brennan, 1990, p. 31).

Fuelling debates about the purpose of PD was increasing emphasis on keeping up to date with new research. In health, the evidence-based medicine movement gained momentum through the 1990s, based on David Sackett's (Sackett, Rosenberg, Gray, Haynes, & Richardson, 1996) hierarchical rules of evidence. Increasingly, double-blind, randomised, controlled clinical trials became the "gold standard" for establishing efficacy in medicine. Sacketts' original nuanced version of evidence-based medicine, as the integration of research evidence with clinical expertise and patients' values, often become debased in its transformation to a generic form of evidence-based practice in professions, from teaching to social work, where evidence cannot be so neatly controlled (Biesta, 2007; Davies, 2003). Even in health, bureaucratic invasion has reduced the original aims to a form of administrative control in some cases (Harrison & Checkland, 2009). Whilst a proponent of the value of evidence-based medicine, Raymond Tallis (2005, p. 35) queries "the notion that medical practice can be reduced to a series of algorithms". Indeed, can any professional practice be reduced in this way?

Linked to the increased focus on evidence-based regulation, evaluation of learning outcomes of PD with respect to performance was increasingly sought. To enable measurement, ways of identifying attributes of professional competence at work were devised (e.g. Gonczi, Hager, & Olivier, 1990). The issue of which attributes were of value, and how they could be assessed, was hotly debated. If competence was reduced to easily assessable domains or skills, does that devalue the process? How do you assess the ability to inspire others, or to empathise? Appreciation of professional competency, as integrated, embodied and context dependent, has developed (Cheetham & Chivers, 2005; Hager & Beckett, 1995), but critique continues about competence being attribute based. Alternative views consider competence to involve discursively constructed ways of being a professional and understanding practice (Sandberg & Dall'Alba, 2006; Sandberg & Pinnington, 2009).

Conceptualisations of competence drew on research into how professional knowledge was used to make judgements in practice. In health, the focus was primarily on rational cognitive processes, analysed within a predominantly positivistic research paradigm (Patel & Arocha, 2000). To help professionals deal with uncertainties of practice, clinical reasoning models were developed as normative guides, often involving complex algorithms. Increasingly, the realisation that multiple dimensions were in play in professional judgement led to broader models, integrating client perspectives, the professional's frame of reference and context for intervention (e.g. Higgs & Jones, 2000). Divergent approaches, acknowledging "professional artistry" and "practice wisdom", emerged (Fish, 1998; Titchen & Higgs, 2001). Drawing on extensive research into PL across professions from the 1990s onwards, Eraut (1994, 2000, 2007) developed several typologies and taxonomies, involving different domains of professional knowledge, modes of cognition, means of learning and factors involved in learning at work. Despite the value of this research and usefulness of learning taxonomies and clinical reasoning models for analysis, it remains difficult to capture the experience of knowing in practice and learning as lived. Professional knowing and learning may not be *experienced* by practitioners as a mixture of domains or factors.

In contrast to a professional climate with an increasing focus on evidence and outcomes, research interest in *learning*, as opposed to training or education, grew. Innovative research explored the situated, social and incidental nature of "moment to moment" learning in practice (Rogoff, 1990). A sociocultural perspective on learning in vocational areas of practice was explored from the 1990s onwards by Stephen Billett (1996, 2001, 2002), suggesting ways that workers could be supported to learn through staged and scaffolded participation in work. Marsick and Watkins's (1990, p. 28) research found that informal learning at work is enhanced by supporting staff to develop agency in seeking learning opportunities, to critically reflect on assumptions and to creatively explore ideas. In his ethnographic study of work, Wenger (1998) extended his theory of learning through social engagement in practice, highlighting interconnections between learning, identity and practice.

Such situated research reverberated within the teaching profession, in concert with interpretive research into the lives of teachers (Goodson & Hargreaves, 1996; Palmer, 1998), leading to innovative ways of supporting PL (Darling-Hammond, 1997; Lieberman & Miller, 2001). By the end of the decade, with a shift in focus from teaching to learning in higher education, innovative pedagogical changes were also introduced into some areas of undergraduate professional education (DeZure & Marchese, 2000). Reflective practice was increasingly recognised as important in learning, in higher education, adult education and the workplace (Moon, 1999). Only rarely was the potential role of reflection in PD critically questioned, however, in terms of challenge to or transformation of assumptions (Cranton, 1996). Despite recognition of the value of reflection in research, in practice many educational or working cultures did not, and still do not, support reflection let alone critique (Brockbank, McGill, & Beech, 2002). If undertaken, the context for reflection was often unexamined, with little consideration of power relationships, privacy issues, emotions or trust (Boud & Walker, 1998).

The legitimacy of situated research into experience culminated in the release of Norman Denzin and Yvonna Lincoln's (1994) "bible" of qualitative researchers, outlining multiple approaches to inquiry relevant to PL. The qualitative researcher was described as a "bricoleur", constructing inquiry into social lives drawing on diverse approaches. Dilemmas of choice almost overcame problems of justification (Kvale, 1994). Postmodernism had an impact on research and social theory through the 1990s, with its rejection of certainties and recognition of multiple, fractured perspectives. With respect to research into PL, it was Jean-Francois Lyotard's (1984) incisive critique of the performative use of knowledge, and Foucault's (1980) links between power, governance and knowledge, that inspired educational research critiquing the impact of neoliberal and economic rationalist policies on learning and work (e.g. Apple, 2000; Usher et al., 1997). By the end of the 1990s, critical research into the workplace as a context for learning questioned the legitimisation of learning for primarily performative ends (e.g. Garrick & Rhodes, 2000).

To support performative goals, the control of quality and pursuit of excellence featured widely in organisational and professional discourse. Tom Peters and Robert Waterman's (1982/2004, p. xx) management exhortation that organisational excellence "require[s] and demand[s] extraordinary performance from the average man" has not changed in the decades between book versions. Coffield questions the relentless pursuit of excellence and "tyranny of momentum" driving organisational learning and continuing education, which has continued through the 1990s to the current day. In the pursuit of good, then best and finally excellent professional practice, will perfection be the next goal (Coffield & Edward, 2009)? Optimistic aspirations towards the emancipatory power of lifelong learning seem to be submerged beneath economic imperatives. Sociologist Anthony Giddens (1999) captured the mood at end of the 1990s by describing the "Runaway World", as doubts surfaced about the unremitting pursuit of ever-continuing growth and progress.

As a working mother from the 1980s onwards, with increasing responsibilities, I understood the time bind and juggling referred to by social researchers of this period, Arlie Hochschild (1997) and Barbara Pocock (2001). I worked in a large government organisation, with responsibility for staff supervision and support of PD. As part of a team, we ran workshops and developed online networks, drawing on the latest in organisational training and professional continuing education. It was postgraduate study in education, however, that introduced me to the extensive research into situated and informal learning and highlighted the gap between research findings and PD practices. New perspectives opened that led me back to academia to undertake the research described in the following chapters of this book.

### 2.3.6 Managing Uncertainty and Complexity

It is difficult to describe the shape of a decade whilst living it. This section considers emerging trends and challenges with respect to the continuing learning of professionals in the first decade of the new millennium. Certainly, a PD industry has emerged, with multiple stakeholders, including consumers, professional associations, universities, workplaces and governments, bringing differing perspectives to questions of purpose and process in PD. In the United Kingdom, there has been intense political focus on the new "Learning Society", with policy aiming towards cohesion, coordination and control of the post-school Learning and Skills sector. Other western governments are moving towards national coordination of sectors involved with education and skills development. Coffield (2000b) offers a thoughtful but incisive critique of this policy development. Although he focus is not specifically on professionals and their learning, much of the research referred to is relevant. Many professionals work in the government sector (e.g. nurses and teachers) or in organisations with defined learning and development goals and strategies to support and evaluate staff performance. Mandatory PD is increasingly linked to a national process of professional registration that must be maintained for practicing professionals, even those in private practice.

There are good reasons to seek such regulation and control. The public needs to be able to trust that the professional they seek advice from is knowledgeable and competent. Employers need to ensure their professional staff are maintaining skills whilst providing fiscal accountability to shareholders or the government. A debate is growing, however, about whether regulation of practice and control of PD will achieve these goals. Coffield (2007, p. 39) critiques the focus of "delivery" of learning to "deficient" practitioners with a resulting tension between "enabling" and "controlling" strategies. It can be argued there will always be tension between political agendas, economic pressures, organisational goals, consumer expectations, educational investments and professional interests (Easterby-Smith et al., 2000, p. 793). Research into PL needs to recognise rather than ignore these tensions and investigate how professionals deal with them whilst engaging in daily practice.

Coexistent with increasing regulation of practice is the sense that both the world and professional practice are becoming more complex and uncertain. With rapid progress in western economies, social theorists, researchers and the community have commented increasingly on a world of uncertainty (Bauman, 2007; Handy, 1996). For professionals, expectations from both their clients and managers have altered, with resulting changes in models of service delivery. Within the health sector for example, there has been a shift from the paradigm of "helping people" achieve goals largely determined by practitioners to "facilitating self-help" by engaging with clients to understand their needs (Trede & Higgs, 2003). Despite the positive nature of this change for clients and most professionals, some practitioners feel unsettled in having their habitual practices questioned. Uncertainty may also be experienced through the proliferation of organisational change processes, often couched in terms of PD. Overall, there is awareness that professionals need to be educated to deal with a world of uncertainty and "supercomplexity" (Barnett, 2000, 2004).

One way of conceptualising this current decade as a context for professional practice and learning is in terms of a tension between certainty and uncertainty (Mullavey-O'Byrne & West, 2001). Evidence-based practice, professional standards and alignment of employee learning with organisational goals, all a focus from the 1990s onwards, aim to enhance the certainty of outcomes through regulation of practice. The drive towards regulation has been described as a quest for the certainty of structural solutions, to resolve complex issues that are not structural in nature (Weil, 1999). Bureaucratic solutions to issues of practice have had limited success, as practice involving human beings is inherently unpredictable (Darling-Hammond, 1997; Fullan, 2007). It is paradoxical to highlight the need for practitioners to question practice in a climate of increasing control of practice (Abrandt Dahlgren, Richardson, & Kalman, 2004). This situation is not unique to health professionals. Similar tensions are described with respect to the PD of teachers (Beijaard, Meijer, Morine-Dershimer, & Tillema, 2005; Groundwater-Smith & Mockler, 2009).

From the turn of the century when challenges for work-related learning were articulated (Boud & Garrick, 1999), this area has experienced an exponential growth of research. From an interest in vocational learning, the field of work-related learning has expanded to involve a wide range of professions and vocations, with particular interest in understanding more about the support of informal learning at work (Colley et al., 2002; Hager & Halliday, 2006). Marsick (2006, p. 52) estimates that up to three-quarters of the learning that takes place at work is informal or incidental. A more critical focus on interrelationships between individual and collective identities and agencies, and the interconnections of workplace context and learning cultures, has extended the organisational learning debates of the 1990s (Billett, 2008a, 2008b; Fenwick, 2008a; Hodkinson, Biesta, & James, 2008). Such debates are often overlooked in the continuing focus of PD on transfer of knowledge. An argument has been made for a move from this primarily epistemological focus to a broader ontological one, with professional undergraduate and continuing education extended to support professional ways of knowing, acting *and* being (Barnett & Coate, 2005; Dall'Alba, 2009).

Current work-related research is critical of assumptions underlying organisational learning. Despite the value of some concepts, their economic and cybernetic origins are reflected in the way proponents may refer to human beings in a dehumanised manner. Coffield (2007, p. 16) argues that a debased, simplified version of human capital theory has been seized upon, with a mechanical discourse of delivery, drivers and leverage. Similar critiques can be made about other concepts, such as systems theory, quality management and even communities of practice. For example, Senge (1990, p. 4) stressed human values in his description of systems learning noting that "real learning gets to the heart of what it means to be human". This emphasis is lost in applications of systems theory as organisational control. The rhetoric of quality management can focus on trivial, but controllable features of working life, sometimes bearing little relationship to ethical professional responsibilities to clients (Groundwater-Smith & Mockler, 2009, p. 69). Despite the value of considering learning through engagement with practice communities, this concept is sometimes reduced to a formulae for project teams (McDermott, 2002), with limited awareness of difficulties in regulating or artificially creating communities (Boud & Middleton, 2003; Marsick, 2006). Increasingly, PD is linked to processes of organisational change, but implementing change is not easy (Alvesson & Sveningsson, 2008). Sustainable change involves complex cultural practices, related to identity, meaning and values, and is not easily amenable to systems control or leveraging of human capacities (Fullan, 2005). Even when organisations focus on values, the emphasis is often on how employees "should be" (Rhodes & Scheeres, 2004). As organisations become leaner, employees may be squeezed as cogs in a machine rather than as individual practitioners and learners.

Sustainability has become a central issue of society following the recent global economic collapse and climate change agendas. Although concern with the triple bottom line (economic, social and environmental outcomes) was raised nearly a decade ago, the idea that sustainability involves interconnections between these areas is more recent. Professional contributions to the social sustainability of communities have been addressed in various contexts, including health, business and education (V. A. Brown, Grootjans, Ritchie, Townsend, & Verrinda, 2005; Limerick, Crowther, & Cunnington, 2002; Willis, McKenzie, & Harris, 2009). Attention has been drawn to the sustainability of organisational change, in terms of durability of outcomes as well as impact on social systems. Coffield (2007, p. 39) asserts that the "heavy hand" of regulation in the Learning Society is focused on short-term outcomes rather than long-term sustainability, arguing that increased professional self-regulation is more likely to result in sustainable learning outcomes. Innovative educational and organisational change can be difficult in a climate of standardisation. When the frenetic surface activity of implementation calms, deeply engrained practices may be found unperturbed on the "unruffled calm of the ocean floor" (Hayward, Priestley, & Young, 2004). For change to be sustainable, it must involve participant ownership and be consistent with "deep values of human purpose" (Fullan, 2005, p. ix). There is an art as well as a science to sculpting organisational change, argue Marsick & Watkins (1999, p. 137), who describe the need to develop cultures with "an enhanced capability for dialogue, inquiry and critical reflection." Michael Fullan (2005) stresses the dynamic nature of sustainable change, in that continual relentless change is unsustainable. Pauses for consolidation are required in what may become iterative erratic cycles. Despite difficulties, many systemic changes offer important steps towards enhancing the lives of people, from students to patients. A balance is required, between centralised informed policy and flexible local implementation, so that improvements that are important to society may be realised (Luke & McArdle, 2009).

Such a balance requires collaborative research partnerships between stakeholders in work-related learning (e.g. Boud, Cressey, & Docherty, 2006). Paradigmatic and methodological research diversity may be required to highlight multiple viewpoints (Borko, 2004; Creswell, 2009). Between macro-quantitative surveys and micro-narrative interviews, there is a need for more intermediate-level research, involving practice communities or activity systems, for example (Easterby-Smith et al., 2000). Where organisational change is investigated, longitudinal studies or those involving ethnographic immersion may prove especially valuable (e.g. Alvesson & Sveningsson, 2008; Gherardi & Nicolini, 2006). Increasingly, there is recognition of the need for creativity and innovation in education and work to address complex societal problems, with value placed on the development of situated, applied transdisciplinary or "mode two" knowledge (Nowotny, Scott, & Gibbons, 2001). Such a collaborative approach to research has been supported by the introduction of Cooperative Research Centres in Australia and elsewhere, increasingly focused on "collaborating to a purpose". That purpose aims towards enhancing the public good in ways that are "sustainable, community-orientated, productive and creative" (Australian Government, 2008).

As this decade draws to a close, echoes of the late 1960s can be discerned. In that era, when sustainability was last widely publicised, it was considered as a radical agenda. Now sustainability is seen as a core concern of education, work, government and society. Another change reflecting concerns of 40 years ago is a renewed interest in secular ethics, the value and meaning of work and the possible contribution that learning can make to transforming lives (e.g. De Botton, 2009; Hamilton, 2008; Prilleltensky & Prilleltensky, 2006). Concerns about social justice and interest in the quality of community life, measured in terms other than gross domestic product, are rising (Sen, 2009; Wilkinson & Pickett, 2009). These community sentiments are marginal but apparent, highlighting possibilities opened through questioning the status quo, that were raised at the end of the 1960s (C. Taylor, 2007, p. 473). Sartre claimed that at that time "imagination was put into power" (Bourges, Sartre, & Cohn-Bendit, 1968).

My re-immersion in academia, after working in government and community sectors, has confirmed for me that concerns expressed over this current decade, about uncertainty and change, managerialism and work intensification, are felt across working contexts in society, including the academe (Rowland, 2006; Winefield, 2008). Academics and researchers are also professionals and learners. Movement back into academia has reminded me of Sartre's claim that ideas can be powerful.

## 2.3.7 Valuing Possibilities of Professionalism

One way of framing future possibilities for the development of professionals is to look behind contexts that have contributed to certainty and uncertainty in professional lives, and research into how learning occurs at work, and consider assumptions underpinning the notion of professionalism. Eliot Freidson (2001) contrasts the ideology and practice of "professionalism" of professionals, with Max Weber's analysis of "managerialism" of bureaucracies, and the "consumerism" of free markets from Adam Smith's conceptions. Freidson's differentiating focus between these theoretical "logics" is the control of work. He argues that the term "professionalism" refers to "circumstances in which the members of occupations, rather than consumers or managers control their work" (p. 12).

Freidson (2001, p. 3) maintains that whilst global changes have led to celebrated triumphs of bureaucracies and markets in producing economic growth, professionals have failed to articulate core principles of professionalism beyond their "rhetoric of good intentions". Principles of professionalism are contrasted by him, with those of bureaucracies, concerned with efficiency and standardisation, and markets, concerned with competition and cost. Researchers have commented on the shift of control of professional practice to workplace organisations and governments, critiquing the resulting managerialism (e.g. Davies, 2003; Felstiner, 2005; Germov, 2005). With respect to the market orientation, in the information age consumers can become experts and, rightly, exercise some control over professional practice. Professionals may feel squeezed between consumer needs and choices, and several levels of organisational bureaucracy and control (Coffield, 2007). Indeed, Gloria Dall'Alba (2009) describes a "crisis of confidence" with respect to how professionals are educated to deal with such issues.

Freidson's theoretical analysis has potential implications for PD. William Sullivan (1995) has also written about the philosophy of professionalism, referring to integrity as a professional responsibility that holds particular promise for addressing society's problems, from environmental degradation to social conflict. Both argue that the core, or "soul" of professionalism as Freidson (2001, p. 213) refers to, is the ability to enhance the public good. Both have made the distinction between professionalization, as credentialism through educational processes, and professionalism, as cultural ways of being professional. The hallmark of this conceptualisation of professionalism involves a nexus between "independent judgement and freedom of action" and responsibility towards clients that reach beyond work towards "transcendent values", such as justice or well-being (Freidson, 2001, p. 122).

Possibilities may exist within a clearly articulated notion of professionalism, focused on society's needs, that the march of professionalisation, overtaken by economic and bureaucratic agendas, cannot adequately address. For example, William Sullivan and Matthew Rosin (2008) argue that professional education needs to be humanistically inspired to integrate professional judgement and technical competence with civic and moral purpose. Perhaps, within a transformed framework of PD, support for professionals could also raise these axiological concerns, in addition to epistemological and ontological issues, in discussions about not only what professionals know and can do but also who they are and what they and society value. With such support, professionals may be able to enhance the difference they already make.

With increasing interest in interdisciplinary and inter-agency collaboration in solving complex problems, diversity of perspectives is important (Meads, Jones, Harrison, Forman, & Turner, 2009). Apart from problems with sustainability of outcomes, in an increasingly standardised professional world, diversity is crushed. Centralised control often neglects the strengths that lie in diversity that may generate creativity and innovation. In 1994, Denzin and Lincoln described five "moments" of qualitative inquiry from traditional ethnography, through modernism's rigour to postmodernist critique. In the current edition of their book (2005), they describe the eighth and ninth moments of the future, as fractured multidimensional research inquiry aligned through a clear sense of social purpose.

## 2.4  Tracing Professional Development

Obvious limitations are imposed by this predominantly linear and abbreviated review. Years of history, research and practice cannot be easily summarised. Decades may form a clumsy organisational tool for review, with influences on and impact of research extending beyond each decade. Mapping seminal research of value to understanding PL and influencing PD, against sociocultural developments in professional practice and the world at large, provides a meta-view however. My own experience through each period colours this review, influencing my choice of focal points, although this is acknowledged through outlining the context of that experience. I acknowledge insights gained through careful reading of the arguments of previous researchers, details of which are often lost in the retelling through reviews. I was not so much climbing onto the "shoulders of giants" but scaling different ladders to view the terrain. The value of a temporal summary is in locating significant threads, tensions or patterns that run through the years. The most obvious observation is that different fields of inquiry related to PD and PL have remained as separate threads until recently.

## *2.4.1  Threads of Inquiry*

The practice of PD and understanding of PL have been informed by multiple areas of research inquiry, influenced by expectations and policies from a range of stakeholders. From the 1970s onwards there have been two main influences on the way that continuing PD has been used to support professionals. One stream was that of continuing professional education, the other being organisational learning.

Continuing professional education drew on models of formal learning influenced by undergraduate professional education, with an emphasis on providing updates of new knowledge and practice. Initially continuing education was controlled by professional associations, with universities contributing from the 1980s. Accountability to, and protection of, the public through supervision of established standards has been the focus (e.g. Golding & Gray, 2006). Evidence-based practice, with positivistic research providing the most legitimate form of evidence, has been influential, particularly in health, but increasingly across other professions. Proof of efficacious practice has been important in supporting the legitimacy and growth of different professional groups. Considerable research has been undertaken to understand more about professional knowledge in attempts to capture the complexity of knowing in practice. Innovative pedagogical changes in undergraduate professional education, such as collaborative or reflective learning, have not had a widespread impact on continuing education after graduation.

The second major influence on PD has been that of organisational learning and human resource management, influenced by andragogy, human capital and systems theories. The control of organisational learning rests with organisations where professionals are employees whose knowledge, skills and performance are of value, particularly if aligned with strategic goals (e.g. Rothwell, 2005). Although organisational learning had developed as a field of practice earlier, it was not until the 1990s that this approach influenced the learning of professionals through training and development programs and performance reviews. As governments adopted organisational frameworks, efficiency of professional service delivery was sought. Despite innovative practices such as action learning developing from within this field, the impact on PD has been limited until recently. The field of continuing professional education has been critiqued for lack of attention to the complexity of professional practice knowledge, whereas the field of human resource development has been critiqued for lack of attention to the cultural complexities of organisational life (Bierema & Eraut, 2004).

From the 1980s onwards, research interest in the social and situated nature of learning, and value of informal and incidental learning, emerged as a work-related learning thread of influence. With increasing research into the complex interrelationships between learning, identity, context and practice, this area of inquiry is challenging and rapidly changing conventional notions of PD, especially in professions, such as teaching, nursing and occupational therapy. Currently, PD provided by professional associations and universities is still primarily focused on education, competence and evidence; that provided by business and government organisations is still focused on training, performance and compliance. Both groups of providers have broadened their strategies to include innovative activities such as mentors, networks and action learning, but tend towards an instructional approach, either as education or as training, as an assumed starting point. The value of instruction in supporting PL has been questioned since Houle's research. Recent research from the work-related area of inquiry highlights the value of self-directed PL with support to structure or guide that learning.

A fourth thread with some influence on theory but, as yet, minimal impact on practice is that of transformative learning (E. W. Taylor, 2008). The emancipatory potential of adult and community education, with the prospect of personal transformation and social change, is emerging as an innovative framework for support of the learning of professional communities (e.g. Grace, 2007; Oakes & Rogers, 2007). For transformation to occur, practitioners need to be involved in truly critical reflective inquiry, where taken-for-granted assumptions and values are foregrounded and challenged. Through dealing with issues of meaning and purpose, sustainable changes in practice may occur, with potential benefits for professionals and society (Cranton, 2006; Willis et al., 2009). Despite research and theory into critical reflection over the past 30 years, this area has gained little traction within PD. Moves towards self-directed and/or transformative learning would entail structural and cultural changes in the working environments of professionals.

## 2.4.2  Patterns of Tensions

Certain tensions have been raised repeatedly over the past 20–30 years, highlighting consistent gaps between research and practice in PD. Related to tensions between certainty and uncertainty in the professional context runs a tension between regulation and innovation. On the one hand is the need for accountability, responsibility, standards and evidence-based practice. On the other is the valuing of self-regulated professional autonomy, agency to seek learning opportunities, creativity to try innovative approaches and support for the development of these capabilities. The difference, with respect to PD aimed at achieving these two sets of outcomes, is essentially between a deficit as opposed to a strengths approach. In noting these tensions in this review, my intention is not to resolve them but to raise questions for research. Learning for performative organisational ends poses a conundrum for advocates of the transformative potential of learning at work, usually educational researchers. Is this a conundrum for professionals? What type of support do professionals say they need?

Thirty years ago, the research of Houle and Schön, in different ways, critiqued formal directed support for PL, recognising the value for professionals of self-directed learning in the former case and reflection in action in the latter. Despite decades of relevant research since, their critiques of didactic instruction delivered within a paradigm of technical rationality remain pertinent today. The assumption underlying much PD, that professionals need careful control, is at odds with current undergraduate education that seeks to enhance independent critical thinking and the ability to form complex judgements. There is a need for research about learning from the perspective of professionals in practice. Instead of undertaking a needs analysis by asking what type of PD delivery or content is required, questions about the experience of learning need to be asked. In particular, how is PL experienced within the complexities of the current workplace? Are the tensions that have been mentioned through the latter part of this review seen as difficulties for professionals with respect to their learning?

In recent years, interest in dialectical rather than dichotomous approaches to dealing with the complexities of learning has emerged. Instead of viewing contradictory concerns as either/or, generative possibilities rather than reductive compromises may be sought. Rather than viewing the needs of the organisation and the individual as always in opposition in a "zero-sum game", a challenge of the future is to find ways to balance needs for productivity with individual quality of life (Boud et al., 2006, p. 3). Boud and colleagues, for example, argue for reframing reflection at work as collaborative and productive in addition to being an individual concern.

Working with, as well as challenging, the context for learning is of value. Instead of outright rejection, for example, evidence-based practice may be reframed as evidence-informed practice. In situations where teachers were encouraged to make their assumptions explicit, examining these, in the light of research evidence as well as evidence from their own practice, led to increasing rather than decreasing autonomy (Cordingley, 2008, p. 45). Whilst arguing for more autonomy and agency in PL, I agree with Andy Hargreaves (1997) who noted that if autonomy is based on "individualism and isolation" it can inhibit rather than enhance innovation in teaching. He maintained that professional autonomy in PD needs to go hand in hand with collaborative, collegial communities of inquiry.

Finally, the notion of "development" in PD has been problematised in research, through comparison with the development of third-world communities, as something delivered by experts to those who are deficient, thus devaluing local knowledge and practices (McWilliam, 2002). Whilst I agree with this premise, if assumptions about learning are not examined, a move to shape interventions as "learning" rather than "development" will not alter the process or outcome. Development could refer to a generative process of growth where professionals are supported rather than controlled (Webb, 1996, p. 32). Learning could refer to an imposed regime of activities unrelated to practice or meaning for the professional. Terminology is important, but clarity and questioning of assumptions are crucial if changes are to be made in PD.

## 2.4.3 Professional Development Terrain

As the section headings in this review of research indicate, the focus of concerns with the continuing learning of professionals could be considered to have moved from authority, through uniformity, evidence and excellence, to a consideration of complexity and possibility. What the review has highlighted is the need for support of PL that considers not only epistemological concerns, changes in knowing or acting, but also ontological concerns, changes in professional ways of being. I have also suggested the need to consider axiological concerns. In what way, for example, are professionals' assumptions and values, about selves, practice or clients, surfaced or challenged in support for PL?

In summarising this review, I do not negate evidence, accountability or standards of professional practice. I am fully aware of their value. Instead I question continuing recourse to traditional PD discourse and practice as the default position for achieving these ends. If this account of PD is compared to a newspaper, traditional PD discourse could be viewed as the abbreviated yet dominating headline: *Professional Development Maintains Standards and Ensures Quality Outcomes!* Valuable research into PL has been relegated to the back page, with some of the interesting stories of practice moved to the colour lifestyle supplement. If the metaphor is continued, what is read in the headlines has a powerful rhetorical impact, but it is in the magazine that people recognise their experiences and often return to read again.

Over the past decades, understanding of learning has moved from analysis of the cognitive acquisition of knowledge to recognition that learning involves an interrelationship between the entire person and their social–cultural context. Increasingly, research into PL has highlighted the importance of active involvement and social interaction in learning, yet there is little significant change in PD practice. When PD stresses keeping up to date, it betrays a concept of the mind as a container for knowledge; the notion of learning as active inquiry is missing. In the perpetuation of the status quo, assumptions are rarely challenged.

There are no easy solutions to mapping a path towards enhancement of PL that takes the needs of all stakeholders into account: from the community, through organisations, to professionals themselves. What is important is that rather than focusing on specific activities or processes, assumptions about learning are foregrounded and critically examined when considering any research into better ways of supporting professionals as they continue to learn.

## 2.5  Setting the Scene

Apart from reviewing the research terrain, the purpose of this chapter has been to frame the context and intent of the research reported in Part III of this book. Problematic issues have been raised about the current context for PL and perceived purpose of PD. Is the environment of the current workplace one that fosters learning? In today's time-pressured environments, there may be limited time for discussion at work and even less for reflection. Does the explicit valuing of competency-based standards and evidence-based practice in professional registration and supervision create dilemmas for professionals? Many PD programmes aim to change the practice of professionals to improve outcomes aligned to organisational goals. Is this considered learning by professionals? Learning in conditions of complex change may exert pressure on individual professionals to make significant shifts in their understanding of practice. Does this raise dilemmas for individual professionals? From the review in this chapter, questions were raised about the experience of PL that underpinned the focus question and directed the design of my research.

A need for "closer scrutiny" of workplace practices and understanding of professional experiences at the "coal face" has been highlighted (Coffield, 2007; Easterby-Smith et al., 2000). Despite interesting and useful research that in some cases seeks to address problematic issues mentioned, much research separates the experience of learning into categories or factors for analysis. Categorisation of knowledge (e.g. domains), learners (e.g. learning styles) and context (e.g. informal and formal) is used as a way of dealing with the diversity and complexity of experience. Phenomenological research takes a holistic rather than atomistic approach to experience. It is difficult to describe a complex phenomenon like APL however, without falling into the usual delineation of factors. To illustrate my contention, two descriptions of learning from the literature are compared. The first is from Peter Jarvis's book *Human Learning: An Holistic Approach*, one of his respected texts on adult learning; the second from Wenger's *Communities of Practice: Learning, Meaning, and Identity*, where he details his social theory of learning.

Jarvis (2005, p. 117) describes learning as an interrelationship between the learner and social structures in the following way:

> [Learning is] the combination of processes whereby the whole person – body (genetic, physical and biological) and mind (knowledge, skills, attitudes, values, emotions, beliefs and senses) – is in a social situation and constructs an experience which is then transformed cognitively, emotionally or practically (or through any combination) and integrated into the individual's own biography.

Despite describing learning as complex and holistic, the language used makes it appear fragmented. As an integral aspect of lived experience, Wenger (1998, p. 5) proposes learning to consist of four intertwined components: meaning (learning as experiencing), practice (learning as doing), community (learning as belonging) and identity (learning as becoming). He describes learning as the development of meaning through a negotiated process between the individual, his or her history and experiences, and the social and cultural community. He does not describe learning as the sum of these features, but essentially maintains that all experiences of learning can be viewed as ways of experiencing, doing, belonging or becoming.

Wenger (1998, p. 141) considers the experience of learning as more than a combination of factors. He describes learning as part of everyday life at work, shaped by shared processes of socialisation and workplace practices, but with a unique quality based on individual ways of understanding experiences. He describes this dialectic:

> Our knowing – even of the most unexceptional kind – is always too big, too rich, too ancient, and too connected for us to be the source of it individually. At the same time, our knowing – even of the most elevated kind – is too engaged, too precise, too tailored, too active, and too experiential for it to be just of a generic size.

The approach Wenger takes to learning is relevant for this research in this book. As an example, I return to the participants' descriptions of PL that open the book, where a dialectic between the shared yet unique nature of learning experiences is exemplified. Nerida's chewing gum incident appears at face value to be a very specific and individualised occasion of PL. However, in seeing the situation as one where she learnt something new about the client, Nerida was drawing on years of shared professional knowledge about communication, based on her own experiences and those of others. Sally's learning through presenting research literature appears at face value to be more of a generalised academic PL. However, her initial interest in the particular technique and her dilemmas in applying it in practice were part of her very specific and personal involvement with her particular clients.

Although Wenger's research is not explicitly phenomenological, his concept of describing the essential features of a complex phenomenon rather than dividing the phenomenon into different elements is congruent with a phenomenological perspective. What is identified in much research as multiple facets of PL (such as cognition, emotion, practice, context or identity) are seen, from a phenomenological perspective, as inseparable, embedded within lived experience, as explained in the following chapter on phenomenology.

# References

Abrandt Dahlgren, M., Richardson, B., & Kalman, H. (2004). Redefining the reflective practitioner. In J. Higgs, B. Richardson, & M. Abrandt Dahlgren (Eds.), *Developing practice knowledge for health professionals* (pp. 15–33). Edinburgh; New York: Butterworth-Heinemann.

Alvesson, M., & Sveningsson, S. (2008). *Changing organizational culture: Cultural change work in progress*. New York: Routledge.

Apple, M. W. (2000). *Official knowledge: Democratic education in a conservative age* (2nd ed.). New York: Routledge.

Argyris, C., & Schön, D. A. (1974). *Theory in practice: Increasing professional effectiveness*. San Francisco: Jossey-Bass Publishers.

Argyris, C., & Schön, D. A. (1978). *Organizational learning: A theory of action perspective*. Reading, MA: Addison-Wesley Publishing Co.

Barnacle, R. (2005). Research education ontologies: Exploring doctoral becoming. *Higher Education Research and Development, 24*(2), 179–188.

Barnett, R. (2000). Supercomplexity and the curriculum. *Studies in Higher Education, 25*(3), 255–265.

Barnett, R. (2004). Learning for an unknown future. *Higher Education Research and Development, 23*(3), 247–260.

Barnett, R., & Coate, K. (2005). *Engaging the curriculum in higher education*. Maidenhead: Open University Press.

Barr, H., Koppel, I., Reeves, S., Hammick, M., & Freeth, D. (2005). *Effective interprofessional education: Argument, assumption and evidence*. Oxford: Blackwell.

Baskett, H. K. M., & Marsick, V. J. (Eds.). (1992). *Professionals' ways of knowing: New findings on how to improve professional education*. San Francisco: Jossey-Bass.

Bauman, Z. (2007). *Liquid times: Living in an age of uncertainty*. Cambridge: Polity Press.

Beijaard, D., Meijer, P., Morine-Dershimer, G., & Tillema, H. (Eds.). (2005). *Teacher professional development in changing conditions*. Dordrecht: Springer.

Belenky, M. F., Clinchy, B. M., Goldberger, N. R., & Tarule, J. M. (1986). *Women's ways of knowing: The development of self, voice, and mind*. New York: Basic Books.

Benner, P. (1984). *From novice to expert: Excellence and power in clinical nursing practice*. Menlo Park, CA: Addison-Wesley Publishing Co., Nursing Division.

Bennett, J. M., Broomham, R., Murton, P. M., Pearcy, T., & Rutledge, R. W. (Eds.). (1994). *Computing in Australia: The development of a profession.* Sydney, NSW: Hale & Iremonger; Australian Computer Society.

Bentley, P., & Dunstan, D. (2006). *The path to professionalism: Physiotherapy in Australia to the 1980s.* Melbourne, VIC: Australian Physiotherapy Association.

Berger, P. L., & Luckmann, T. (1966/1981). *The social construction of reality: A treatise in the sociology of knowledge.* Middlesex: Penguin Books.

Bierema, L. L., & Eraut, M. (2004). Workplace-focused learning: Perspective on continuing professional education and human resource development. *Advances in Developing Human Resources, 6*(1), 52–68.

Biesta, G. (2007). Why "what works" won't work: Evidence-based practice and the democratic deficit in educational research. *Educational Theory, 57*(1), 1–22.

Biggs, J. (2003). *Teaching for quality learning at university: What the student does* (2nd ed.). Philadelphia, PA: Society for Research into Higher Education & Open University Press.

Billett, S. (1996). Towards a model of workplace learning: The learning curriculum. *Studies in Continuing Education, 18*(1), 45–58.

Billett, S. (2001). *Learning in the workplace: Strategies for effective practice.* Crows Nest, NSW: Allen & Unwin.

Billett, S. (2002). Towards a workplace pedagogy: Guidance, participation, and engagement. *Adult Education Quarterly, 53*(1), 27–43.

Billett, S. (2008a). Learning throughout working life: A relational interdependance between personal and social agency. *British Journal of Educational Studies, 56*(1), 39–58.

Billett, S. (2008b). Subjectivity, learning and work: Sources and legacies. *Vocations and Learning, 1*(2), 149–171.

Borko, H. (2004). Professional development and teacher learning: Mapping the terrain. *Educational Researcher, 33*(8), 3–15.

Boud, D. (2006). 'Aren't we all learner-centred now?': The bittersweet flavour of success. In P. Ashwin (Ed.), *Changing higher education: The development of learning and teaching* (pp. 19–32). London: Routledge.

Boud, D., Cressey, P., & Docherty, P. (Eds.). (2006). *Productive reflection at work: Learning for changing organizations.* New York: Routledge.

Boud, D., & Garrick, J. (Eds.). (1999). *Understanding learning at work.* London: Routledge.

Boud, D., Keogh, R., & Walker, D. (Eds.). (1985). *Reflection: Turning experience into learning.* London: Kogan Page.

Boud, D., & Middleton, H. (2003). Learning from others at work: Communities of practice and informal learning. *Journal of Workplace Learning, 15*(5), 194–202.

Boud, D., & Solomon, N. (Eds.). (2001). *Work-based learning: A new higher education?* Philadelphia, PA: Society for Research into Higher Education & Open University Press.

Boud, D., & Walker, D. (1998). Promoting reflection in professional courses: The challenge of context. *Studies in Higher Education, 23*(2), 191–206.

Bourdieu, P. (1977). *Outline of a theory of practice.* Cambridge: Cambridge University Press.

Bourdieu, P. (1990). *The logic of practice* (R. Nice, Trans.). Cambridge: Polity Press.

Bourges, H., Sartre, J.-P., & Cohn-Bendit, D. (1968). *The French student revolt: The leaders speak* (B. Brewster, Trans.). New York: Hill and Wang.

Boyce, R. (2006). Emerging from the shadow of medicine: Allied health as a "professional community" subculture. *Health Sociology Review, 15*(5), 520–534.

Brennan, B. (Ed.). (1990). *Continuing professional education: Promise and performance.* Hawthorn, VIC: Australian Centre for Education Research.

Brint, S. (1993). Eliot Freidson's contribution to the sociology of professions. *Work and Occupations, 20*(3), 259–278.

Brockbank, A., McGill, I., & Beech, N. (Eds.). (2002). *Reflective learning in practice.* Aldershot, England; Burlington, VT: Gower.

Brookfield, S. (1987). *Developing critical thinkers: Challenging adults to explore alternative ways of thinking and acting*. San Francisco: Jossey-Bass.

Brown, J. S. (1989). Situated cognition and the culture of learning. *Educational Researcher, 18*(1), 32–42.

Brown, V. A., Grootjans, J., Ritchie, J. E., Townsend, M., & Verrinda, G. (Eds.). (2005). *Sustainability and health: Supporting global ecological integrity in public health*. Crows Nest, NSW: Allen & Unwin.

Burnham, J. C. (1998). *How the idea of profession changed the writing of medical history*. London: Wellcome Institute for the History of Medicine.

Cervero, R. M. (2001). Continuing professional education in transition, 1981–2000. *International Journal of Lifelong Education, 20*(1–2), 16–30.

Checkland, P., & Scholes, J. (1990). *Soft systems methodology in action*. Chichester: John Wiley & Sons.

Cheetham, G., & Chivers, G. (2005). *Professions, competence and informal learning*. Cheltenham; Northampton, MA: Edward Elgar.

Coffield, F. (2000a). Introduction: A critical analysis of the concept of a learning society. In F. Coffield (Ed.), *Differing visions of a learning society: Research findings* (pp. 1–38). Bristol: The Policy Press.

Coffield, F. (Ed.). (2000b). *Differing visions of a learning society: Research findings* (Vol. 1). Bristol: The Policy Press.

Coffield, F. (2007). *Running ever faster down the wrong road: An alternative future for education and skills*. London: Institute of Education, University of London.

Coffield, F., & Edward, S. (2009). Rolling out 'good', 'best' and 'excellent' practice. What next? Perfect practice? *British Educational Research Journal, 35*(3), 371–390.

Colley, H., Hodkinson, P., & Malcolm, J. (2002). *Non-formal learning: Mapping the conceptual terrain. A consultation report*. Leeds: University of Leeds Lifelong Learning Institute.

Cook, S. D., & Brown, J. S. (1999). Bridging epistemologies: The generative dance between organizational knowledge and knowing. *Organization Science, 10*(4), 381–400.

Cordingley, P. (2008). Research and evidence-informed practice: Focusing on practice and practitioners. *Cambridge Journal of Education, 38*(1), 37–52.

Cowan, J. (2006). *On becoming an innovative university teacher: Reflection in action* (2nd ed.). Buckingham; New York: Society for Research into Higher education & Open University Press.

Cranton, P. (1996). *Professional development as transformative learning: New perspectives for teachers of adults*. San Francisco: Jossey-Bass Publishers.

Cranton, P. (2006). *Authenticity in teaching*. San Francisco: Jossey-Bass.

Creswell, J. W. (2009). Mapping the field of mixed methods research. *Journal of Mixed Methods Research, 3*(2), 95–108.

Crotty, M. (1998). *The foundations of social research: Meaning and perspective in the research process*. St Leonards, NSW: Allen & Unwin.

Dall'Alba, G. (2004). Understanding professional practice: Investigations before and after an educational programme. *Studies in Higher Education, 29*(6), 679–692.

Dall'Alba, G. (2009). *Learning to be professionals*. Dortrecht: Springer.

Dall'Alba, G., & Sandberg, J. (2006). Unveiling professional development: A critical review of stage models. *Review of Educational Research, 76*(3), 383–412.

Damasio, A. R. (1994). *Descartes' error: Emotion, reason, and the human brain*. New York: G.P. Putnam's Sons.

Darling-Hammond, L. (1997). *The right to learn: A blueprint for creating schools that work*. San Francisco: Jossey-Bass.

Davies, B. (2003). Death to critique and dissent? The politics and practices of new managerialism and of "evidence-based practice". *Gender and Education, 15*, 91–103.

De Botton, A. (2009). *The pleasures and sorrows of work*. London: Hamish Hamilton, Penguin Books.

DeZure, D., & Marchese, T. J. (Eds.). (2000). *Learning from change: Landmarks in teaching and learning in higher education from Change magazine, 1969–1999*. London: Sterling, VA: Kogan Page; American Association for Higher Education.

Delors, J. (1996). *Learning, the treasure within: Report to UNESCO of the International Commission on Education for the Twenty-first Century*. Paris: UNESCO.

Denzin, N. K., & Lincoln, Y. S. (1994). *Handbook of qualitative research*. Thousand Oaks, CA: Sage Publications.

Denzin, N. K., & Lincoln, Y. S. (Eds.). (2005). *The SAGE handbook of qualitative research* (3rd ed.). Thousand Oaks, CA: Sage.

Dewey, J. (1929/1960). *The quest for certainty: A study of the relation of knowledge and action*. New York: Putnam.

Dewey, J. (1933). *How we think: A restatement of the relation of reflective thinking to the educative process*. Boston: Heath.

Dreyfus, H. L., & Dreyfus, S. E. (1986). *Mind over machine: The power of human intuition and expertise in the era of the computer*. New York: Free Press.

Drucker, P. F. (1992). *Managing for the future*. Oxford: Butterworth-Heinemann.

Easterby-Smith, M., Crossan, M., & Nicolini, D. (2000). Organizational learning: Debates past, present and future. *Journal of Management Studies, 37*(6), 783–796.

Engeström, Y. (1999). Activity theory and individual and social transformation. In Y. Engeström, R. Miettinen, & R.-L. Punamäki-Gitai (Eds.), *Perspectives on activity theory* (pp. 1–38). Cambridge; New York: Cambridge University Press.

Eraut, M. (1994). *Developing professional knowledge and competence*. London: Falmer Press.

Eraut, M. (2000). Non-formal learning and tacit knowledge in professional work. *British Journal of Educational Psychology, 70*, 113–136.

Eraut, M. (2004). Informal learning in the workplace. *Studies in Continuing Education, 26*(2), 247–273.

Eraut, M. (2007). Learning from other people in the workplace. *Oxford Review of Education, 33*(4), 403–442.

Etzioni, A. (1969). *The semi-professions and their organization*. New York: Free Press.

Felstiner, W. L. F. (Ed.). (2005). *Reorganization and resistance: Legal professions confront a changing world*. Portland, OR: Hart.

Fenwick, T. (2008a). Understanding relations of individual collective learning in work: A review of research. *Management Learning, 39*(3), 227–243.

Fenwick, T. (2008b). Workplace learning: Emerging trends and new perspectives. In S. B. Merriam (Ed.), *Third update on adult learning theory* (pp. 17–26). San Francisco: Jossey-Bass.

Fish, D. (1998). *Appreciating practice in the caring professions: Refocusing professional development and practitioner research*. Oxford: Butterworth Heinemann.

Foucault, M. (1980). *Power/knowledge: Selected interviews and other writings, 1972–1977* (C. Gordon, Trans.). New York: Pantheon Books.

Foucault, M. (1984). Nietzsche, genealogy, history. In P. Rabinow (Ed.), *The foucault reader* (pp. 76–100). London: Penguin.

Freidson, E. (1970). *Professional dominance: The social structure of medical care*. New York: Atherton Press.

Freidson, E. (1986). *Professional powers: A study of the institutionalization of formal knowledge*. Chicago: University of Chicago Press.

Freidson, E. (2001). *Professionalism: The third logic*. Chicago: University of Chicago Press.

Freire, P. (1996). *Pedagogy of the oppressed* (New rev. ed.). London: Penguin.

Friedman, A., & Phillips, M. (2004). Continuing professional development: Developing a vision. *Journal of Education and Work, 17*(3), 361–376.

Fullan, M. (2005). *Leadership & sustainability: System thinkers in action*. Thousand Oaks, CA: Corwin Press.

Fullan, M. (2007). *The new meaning of educational change* (4th ed.). New York: Teachers College Press.

Gabe, J., & Calnan, M. (Eds.). (2009). *The new sociology of the health service*. Abingdon, New York: Routledge.

Gadamer, H. G. (1965/1979). *Truth and method* (2nd ed.). London: Sheed & Ward.

Garet, M., Porter, A., Desimone, L., Birman, B., & Yoon, K. S. (2001). What makes professional development effective? Results from a national sample of teachers. *American Educational Research Journal, 38*(4), 915–945.

Garrick, J., & Rhodes, C. (2000). Legitimising knowledge at work. In J. Garrick & C. Rhodes (Eds.), *Research and knowledge at work* (pp. 1–12). London; New York: Routledge.

Gee, J. P. (1990). *Social linguistics and literacies: Ideology in discourses*. London; New York: Falmer Press.

Gergen, K. J. (2001). *Social construction in context*. London: Sage Publications.

Germov, J. (2005). Managerialism in the Australian public health sector: Towards the hyper-rationalisation of professional bureaucracies. *Sociology of Health and Illness, 27*(6), 738–758.

Germov, J. (2009). Challenges to medical dominance. In J. Germov (Ed.), *Second opinion: An introduction to health sociology* (pp. 392–415). Melbourne: Oxford University Press.

Gherardi, S., & Nicolini, D. (2006). *Organizational knowledge: The texture of workplace learning*. Malden, MA: Blackwell Publications.

Giddens, A. (1999). *Runaway world: The Reith lectures revisited*. Retrieved 24 April, 2006, from http://www.globalpolicy.org/globaliz/define/1999/1110giddens.pdf

Giorgi, A. (1970). *Psychology as a human science: A phenomenologically based approach*. New York: Harper & Row.

Golding, L., & Gray, I. (Eds.). (2006). *Continuing professional development for clinical psychologists: A practical handbook*. Malden, MA; Oxford: BPS Blackwell.

Gonczi, A., Hager, P., & Olivier, L. (1990). *Establishing competency standards in the professions*. Canberra: Australian Government Publishing Service.

Goodson, I., & Hargreaves, A. (1996). *Teachers' professional lives*. London; Washington: Falmer Press.

Australian Government. (2008). *Collaborating to a purpose: Review of the Cooperative Research Centres program*. Canberra: Department of Innovation Industry Science and Research.

Grace, A. P. (2007). Envisioning a critical social pedagogy of learning and work in a contemporary culture of cyclical lifelong learning. *Studies in Continuing Education, 29*(1), 85–103.

Greenwood, D. J., & Levin, M. (2007). *Introduction to action research: Social research for social change* (2nd ed.). Thousand Oaks: Sage Publications.

Groundwater-Smith, S., & Mockler, N. (2009). *Teacher professional learning in an age of compliance: Mind the gap*. Dordrecht: Springer.

Habermas, J. (1973). *Theory and practice*. Boston: Beacon Press.

Hager, P. (2004). Conceptions of learning and understanding learning at work. *Studies in Continuing Education, 26*(1), 3–17.

Hager, P., & Beckett, D. (1995). Philosophical underpinnings of the integrated conception of competence. *Educational Philosophy and Theory, 27*(1), 1–24.

Hager, P., & Halliday, J. (2006). *Recovering informal learning: Wisdom, judgement and community*. Dortrecht: Springer.

Hamilton, C. (2008). *The freedom paradox: Towards a post-secular ethics*. Crows Nest, NSW: Allen & Unwin.

Handy, C. B. (1996). *Beyond certainty: The changing worlds of organizations*. Boston: Harvard Business School Press.

Hargreaves, A. (1997). The four ages of professionalism and professional learning. *Unicorn, 23*(2), 86–114.

Harrison, S., & Checkland, K. (2009). Evidence-based practice in UK health policy. In J. Gabe & M. Calnan (Eds.), *The new sociology of the health service* (pp. 121–142). Abingdon; New York: Routledge.

Hayward, L., Priestley, M., & Young, M. (2004). Ruffling the calm of the ocean floor: Merging practice, policy and research in assessment in Scotland. *Oxford Review of Education, 30*(3), 397–415.

Hewison, J., Dowswell, T., & Millar, B. (2000). Changing patterns of training provision in the National Health Service: An overview. In F. Coffield (Ed.), *Differing visions of a learning society: Research findings* (pp. 167–197). Bristol: The Policy Press.

Higgs, J., & Jones, M. A. (Eds.). (2000). *Clinical reasoning in the health professions* (2nd ed.). Oxford; Boston: Butterworth-Heinemann.

Higgs, J., Richardson, B., & Abrandt Dahlgren, M. (Eds.). (2004). *Developing practice knowledge for health professionals.* Edinburgh; New York: Butterworth-Heinemann.

Higgs, J., & Titchen, A. (Eds.). (2001). *Practice knowledge and expertise in the health professions.* Boston: Butterworth-Heinemann.

Hochschild, A. R. (1983). *The managed heart: Commercialization of human feeling.* Berkeley: University of California Press.

Hochschild, A. R. (1997). *The time bind: When work becomes home and home becomes work.* New York: Metropolitan Books.

Hodkinson, P., Biesta, G., & James, D. (2008). Understanding learning culturally: Overcoming the dualism between social and individual views of learning. *Vocations and Learning, 1,* 27–47.

Houle, C. O. (1980). *Continuing learning in the professions.* San Francisco: Jossey-Bass Publishers.

Illich, I. (1971). *Deschooling society.* London: Calder and Boyars.

Illich, I. (1975). *Medical nemesis: The expropriation of health.* London: Calder & Boyars.

Jarvis, P. (2005). Human learning: The interrelationship of the individual and the social structures. In P. Jarvis & S. Parker (Eds.), *Human learning: An holistic approach* (pp. 116–127). Milton Park, Abingdon; New York: Routledge Falmer.

Kanter, R. M. (1995). *World class: Thriving locally in the global economy.* New York: Simon & Schuster.

Kemmis, S., & McTaggart, R. (1988). *The action research planner* (3rd rev. ed.). Waurn Ponds, VIC: Deakin University.

Knowles, M. S. (1973). *The adult learner: A neglected species.* Houston, TX: Gulf.

Knowles, M. S., Holton, E. F., & Swanson, R. A. (2005). *The adult learner: The definitive classic in adult education and human resource development* (6th ed.). Amsterdam: Elsevier/Buttrworth Heinemann.

Kolb, D. (1984). *Experiential learning: Experience as the source of learning and development.* Englewood Cliffs, NJ: Prentice-Hall.

Kvale, S. (1994). Ten standard objections to qualitative research interviews. *Journal of Phenomenological Psychology, 25*(2), 147–173.

Larson, M. S. (1977). *The rise of professionalism: A sociological analysis.* Berkeley: University of California Press.

Lave, J. (1988). *Cognition in practice: Mind, mathematics, and culture in everyday life.* Cambridge; New York: Cambridge University Press.

Lave, J., & Wenger, E. (1991). *Situated learning: Legitimate peripheral participation.* Cambridge: Cambridge University Press.

Lee, A., Manathunga, C., & Kandlbinder, P. (Eds.). (2008). *Making a place: An oral history of academic development in Australia.* Milpera, NSW: Higher Education Research and Development Society of Australasia.

Leighninger, L. (Ed.). (2000). *Creating a new profession: The beginnings of social work education in the United States.* Alexandria, VA: Council on Social Work Education.

Lewin, K. (1951/1997). *Resolving social conflicts and field theory in social science.* Washington: American Psychological Association.

Lieberman, A., & Miller, L. (Eds.). (2001). *Teachers caught in the action: Professional development that matters.* New York: Teachers College Press.

Limerick, D., Crowther, F., & Cunnington, B. (2002). *Managing the new organisation: Collaboration and sustainability in the postcorporate world* (2nd ed.). Crows Nest, NSW: Allen & Unwin.

Linn, R. (1996). *Power, progress & profit: A history of the Australian accounting profession.* Melbourne: Australian Society of Certified Practising Accountants.

Luke, A., & McArdle, F. (2009). A model for research-based State professional development policy. *Asia-Pacific Journal of Teacher Education, 37*(3), 231–251.

Lyotard, J.-F. (1984). *The postmodern condition: A report on knowledge.* Minneapolis, MN: University of Minnesota Press.

Marsick, V. J. (2006). Informal strategic learning in the workplace. In J. N. Streumer (Ed.), *Work-related learning* (pp. 51–69). Dortrecht: Springer.

Marsick, V. J., & Watkins, K. E. (1990). *Informal and incidental learning in the workplace.* London; New York: Routledge.

Marsick, V. J., & Watkins, K. E. (1999). *Facilitating learning organizations: Making learning count.* Aldershot, Hampshire, England: Gower.

Marton, F., & Säljö, R. (1976). On qualitative differences in learning: I. Outcome and process. *British Journal of Educational Psychology, 46*, 4–11.

McDermott, R. (2002). Measuring the impact of communities. *Knowledge Management Review, 5*(2), 26–30.

McWilliam, E. (2002). Against professional development. *Educational Philosophy and Theory, 34*(3), 289–299.

Meads, G., Jones, I., Harrison, R., Forman, D., & Turner, W. (2009). How to sustain interprofessional learning and practice: Messages for higher education and health and social care management. *Journal of Education and Work, 22*(1), 67–79.

Mezirow, J. (1963). *Dynamics of community development.* New York: Scarecrow Press.

Mezirow, J. (1991). *Transformative dimensions of adult learning.* San Francisco: Jossey-Bass.

Mishler, E. G. (1984). *The discourse of medicine: Dialectics of medical interviews.* Norwood, NJ: Ablex Publishing Corporation.

Moon, J. A. (1999). *Reflection in learning and professional development: Theory and practice.* London: Kogan Page.

Mullavey-O'Byrne, C., & West, S. (2001). Practising without certainty: Providing health care in an uncertain world. In J. Higgs & A. Titchen (Eds.), *Professional practice in health, education and the creative arts* (pp. 49–61). Oxford: Blackwell Science.

Nowotny, H., Scott, P., & Gibbons, M. (2001). *Re-thinking science: Knowledge and the public in an age of uncertainty.* Cambridge: Polity Press.

O'Neil, J., & Marsick, V. J. (2007). *Understanding action learning.* New York: American Management Association.

OECD. (1996). *Information technology and the future of post-secondary education.* Paris: Organisation for Economic Co-operation and Development.

OECD. (1998a). *Human capital investment: An international comparison.* Paris: Organisation for Economic Co-operation and Development.

OECD. (1998b). *Lifelong learning: A monitoring framework and trends in participation.* Paris: Organisation for Economic Co-operation and Development.

Oakes, J., & Rogers, J. (2007). Radical change through radical means: Learning power. *Journal of Educational Change, 8*, 193–206.

Palmer, P. J. (1998). *The courage to teach: Exploring the inner landscape of a teacher's life.* San Francisco: Jossey-Bass.

Patel, V. L., & Arocha, J. F. (2000). Methods in the study of clinical reasoning. In J. Higgs & M. A. Jones (Eds.), *Clinical reasoning in the health professions* (pp. 78–91). Oxford; Boston: Butterworth-Heinemann.

Penuel, W. R., Fishman, B. J., Yamaguchi, R., & Gallagher, L. P. (2007). What makes professional development effective? Strategies that foster curriculum implementation. *American Educational Research Journal, 44*(4), 921–958.

Perrucci, R., & Gerstl, J. E. (1969). *Profession without community: Engineers in American society.* New York: Random House.

Perry, W. G. (1970). *Forms of intellectual and ethical development in the college years.* New York: Rinehart & Winston.

Peters, T., & Waterman, R. H. (1982/2004). *In search of excellence: Lessons from America's best run companies.* New York: Harper Business Essentials.

Pocock, B. (2001). *Having a life: Work, family, fairness and community in 2000.* Adelaide: Centre for Labour Research, Dept. of Social Inquiry, Adelaide University.

Polanyi, M. (1967). *The tacit dimension.* Garden City, NY: Doubleday.

Prilleltensky, I., & Prilleltensky, O. (2006). *Promoting well-being: Linking personal, organizational, and community change.* Hoboken, NJ: John Wiley.

Putnam, R., & Borko, H. (2000). What do new views of knowledge and thinking have to say about research on teacher learning? *Educational Researcher, 29*(1), 4–15.

Revans, R. W. (1965). *Science and the manager.* London: Macdonald.

Rhodes, C., & Scheeres, H. (2004). Developing people in organizations: Working (on) identity. *Studies in Continuing Education, 26*(2), 175–193.

Rogoff, B. (1990). *Apprenticeship in thinking: Cognitive development in social context.* New York; Oxford: Oxford University Press.

Rorty, R. (1982). *Consequences of pragmatism: Essays, 1972–1980.* Minneapolis, MN: University of Minnesota Press.

Rothwell, W. J. (2005). *Beyond training and development: The groundbreaking classic on human performance enhancement* (2nd ed.). New York: American Management Association.

Rowden, W. R. (1996). *Workplace learning: Debating five critical questions of theory and practice.* San Francisco: Jossey-Bass Publishers.

Rowland, S. (2000). *The enquiring university teacher.* Buckingham: Society for Research into Higher Education & Open University Press.

Rowland, S. (2006). *The enquiring university: Compliance and contestation in higher education.* Maidenhead, England; New York: Open University Press; Society for Research into Higher Education.

Sackett, D. L., Rosenberg, W. M., Gray, J. A., Haynes, R. B., & Richardson, W. S. (1996). Evidence-based medicine: What it is and what it isn't. *British Medical Journal, 312,* 71–72.

Sandberg, J., & Dall'Alba, G. (2006). Re-framing competence development at work. In R. Gerber, G. Castleton, & H. Pillay (Eds.), *Improving workplace learning: Emerging international perspectives* (pp. 107–121). New York: Nova Publishers.

Sandberg, J., & Pinnington, A. H. (2009). Professional competence as ways of being: An existential ontological perspective. *Journal of Management Studies, 46*(7), 1138–1170.

Sawchuk, P. H. (2008). Theories and methods for research on informal learning and work: Towards cross-fertilization. *Studies in Continuing Education, 30*(1), 1–16.

Schatzki, T. R., Knorr-Cetina, K., & von Savigny, E. (Eds.). (2001). *The practice turn in contemporary theory.* London: Routledge.

Schwandt, T. A. (2000). Three epistemological stances for qualitative inquiry: Interpretivism, hermeneutics and social constructionism. In N. K. Denzin & Y. S. Lincoln (Eds.), *The handbook of qualitative research* (pp. 189–213). Thousand Oaks, CA: Sage Publications.

Schön, D. A. (1983). *The reflective practitioner: How professionals think in action.* Aldershot, England: Arena.

Schön, D. A. (1987). *Educating the reflective practitioner: Toward a new design for teaching and learning in the professions.* San Francisco; London: Jossey-Bass.

Schön, D. A. (1995). Knowing-in-action: The new scholarship requires a new epistemology. *Change, 27*(6), 27–35.

Sen, A. K. (2009). *The idea of justice.* London; New York: Allen Lane/Penguin Books.

Senge, P. M. (1990). *The fifth discipline: The art and practice of the learning organization.* New York: Doubleday; Currency.

Spradley, J. P. (1979). *The ethnographic interview.* New York: Holt Rinehart and Winston.

Stenhouse, L. (1981). What counts as research? *British Journal of Educational Studies, 24*(2), 103–114.

Streumer, J. N. (Ed.). (2006). *Work-related learning*. Dortrecht: Springer.

Sullivan, W. M. (1995). *Work and integrity: The crisis and promise of professionalism in America*. New York: HarperCollins.

Sullivan, W. M., & Rosin, M. S. (2008). *A new agenda for higher education: Shaping a life of the mind for practice*. San Francisco: Jossey-Bass; Carnegie Foundation for the Advancement of Teaching.

Tallis, R. (2005). *Hippocratic oaths: Medicine and its discontents*. London: Atlantic.

Taylor, C. (2007). *A secular age*. Cambridge, MA: Belknap Press of Harvard University Press.

Taylor, E. W. (2008). Transformative learning theory. In S. B. Merriam (Ed.), *Third update on adult learning theory* (pp. 5–15). San Francisco: Jossey-Bass.

Titchen, A., & Higgs, J. (2001). Towards professional artistry and creativity in practice. In J. Higgs & A. Titchen (Eds.), *Professional practice in health, education and the creative arts* (pp. 273–290). Oxford: Blackwell Science.

Trede, F., & Higgs, J. (2003). Reframing the clinician's role in collaborative clinical decision making: Re-thinking practice knowledge and the notion of clinician-patient relationships. *Learning in Health and Social Care, 2*(2), 66–73.

Tripp, D. (1998). Critical incidents in action inquiry. In G. Shacklock & W. J. Smyth (Eds.), *Being reflexive in critical educational and social research* (pp. 36–49). London: Falmer Press.

Usher, R., Bryant, I., & Johnston, R. (1997). *Adult education and the postmodern challenge: Learning beyond the limits*. London; New York: Routledge.

van Manen, M. (1977). Linking ways of knowing with ways of being practical. *Curriculum Inquiry, 6*(3), 205–228.

Vygotsky, L. S. (1962). *Thought and language*. Cambridge: MIT Press.

Vygotsky, L. S. (1978). *Mind in society: The development of higher psychological processes*. Cambridge: Harvard University Press.

Webb, G. (1996). *Understanding staff development*. Buckingham; Bristol, PA: Society for Research into Higher Education & Open University Press.

Webster-Wright, A. (2009). Reframing professional development through understanding authentic professional learning. *Review of Educational Research, 79*(2), 702–739.

Weil, S. (1999). Re-creating universities for 'Beyond the stable state': From 'Dearingesque' systematic control to post-dearing systematic learning and inquiry. *Systems Research and Behavioral Science, 16*(2), 171–194.

Wenger, E. (1998). *Communities of practice: Learning, meaning, and identity*. Cambridge; New York: Cambridge University Press.

Wilkinson, R. G., & Pickett, K. (2009). *The spirit level: Why more equal societies almost always do better*. London: Allen Lane.

Williams, L. (2009). Jostling for position: A sociology of allied health. In J. Germov (Ed.), *Second opinion: An introduction to health sociology* (pp. 452–475). Melbourne: Oxford University Press.

Willis, P., McKenzie, S., & Harris, R. (Eds.). (2009). *Rethinking work and learning: Adult and vocational education for social sustainability*. Netherlands: Springer.

Winefield, A. H. (2008). *Job stress in university staff: An Australian research study*. Bowen Hills, QLD: Australian Academic Press.

# Chapter 3
# A Phenomenological Perspective

In choosing and using a research perspective, conceptual congruence and clarity are vital. Thus the research purpose should be congruent with the research approach and methods chosen; the assumptions underpinning the research approach should be clear and consistent in their use throughout the research. This chapter highlights conceptual underpinnings in outlining the phenomenological perspective taken in this book. For readers unfamiliar with phenomenology, an overview of key concepts is presented; for others cognizant of the complexity of phenomenology, the philosophical assumptions of the particular approach I have used are clarified.

Phenomenology was introduced in Part I as a way of investigating this research area, because of its focus on everyday lived experience of phenomena and its underlying philosophical assumptions. This research approach allows conceptualisation of the experience of PL as inextricably interrelated with its lived context. Chapter 3 clarifies how I have understood and used phenomenology in this research, as an overall conceptual framework as well as an empirical methodology.

## 3.1 Wondering About Phenomenology

The question "What is phenomenology?" was asked by Maurice Merleau-Ponty (1945/2002) at the beginning of his classic text "The Phenomenology of Perception". Sixty years later it is still worth asking this question as the phenomenological project is widely recognised as being complex, multifaceted and continually evolving. Phenomenological research can take many forms. As Martin Heidegger (1975/1982, p. 328), arguably the most influential phenomenological philosopher of the last century, commented, "There is no such thing as *the one* phenomenology".

There is debate, therefore, as to what constitutes "true" phenomenological research in the social sciences (Caelli, 2001; Giorgi, 2000a). Partly this is because phenomenology is a philosophy as well as a methodological approach to studying experience. It is essential therefore to clarify the phenomenological philosophy on which any phenomenological inquiry draws, especially in interdisciplinary research.

Underpinning phenomenology's place as a philosophy and a methodology, it is first and foremost a way of thinking about or approaching experience, whose

A. Webster-Wright, *Authentic Professional Learning*, Professional and Practice-based Learning 2, DOI 10.1007/978-90-481-3947-7_3, © Springer Science+Business Media B.V. 2010

primary task is "to reveal the mystery of the world" (Merleau-Ponty, 1945/2002, p. xxiv). Therefore as Robyn Barnacle (2001, p. 3) asserts: "phenomenology begins with wonder". Both statements refer to the intent of phenomenology to uncover the taken-for-granted nature of everyday experience and look with fresh eyes at the world. I clarify, below, how I have "wondered" about continuing PL through a phenomenological perspective as a philosophical and empirical approach to research.

## 3.2 Phenomenology as a Conceptual Framework

There is a confusing multiplicity of ways in which phenomenology is drawn upon in research. Terms used in phenomenology, such as "being", "life-world" and "everyday lived experience", are pervasive in the literature of social sciences, often used without specification of their meaning. Moreover, in initially clarifying my research approach, I found potential contradictions in the philosophical basis of methodologies I chose and in some research literature I drew upon. For example, Amedeo Giorgi's empirical methodology has its philosophical origins in Edmund Husserl's work, whereas the other methodology I drew from, that of Max van Manen's, was based on Heidegger. Phenomenological researchers whose work I draw upon later in the book have extrapolated from Merleau-Ponty's focus on the embodied nature of experience, Hans-Georg Gadamer's focus on the dialogic nature of understanding and Alfred Schutz's focus on the intersubjective construction of meaning. The brief outline of phenomenological philosophy presented below is intended to contextualise the way key phenomenological concepts are understood and used throughout the book.

### 3.2.1 Phenomenological Philosophy

Phenomenology as a contemporary movement evolved a century ago from the work of Husserl. A crucial ontological tenet of Husserl's work is the rejection of the Cartesian duality of subject and object, through his concept of the "life-world". In the life-world, subject and object are inextricably linked through the subject's lived experience. This ontological stance is the basis of the social constructionist perspective of learning mentioned in Chapter 2. Peter Berger and Thomas Luckmann (1966/1981) acknowledge the foundations of their work in the phenomenology of Schutz who extended Husserl's notion of the life-world.

The basic tenet of Schutz's social phenomenology is that what appears to be an objective reality is intersubjectively constructed and interpreted as subjectively meaningful: "Everyday life presents itself as a reality interpreted by men and subjectively meaningful to them as a coherent world" (Berger & Luckmann, 1966/1981, p. 33). This everyday life is shared with others although everyone experiences it from a slightly different perspective. In everyday life, there is a continual dialectic between perceived (subjective) reality and intersubjectively shared (objective) reality. Reality is constructed through shared social activity, which is simultaneously externalised as objective (existing outside ourselves) as well as internalised as our own subjective reality (p. 149). Thus any analysis of experience that considers only one aspect of reality is considered inadequate.

As a philosophy, phenomenology rejects the ontological extremes of both subjectivism and objectivism (Merleau-Ponty, 1945/2002). Although phenomenology examines phenomena as they are experienced, it is not pure subjectivism. The person experiencing a situation is never isolated from the world, but always enmeshed in it. Similarly phenomenology rejects the notion that the world consists of a fixed objective reality, maintaining that a situation can only be understood with reference to the different meanings that are created through people's experiences. Thus in phenomenology, "subjectivity must be understood as inextricably involved in the process of constituting objectivity" (Moran, 2000, p. 15).

In fact phenomenology questions the whole notion of division of the world into dichotomies (e.g. subject/object, body/mind, cognition/emotion), an idea pervading much research. Phenomenology maintains that the world of experience is given as a whole rather than perceived as artificially divided. From a phenomenological perspective therefore, the experience of continuing PL cannot be meaningfully studied in an atomistic way.

A crucial figure in discussing the phenomenological analysis of experience is Heidegger. He queried the detached stance on knowledge suggested by Husserl. Heidegger maintained that phenomenological understanding of the world should involve an ontological investigation rather than a purely epistemological one, stemming from analysis of being rather than of knowing. That is, before one can ask what it is to know, the matter of who asks the question needs to be investigated. Heidegger (1927/1962, p. 31) presented a radical version of ontology in his magnum opus "Being and Time", maintaining that the question of the "meaning of being", especially what it is to be human, is the primary task of phenomenology and ontology. Heidegger made a distinction between an "ontic" analysis of being that describes various elements of being and an "ontological" analysis that describes ways of being or the essential experience of being (Dreyfus & Wrathall, 2002, p. xiii). This distinction is also pertinent to my critique of atomistic research with its focus on separate elements.

Heidegger described "being-in-the-world" in the sense of not just being located in the world, but being always inextricably immersed and involved with it. His phenomenological analysis is attentive to the historic and temporal features of being and has had considerable impact on social theories in the later twentieth century, including postmodern and deconstructionist theories (Dreyfus, 1991, p. 9). Under Heidegger, hermeneutics and phenomenology were brought together to understand the nature of humans as our way of being. Hermeneutics is the study of interpretation; originally of texts, but later becoming the study of understanding or interpretation of meaning in a broader sense. Heidegger transformed phenomenology, incorporating hermeneutics and changing the focus from the descriptive, epistemological project of Husserl to an interpretative, ontological one.

Gadamer also identified an essential connection between phenomenology and hermeneutics, maintaining that understanding experience was a concern of both projects (Moran, 2000, p. 248). In analysing how science attempts to understand human experience, in "Truth and Method" Gadamer (1965/1979) investigated the nature of understanding. His hermeneutic focus emphasised understanding as basic to any consideration of human experience, as understanding pervades all human interactions with the world. The concept of "understanding" has a central place in this book about APL; as not only is this research an attempt to understand more about professionals' experiences of learning, but understanding also emerges in the findings as central to that learning.

Finally, in common with the foregoing philosophers, Merleau-Ponty's work also places emphasis on the unity inherent in all experience, although with a different focus. His particular contribution to phenomenology was to highlight the embodied nature of being human, stating, "The world is not what I think but what I live through" (1945/2002, p. xviii). We perceive the world and our participation in it as a whole. He described a "chiasmic intertwining" between humans and the world through the reality of lived bodily experience (Merleau-Ponty, 1968, p. 249). It is through our bodies, argued Merleau-Ponty, that we experience the world, yet the body is taken for granted in habitual activities. In other words having a body is necessary for acting in the world, at the same time as subjectively experiencing or having any understanding of that world. Merleau-Ponty maintains that all higher levels of existence such as imagination, knowing, emotions or learning are built upon the perceptual experience of embodied being in the world.

## 3.2.2 Phenomenological Concepts

The phenomenological perspective used in framing this research involved specific concepts mentioned in the foregoing overview of phenomenological philosophy. The assumptions underlying these concepts need further elucidation. Whilst none of the concepts has a specific focus on the experience of learning, they all have a bearing on this research. The concepts described are life-world, being-in-the-world, embodied knowing, construction of meaning and understanding.

### 3.2.2.1 Life-World

Husserl referred to the "life-world" and all phenomenologists draw on this notion in some way. The idea of phenomenology as referring to the study of lived experience stems from the widely accepted yet poorly defined notion of life-world (Barnacle, 2004; Sandberg & Dall'Alba, 2009). Although the life-world refers to everyday experience, it refers to more than what is present in the world as we consciously survey our surroundings. In what Husserl termed the "horizon" of experience are "real" or concrete objects and "ideal" or abstract objects such as ideas (Giorgi, 2005a; Toombs, 1992). Even absences and possibilities are present in our experience. Thus the everyday life-world includes ideas, dreams, fantasies, reflection, concrete action or scientific analysis.

The life-world is a shared world that is structured in both spatial and temporal ways. In this shared world we develop meanings with others through communication. Communication thus presupposes commonalities in our shared experiences. "The everyday life-world is therefore fundamentally intersubjective; it is a social world", state Schutz and Luckmann (1973, p. 16). They explain that understanding is fundamental with respect to our relationship with other people. Spatially, the life-world can be conceptualised as zones, with the zone of immediacy being the one in which people can act, which is different from, but overlaps and interacts with, other people's zones of immediacy. The life-world has temporal aspects, some of which are shared and intersubjectively available like dates or seasons, and others which are experienced internally and vary with experience (Berger & Luckmann, 1966/1981, p. 40).

Referring back to the vignette in Chapter 1 as an example, as Gina enters her room to greet a client in the morning, her life-world includes more than what happens in the room. She may notice the absence of some equipment she was about to use and conjecture a possible reason for that absence. She may be annoyed that it is difficult to order new equipment in this organisation. She may rue her late arrival due to family reasons so that she now has no time to change plans for the session. She would remember what she had meant to do with the client and think of other ways of proceeding, including asking her colleague for suggestions. This means that social interaction, time and place are part of her horizon of experience. Her perception of the temporal and spatial structures of her life-world is affected by what she is doing and the meaning that experience holds for her. Thus, when driving to work whilst worrying about being late, time and distance take on a different perspective than they do when driving on a holiday.

There is a dynamic interaction between a person and the world as experienced. "The life-world is thus a reality which we modify through our acts and which, on the other hand, modifies our actions" (Schutz & Luckmann, 1973, p. 6). Through her actions, the professional both alters her life-world and is altered by it. Although the horizons of experience offer many possibilities, because of the taken-for-granted nature of many aspects of everyday life, only a certain number of possible actions make sense for that professional in a particular context. Heidegger referred to these possibilities in his analysis of being-in-the-world, described below.

### 3.2.2.2 Being-in-the-World

Most of Heidegger's work has, at its core, the analysis of being, in particular what it means to be human (or "Dasein"). As a term, Dasein refers neither to a single human nor to generic mankind but to the essence of "being human"; the "expression of its Being" (Heidegger, 1927/1962, p. 33). Heidegger maintained that the primary fact of being human is existence, which he described in terms of "possible ways for it to be" rather than separate characteristics (p. 67). Heidegger constantly reinforced the holistic nature of the experience of being human as a "unitary phenomenon" expressed by him as "Being-in-the-world" (p. 78).

As explained, Dasein is inextricably immersed within this shared world, always involved in specific circumstances. It is only because human beings are actively absorbed, that the world and its activities have significance and meaning for them (Inwood, 2000, p. 59). Through absorption in activities and interaction with others, human beings are constantly making sense of the world, everyday activities and themselves. As (Heidegger, 1975/1982, p. 159) explained, "We understand ourselves and our existence by way of the activities we pursue and the things we take care of". Through this familiarity with the world, enabling Dasein to make sense of the world whilst acting within it, Dasein has an inherent "understanding of being" (Heidegger, 1927/1962, p. 119). Without this understanding, people would not be able to function in everyday life.

Thus Heidegger described human beings as self-interpreting in that what people do makes sense to them, in particular social situations. He uses a term "for-the-sake-of-which" to describe the general direction that people take in their activities as part of a particular way of being into which they have been socialised (Heidegger, 1927/1962, p. 119). He is not describing a goal of any particular activity but rather the way that social roles, such as being a parent or consumer, have assumed norms that shape activities, determining what is seen as possible in given situations (Dreyfus, 1991, p. 95). In my research, participants were asked to describe situations where they learnt "as a professional". It is because of their immersion in the professional life-world that such learning experiences hold meaning for them. Thus their descriptions of learning are from the perspective of "being a professional".

Another aspect of Heidegger's holistic analysis of being, pertinent to framing this study, is his critique of the concept of knowledge as separate from the knower. In a cogent and evocative description, Heidegger (1927/1962, p. 89) stated: "The perceiving of what is known is not a process of returning with one's booty to the 'cabinet' of consciousness after one has gone out and grasped it". His description parallels the way that learning is traditionally conceptualised: as a person venturing outside themselves into a separate world (maybe a PD activity) and "grasping" a commodity called "knowledge" that is put into the mind. His critique of a dualist ontology and objectivist epistemology predates research referred to in Chapter 2.

Although Heidegger did not foreground the body in his analysis, he certainly implied its existence. Dasein, as being-in-the-world, expresses an embodied connection through absorbed actions in the world. It was Merleau-Ponty however who highlighted that human beings are "primarily an active living body" as they act in and experience the world (Moran & Mooney, 2002, p. 423).

### 3.2.2.3  Embodied Knowing

For Merleau-Ponty, the body is an object as well as a subject. In other words we have a body that exists in the world, but it is also the source of our intersubjective knowing of the world. This body is the means of perceiving, experiencing, knowing and acting in the world, yet it is usually taken for granted. Thus a researcher does not think of her fingers moving as she types, but is absorbed in the content and meaning of that typing. Through discomfort from long periods of typing, however, the body may present itself for attention.

Through their body, people extend into the world, interacting with and understanding it, not as something separate but as part of the world. Gloria Dall'Alba and Robyn Barnacle (2005) raise this idea of extension in Merleau-Ponty's work in their notion of "embodied knowing", explaining how, through the body, people experience and know the world beyond the boundaries of the physical body. Merleau-Ponty drew from Jean-Paul Sartre, who referred to this notion of extension, describing his body "at the end of the telescope which shows me the stars" (Moran, 2000, p. 423). A number of professionals in my research spoke about using tools in learning such as the internet. It is through their embodied interaction with the computer that they extend into the world of other people and ideas. Their learning is embodied.

Embodied knowing refers to a holistic perception of experience. As Dall'Alba and Barnacle (2005, p. 724) note, "There is an inextricable adhesion and overlapping in Merleau-Ponty's ontology between the perceiver and that which is perceived". Thus a therapist making a splint for a client, for example, does not focus on the feeling of heat in the material, but feels it as just malleable enough to mould now for a particular purpose. Even communication with the client whilst fitting the splint is embodied, as speech "accomplishes" thought (Merleau-Ponty, 1945/2002, p. 207). That is, the body is the nexus of the professional's relationship with the world.

Within his analysis of our embodied relationship with the world, Merleau-Ponty questioned the privileged position of rationality in ways of knowing the world. He argued that even theoretical or abstract ideas arise out of a less-articulated form of experience, that of perception. Mark Johnson (1987, 2007) draws on Merleau-Ponty's ideas, combined with neuroscience, to describe a concept of the "embodied mind" as not just located in the body but formed by bodily perceptions and actions. Through empirical research he describes how all concepts, metaphors and images develop from and are dependent on embodied experience in the world (Lakoff & Johnson, 1999). Arguing that perception is the foundation of rationality but does not "destroy" rationality, Merleau-Ponty (1964, p. 13) noted that such a perspective "only tries to bring [rationality] down to earth".

Through the phenomenological framework used in this book, learning is therefore not conceptualised as confined to the mind, but includes the whole professional as an embodied being. This embodied being is always involved within a shared and meaningful world. Thus meaning is constructed by and embodied in a professional's activities in interaction with others.

### 3.2.2.4 Construction of Meaning

As noted above, lives revolve around meaning. Merleau-Ponty (1945/2002, p. xxii) maintained that "because we are in the world, we are condemned to meaning". In other words people constantly make sense of and construct meaning through their intersubjective experiences. Everything people do is meaningful to them. Merleau-Ponty noted: "There is not a human word, not a gesture, even one which is the outcome of habit or absent mindedness, which has not some meaning" (p. xx).

One of the chief aims of phenomenology is to investigate how people understand and make meaning of their lived experience. As previously discussed, phenomenology views meaning as intersubjectively constituted within the shared and inherently meaningful life-world. Meaning is attributed to objects (from concrete matter to abstract words) through a shared cultural history as well as from the individual's unique experiences. Thus meaning is constructed in the dialectic between the world and the person, and does not reside within an individual, a culture or a particular object. Although not referring to phenomenology, Etienne Wenger (1998) drew similar conclusions about the social experience of learning as both unique and shared as indicated in Chapter 2.

Meaning accrues through lived experience, therefore. As I have stressed, experience is perceived as a whole. That is, people see meaning in communicating with someone, not facial or bodily movement; they hear meaning, not noise. As Merleau-Ponty (1968, p. 155) described so eloquently: "The meaning is not on the phrase like the butter on the bread, like a second layer of 'psychic reality' spread over the sound: it is the totality of what is said".

As the same experience can be interpreted in many ways, meanings are always polyvalent. Yet meanings are constituted within certain horizons of possibility. When a professional enters a room, the horizons of her[1] experience consist of all the possible ways that she may experience what happens within it. But, as mentioned earlier, only certain possibilities present themselves as meaningful and able to be done in given circumstances. Depending on her involvement with a situation, previous understanding of it and its significance for her, she may do certain things as a professional. Thus the meaning she makes of the situation is open to many possibilities yet constrained. Meaning is structured in certain ways.

Many authors have used this idea of "structures of meaning", which directs what people are likely to do in certain circumstances (Bullington, 1999; Dall'Alba & Sandberg, 1996; Toombs, 1992). These structures become sedimented as habitual ways of thinking and acting. In fact Pierre Bourdieu (1990) extends this notion into his expression of "habitus" as socially acquired embodied dispositions. Merleau-Ponty described such "structures" that determine behaviour as dimensions of reality, "neither thing nor idea" that enable understanding or sense making of experience (Giorgi, 2000b, p. 64).

In Gadamer's (1965/1979, p. 273) analysis of how meaning is shared, or understanding is possible between people, he spoke of a "fusion of horizons". When we understand another person, even if we disagree with that view, it is because we can see "the standpoint and horizon of the other" (p. 270). Gadamer stressed the dialogic and hermeneutic nature of understanding, so that understanding is not fixed, but fluid. As mentioned, the notion of understanding is integral not only to

---

[1]To avoid the clumsy use of his or her, the generic professional will be referred to as female to reflect the gender balance of the participants in the study (F:M; 4:1).

my research but also to any phenomenological project. I describe below the way I have interpreted understanding, drawing on hermeneutics in general and Heidegger in particular.

### 3.2.2.5 Understanding

Drawing on Heidegger, Mats Alvesson and Kaj Sköldberg (2000, p. 56) describe understanding as "a basic way of existing for every human being, since we must continually keep orientating ourselves in our situation simply in order to stay alive". This understanding is part of the taken-for-granted aspects of everyday life, so that it is rarely made explicit, articulated or analysed. It is integral to being able to proceed with everyday life, in particular social roles. An everyday understanding is implied so that people know how to do certain things, such as understanding the appropriate way for a professional to greet a client.

From this perspective, understanding is not purely a cognitive function, but is fundamental to being human and involved in the world. Understanding "is a basic form of human existence in terms of something we do and at the same time are" (Sandberg, 2001, p. 18). Understanding is more primordial than any distinction between cognition and action, allowing the possibility of both (Dreyfus, 1991, p. 185). All other ways of approaching the world, such as knowing, valuing, interpreting or explaining, presuppose understanding.

Heidegger described how understanding, as embodied, is revealed in action. For example, the therapist making the splint for a client reveals a certain understanding about what a splint is for, why she would want to use it and how it is made. This doesn't mean she knows everything about using splints. Her understanding of using the splint is part of her current understanding of being a professional therapist.

Understanding does not remain static. As described, people affect the life-world through activities within it and are affected by this shared world. Understanding changes through this dialectic as people continually reorientate to changing circumstances. Yet through doing so in certain social–cultural settings, habitual structures develop that shape and constrain people's understanding of the world. People bring these structures as their preunderstanding to each situation. Heidegger spoke of the preunderstanding everyone has in all activities, referring to the hermeneutic circle.

The concept of the hermeneutic circle was originally referred to with regard to understanding texts, but also is a way of describing the understanding of experience (Schwandt, 2000). In reading a text, there is continuous dialectic interplay between our prior understanding and changing understanding, as well as between parts and whole in understanding the meaning of the text. Richard Palmer's (1969, p. 87) description of the hermeneutic circle clarifies this dialectic:

Understanding is a basically referential operation; we understand something by comparing it to something we already know.... An individual concept derives its meaning from a context or horizon within which it stands; yet the horizon is made up of the very elements to which it gives meaning. By dialectical interaction between the whole and the part, each gives the other meaning; understanding is circular, then. Because within this "circle" the meaning comes to stand, we call this the "hermeneutic circle".

Palmer described the inherent contradiction in this statement, that is, how we can understand parts that make up the whole as well as understanding the whole? It becomes apparent that "logic cannot fully account for the workings of understanding" and that understanding is comparative and partly intuitive (p. 87). There is also the paradox of the relationship of prior or "preunderstanding" to understanding. "To understand presupposes preunderstanding, but at the same time preunderstanding is an obstacle to understanding" (Alvesson & Sköldberg, 2000, p. 84). Yet Heidegger referred to the circle of understanding as not a "vicious" circle, but a basic feature of being human. All phenomenology for Heidegger is interpretative and hermeneutic. In any investigation of human experience, he states we must "endeavour to leap into the 'circle'" in the right way (Heidegger, 1927/1962, p. 363).

Thus as a phenomenological researcher I needed to be aware of my preunderstanding of PL and attempt to bring aspects to conscious awareness as the research was undertaken. I deal with this issue of accounting for myself in Chapter 4. This consideration of preunderstanding is also pertinent to the participants of the research. Regardless of how a professional may be theoretically defined, all participants in this research considered themselves to be professionals. Thus from the phenomenological perspective used to frame this study, they embodied a certain understanding of being a professional. They act in the life-world of professional practice, not only situated in it but also inseparable from it. In addition, the professional life-world is a shared world that is intersubjectively meaningful. When I asked participants of the study through the interviews to describe situations where they have learnt as a professional, it is from this understanding of "being a professional" that they answered.

## 3.2.3 Philosophical Assumptions of This Research

All research involves philosophical assumptions. As the researcher operates from a particular socially constructed perspective, taken-for-granted assumptions will always be present. By foregrounding the philosophical basis of this book, assumptions underpinning the framing and undertaking of the research are made explicit.

The phenomenological perspective used here is one way of looking at a research problem. This perspective draws on ontological and epistemological assumptions underlying particular expressions of phenomenology. These assumptions, about the holistic nature of experience, our embodied being-in-the-world, the intersubjective construction of meaning, and the hermeneutic nature of understanding, form the conceptual framework of this research. Thus continuing PL is conceptualised as involving the whole professional inextricably intertwined in the world through embodied experience with others as she learns.

Furthermore, in phenomenological research, experience is conceptualised as open to multiple interpretations. From a phenomenological perspective, there are many ways of interpreting the findings of research. Interpretations are contingent not only on the research design and finished text but also on the socially constructed preunderstandings of the researcher and the academic or professional audience.

## 3.3 Phenomenology as a Methodological Approach

Whilst it is important for all researchers to be aware of their assumptions, in phenomenological research this need is made explicit. Although a critically questioning and reflexive approach is also highlighted in other interpretative research, there are specific processes undertaken when considering phenomenology as a methodological approach.

### 3.3.1 Principles of Phenomenological Research

Whether the phenomenological project is one of philosophical reflection on experience (as Heidegger did) or involves the gathering of other people's descriptions of experience (as in empirical phenomenology), the following two principles are crucial for the enterprise to be considered phenomenological. They are adopting a "phenomenological attitude" and seeking a "phenomenological essence".

#### 3.3.1.1 Phenomenological Attitude

Integral to a phenomenological approach to research is the taking up of the "phenomenological attitude", also referred to as a process of reduction or bracketing (Creswell, 2007; Moustakas, 1994). Fundamentally, assuming the phenomenological attitude is a way of being open to phenomena as they present. This concept of phenomenological bracketing is perhaps the most misunderstood and debated phenomenological precept. Nevertheless taking up a phenomenological attitude is claimed by phenomenologists, philosophers and empirical researchers alike, to be the basis of phenomenology. Without it the process of reflection or research cannot be considered to be phenomenological (Giorgi, 2009; Merleau-Ponty, 1945/2002; van Manen, 2001).

The phenomenological attitude may best be described by contrasting it with our everyday "natural attitude". Schutz described the privileged position of our everyday life as our "fundamental and paramount reality" (Schutz & Luckmann, 1973, p. 3). Within the everyday "natural attitude" the world is "taken for granted and self-evidently 'real'" (p. 4). That is, within everyday lived experience we do not question many features of our world. Thus, as Heidegger described it, we may not notice the glasses on our nose although we see the world through them. Nor may we notice features of our general surroundings or social context except if they suddenly alter.

The phenomenological attitude is often mistakenly considered to be a transcendental withdrawal from the world, with a suspension of our connection and knowledge of it. Yet this is impossible from a phenomenological perspective, as we are, and always will be, in the world. It is because of this consistent being-in-the-world, that the everyday world and phenomena within it are so taken for granted by us. Merleau-Ponty (1945/2002, p. xv) maintained that in order to see the world phenomenologically we need to "break with our familiar acceptance of it", not to withdraw from it, but to step back temporarily and watch "filled with wonder" at its mysteries and paradoxes. He maintained that this "radical reflection amounts to a consciousness of its own dependence on an unreflective life which is its initial situation" (p. xvi). That is, we need to be aware of the natural attitude to step back from it.

Yet how to do this in empirical phenomenology is neither easily described nor practiced. As I have maintained, it is more about taking an attitude or an approach to doing research than a specific analytic tool. One thing is clear, reduction is always only partial (Merleau-Ponty, 1945/2002, p. xv). What is important as part of any phenomenological method is evidence of a legitimate attempt to step aside from the usual natural attitude to be open to the phenomenon as presented. I discuss practical issues about taking up the phenomenological attitude in this research in the following section and in Chapter 4.

### 3.3.1.2 Phenomenological Essence

The "essence" of a phenomenon, the identification of which is the key outcome of any phenomenological enquiry, is another misunderstood concept. In phenomenology, the term is not used in the Platonian sense of being the core, singular meaning, nor is elucidating it a reductive process such as in many qualitative thematic analyses. It is best described as the essential meaning of the experience (Giorgi, 1997). In this study, for example, the essence of APL is a description of what is essential for an experience to be considered a PL experience. What is important to note is that this essence is a network of relationships that can be expressed in terms of a complex structure of constituents and sub-constituents. For this reason, Giorgi uses the term phenomenological "structure" rather than "essence" (Giorgi & Giorgi, 2003).

Free imaginative variation is the method used for elucidating the essence in phenomenological philosophy (Moustakas, 1994; Sokolowski, 2000). Every experience exists within a horizon of possibilities. The phenomenologist reflects on possible ways that features of a phenomenon may be varied. Whilst varying different features he notes whether the phenomenon remains intact. In other words if a certain feature is changed and the phenomenon collapses, it must be an essential feature; however, if another feature is removed and the phenomenon holds, it means that feature is not an essential constituent. For example, colour is not an essential constituent of a chair, whereas the ability to support a sitting body is essential.

In the empirical approach used in this study, following Giorgi (1997, 2009), the essential structure of a phenomenon is developed in a manner similar to phenomenological philosophy, but the variation is derived from diverse empirical descriptions from people experiencing that phenomenon (in this case, continuing PL). The structure reflects, in its written description, the richness and variability of the phenomenon as lived by those participants. It is a way of understanding the meaning of a phenomenon, but makes no claims to be a complete description of reality, as no descriptions can ever capture the life-world as experienced.

### *3.3.2 Empirical Phenomenology*

Empirical phenomenology draws on the philosophy of phenomenology whilst using empirically based research methods. The method used in such studies varies, but the researchers seek to understand experiences as lived. Accordingly, the aim of any empirical phenomenological study is exploration of the meaning of a phenomenon, through examining the complexity of lived experience of the phenomenon.

Husserl conceived of phenomenological philosophy as a "rigorous science" that attempted to describe the life-world as closely as possible to actual experience. When I initially undertook phenomenological research, the search for scientific rigour and the evocation of people's experiences appeared to be somewhat paradoxical goals. When examining empirical phenomenological approaches, I found that different aspects of method are foregrounded in the work of different researchers. Some emphasise systematic, analytical rigour, and others the sensitive, evocation of experience.

Empirical phenomenological approaches share an attempt to take a middle path between empirical objectivism and subjective reflection. That is, they reject a positivist focus on objective analysis and a world with fixed truths waiting to be discovered. They also reject purely subjective, reflective conjecture. Therefore, all analyses are grounded in lived experience of a phenomenon, but involve stepping back from the taken-for-granted nature of that experience by adopting the phenomenological attitude. A text is produced that in some way conveys the essence of the phenomenon studied. Sometimes this text is analytical and precise in language (e.g. Giorgi, 1999; Kleiman, 2004; Koivisto, Janhonen, & Vaisanen, 2002; Parse, 2003); at other times it captures an experience with verisimilitude, conveying a vivid sense of "being there" to the reader (e.g. Bullington, 1999; Sells, Topor, & Davidson, 2004; Toombs, 1992; van Manen, 2002).

In referring to Husserl's somewhat paradoxical aims, Merleau-Ponty (1945/2002) claimed that phenomenology can only be understood through undertaking it. He added that practicing phenomenology is less a matter of rational weighing up of different phenomenological ideas than "determining and expressing in concrete form this phenomenology for ourselves" (p. viii). Accordingly, in my approach to this research, I have traversed my own path, drawing closely but not exclusively on the work of two currently active and internationally respected phenomenologists, Giorgi and van Manen. To explain how and why, I compare features of their work pertinent to the needs of my research.

Giorgi (2000a), a psychologist, originally came from a quantitative research background but was dissatisfied with its limitations. After studying philosophy he investigated a way of applying phenomenological philosophy in a scientific way to psychological research. He was searching for a rigorous way to analyse and describe human experience that maintained the complexity of that experience. He refers to the empirical methodology that he began to develop in the 1970s as scientific phenomenology. It is grounded in the phenomenological philosophy of Husserl and influenced by Merleau-Ponty.

Van Manen, originally a teacher, turned to phenomenology in the 1980s when searching for a pedagogical approach that was grounded in everyday teaching experiences. His phenomenology of practice is a highly reflective inquiry into professional practice that is grounded in, sensitive of and aims to provide insights into the richness of lived professional experiences and their meaning. He places particular emphasis on the evocation of these experiences through close attention to the redolent qualities of the textual outcome. He draws from the hermeneutic phenomenology of Heidegger and from Merleau-Ponty.

Thus although both Giorgi's and van Manen's approaches are grounded in different philosophies, they have a similar intent: to enquire into lived experience. They differ in emphasis with the focus of the former on rigorous precision and the latter on evocative imagery. Giorgi claims to use a descriptive phenomenological approach, whereas van Manen describes his as hermeneutic or interpretative. Beyond any similarities, they are very different in method and outcome. Particular differences are to be found in the processes used to access lived experience, and the analysis and presentation of these experiences. Below, I describe the features of each approach that I have drawn upon in my methodology, with a full description of that methodology given in Chapter 4.

### 3.3.2.1  Phenomenology as a Scientific Method

Perhaps the most widely used phenomenological empirical research methodology is that of Giorgi and colleagues (Creswell, 2007; Moustakas, 1994). Giorgi (1990, 1997, 2005b, 2009) describes his work as modifying Husserl's philosophical phenomenological method by seeking concrete and contextual descriptions of phenomena from empirical subjects. The strength of Giorgi's method for my research was his focus on a systematic method of seeking and analysing people's experiences. His approach has a strong emphasis on rigour whilst remaining faithful to participants' descriptions of experiences in their full complexity (Giorgi, 2009). His approach is widely used in the social sciences and amongst health professionals for this reason. However, his approach has been criticised as being removed from its philosophical origins and for relying too much on analysis of textual data rather than on other means of investigating experiences (Crotty, 1998; Paley, 1997). He defends his method as being more likely to develop new insights than more interpretative approaches for reasons described below (Giorgi, 2000d).

Giorgi (2009) articulates his descriptive phenomenology as aligned with Husserl in that he limits himself to describing experience within the constraints of presentational evidence. For Giorgi the evidence is usually presented in the form of interview transcripts. He places high value on remaining faithful to the data as given and describes methods of doing so, involving rigorous criteria of bracketing existing knowledge and withholding knowledge claims. In interpretative (hermeneutic) empirical phenomenology, he argues, the researcher goes beyond the data so that theories, reflections or other research are drawn upon (Giorgi, 2000c). Giorgi acknowledges the possible usefulness of interpreting findings, but notes the importance of being explicit about doing so, separating such interpretations from the descriptive analysis.

I based my methodology on Giorgi's approach for the following reasons. As a well-established method, it was ideal for the purposes of carrying out interdisciplinary research, because of his clearly demonstrable emphasis on rigour and systematic approach to obtaining and analysing data. Giorgi attempts to combine rigour with fidelity to the participants' experiences as far as possible. When gaining descriptions from participants he focuses on obtaining rich descriptions of concrete situations where the phenomenon was experienced, rather than espoused theories (Giorgi, 1989).

Despite using Giorgi's approach, I did have dilemmas accounting for myself as a professional and "insider" to the research. Although the participants' experiences of PL were diverse, many descriptions resonated with similar experiences of mine at some stage in my career. I therefore had to be particularly vigilant and critical of my preunderstanding. To some extent, Giorgi's rigorous approach was useful in supporting my adoption of the phenomenological attitude, but I needed to modify his method to make my preunderstanding more transparent, as described in Chapter 4.

I also found the outcomes of Giorgi's approach, as it is usually followed, lacked evocation of the lived experience described (e.g. Giorgi, 1999; Kleiman, 2004). Although the descriptive structure is detailed and precise, the analytical language used does not evoke a sense of meaning. It is difficult to sense the experience as can be done when reading van Manen's texts. In addressing this limitation, I was influenced by van Manen, as outlined below.

### 3.3.2.2 Phenomenology as Evocation of Lived Experience

Van Manen (1997b) describes phenomenology as a deeply reflective inquiry into human meaning. His approach is unavowedly hermeneutic, being interpretative rather than purely descriptive. In hermeneutic phenomenology meaning is foregrounded rather than method (Sharkey, 2001; van Manen, 1997a). For van Manen, as for Giorgi, lived experience is the starting point for phenomenological research. Van Manen describes his phenomenology of practice as a way of researching and understanding issues of everyday professional practice that arises from and remains connected to the lived moment of the "now". In referring to Wilhelm Dilthey's evocation of lived experience being to the soul what breathing is to the body, van Manen (1997b, p. 36) describes lived experience as "the breathing of meaning".

Van Manen (2002) focuses particularly on vocative aspects of phenomenology through writing, which portrays meanings embedded within professional experience. His aim in phenomenological research is to transform lived experience into a textual expression of its essence that a reader can identify with her own experience. Credibility and authenticity of the phenomenological text are achieved if readers are able to recognise the description of the phenomena as mirroring aspects of their experience (van Manen, 1997b). The literary term verisimilitude describes this appearance of truthfulness when a reader experiences "being there" (Richardson, 2000).

Yet van Manen acknowledges the difficulty of attempting to capture the ambiguity, complexity and immediacy of lived experience. Although he describes how language "tends to intellectualize our awareness" because language is cognitive, he attempts to "evoke understandings through language that in a curious way seem to be non-cognitive" (van Manen, 1997b). Van Manen uses the specific language of professionals' lived experiences in the text, but through reflective awareness as a phenomenological researcher, he "thickens" and intensifies the final text so that it is concrete yet evocative. Other phenomenologists also attempt evocation in text (Todres & Galvin, 2008). This enables the reader to break from taken-for-granted ways of looking and to see everyday phenomena in a new and insightful way. Van Manen's aim of evoking the essence of an experience through text appears tantalisingly simple, yet is difficult to achieve.

### 3.3.2.3  Phenomenology as Rigorous Yet Evocative

In modifying Giorgi's empirical phenomenological methodology, through drawing on van Manen's emphasis on evocative textual descriptions, I aimed to maintain the rigour of descriptive phenomenological analysis, without stripping away the evocative nature of the professionals' experiences. Thus I used participants' words in the text and vignettes throughout the description of the essential structure of APL. I aimed to reveal the essence of APL in a way that speaks to professionals with verisimilitude, whilst realising that no analysis and text can match lived experience.

In addition, through contextualising the structure of authentic PL with observations and documentations gained from the field, I aimed to intensify the textual evocations whilst remaining faithful to the participants' descriptions gathered through interviews. Also, as I account for my own preunderstanding, the entire project is more co-constructed with participants than Giorgi's approach suggests. This reflexivity is reported throughout the book, as discussed earlier and detailed in the next chapter.

As justification for these adaptations of approaches to empirical phenomenology, I offer Merleau-Ponty's (1945/2002, pp. xvi–xvii) assertion that revealing the essence of a phenomenon is "not the end but the means" of doing phenomenology and that doing so is a way of "bringing the world to light". My hope is that the end justifies the means.

## 3.4  Summary of Phenomenological Perspective

In summary, this chapter demonstrates how phenomenology, as a theoretical perspective that is both complex and multi-layered, offers an approach to investigating PL that addresses issues raised in Chapter 2. The philosophical assumptions described in Section 3.2 form the basis of this phenomenological perspective, enabling continuing PL to be conceptualised in a way that is different from most research into PD. This conceptual framework focuses on the holistic experience of learning through the professional's embodied being-in-the-world as she intersubjectively constructs meaning. This is in stark opposition to research, which reduces such complexity to a set of factors involved in the development of professionals.

I am wary of labelling this research, other than to say it is phenomenological. As Thomas Schwandt (2000, p. 205) cautions, in describing differences in philosophical traditions, labels are dangerous. When labels are used, it is easy to overlook common concerns and tensions that run across traditions. Thus, this research involves empirical studies of continuing PL, drawing from concrete experiences of being practicing professionals. It is informed by phenomenological philosophy as a conceptual framework, drawing on a number of its basic assumptions. This study uses an empirical phenomenological methodology, adapted from Giorgi's descriptive approach. It draws on hermeneutic and phenomenological insights, especially from Heidegger, Gadamer and Merleau-Ponty in the interpretation of the empirical findings.

Besides entailing a shift in perspective on learning and knowledge, as discussed, a phenomenological perspective offers "a theoretical framework that engenders wonder or openness in the way that we understand the world and enables thought to linger in the presence of possibility" (Barnacle, 2001, p. 13). How I sought to walk the tightrope of maintaining rigour whilst remaining open to the evocation of experience is detailed in the following chapter.

# References

Alvesson, M., & Sköldberg, K. (2000). *Reflexive methodology: New vistas for qualitative research,* London; Thousand Oaks, CA: Sage Publications.

Barnacle, R. (2001). Phenomenology and wonder. In R. Barnacle (Ed.), *Phenomenology* (pp. 1–15.) Melbourne: RMIT University Press.

Barnacle, R. (2004). Reflection on lived experience in educational research. *Educational Philosophy and Theory, 36*(1), 57–67.

Berger, P. L., & Luckmann, T. (1966/1981). *The social construction of reality: A treatise in the sociology of knowledge.* Middlesex: Penguin Books.

Bourdieu, P. (1990). *The logic of practice* (R. Nice, Trans.). Cambridge: Polity Press.

Bullington, J. (1999). *The mysterious life of the body: A new look at psychosomatics* (Vol. 190). Linkoping, Sweden: The TEMA Institute, Department of Health and Society.

Caelli, K. (2001). Engaging with phenomenology: Is it more of a challenge than it needs to be? *Qualitative Health Research, 11*(2), 273–281.

Creswell, J. W. (2007). *Qualitative inquiry & research design: choosing among five approaches* (2nd ed.). Thousand Oaks, CA: Sage Publications.

Crotty, M. (1998). *The foundations of social research: Meaning and perspective in the research process.* St Leonards, NSW: Allen & Unwin.

Dall'Alba, G., & Barnacle, R. (2005). Embodied knowing in online environments. *Educational Philosophy and Theory, 37*(5), 719–744.

Dall'Alba, G., & Sandberg, J. (1996). Educating for competence in professional practice. *Instructional Science, 24,* 411–437.

Dreyfus, H. L. (1991). *Being-in-the-world: A commentary on Heidegger's Being and time, division i.* Cambridge, MA: MIT Press.

Dreyfus, H. L., & Wrathall, M. A. (Eds.). (2002). *Heidegger reexamined. Volume 1: Dasein, authenticity and death.* New York; London: Routledge.

Gadamer, H. G. (1965/1979). *Truth and method* (2nd ed.). London: Sheed & Ward.

Giorgi, A. (1989). An example of harmony between descriptive reports and behaviour. *Journal of Phenomenological Psychology, 20*(1), 60–88.

Giorgi, A. (1990). Phenomenology, psychological science and common sense. In G. R. Semin & K. J. Gergen (Eds.), *Everyday understanding: Social and scientific implications* (pp. 64–82). London: Sage Publications.

Giorgi, A. (1997). The theory, practice and evaluation of the phenomenological method as a qualitative research procedure. *Journal of Phenomenological Psychology, 28*, 235–260.

Giorgi, A. (1999). A phenomenological perspective on some phenomenographic results on learning. *Journal of Phenomenological Psychology, 30*(2), 68–93.

Giorgi, A. (2000a). Concerning the application of phenomenology to caring research. *Scandinavian Journal of Caring Sciences, 14*, 11–15.

Giorgi, A. (2000b). Psychology as a human science revisited. *The Journal of Humanistic Psychology, 40*(3), 56–73.

Giorgi, A. (2000c). The similarities and differences between descriptive and interpretative methods in scientific phenomenological psychology. In B. Gupta (Ed.), *The empirical and the transcendental: A fusion of horizons* (pp. 61–75) New York: Rowman & Littlefield.

Giorgi, A. (2000d). The status of Husserlian phenomenology in caring research. *Scandinavian Journal of Caring Sciences, 14*, 3–10.

Giorgi, A. (2005a). The phenomenological movement and research in the human sciences. *Nursing Science Quarterly, 18*(1), 75–82.

Giorgi, A. (2005b). Remaining challenges for humanistic psychology. *Journal of Humanistic Psychology, 45*(2), 204–216.

Giorgi, A. (2009). *The descriptive phenomenological method in Psychology: A modified Husserlian approach.* Pittsburgh, PA: Duquesne University Press.

Giorgi, A., & Giorgi, B. (2003). Phenomenology. In J. A. Smith (Ed.), *Qualitative psychology: A practical guide to research methods* (pp. 25–50) London: Sage Publications.

Heidegger, M. (1927/1962). *Being and time* (J. Macquarrie & E. Robinson, Trans., 1st English ed.). London: SCM Press.

Heidegger, M. (1975/1982). *The basic problems of phenomenology* (A. Hofstadter, Trans.). Bloomington, IN: Indiana University Press.

Inwood, M. J. (2000). *Heidegger: A very short introduction.* Oxford; New York: Oxford University Press.

Johnson, M. (1987). *The body in the mind: The bodily basis of meaning, imagination, and reason.* Chicago; London: University of Chicago Press.

Johnson, M. (2007). *Embodied meaning and aesthetic experience.* Chicago: University of Chicago Press.

Kleiman, S. (2004). Phenomenology: To wonder and search for meanings. *Nurse Researcher, 11*(4), 7–19.

Koivisto, K., Janhonen, S., & Vaisanen, L. (2002). Applying a phenomenological method of analysis derived from Giorgi to a psychiatric nursing study. *Journal of Advanced Nursing, 39*(3), 258–265.

Lakoff, G., & Johnson, M. (1999). *Philosophy in the flesh: The embodied mind and its challenge to Western thought.* New York: Basic Books.

Merleau-Ponty, M. (1945/2002). *Phenomenology of perception.* London; New York: Routledge Classics.

Merleau-Ponty, M. (1964). An unpublished text by Maurice Merleau-Ponty: A prospectus of his work. In J. M. Edie (Ed.), *The primacy of perception and other essays on phenomenological psychology, the philosophy of art, history, and politics* (pp. 3–11). Evanston, IL: Northwestern University Press.

Merleau-Ponty, M. (1968). The visible and the invisible (A. Lingis, Trans.). In C. Lefort (Ed.), *The visible and the invisible: Followed by working notes.* Evanston, IL: Northwestern University Press.

Moran, D. (2000). *Introduction to phenomenology*. London; New York: Routledge.

Moran, D., & Mooney, T. (2002). *The phenomenology reader*. London; New York: Routledge.

Moustakas, C. E. (1994). *Phenomenological research methods*. Thousand Oaks, CA; London: Sage Publications.

Paley, J. (1997). Husserl, phenomenology and nursing. *Journal of Advances in Nursing, 26,* 187–193.

Palmer, R. E. (1969). *Hermeneutics: Interpretation theory in Schleiermacher, Dilthey, Heidegger, and Gadamer*. Evanston, IL: Northwestern University Press.

Parse, R. (2003). The lived experience of feeling very tired: A study using the Parse research method. *Nursing Science Quarterly, 16*(4), 319–325.

Richardson, L. (2000). Writing: A method of inquiry. In N. K. Denzin & Y. S. Lincoln (Eds.), *The handbook of qualitative research* (2nd ed., pp. 923–948). Thousand Oaks, CA: Sage Publications.

Sandberg, J. (2001). Understanding the basis for competence development. In C. Velde (Ed.), *International perspectives on competence in the workplace* (pp. 9–25). Dordrecht: Kluwer Academic Press.

Sandberg, J., & Dall'Alba, G. (2009). Returning to practice anew: A life-world perspective. *Organization Studies, 30*(12), 1349–1368.

Schutz, A., & Luckmann, T. (1973). *The structures of the life-world*. Evanston, IL: Northwestern University Press.

Schwandt, T. A. (2000). Three epistemological stances for qualitative inquiry: Interpretivism, hermeneutics and social constructionism. In N. K. Denzin & Y. S. Lincoln (Eds.), *The handbook of qualitative research* (pp. 189–213). Thousand Oaks, CA: Sage Publications.

Sells, D., Topor, A., & Davidson, L. (2004). Generating coherence out of chaos: Examples of the utility of empathetic bridges in phenomenological research. *Journal of Phenomenological Psychology, 35*(2), 253–271.

Sharkey, P. (2001). Hermeneutic phenomenology. In R. Barnacle (Ed.), *Phenomenology* (pp. 16–37). Melbourne: RMIT University Press.

Sokolowski, R. (2000). *Introduction to phenomenology*. Cambridge; New York: Cambridge University Press.

Todres, L., & Galvin, K. (2008). Embodied interpretation: A novel way of evocatively re-presenting meanings in phenomenological research. *Qualitative Research, 8*(5), 568–583.

Toombs, S. K. (1992). *The meaning of illness: A phenomenological account of the different perspectives of physician and patient*. Dordrecht; Boston: Kluwer Academic Publishers.

van Manen, M. (1997a). From meaning to method. *Qualitative Health Research, 7*(3), 345–369.

van Manen, M. (1997b). *Researching lived experience: Human science for an action sensitive pedagogy* (2nd ed.). London: Althouse Press; University of Western Ontario.

van Manen, M. (2001). Professional practice and 'doing phenomenology'. In S. K. Toombs (Ed.), *Handbook of phenomenology and medicine* (pp. 457–474). Dordrecht: Kluwer Press.

van Manen, M. (Ed.). (2002). *Writing in the dark: Phenomenological studies in interpretive inquiry*. London: Althouse Press.

Wenger, E. (1998). *Communities of practice: Learning, meaning, and identity*. Cambridge; New York: Cambridge University Press.

# Chapter 4
# Delving into Methodology

This chapter on methodology begins by reviewing the increasing dissent amongst social researchers about close adherence to research method. I then outline my own position on method in this research, drawing on Mats Alvesson's argument about the need for "reflexive interpretation" in most empirical research (Alvesson & Sköldberg, 2000; Alvesson, 2002). Following this theoretical and reflexive positioning, issues of quality that influenced the research design and choice of methods are described. The design involves an adapted and extended version of Amedeo Giorgi's methodology, with some influence from Max van Manen. Most of this chapter describes the research process, from data gathering through analysis to integration, paying close attention to rigour, reflexivity and relevance as the chosen criteria of quality.

For readers new to empirical phenomenology, this chapter includes my reflexive viewpoint about how methodological choices were made. Considerable detail about analysis is included as phenomenological texts are notoriously light on explicit detail, making empirical phenomenological analysis appear more esoteric than necessary. Readers familiar with this methodology or more focused on the findings may wish to glance at the first three sections only.

## 4.1 Reflexive Methodology

Hans-Georg Gadamer (1965/1979) powerfully critiques method in the social sciences, when he questions certainty of method as the guaranteed path to truth. Using a hermeneutic approach he sought to understand what the human sciences were about, "beyond their methodological self-consciousness", questioning how scientific investigations seek to explore human experience (p. xiii). Both Gadamer and later van Manen (1997a) highlight understanding and meaning as the key focus in investigating human experience, rather than method.

Recent critique of method in social research is diverse (e.g. Paul & Marfo, 2001). At one end of the spectrum of critique is a general warning against strict adherence to method as the sure path to quality in research (e.g. Denzin & Lincoln, 2005; Silverman, 2005). At the other end is postmodernism, often portrayed in research as a questioning and rejection of most methodological conventions (e.g. Alvesson, 2002; Edwards & Usher, 2000). In between, critiques focus on the role of the researcher, especially tension between involvement in data construction and disengagement in data analysis (e.g. Chesney, 2001; Halling, 2005). Referring to this tension, Erica McWilliam (2004, p. 122) notes that usually "method cannot imagine both disinterestedness and interestedness within the one study".

The crux of the problem with method in social research is the ambiguous and constructed nature of social reality and the "notoriously ambivalent relation" of the final research product to the experiences studied (Alvesson & Sköldberg, 2000, p. vii). Alvesson (2002, p. 9) argues that "following methodological guidelines is totally insufficient for good research, and ... complexities and uncertainties involved must be taken seriously and addressed [with] elements of self-doubt ... built into the research process and the text". Social research is described as a "provisionally rational project" in which the basis of that rationality is reflection rather than process (Alvesson & Sköldberg, 2000, p. 287). My aim in this research was to establish a sound methodological approach rather than rely on prescriptive method.

As described in Chapter 3, I aimed to balance rigour of analysis and evocation of experience in using empirical phenomenology, whilst accounting for my role as a researcher-practitioner. In doing so, I found Alvesson's notion of "reflexive interpretation" helpful. Alvesson (2002) argues for a reflexive approach to empirical social research and re-envisages social research in the space between abstract theory and empirical method in a coherent, provocative and thoughtful manner. In "Reflexive Methodology" (Alvesson & Sköldberg, 2000) I found a framework, or meta-methodology to use the authors' term, to structure the doubts and misgivings that emerged while undertaking this research. These doubts centred on an awareness of the inherent interpretative and political nature of social research. In my case, doubts revolved around the interpretative nature of my entire project, concerns about the nature of hidden, implicit discourses within the participants' descriptions and how I could deal with these issues within Giorgi's rigourous methodological processes.

First, from a phenomenological perspective, my participants and I brought preunderstandings about PL that are historically, culturally and professionally influenced. Preunderstanding is given, yet needs addressing as I have stated, through critical reflexivity and use of the phenomenological attitude. Despite care structuring the data collection, in my interactions with participants my preunderstanding influenced and to some degree co-constructed those data. As my own understanding of continuing PL evolved in a hermeneutic manner through the research, demanding transparency about how I drew conclusions, the entire study has an interpretative nature. However Giorgi's method is unavowedly descriptive rather than interpretive, staying close to the participants' written transcripts.

Second, from a phenomenological perspective, APL is embedded in the lived experience of being a professional, so the structure of APL that emerged would reflect this professional context. Was this sufficient though to illuminate some of the hidden political features of professional discourse that flavoured the data? I saw the need for further interpretation of the APL structure if the original research problem about the lack of change in PD activities was to be addressed. In other words, there was a need for data additional to interviews, such as workplace observations and documents, to illuminate implicit conceptual features.

In reflecting on these doubts, I agree with Mats Alvesson and Kaj Sköldberg (2000) that it is possible to remain grounded in empirical data whilst being aware of and attentive to uncertainties about research through "reflexive interpretation". I draw on reflexivity therefore as a specific methodological strategy. I report on empirically grounded research, paying close attention to rigour of data collection and analysis, whilst articulating the inchoate nature of my role as researcher and the indeterminate nature of conclusions drawn. Following Alvesson, I link empirical data and theoretical perspectives using my reflexivity as a bridge, so that philosophical insights can be brought to bear on issues of workplace practice.

Strategies that assisted this reflexive journey included my own questioning, dialogue with others and keeping a research journal. Other researchers have similar dilemmas (D'Cruz, 2001; Etherington, 2004). One researcher, Judi Marshall (2001, p. 433), discusses the need for qualitative researchers to make judgements about "when to be focused and directed and when to be open and receptive". Consequently, I moved dialectically between close attention to detail and a more reflective meta-methodological view, articulating reflexive dilemmas at appropriate stages throughout the book. I agree with Nicky Solomon and colleagues (Solomon, Boud, Leontios, & Staron, 2001) who argue that when undertaking research into continuing learning it behoves researchers to reflect on their own learning through the process.

## 4.2   Criteria of Quality in Research

If strict adherence to method is not the path to good research, then what is? Alvesson and Sköldberg (2000) argue that high-quality research involves the interplay of philosophical theories, empirical work and creative inspiration. They describe it as featuring inspired interaction and interpretations of the data, credible empirical arguments and critical reflection that opens the possibility of different interpretations (p. 276). Even if agreeing with these researchers, however, the reader will be left with the key question underlying all research evaluation. That is, can the findings be relied upon sufficiently by the research community to act upon them?

The current research climate of competitive funding favours the use of widely accepted criteria such as validity and reliability. The problem with such terms is their positivistic overtones from decades of established use. Validity and reliability, as they are applied in quantitative research, are based on the assumption of establishing objective truth; hence they are inappropriate for qualitative inquiry. However, there is a variety of opinion amongst qualitative researchers as to what constitute criteria of high-quality research (Angen, 2000; Giorgi, 1988; Mays & Pope, 2000; Sparkes, 2001).

Some qualitative researchers invoke criteria of credibility, authenticity or trustworthiness and talk about notions of validation rather than validity and confidence rather than reliability (e.g. Byrne-Armstrong, Higgs, & Horsfall, 2001; Denzin & Lincoln, 2005). Other qualitative researchers adapt the criteria of validity and reliability in a way that is appropriate for qualitative inquiry (e.g. Cope, 2004; Silverman, 2005). Jörgen Sandberg (2005), for example, elegantly articulates how validity and reliability in knowledge claims can be demonstrated from a phenomenological perspective.

In addition to Alvesson, I have been influenced by Sandberg's interpretation of criteria within a phenomenological framework. I agree with these authors, and others, that it is possible to justify knowledge claims within interpretative research. In this research, however, I circumvented ambiguous nomenclature by addressing issues of quality using criteria that underlie the concerns of validity and reliability; that is, does the research fulfil its stated purpose, and are the conclusions justifiable and able to be trusted? This research used the criteria of rigour, relevance and reflexivity. In using these criteria, my aim was that the results of a well-designed and conceptualised study are interpreted thoughtfully to be relevant to the reality of participants' lives.

Reflexivity has been addressed above with reference to Alvesson's work. Rigour is a broad term defining high-quality empirical research that is applicable across disciplines and methods (Grbich, 1999; Patton, 2002). Rigour may be addressed by demonstrating firstly well-structured and justifiable research design and systematic data processes and secondly conceptual congruence and appropriate evidence for knowledge claims (Guba & Lincoln, 2005, p. 205). I refer to these two concepts as structural rigour and conceptual rigour.

Calls for research to be more relevant to practice have been made (Kezar & Eckel, 2000; Schwandt, 2005). Relevance can be viewed as the means of crossing the research practice divide, to address issues of real concern to participants. The argument has been put, that by paying extreme attention to the rigour of procedures, research can be stripped of its context and meaning, and therefore its relevance (Guba & Lincoln, 2005). Donald Schön (1983, p. 42) highlights the tension between the "high, hard ground" of rigorous pursuit of tightly focused concerns and the "swampy lowlands" of investigation of issues of real relevance. Although such a tension exists, it is possible to be both rigorous and relevant (Schön, 1995).

Means of meeting all three criteria are described in the following data sections. Before doing so, the research design is summarised, extending the discussion in Chapter 3 about my adaptation of Giorgi's empirical methodology.

## 4.3  Research Design

The overall design of the study is summarised in Fig. 4.1, although the process was not as linear as the figure suggests. Before outlining adaptations to Giorgi's methodology and details of methods used in this study, I summarise Giorgi's approach. As mentioned, Giorgi's methodology emphasises rigour in the collection and analysis of descriptions of people's experiences, remaining as faithful as possible to those experiences as they are presented. The focus of his data collection is gaining

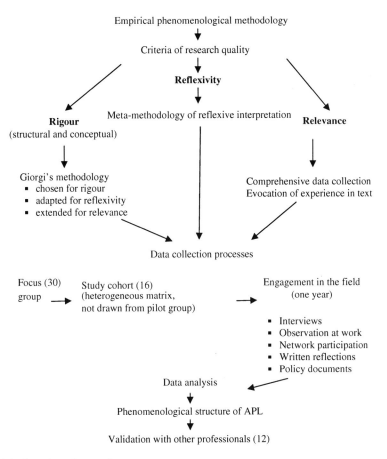

**Fig. 4.1**  Overview of research process

rich descriptions of concrete experiences by interviewing people who have experienced the phenomenon. Although he states that data other than transcripts of retrospective descriptions may be used (Giorgi & Giorgi, 2003b), in practice most research following Giorgi's approach uses interview transcripts as the sole source of data. Through open questions facilitating the description of concrete situations, Giorgi (1989, 1990) aims to avoid the participant espousing theories about the phenomenon. In my original research, descriptions of learning situations were gained during semi-structured, lengthy interviews with 16 participants, in response to the prompt question: *Describe a situation where you felt you learnt something as a professional.*

Giorgi's data analysis proceeds in four steps (see Section 4.6), but is holistic in its iterative movement between them (Giorgi & Giorgi, 2003a, 2003b). It begins with the researcher assuming the phenomenological attitude (Giorgi uses the term bracketing) and ends with the development of a structure of the phenomenon being investigated. The structure describes not only the essential constituents of the phenomenon but also the complex interrelationship between constituents.

As explained in the following section, I adapted Giorgi's methodology. This adaptation included more engagement with the participants involving a comprehensive range of methods of data collection. These included two rounds of interviews, observation of participants at work, observation of participants at network and PD meetings, collection of written reflections from participants and collection of policy documents about learning from the employing organisations, professional associations and registration boards involved.

The interview data were analysed whilst adapting Giorgi's analysis to account for my preunderstanding (see Sections 4.4 and 4.6.2). The analysis identified the essential structure of the diverse experiences of APL, with descriptions of the constituents and their interrelationships, including vignettes evoking participants' experiences. The other data were analysed thematically and drawn upon to contextualise the phenomenological analysis. Feedback on the findings was sought from a further 12[1] professionals, from diverse professional backgrounds, in order to gauge the verisimilitude of the descriptions. These professionals were asked to comment on how the findings related, or did not relate, to their own experiences of PL and their knowledge of PL based on interaction with other professionals.

## 4.4  Rigour, Relevance and Reflexivity

Essentially Giorgi's methodology was chosen for rigour, adapted for reflexivity and extended for relevance. As a methodology it satisfies scientific criteria of rigour at the same time as being aligned with phenomenological philosophical assumptions. As mentioned in Chapter 3, this is what Giorgi specifically designed his approach to achieve in response to a predominantly positivistic research culture within psychology. It has been soundly tested and adapted over decades, within psychology, health, education and management (e.g. Ivarsson, Söderback, & Ternestedt, 2002; Kleiman, 2004; Rydahl-Hansen, 2005; Van der Mescht, 2004). Giorgi has responded to critique of the method (2000a, 2000b, 2005). It meets criteria of conceptual and structural rigour in ways described below.

Conceptually, Giorgi's methodology was well suited to my research purpose, allowing the investigation of experiences of continuing PL as grounded in practice. Conceptual rigour is also demonstrated by Giorgi's careful attention to the key principle underpinning phenomenological research, that of the phenomenological attitude or bracketing. Empirically, Giorgi describes this as a process of suspending pre-conceptions about the phenomenon both in collecting data and in analysis. He pragmatically notes that complete bracketing of pre-conceptions about the phenomenon is neither possible nor desirable, but that a conscious effort is made to temporarily disengage from them. Giorgi argues that this allows the researcher to

---

[1] This research continues to be validated with professionals in different contexts.

be "fresh and maximally open" to the experience as described (Giorgi & Giorgi, 2003b, p. 32). He states that "subjectivity cannot be eliminated, and it shouldn't be, but subjectivity in the pejorative sense can be transcended" (Giorgi, 1994, p. 205). In other words, subjectivity is an essential element of phenomenology. This close attention to bracketing means that Giorgi stresses withholding knowledge claims until analysis is complete, with such claims always being provisional.

Second, using Giorgi's methodology allowed me to demonstrate evidence of structural rigour through use of systematic, transparent and traceable processes for gathering, analysing and evaluating data. The most important aspect of structural rigour for phenomenology is "fidelity to the phenomena" (Giorgi & Giorgi, 2003b; Kvale, 1994). This means capturing, as clearly as possible, the way in which a phenomenon appears in lived experience. Giorgi's methodology carefully details processes that aim to remain faithful to participants' experiences, involving extensive "dwelling with the data" before analysis, constant return to the data and critical questioning throughout the analysis (Giorgi, 1997, 2009).

Despite the conceptual and structural rigour of Giorgi's method, it was insufficient to fulfil my intentions with respect to the reflexivity of the process and relevance of the outcomes. I deal first with reflexivity. Despite attention being paid to the setting aside of pre-conceptions, Giorgi (2003)[2] warns against use of his method when the researcher is closely related to the experiences described. As mentioned previously his methodology provides no means of accounting for self as an insider in the professional life-world with similar experiences, nor for the issues this raises, both positive and negative. Thus I adapted the method to account for myself, adding another stage to the transformation of data as described in Section 4.6.2.

This reflexive dilemma is related to a tension between descriptive and interpretative methods in phenomenological research. Giorgi's methodology is descriptive, staying close to participants' descriptions. This is a strength of his method, underpinning its rigour. As the research evolved, however, I came to recognise that all descriptions involve interpretation (Alvesson & Sköldberg, 2000). Gunnar Karlsson (1993) raises similar concerns surrounding preunderstanding when using Giorgi's methodology. I dealt with this issue by consciously questioning my own interpretations as they arose during the analysis using the additional stage in the data analysis referred to above. I also attempted to structurally separate further interpretation of the APL structure, in the light of other philosophy and research, locating this in Part IV following the phenomenological analysis in Part III. Thus I have taken the unusual step of using a descriptive phenomenological methodology within an interpretative philosophical framework.

Finally, regarding relevance, I gauged the final outcome of a descriptive structure of APL as being insufficient to meet my needs for two reasons: one related to context and the other to text. To adequately address the research problem about lack of change in PD, I needed additional contextual data, as relevance is related

---

[2]Some of the detail referred to in this chapter was obtained through participation in a live-in research workshop with Giorgi and is not widely available in print.

to a thorough exploration of the context in which the research problem is situated. To enhance relevance, I collected data from a variety of sources that could clarify participants' experiences of continuing PL with respect to the research questions.

Alvesson and Sköldberg (2000, p. 78) refer to the value of multiple data sources as a means of providing corresponding sources of information for some interviewees' observations, as is done in historical research. Some researchers describe multiple sources of data in terms of triangulation, as a means of enhancing rigour in interpretative research (Grbich, 1999; Patton, 2002). Such a concept is related to a positivistic assumption that an objective "truth" can be found through the corroboration of convergent methodological approaches. David Silverman (2005) and many other interpretative researchers argue against triangulation of this kind. They talk instead of comprehensiveness of data. In this study, my aim through multiple data collection was to enhance relevance, as well as rigour, through further contextualisation. It is never possible, however, to get a complete picture of any phenomenon no matter how much data are collected.

In order to gauge the verisimilitude of the study's outcomes by sharing findings with other professionals, I paid attention to the evocative qualities of the text, examining ways of presenting findings drawing on van Manen's (2001, 2002) phenomenological writing. I was looking for a way to resolve tension between a precise, analytical structure and an evocative, rich texture in describing the experience of APL. Leslie Todres (1998) reports a similar dilemma with textual outcomes using Giorgi's method. I adapted the description of the structure of APL by drawing substantially on participants' language, collating descriptive vignettes and using present tense as a rhetorical device. The credibility and relevance of the results were evaluated through dissemination of the written findings to a range of professionals to gauge whether they were able to relate my description of APL to their own experience (van Manen, 1997b, 2001). Thus my adaptation of Giorgi's methodology takes van Manen's and Alvesson's work into account, aiming to address issues of rigour, reflexivity and relevance as they apply to this research.

## 4.5  Engaging with the Participants

In the early stages of the research, a focus group was held to discuss experiences of continuing PL, with 30 therapists attending, similar to those later recruited for the study. The group discussion demonstrated that the interest level and relevance of this topic were high. Participants were invited to leave their anonymous written responses to the discussion. Besides helping frame the interview questions, the discussion and responses reinforced the need to seek diversity in participant selection.

Two large government organisations, A and B, and two small non-government organisations, C and D, employing therapists to work in community settings from urban to rural were approached, and a call for volunteers made. Community settings rather than hospitals were chosen, because literature and experience suggest that in the community therapists were often challenged to adapt their practice (Williams, 2005). Thus PL experiences were expected to be a feature of such work. As there

**Table 4.1** Participant selection matrix

Organisational and professional affiliation

|  | Occupational therapists | Physiotherapists | Speech pathologists | Total number |
|---|---|---|---|---|
| Government organisation A | 3 | 3 | 1 | 7 |
| Government organisation B | 1 | 2 | 3 | 6 |
| Non-government organisation C and D | 1 | 1 | 1 | 3 |
| Total number | 5 | 6 | 5 | 16 |

Variations in professional experience (other than organisational and professional affiliation)

| Gender | Female: 13 | Male: 3 | |
|---|---|---|---|
| Experience | Seniors: 6 (designated title) | Experienced: 7 (3 or more years of experience) | New graduates: 3 (up to 3 years of experience) |
| Place of work | City: 8 | Urban: 6 | Rural: 2 |
| Hours of work | Full time: 9 (30–40 h) | Part time: 7 (less than 30 h) | |

is a move in health delivery towards community-based services, such a focus was warranted (Baum, 2005).

The most important aspect of participant selection in phenomenology is that they have experienced the phenomenon. Purposeful sampling was undertaken to incorporate diverse experiences of continuing PL, using a stratified heterogeneous matrix to ensure a mix of different therapies, organisations, locations and types of experience (Grbich, 1999). Approximately equal numbers were allocated across organisations and therapies, with a gender balance of 80/20 (F/M) that reflected staffing ratios. Participant selection is illustrated in Table 4.1.

A problem with selection through volunteering was that volunteers may have been enthusiastic about learning and/or had particular issues that concerned them. As sufficient diversity was not found initially, a snowball technique was used to contact more rural practitioners and an additional male (Brace-Govan, 2004). Thus not all those recruited had volunteered initially. I was able to include a "negative case" in that a therapist was frank about his growing disinterest in PL and gave interesting descriptions of situations where he had failed to learn. Sixteen participants were recruited overall in this first cohort, with a diverse range of experience and work contexts.

As mentioned, a variety of data were gathered. Interview data were contextualised through fieldwork involving site visits, network meetings, perusal of organisational policies and collection of written feedback on learning from participants via email. Data collection occurred over a 12-month period. Finding suitable times to interview and observe participants were problematic as most participants had heavy case loads and tight time schedules. Nevertheless once time was available, participants were generous with their descriptions and all gave feedback that they valued the opportunity to discuss their PL. A second round of interviews explored and clarified issues that arose from the first interviews and fieldwork.

The primary source of data involved semi-structured interviews, with questions related to concrete work situations, where participants considered they had learnt as a professional. Pilot interviews confirmed the value of Giorgi's (2003) focus on continually bringing the interview back to concrete situations where detailed descriptions of experiences could be gained through judicious questioning. This avoided straying into areas of "espoused theory" where the therapists intoned definitions of continuing PL (Argyris & Schön, 1974).

It is widely accepted that any interviewing regardless of method involves joint construction of data (Fontana & Frey, 2000; Silverman, 2001). At the very least, all involve interactive conversation where meaning is shared and constructed (Atkinson & Silverman, 1997; Holstein & Gubrium, 1995). For example, in my interviews, participants knew that the focus was on continuing to learn as a professional. To be able to have a conversation at all, we both had to have some understanding of the phenomenon of continuing PL. All the people I interviewed had no trouble describing a situation where they had learnt as a professional. Often they qualified the description asking: Is this what you want? By doing so they were checking with my purpose and my understanding of the phenomenon.

On my part, I tried to be as attentive to the participant's meaning as possible, following up on nuances expressed, using open questioning to probe what I did not understand. Sandberg (2005, p. 54) refers to an attempt at genuine dialogue during the interview as a form of "communicative validity". I also asked for elaboration with concrete descriptions: a process that Sandberg refers to as a form of "pragmatic validity" (p. 56). In other words, I sought to assume the phenomenological attitude in interviewing: an open attitude that seeks to fully explore the descriptions of the participants. This enhances the rigour of the interview process whilst recognising it as two-way communication.

There were positive and negative issues in the interviewing related to my "insider" status. On the one hand, I found our shared therapy background allowed participants to be forthright and open with me and was an asset allowing me to probe issues. For example, when I arrived for one interview, the therapist seemed uneasy and said her time was limited. As we talked, it became evident that she thought I was "checking up" on her to see if she was meeting her PD points target required by the association. Once my aims were clarified the interview that followed was full and frank. Had I not known about PD points accumulation, the interview outcome could have differed. Elliot Mishler (1984, p. 60) describes the "shared and tacit understandings" that allow interviews between those from the same culture to proceed in a "contextually appropriate" manner. Shared understandings allow such issues of relevance to be followed more closely.

On the other hand, our shared understanding may have meant that my assumptions limited my awareness of other possibilities as I interviewed. Here I relied on critical reflection after the interviews and during analysis of data, as detailed in Section 4.6.2. In addition, because of a shared background, there was always the possibility that participants may have said what they thought I wanted to hear. I relied on what Pierre Bourdieu (1996, p. 18) describes as a "reflex reflexivity" attempting to monitor these issues intuitively throughout the interview, as in the example of the PD discussion raised in the previous paragraph. Where possible, I continually refocused participants' discussions back towards concrete descriptions.

Although access difficulties, including issues of client confidentiality, prevented observation in some cases, visits were made to most participants' workplaces. The aim was to gain extra contextual information about the situation in which the participants practiced and to discuss learning experiences with them in connection with a period of observation. Visits were also made to three informal network meetings concerned with PD, to observe interactions within the professional communities. I also attended a full-day formal PD seminar, observing sessions and discussing learning with participants during breaks.

I collected publicly available policy documents relating to PL or staff development from the organisations involved. The smaller organisations C and D had no such documentation. Similar documents relating to PD policies were collected from the Health Practitioners Registration Board and three relevant professional associations. Official documents provided important contextual information regarding expectations from employers and professional organisations about continuing learning of professionals: part of the implicit professional discourse (Atkinson & Coffey, 2004). After visits, I asked participants to email me if they had further thoughts about our conversations. Some particularly insightful written reflections were sent to me that added contextual information to the interview data.

## 4.6  Data Analysis

Although the interviews, as the main source of data in this study, are the primary focus of this data analysis section, additional data were used in three methodologically inclusive ways through the research process (Suri & Clarke, 2009). First, they gave insight into the context that the professionals were describing in the interviews. Through the phenomenological analysis of those interviews, I was able to draw on observations and discussions to make explicit some implicit contextual details. An example is given later in this section. Second, I drew on all the contextual data to sketch the professional life-world of the participants that is presented at the beginning of Chapter 5. This allows the reader to comprehend the context in which the continuing PL occurred that is mentioned, but not detailed in the structure. Third, I drew on policy documents from work organisations and professional associations to verify details about official professional expectations mentioned by participants.

I undertook a phenomenological analysis of the 16 first-round interview transcripts. In phenomenology, data analysis involves an extensive iterative process. Significant time is spent reading and reflecting on the data before transforming them. As mentioned, Giorgi's methodology involves four stages: reading the entire transcript, division of the transcript into meaning units, transformation of data in these units and developing the structure of the phenomenon. Although I describe these in a linear fashion below, the process of data analysis is more fluid than this textual account reveals.

Giorgi's process is rigorous yet creative in a way that I do not think is clear in his own written accounts, but is apparent when working with him (2003). It is an active and engaged process that continually returns to the data. There is a to-ing and fro-ing not only between different stages of the data analysis but also between thinking, reading and writing, with each giving the other meaning in a process reflective of the hermeneutic circle.

### 4.6.1 Dwelling with the Data

Giorgi's method is holistic in nature with analysis of one transcript at a time being undertaken as a single entity initially. In this first stage the entire transcript is read several times to gain an overall sense of the experiences described. Peter Willis (2001, p. 3) describes how "phenomenology wants to slow the researcher down and hold his or her gaze on the phenomenon". Giorgi's process achieves that end. I experienced this stage as listening to the text, reinvoking for me the interview experiences.

After gaining an overall sense of the experience described, the second stage involves dividing the transcript into meaning units. This is undertaken from the researcher's particular research perspective. That is, as I read I began to sense where the meaning with respect to continuing PL changed, marking that division. This is a practical rather than an analytical stage, with the aim of dividing data into meaningful, manageable chunks for analysis. Giorgi's (2009) recent book has descriptions of meaning units, but for only small transcripts. My interview data usually contained between 30 and 40 meaning units.

Giorgi (2003) stresses that all data in all meaning units have equal value. To discard seemingly irrelevant data as is done in some thematic qualitative research is to risk decontextualising it. This may mean that slight nuances about the experience gained from an aside remark or repetitious comment may be missed. My experience leads me to concur with Giorgi.

### 4.6.2 Transformation of Data

To assist the process of systematic analysis, Giorgi uses transformation tables. Table 4.2, demonstrates the transformation of one complete meaning unit (MU) through stages using six columns. As analysis is done on a transcript in its entirety, with reference backwards and forwards between meaning units, and no meaning discarded, this does not completely represent the process. Nevertheless, for reasons of space I have chosen a meaning unit that can be understood without undue reference to the entire transcript.

**Table 4.2** Transformation of meaning unit

| 1 Original transcript | 2 First transformation | 3 Second transformation | 4 Final transformation | 5 Reflections and contextual information | 6 My queries and critique |
|---|---|---|---|---|---|
| **MU17** | **TMU17** | **TMU17** | **TMU17** | 154. 155 S talks about her work at home as another job. She also is a volunteer on her days off. She implied that she was involved in other activities as well ie children's school. She had told me this on a previous occasion | 158 She saw the issue of time as being her own problem linked to her own personality and didn't question that it could be a wider workplace issue despite probing. (*I'm probably my own worst enemy*) Is this a gender issue? Some other participants spoke about – *we're all so busy here* rather than seeing it as a personal issue |
| 153. I. Is there anything in your work situation that would make learning and the things we've talked about easier? Is there anything in your work situation that you'd like to improve or change? | When asked what she would like to change to make learning easier, S said she always *struggled with time*, and felt she didn't have enough time to do everything she was involved with. She left work quickly to *race home in time* for her children's return from school and begin her other 'job' of being a parent | S raised the issue of time as a difficulty with respect to her continuing learning as a professional. A perceived lack of time was an overall issue in her life. She said she always *struggled* with time, and felt she didn't have enough time to fulfil commitments of her multiple life roles | A perceived lack of time and busyness was an overall issue in S's life. S was aware of her yearning for her own, quiet time alone to think, read and study about personal and professional issues. Despite her recognition of the value for her of reflective time, she had a certain acceptance of the situation as being her own problem | 154 I'm just part time – What does this say about the status of part timers? Being part time exacerbates this issue as most work with the clients is done between 9 and 3 and any possible quiet time is taken by full time staff after 3 which is when S goes home | |
| 154. S. I always *struggle with time*. If I had *more time* and didn't have to get in my car and *race home to my other job* at a quarter to three. You know that would be... I'm *just part time* and I do have lots of other things. Like I'm probably *my own worst enemy* with all the other things that I do | Being '*just*'? part time at work she was involved with a many other activities and felt she managed to do it all by '*just going flat out*' | Despite questioning the desirability of this situation where she was '*going flat out*' to get everything done, she felt being so involved was just the way she was, and had a certain acceptance? resignation? of the situation | S saw no opportunity at work to take time to reflect, because her working hours were busy and noisy, doing things with others, and S finds it difficult to learn in that environment. She would like a few hours of quiet time alone at work to reflect and get ideas by *going inside* her head. Instead S takes work home and makes time in the early morning | 158 Its 'just my personality' – an acceptance of its just who she is – her husband has more trouble accepting it than her | |
| | | | | 160 Later MU 23 talks about how she is always 'doing' and feels she cant take time to sit at work | |

**Table 4.2** (continued)

| 1 Original transcript | 2 First transformation | 3 Second transformation | 4 Final transformation | 5 Reflections and contextual information | 6 My queries and critique |
|---|---|---|---|---|---|
| 155. I. Because you're so involved? | Both she and her husband had questioned the desirability of this situation, but S wondered if he had more difficulty with her busyness than she did. S wondered to herself if she was her '*own worst enemy*' and could change something to improve the situation, but felt that she had a personality that? was interested in getting involved in lots of things | With respect to professional learning, S wanted a few hours of quiet time alone after work at her desk She would like this time to reflect about work and *get ideas by going inside* her head. Her working hours are busy and noisy, doing things and interacting with people, and S finds it difficult to reflect or learn in that environment. (see also MU23) | | | 160, 174 Time seems to be a broader issue here than time for learning – it seems to be a deeply felt need/yearning (*that would be would be...*) for time alone to think generally – *my time* as opposed to time where she meets other demands/ expectations. *Where I've always wanted to be* – implying this is something she's wanted for a long time – maybe back to pre professional years |
| 156. S. Yeah | | | | | |
| 157. I. So how do you manage it – your time | | | | | |
| 158. S. Um, *just go flat out...I think just my personality* I can...just ask my husband, he probably has more trouble *managing my busy schedule than I do.* He says do you want to go down this road? | What she would like to do is to be able to have a few hours of quiet time alone after work at her desk. She would like this time to think, '*go inside her head*' where *she gets all her ideas.* | She feels she's always needed this sort of personal reflective time, but doesn't get it at work so she builds it into her early morning routine at home to think, read and study for personal and professional purposes | | | |
| 159. I. Yes, I mean time seems to be a factor for so many of the professionals that I talk to | | | | | |
| 160. S. Well I'd like to be able to stay till five o'clock and *just have my time, sitting at my desk, going inside my head where I get all my ideas.* | | | | | |

**Table 4.2** (continued)

| 1 Original transcript | 2 First transformation | 3 Second transformation | 4 Final transformation | 5 Reflections and contextual information | 6 My queries and critique |
|---|---|---|---|---|---|
| *Where I've always wanted to be quiet by myself and I don't get that time. And when I'm there eight till three, there's people around and I don't learn enough in the busy environment. I can't switch off and I need it. I take my notes home and I sit at the desk at home and I go inside my head and just think about it* | Her working hours are busy and noisy, with people around and things to do, and S finds it difficult to learn enough in that environment. (also MU23) I can't switch off and I need it | | | | |
| 161. I. And so do you get any of that time at all? Like at home or work? That sort of head time? | She feels she's always needed this sort of personal reflective time, but doesn't get it at work so she takes her work notes home | | | | |
| 162. S. Professionally? | S has an established routine on many mornings when she gets up very early, so she has time alone at home to read and think. She uses this time for reading or professional work issues | | | | |
| 163. I. Or just, yeah | | | | | |

**Table 4.2**  (continued)

| 1 Original transcript | 2 First transformation | 3 Second transformation | 4 Final transformation | 5 Reflections and contextual information | 6 My queries and critique |
|---|---|---|---|---|---|
| 164. S. I get up early in the morning. R gets up at 5:30 and at 6:10 I do sit down till 7:00. Not *professionally* but *personal* time? | S loves quiet time alone to think, read or study, but more than that its 'her time' *I go inside my head and just think about it* | | | | |
| 165. I. Your own | | | | | |
| 166. S. Yeah, reading | | | | | |
| 167. I. And so, you've done that for quite a while? | | | | | |
| 168. S. I've been reading for about 20 years. I wouldn't do it every morning | | | | | |
| 169. I. But it's quite a routine | | | | | |
| 170. S. But more than half of the week | | | | | |
| 171. I. And what does that give you and what do you miss if you don't get it? | | | | | |
| 172. S. This is probably more personal sort of stuff | | | | | |

**Table 4.2**  (continued)

| 1 Original transcript | 2 First transformation | 3 Second transformation | 4 Final transformation | 5 Reflections and contextual information | 6 My queries and critique |
|---|---|---|---|---|---|
| 173. I. Because I can understand what you're saying about needing to go inside my head | | | | | |
| 174. S. Yeah, *I love that time. It's my time that I can just study* | | | | | |
| 175. I. So your focus is usually on your personal studies | | | | | |
| 176. S. Yes, but I can use it sometime on my work | | | | | |

For S, the experience of APL includes the following:

1. An awareness of the value for her, both personally and professionally, of having time alone to think, read and study (learn).
2. That time alone is when she goes inside her head and generates/*gets ideas.*
3. She sees the lack of time for reflection as her personal problem related to her doing too much rather than being a professional or workplace issue.
4. She perceives there as being no opportunities for that at work, as she is busy doing things with people and she can't learn in that environment.
5. The feeling of having a lack of time is an issue that pervades many aspects of her life.
6. She accepts this issue to some extent and takes work home to spend time alone thinking or studying.

In Table 4.2, column 1 consists of the original transcript, verbatim, where meaning is expressed in the language of the participant. The transcript is transformed through a number of phases, so that everyday language is expressed in the language of the researcher's discipline in a way that reveals the essence of the phenomenon. Giorgi (1994, p. 209) describes this phase as "intuiting disciplinary meanings". Giorgi's (2009) published work demonstrates two phases of the transformation, but in practice an indeterminate number of phases may be needed. The final transformation (column 4) is used with other transcripts to develop the common structure for the phenomenon.

### 4.6.2.1  First Transformation

Giorgi describes the first transformation as expressing the original description of the experience in a disciplinary sensitive way. The participant spoke about her learning experience from the everyday attitude, which is always fuller and richer than the phenomenological perspective. In the transformations I foreground the educational perspective of the experience, but retain all other features of the experience in the background. As can be seen in the transformed meaning unit (TMU) in Table 4.2, column 2, all data remain and are accounted for. Where possible, the words of the participant are kept and I am careful to avoid introducing theoretical terms.

In the first transformation, column 2 of the example, I seek to make explicit the implicit or assumed nature of many aspects of the description. These were often not described in detail because they were taken for granted by the participant and myself. For example, referring to line 154, I knew from previous discussions that her "other job" was being a parent. The text is also altered from the first to the third person, as a step away from the particularity of that experience towards a general structure of APL. I use italics to highlight original words of the participant for clarity when accessing the data later. In many ways, the first transformation expands the data set rather than reduces it. The description is clarified through this initial transformation.

As mentioned earlier I added two columns to Giorgi's process to make my awareness of my preunderstandings (or reflexive interpretations) as transparent as possible. These are columns 5 and 6 in Table 4.2. From field visits I had ready access to a number of important contextual features that helped clarify the implicit nature of some aspects of descriptions. I added these to column 5, so that their source was apparent. I also used column 5 to record tension between attempts to bracket my preunderstanding and previous experience. Column 6 is described in the next transformation.

### 4.6.2.2  Second Transformation

In the second transformation, column 3, I ask the question, adapted from Giorgi (1994, p. 208): What is the meaning-for-the-professional insofar as it is relevant to, and revelatory of, the experience of continuing learning as a professional? This is the creative part of the method, where possibilities are explored, but there is no creativity without risk. Whilst adopting a critical attitude, there is a need to do several sweeps of the data, refining and questioning: going back to the original data to check whether the transformation remains faithful.

The meaning of a particular segment of the transcript, with respect to learning, may seem ambiguous initially but becomes clearer with repeated iterative cycles of the entire transcript. Thus the meaning is revealed within the circumscribed boundaries of the whole description. I attempted to rigorously interrogate the transformations by seeking other possible meanings, remaining faithful to the participant's description as much as possible. I took care to avoid making early knowledge claims. The transformed data presents the best judgement I could make about the meaning of continuing PL for this participant. The sixth column was useful for questioning other possibilities or expressing ambiguity or doubt in a way that was still linked to specific data. This column makes such attempts at rigour transparent.

For example, in column 6, I note that this participant's statement about being her *own worst enemy* with respect to time issues was very different from the way that some other professionals expressed concern about time. In particular some male participants had seen it as purely an employer issue of under-staffing rather than a personal deficiency. The question of gender was raised, but I put it aside at the time, taking care to stay within the constraints of the evidence as presented at this stage of analysis.

Care is taken to retain meaning whilst transforming. In moving from the original data it is easy for assumptions about the experience to enter inadvertently. In the example (line 160), the participant talks about *getting all my ideas* by *going inside my head*. At one stage in the second transformation I found I had changed this to "generate ideas": a very different representation to that of "getting ideas". This is when I began to keep participants' words in italics as a way of crosschecking unintended changes in meaning. Transformation is a gradual refining process that shouldn't be rushed.

### 4.6.2.3  Final Transformation

Regardless of the number of transformations, the final one is compared with those of other participants to construct the meaning structure of the phenomenon. By this final stage, the transcript has moved as far as possible from the particularity of the experience for this professional to the structure of the phenomenon.

Clarity was enhanced and ambiguity diminished with each iteration. Giorgi (2003) states that the analysis is a self-correcting procedure to some extent, as small nuances become clearer as you progress through the process. By the final transformation each meaning unit was imbued with a sense of the whole transcript. For example (line 160), the participant refers to the *busy environment*. By referring to other meaning units it became clear that she was referring not only to other people being around but also to noise and her own busyness. She comments in later meaning units that: *I do tend to be a doer rather than actually sit there in work time. I think oh, I should be doing something*. Although Giorgi describes his work as descriptive not hermeneutic, the process reflects the hermeneutic circle where understanding involves both part and whole in a dialectic relationship.

Finally, the process of transformation of data involves what I call horizontal and vertical iterations. Re-reading the entire transcript is a vertical iteration that clarifies ambiguous meaning units over time, as described with respect to the "busy environment". At the same time, there is a horizontal iteration in the sense that within the transcript table later transformations are checked against the original data to make sure meaning is not altered as described with respect to "getting ideas". The final transformed meaning units for all transcripts are considered equally in the building of the structure of the phenomenon.

## *4.6.3  Developing the Structure*

As previously stated, the aim of phenomenological analysis is to step back from the natural attitude towards the world to allow the essential meaning of the experiences described to emerge. The essential meaning is usually a complex interaction of a number of constituents and sub-constituents. Although determination of what the constituents are and how they are related in the structure occurs in tandem as the structure emerges, I describe them separately for clarity.

### 4.6.3.1  Determining the Constituents

The constituents of the meaning structure are determined by comparing the final TMUs across several participants, to consider what it is that makes an experience one of continuing PL. Illumination of the essential nature of each constituent is achieved through the consideration of other possibilities, varying aspects of the experience one at a time: a process called free imaginative variation (Giorgi, 2009, p. 132). Variation is explored across participants in empirical phenomenology. Each participant's experience of PL is a profile or perspective on the phenomenon of APL (Sokolowski, 2000). That is, different people may experience PL in different ways. Not only do they view it from different perspectives, but different meanings are conveyed from past experiences.

Through comparing and contrasting diverse experiences, a fuller and richer sense of APL was gained. Once four transcripts were transformed, I began to build a temporary structure of APL by comparing the final TMUs on the basis of commonalities and variation. I was initially struck by the differences and uniqueness of each participant's description rather than commonalities, which is not surprising as maximum variability was an aim of the participant selection. A constituent of a phenomenon must be present in some way across all participants to become part of the structure. Some aspects are clearly present in the descriptions; others are strongly implied.

The nature of the constituents in the temporary structure of APL altered as I added further transformed transcripts. In describing the constituents I tried to use words from the everyday professional language of the transcripts in order to stay as close as possible to the experience evoked. Each constituent was interrogated to find what was essential and what was contingent. With more subjects the structure became clearer. The greater the variation, the easier it is to see what is common. Variations were noted and accounted for as part of the description of each constituent. All constituents are complex, so that I used sub-constituents to describe them in detail.

### 4.6.3.2  Creating the Structure

In determining the structure I needed to step back from the details of the TMUs to a meta-level of analysis. Over time the picture became clearer, making it easier to see essential constituents. A useful metaphor is Annie Lamont's (1995) comparison of the process of creative writing to the development of a Polaroid picture, where a sense of the picture is glimpsed before specific features become clear. From the meta-level, I revisited the data of each participant continually to see whether the tentative constituents I was developing were an accurate reflection of each person's experience of APL. Each time, I altered the emerging structure slightly through expansion or refinement of some constituent until all TMUs were accounted for.

As an example of this process I refer to the issue of time. As I examined the TMUs of participants, many referred to problems with time related to their experience of APL, as is seen in the example in Table 4.2. In my initial groupings of TMUs, I considered time issues as a possible constituent, as such issues had confronted me from my early collection of the data. As the structure became clearer, I saw that time featured as an aspect of several constituents. Time held several meanings with respect to APL, depending on the particular professional and the context of the experience she was discussing. This is illustrated in the findings in Chapter 5.

Thus I moved in an iterative way between distance from and closeness to specific transformations until the constituents were clarified. Sandberg (2005, p. 50) describes a similar iterative process as the fulfilment of intention whereby the researcher's changing interpretation of the data eventually matches the "meaning given in lived experience". Although not referring to phenomenology as such, Alvesson (2002 p. 62) also refers to "a dialectic between distance and familiarity" in describing the hermeneutic process of interpretation of meaning of texts.

When justifying the choice of phenomenological analysis as a holistic method, I contrast it to dealing with complex phenomena by division into factors or elements. Constituents of a phenomenological structure are very different from factors. Each constituent is inextricably interrelated with the others. Not only are all constituents interdependent, as could also be argued with some descriptions of factors, but phenomenological constituents can be described as a holographic representation (Willis, 2001, p. 12). Thus each constituent expresses the entire experience viewed from a particular perspective, foregrounding one aspect whilst including the other constituents in the background.

After eight transcripts redundancies became apparent, whereby the structure remained the same despite additional data, I carefully examined the final eight transcripts checking against the structure for additional information or variation that would alter the essential meaning. All 16 transcripts were thus analysed and are reflected in the final structure. The second round of interviews only added contextual description, but did not alter the structure.

### 4.6.3.3  Evoking the Structure

Once I had a viable structure as a set of constituents, I refined the relationship between the constituents and sub-constituents through a full textual description. It is the text that solidifies the meaning of the experience for the audience of research. Production of text can therefore be described as part of the methodology, involving an "imagined dialogue" with the reader (Alvesson, 2002, p. 62).

In describing the structure, I aimed to produce a text that reflects the essence of the lived experience of APL. As Willis (2001, p. 3) suggests, I was seeking "to illuminate its specific quality as an experience" rather than to "locate it in an abstract matrix". Through vignettes and experiential accounts from participants in the description of the structure, I intended to bring it to life in a way that expresses the "phenomenological meaning" of the experience of continuing learning for these professionals.

The inter-subjective meanings evoked through my text are reflective of shared experiences within the professional life-world. I have – and continue to – present these ideas and related research to colleagues at conferences, gaining feedback that helps coalesce my findings. Alvesson (2002, p. 62) describe such dialogue as part of the hermeneutic process of reflexive interpretation. Sandberg (2005, p. 55) also describes discussion of findings with colleagues as a way of establishing communicative validity.

In keeping with the dialogic nature of the research, I sent the completed findings to 12 professionals, from a mix of therapy and education backgrounds with academic and workplace experiences. I asked whether any of the experiences described either reflected or were different from their own experiences of PL. There was agreement that the findings reflected widely shared experiences.

## 4.7  Looking Back

As with any project, in hindsight changes could have been made. What was intended was not always enacted. Professionals' days would suddenly alter so that systematically planned observations would be limited. Such difficulties are part of the quest to investigate learning as lived. Willis (2001, p. 12) notes two specific concerns for phenomenological researchers investigating lived experience, reflecting my concern about balancing rigour and evocation:

> The first [concern] is to cultivate an active suspicion of assumptions and prejudices that might tacitly influence and subvert honest inquiry. The second ... is the importance of understanding and developing expressive approaches to inquiry which can complement and underpin analytic or explanatory approaches.

In this chapter I have described how I drew upon criteria of rigour, reflexivity and relevance, aiming to enhance the quality of the research. I demonstrate rigour through attention to a systematic and transparent procedure. The procedure involved a reflexive critique of assumptions as an iterative process between the distance of a meta-methodological view and closeness to detail. The design and reporting of this research attempt to be relevant to real issues of concern for professionals in current practice. My intention is that the structure is faithful to the participants' experiences, whilst being justifiable from a methodological perspective. The phenomenological structure of APL described in the following section is a way of understanding how professionals learn in and through their practice.

# References

Alvesson, M. (2002). *Postmodernism and social research*. Philadelphia, PA: Open University.

Alvesson, M., & Sköldberg, K. (2000). *Reflexive methodology: New vistas for qualitative research*. London; Thousand Oaks, CA: Sage Publications.

Angen, M. J. (2000). Evaluating interpretive inquiry: Reviewing the validity debate and opening the dialogue. *Qualitative Health Research, 10*(3), 378–395.

Argyris, C., & Schön, D. A. (1974). *Theory in practice: Increasing professional effectiveness*. San Francisco: Jossey-Bass Publishers.

Atkinson, P., & Coffey, A. (2004). Analysing documentary realities. In D. Silverman (Ed.), *Qualitative research: Theory, method and practice* (2nd ed., pp. 56–75). London; Thousand Oaks, CA: Sage Publications.

Atkinson, P.,& Silverman, D. (1997). Kundera's "Immortality": The interview society and the invention of the self. *Qualitative Inquiry, 3*(3), 304–318.

Baum, F. (2005). Community health services in Australia. In J. Germov (Ed.), *Second opinion: An introduction to health sociology* (pp. 373–396). Melbourne: Oxford University Press.

Bourdieu, P. (1996). Understanding. *Theory, Culture and Society, 13*(2), 17–38.

Brace-Govan, J. (2004). Issues in snowball sampling: The lawyer, the model and ethics. *Qualitative Research Journal, 4*(1), 52–60.

Byrne-Armstrong, H., Higgs, J., & Horsfall, D. (Eds.). (2001). *Critical moments in qualitative research*. Oxford: Butterworth-Heinmann.

Chesney, M. (2001). Dilemmas of self in the method. *Qualitative Health Research, 11*(1), 127–135.

Cope, C. (2004). Ensuring validity and reliability in phenomenographic research using the analytical framework of a structure of awareness. *Qualitative Research Journal, 4*(2), 5–18.

D'Cruz, H. (2001). The fractured lens: Methodology in perspective. In H. Byrne-Armstrong, J. Higgs, & D. Horsfall (Eds.), *Critical moments in qualitative research* (pp. 17–29). Oxford: Butterworth-Heinmann.

Denzin, N. K., & Lincoln, Y. S. (Eds.). (2005). *The SAGE handbook of qualitative research* (3rd ed.). Thousand Oaks, CA: Sage Publications.

Edwards, R., & Usher, R. (2000). Research on work, research at work: Postmodern perspectives. In J. Garrick & C. Rhodes (Eds.), *Research and knowledge at work: Perspectives, case-studies and innovative strategies* (pp. 32–50). London; New York: Routledge.

Etherington, K. (2004). *Becoming a reflexive researcher: Using our selves in research*. London; Philadelphia, PA: Jessica Kingsley Publishers.

Fontana, A., & Frey, J. H. (2000). The interview: From structured questions to negotiated text. In N. K. Denzin & Y. S. Lincoln (Eds.), *The handbook of qualitative research* (pp. 645–672).

Gadamer, H. G. (1965/1979). *Truth and method* (2nd ed.). London: Sheed & Ward.

Giorgi, A. (1988). Validity and reliability from a phenomenological perspective. In W. J. Baker, L. P. Mos, H. V. Rappard, & H. J. Stam (Eds.), *Recent trends in theoretical psychology* (pp. 167–176). New York: Springer-Verlag.

Giorgi, A. (1989). An example of harmony between descriptive reports and behaviour. *Journal of Phenomenological Psychology*, *20*(1), 60–88.

Giorgi, A. (1990). Phenomenology, psychological science and common sense. In G. R. Semin & K. J. Gergen (Eds.), *Everyday understanding: Social and scientific implications*. London: Sage Publications.

Giorgi, A. (1994). A phenomenological perspective on certain qualitative research methods. *Journal of Phenomenological Psychology*, *25*(2), 190–220.

Giorgi, A. (1997). The theory, practice and evaluation of the phenomenological method as a qualitative research procedure. *Journal of Phenomenological Psychology*, *28*, 235–260.

Giorgi, A. (2000a). Concerning the application of phenomenology to caring research. *Scandinavian Journal of Caring Sciences*, *14*, 11–15.

Giorgi, A. (2000b). Psychology as a human science revisited. *The Journal of Humanistic Psychology*, *40*(3), 56–73.

Giorgi, A. (2003). *Workshop on phenomenology: The philosophy and the method*. Quebec: University of Quebec.

Giorgi, A. (2005). The phenomenological movement and research in the human sciences. *Nursing Science Quarterly*, *18*(1), 75–82.

Giorgi, A. (2009). *The descriptive phenomenological method in Psychology: A modified Husserlian approach*. Pittsburgh, PA: Duquesne University Press.

Giorgi, A., & Giorgi, B. (2003a). The descriptive phenomenological psychological method. In P. M. Camic, J. E. Rhodes, & L. Yardley (Eds.), *Qualitative research in psychology: Expanding perspectives in methodology and design* (pp. 243–273). Washington, DC: American Psychological Association.

Giorgi, A., & Giorgi, B. (2003b). Phenomenology. In J. A. Smith (Ed.), *Qualitative psychology: A practical guide to research methods* (pp. 25–50). London: Sage.

Grbich, C. (1999). *Qualitative research in health: An introduction*. St Leonards, NSW: Allen & Unwin.

Guba, E. G., & Lincoln, Y. S. (2005). Paradigmatic controversies, contradictions, and emerging confluences. In N. K. Denzin & Y. S. Lincoln (Eds.), *The SAGE handbook of qualitative research* (3rd ed., pp. 191–215). Thousand Oaks, CA: Sage.

Halling, S. (2005). When intimacy and companionship are at the core of the phenomenological research process. *Indo-Pacific Journal of Phenomenology*, *5*(1), 1–11.

Holstein, J. A., & Gubrium, J. F. (1995). *The active interview*. Thousand Oaks, CA: Sage Publications.

Ivarsson, A.-B., Söderback, I., & Ternestedt, A.-M. (2002). The meaning and form of occupational therapy as experienced by women with psychoses. *Scandinavian Journal of Caring Sciences*, *16*(1), 103–110.

Karlsson, G. (1993). *Psychological qualitative research from a phenomenological perspective*. Stockholm: Almqvist & Wiksell International.

Kezar, A., & Eckel, P. (Eds.). (2000). *Moving beyond the gap between research and practice in higher education*. San Francisco: Jossey-Bass.

Kleiman, S. (2004). What is the nature of nurse practitioners' lived experiences interacting with patients? *Journal of the American Academy of Nurse Practitioners*, *16*(6), 263–269.

Kvale, S. (1994). Ten standard objections to qualitative research interviews. *Journal of Phenomenological Psychology*, *25*(2), 147–173.

Lamont, A. (1995). *Bird by bird: Some instructions on writing and life*. New York: Random House.

Marshall, J. (2001). Self-reflective inquiry practices. In P. Reason & H. Bradbury (Eds.), *Handbook of action research: Participative inquiry and practice* (pp. 433–439). London; Thousand Oaks, CA: Sage Publications.

Mays, N., & Pope, C. (2000). Qualitative research in health care: Assessing quality in qualitative research. *British Medical Journal*, *320*(7226), 50–52.

McWilliam, E. (2004). W(h)ither practitioner research. *The Australian Educational Researcher*, *31*(2), 113–126.

Mishler, E. G. (1984). *The discourse of medicine: Dialectics of medical interviews.* Norwood, NJ: Ablex Publishing Corporation.

Patton, M. Q. (2002). *Qualitative research and evaluation methods* (3rd ed.). Thousand Oaks, CA: Sage Publications.

Paul, J. L., & Marfo, K. (2001). Preparation of educational researchers in philosophical foundations of inquiry. *Review of Educational Research, 71*(4), 525–547.

Rydahl-Hansen, S. (2005). Hospitalized patients experienced suffering in life with incurable cancer. *Scandinavian Journal of Caring Sciences, 19,* 213–222.

Sandberg, J. (2005). How do we justify knowledge produced within interpretive approaches? *Organizational Research Methods, 8*(1), 41–68.

Schwandt, T. A. (2005). A diagnostic reading of scientifically based research for education. *Educational Theory, 55*(3), 285–305.

Schön, D. A. (1983). *The reflective practitioner: How professionals think in action.* Aldershot, England: Arena.

Schön, D. A. (1995). Knowing-in-action: The new scholarship requires a new epistemology. *Change 27*(6), 27–35.

Silverman, D. (2001). *Interpreting qualitative data: Methods for analysing talk, text and interaction* (2nd ed.). London: Sage Publications.

Silverman, D. (2005). *Doing qualitative research: A practical handbook* (2nd ed.). London: Sage Publications.

Sokolowski, R. (2000). *Introduction to phenomenology.* Cambridge; New York: Cambridge University Press.

Solomon, N., Boud, D., Leontios, M., & Staron, M. (2001). Researchers are learners too: Collaboration in research on workplace learning. *Journal of Workplace Learning, 13*(7/8), 274–282.

Sparkes, A. C. (2001). Myth 94: Qualitative health researchers will agree about validity. *Qualitative Health Research, 11*(4), 538–552.

Suri, H., & Clarke, D. (2009). Advancements in research synthesis methods: From a methodologically inclusive perspective. *Review of Educational Research, 79*(1), 395–430.

Todres, L. (1998). The qualitative description of human experience: The aesthetic dimension. *Qualitative Health Research, 8*(1), 121–127.

Van der Mescht, H. (2004). Phenomenology in education: A case study in educational leadership. *Indo-Pacific Journal of Phenomenology, 4*(1), 1–16.

Williams, L. (2005). Jostling for position: A sociology of allied health. In J. Germov (Ed.), *Second opinion: An introduction to health sociology* (pp. 349–372). Melbourne: Oxford University Press.

Willis, P. (2001). The 'Things Themselves' in phenomenology. *Indo-Pacific Journal of Phenomenology, 1*(1), 1–14.

van Manen, M. (1997a). From meaning to method. *Qualitative Health Research, 7*(3), 345–369.

van Manen, M. (1997b). *Researching lived experience: Human science for an action sensitive pedagogy* (2nd ed.). London, ON: Althouse Press; University of Western Ontario.

van Manen, M. (2001). Professional practice and 'Doing Phenomenology'. In S. K. Toombs (Ed.), *Handbook of phenomenology and medicine* (pp. 457–474). Dordrecht: Kluwer Press.

van Manen, M. (Ed.). (2002). *Writing in the dark: Phenomenological studies in interpretive inquiry.* London, ON: Althouse Press.

# Part III
# Understanding

This part contains the pivotal chapter of the book, Chapter 5, "Authentic Professional Learning" (APL), which describes the experience of professionals as they continue to learn in their daily lives through their professional career. In this chapter, I return to the metaphorical "lens" of phenomenology used to frame this investigation, altering the depth of field of that lens to determine what aspect of experience is in focus. Doing this highlights three ways that the experience of APL can be discussed. These are: the experience of a specific learning situation, the experience of continuing to learn as a professional and learning as part of the overall experience of "being a professional".

There are four parts to Chapter 5. Before describing the three perspectives on APL as viewed through a multi-focal lens, a broad sweep of the data corpus is presented (Section 5.1). This sketches the professional life-world of the participants to contextualise the detailed experiences for the reader. During engagement with participants I asked for detailed descriptions of concrete situations where each considered he or she had learnt as a professional. A "close-up" view (Section 5.2) of these specific learning situations highlights the type of situations discussed and their diversity. It became clear early in the research, that the experience of continuing to learn as a professional is never limited to single situations.

The bulk of Chapter 5 is focused on describing the phenomenological structure of APL (Section 5.3). A phenomenological analysis allows a "mid-range" perspective looking across diverse learning situations, revealing commonalities in lived experiences that were essential for situations to be described by the participants as professional learning experiences. The structure of APL details inter-related constituents and sub-constituents so that not only commonalities but also variability between experiences is accounted for. Vignettes of participants' stories exemplify different ways that the structure of APL manifests within different professionals' lived experiences.

Finally, the "wide-angled" view (Section 5.4) takes a broad perspective in considering how experiences of APL contribute to life as a practicing professional. Despite commonalties in the experiences of APL, there is a unique quality to each professional's learning, reflecting his or her "way of being a professional". Meaning is constituted through learning at work in idiosyncratic ways that shape (and are shaped by) each professional's way of being.

# Chapter 5
# Authentic Professional Learning

## 5.1 Professional Life-World

From the holistic perspective taken in this research, the descriptions of APL throughout this chapter are imbued with nuances of the professional life-world, but because the focus is on the experience of learning, some life-world details are lightly sketched. To contextualise the phenomenological structure of APL, this chapter begins with a description of the professional life-world drawn from the complete data corpus, with respect to three aspects of the professional context: professional affiliations, employer organisations and local workplaces.

### 5.1.1 Professional Affiliations

Most clearly identified themselves as an occupational therapist, a physiotherapist or a speech pathologist before thinking of themselves as an employee of an organisation. That is, their professional affiliation seemed stronger than their employer connections. Participants were aware of common expectations about a professional's responsibility with respect to continuing learning. They repeated, almost word for word, their perceived professional responsibilities to *keep up-to-date with new knowledge and practices, maintain a quality service, be accountable* and *use evidence-based practice.*

These perceptions tally with documentation available from most professional associations. As only half of the participants were members of their association, this shared perception was presumably gained through interaction with the wider professional community. Professional association websites stressed continuing PD, with terminology such as "knowledge acquisition" and "updating knowledge" used rather than PL. Although learning is implied in many of the PD statements, the focus of these documents was, and still is, on public accountability through maintenance of professional standards, delivery of PD activities and supervision of practice.

In the current climate of accountability and litigation, there are moves towards mandatory and auditable PD as a requirement of yearly registration for all health (and many other) professionals. The professional associations award points for attendance at accredited courses as well as for other forms of individual PD, such as reading articles or presenting to colleagues, requiring written evidence of such activities. Many participants mentioned that public acknowledgement of their knowledge and skills, by their peers, offered professional credibility and was necessary for career progression.

The second focus of documents from professional associations was on delivery of PD. Associations survey members to identify preferred content and method of delivery. Practical courses and staying up to date with research were stressed, with a move towards more flexible delivery of programmes through self-paced learning modules. Access to databases of critically appraised evidence of practice is often provided, with access to relevant scientific journals. Participants valued their professional journal when the content was relevant to their practice. Despite this, many admitted to leaving them *unread by the bed* or *sitting at the bottom of the briefcase* because of lack of time. One participant noted that journals were often perceived as unrelated to problems of practice, explaining:

> *I think that there is probably a role for a journal, or at least a section of one, which encourages clinician's viewpoints without the expectation that papers are well researched, referenced and scientific in nature. The present state of our current national journal does little to encourage the masses to contribute to discussions. I repeat what I said before, the cutting edge is in clinical practice, not in the universities.* (Dom)

Finally, all associations stressed the need for supervision of therapists and offered varying degrees of support through mentor programmes. The terms "supervision", "mentoring" and "support" are often used interchangeably. Participants also used these words interchangeably in the interviews despite the different inferences of the terms. For example, statements such as *I really need supervision to help me know what to do* were made in situations where a need for support or mentoring was implied.

## 5.1.2 Employer Organisations

The two large government organisations, who employed 13 of the 16 participants, published clearly identifiable strategic directions and goals that included staff development, as do most public organisations. One also had a learning and development policy for employees involving individual learning plans aligned with workplace priorities. None of these 13 participants mentioned or seemed aware of these policies. Some did comment, however, that these two organisations valued the professionals' ability to *be accountable, develop measurable outcomes* and *meet goals in a timely manner*.

Both organisations encouraged performance reviews by the line manager who was usually not from the same profession. When participants mentioned a review, they did not generally see it as relevant to their ongoing PL. For example Nola noted: *My manager doesn't really understand what a therapist does. I've tried to give him some information but he's not that interested. He doesn't have a clue what I do.* In the two large organisations, therapists as a group comprised only a small percentage of the employees. Participants commented on this minority status.

*One of my colleagues said that it's like, it's us and them but we're never us, as therapists, we're always them. I don't feel that the organisation understands why they need to have therapists, the decision makers don't know, don't really have any contact with therapists about decisions.* (Nerida)

A few participants expressed a strong feeling of frustration at what they saw as an abrogation of a social justice agenda, describing the organisation's main focus as fiscal rather than client-centred, despite rhetoric to the contrary. Most participants were quite explicit in their feelings that neither they nor their contribution was valued. For some, this resulted in resignation. Sam noted, *I'm leaving due to frustration, dissatisfaction and feeling totally undervalued. It has become very evident that I am just a position number.* Others pragmatically stated they loved what they did in their work but that *being appreciated would be the icing on the cake* (Mary).

The two smaller non-government agencies had no published policies on PL, nor did the three participants from these organisations mention many of the workplace concerns commented on above by other participants. None of these three participants alluded to feeling that they or their work was unvalued.

All four organisations supported staff to attend some PD activities within budget constraints. Participants reported attending a variety of PD activities provided by the workplace, professional associations or private providers, both within and outside working hours. Sometimes the organisations funded activities but all professionals attended self-funded activities as well. Two participants mentioned they were not granted organisational approval for funds or leave to attend PD that had a specific therapy focus, as this focus did not align with organisational goals. The three workplace PD sessions I attended were enthusiastically received, according to my observations and to organisational satisfaction surveys. The focus was on clinical practice, with client examples, preceded by theoretical background. They were delivered to a seated audience in a traditional didactic manner, but interaction and interjection were encouraged and did occur.

Formal professional networks were supported to some degree by all organisations and participants agreed on the value of these networks for their PL. The networks were usually organised on the basis of location and profession, although some informal networking based on shared interests was reported. The network meetings I observed varied according to who facilitated the group. When a senior professional supervisor facilitated, the proceedings were reasonably formal. Participants tended to speak in turn, looked for the supervisor to lead and waited for her comments before proceeding. When the local network met without a supervisor the discussions were more informal with interaction between multiple participants. In particular, I observed more readiness of participants to admit failure or doubt in the latter situation. This was not observed when the supervisor was present.

### 5.1.3 Local Workplaces

From the workplace visits and interviews, it became obvious that the structure of the local workplace had particular impact on continuing PL experiences. Participants commented, in particular, on the impact of opportunities for interactions with other people and the value of flexibility in schedules and timetabling.

All the participants worked with other staff. Usually this includes other therapists as well as psychologists, teachers, nurses, residential care workers and administrative staff. Of the 16 participants, 10 worked in multi-disciplinary teams with regular interaction. The other six had minimal interaction with team members, because they worked on different days or because of staff shortages and unfilled vacancies. In addition to interaction with clients, who ranged from children to adults, most of the therapists interacted with the clients' families. When I observed teams sharing space and time during the day, such as over lunch breaks, I noted significant interaction between them, described by them generally as *catching up socially, sharing humour as a safety valve* or *brainstorming ideas about work.*

The pace, intensity and busyness of the professionals' work situations were commented on in a negative way by most participants, especially in the large organisations, if they had limited autonomy. Even when participants reported coping with the workload, they used phrases such as *we're just run off our feet* or *we just dig away at the mountain of work.* Some participants reported working extended hours and having difficulty taking leave because of their perception of unmet client need and a high level of commitment to their clients. Many found that work intrudes on their personal lives. One younger professional commented: *How does having a family fit in as well as maintaining our professional career? That worries me* (Nola). The high workload of frontline staff has been commented on in public enquiries into similar government organisations.

Participants discussed a range of strategies for dealing with the intensity of work. A process of prioritisation of client service was in place in one organisation with varying degrees of success according to participants. In the other organisations prioritisation was decided locally. The working days of four participants were particularly tightly scheduled. After I finished an interview with one of these professionals to the sounds of the next client crying outside the door, the irony of a union notice about workload on the staffroom wall did not escape me. It stated in bold print: "Say no to work overload. Speak up when you have too much to handle".

## 5.2 Situations Where Professionals Learn

Within the contexts described above, there were many different situations where professionals considered they had learnt. After describing their everyday work in the interviews, participants gave detailed descriptions of several learning situations. They described situations where, either at the time or in hindsight, they identified that *something happened*, resulting in learning. Using a term from one participant, I call these *transition situations* where the professional's awareness of the situation changed. As expected, there were many types of transition situations. Some were relatively straightforward involving a chance encounter with a client or talking with a colleague. Others were complex, such as dealing with a client with multiple needs or resolving a difficult organisational dilemma. In all cases, the descriptions of one situation led to descriptions of others that were related in some way.

Most participants discussed learning through clinical problem solving with clients, especially when the client had complex or unusual problems. A transition in awareness, where the therapist *understood what was happening* or *saw the situation in a different way*, occurred through various means. Feedback from the client, the addition of new information or discussion with others was involved in this change. Sometimes the situation was clear-cut, such as learning to apply a new technique with a client. Many learning situations, however, involved multiple shifts in awareness and concerned broader issues with clients, where professionals described moving over time to a *more holistic* or *long-term perspective* about practice issues.

About half the participants began their descriptions of learning situations by discussing a PD course. Invariably it was one attended some years ago but remembered because it was a significant learning experience. This is in contrast with general comments that participants learnt little from many PD courses because they were either not relevant or forgotten if not incorporated into practice. When probed further about PD courses considered to be learning experiences, it became apparent that the course was only part of the learning experience, being always linked to other situations. For example, a transition in awareness sometimes occurred after a course when working with clients or talking with others. It is then that *it all made sense*, or *the pieces fell into place*. Only one professional described a transition in awareness during a course when she suddenly saw *a whole new way of looking at my practice* (Gina). Some described transitions in awareness through several situations before a course, noting how the course confirmed an emerging change in their understanding.

Many significant transition situations were described where the focus of the shift in awareness was interaction with others. Every participant mentioned learning to work with others as part of their PL experience, described as learning *interpersonal skills*, *communication skills* or *conflict resolution*. The majority mentioned this as a crucial part of learning once a professional is in the workforce and one they generally felt unprepared for. Learning to work with others was ongoing, as even experienced therapists recounted significant learning experiences in this area. Learning through interaction with others also included learning from the experience of teaching others or presenting to peers and of being mentored and mentoring others.

The learning situations described by the two least experienced therapists, working for less than two years, were focused on learning what to do as a professional. They explained what had helped them to learn initially and what difficulties they faced. The transition situations they described included learning *where to start* in complex situations and learning how to put the theory they knew *into practice*.

Finally, some descriptions of learning were about moral or ethical dilemmas and what was learnt through their resolution. Almost half the participants recounted how they learnt about themselves through PL and two spoke of learning about learning. Thus descriptions of learning situations led to general comments about learning: what helps, what hinders, what is valued and which strategies are used. All participants expressed varying preferences for different ways of learning.

The type of learning situations described through the pilot study did not differ from those in the interviews. This indicates that the PL experiences of the 16 interviewees were similar to the larger group. Similarly, the types of learning situations from the second round of interviews a year later were similar to those mentioned already. Further clarification was gained from the second interviews about what supported the professionals to continue learning and what they, their profession and the workplace valued about learning. In two cases further contextual information about the local workplace was gained. In these cases, workplace dilemmas had worsened, resulting in frustration and anger on behalf of clients by one professional and disillusionment and stress leave for the other.

From this overview of learning situations, the diversity and complexity of the experience of PL can be glimpsed. The problem with research that remains with specific instances of learning, describing specific factors that may encourage learning, is that similar situations support learning for one person but not for another. In this research, the intention of asking participants to describe concrete situations where they had learnt as professionals was to draw out rich descriptions of the experience of PL. Viewing these descriptions from a phenomenological perspective allows constituents of an experience rather than elements of a specific situation to be seen. The value of a phenomenological approach to studying complex experiences is demonstrated in the following section.

## 5.3 Phenomenological Structure of APL

What is it about the various situations described above that make them identifiable to the participants, to other professionals and to myself as PL? From the phenomenological analysis, four constituents, *understanding*, *engagement*, *interconnection* and *openness*, were identified as essential to the experience of APL. All of these constituents were present in each participant's description of their PL experiences. As mentioned in Chapter 4, the essential structure of a complex experience revealed through phenomenological analysis is holographic, with each constituent incorporating the experience as a whole. The constituents are interdependent, but are separated below for the purpose of description. Their interdependence is evident in the short vignette of participants' experiences, following each constituent.

### 5.3.1  Overview of Authentic Professional Learning

The experience of continuing to learn as a professional involves change in professional understanding through different types of learning transitions (constituent 1). Such transitions occur when the professional is actively engaged in aspects of professional practice they care about, perceive as uncertain and see as novel (constituent 2). Through multiple transitions, the experiences of professionals are interconnected over time with experiences of others as an iterative, circuitous and imaginative web

**Table 5.1**  Constituents and sub-constituents of the structure of APL

---

**Constituent 1: Understanding**

*Change in professional understanding*
- from *prior understanding* through learning *transitions* to *changed understanding* as a professional

Variation in the type of transition(s), involving:
- knowing what to do;
- thinking about what to do; and
- questioning what is done.

---

**Constituent 2: Engagement**

*Engagement in professional practice*
- *actively* engaged in some way;
- *cared about* aspects of professional practice;
- perceived aspects as *uncertain*; and
- aspects of professional practice perceived in a *novel* way.

Variation in engagement in different aspects of professional practice and ways in which uncertainty is perceived by the professional.

---

**Constituent 3: Interconnection**

*Interconnection of experiences over time*
- multiple experiences interconnected in a *circuitous iterative web*;
- *imagination draws together* past, present and future; and
- through *dynamic interaction* with others.

Variation in the type of interactions and the extent of shared experiences and understanding.

---

**Constituent 4: Openness**

*Openness to possibilities that is circumscribed*
- *process* of APL is *open ended* requiring *openness of attitude*;
- *opportunities and constraints of professional context* shapes APL; and
- *resolution of tensions* between openness and context.

Variation in ways of resolving tensions, providing a unique quality imbuing the shared structure of APL

---

(constituent 3). Through these interconnections, continual PL is experienced as a process that is open to possibilities yet circumscribed by the professional's particular working context (constituent 4). An overview of the structure is shown in Table 5.1 and in the following paragraphs. Each *constituent* is outlined with *sub-constituents* that comprise it. Variation is accounted for in each constituent.

In constituent 1, *change* in *professional understanding* involves more than cognitive knowing, encapsulating all that a professional embodies and expresses through being a professional in practice. In situations where professionals describe having learnt, the *prior understanding* they bring to the situation is insufficient for the requirements of that situation, but *changes* through learning *transition(s)*. Variation in this constituent is related to different types of transitions involving knowing what to do, thinking about what to do or questioning what is done.

Constituent 2 describes how such change in understanding occurs, through the professional's *active engagement in* aspects of *professional practice* that they *care about* and perceive as *uncertain*. Here professional practice pertains to a broad range of activities related to being a professional. Through learning, a feature of professional practice is perceived in a *novel* way as professional understanding changes. Variation in this constituent is related to engagement in different aspects of practice and ways in which uncertainty in practice is perceived by the professional.

Constituent 3 describes how multiple experiences of learning are *interconnected over time* in APL. Professionals learn through *dynamic interaction* with a range of other people in an ongoing, *circuitous and iterative* manner that creates a *web* of interconnected experiences. In this process, the professional's *imagination draws together* recollections of past experiences, awareness of the present situation and anticipation of future possibilities. This constituent accounts for and integrates the complex social and temporal dimensions of APL. Variation in this constituent is related to the type of interactions that occur and the extent to which experience and understanding is shared.

Constituent 4 describes how APL is experienced as a process that is *open to* many *possibilities* because it occurs through engagement with others in the complexities of practice over time. APL is *open ended* with no clear beginning or predetermined outcome, requiring an *openness* or flexibility *of attitude* on the part of the professional to cope with the inherent uncertainty of the process. Yet this openness is not infinite, but is *circumscribed* and shaped by the *opportunities and constraints* of the *professional*'s working *context*. There are tensions between the possibilities inherent in APL and the circumscription of context. Variation in this constituent is related to the way in which different professionals *resolve these tensions*. This resolution shapes the professional's experience of APL, so that the learning of each professional has a unique quality although the structure of that experience is common to all the professionals.

*Change in professional understanding* is the core constituent. Active *engagement in professional practice* and *interconnection of experiences over time* describe in a chiasmic manner how such change in understanding occurs. *Circumscribed openness to possibilities* describes the way that the overall experience of APL is shaped so that changes in understanding in APL are experienced and expressed by professionals in unique ways. All four constituents interact dynamically.

In every experience of APL there is the recognisable thread of all four constituents. As I describe each constituent in detail in the following four sections, I refer to other constituents as appropriate. Similarly the vignettes at the end of each section contain elements of all four constituents although one is highlighted. Throughout the descriptions I draw on participants' words, shown in italics.

## 5.3.2 Learning as Change in Professional Understanding

Constituent 1, the keystone of the structure of APL, describes how learning is essentially about change in professional understanding. In the study, professionals were asked to describe particular situations where they learnt as a professional (occupational therapist, physiotherapist or speech pathologist). Through exploring such concrete situations, participants spoke about how their understanding as professionals changed through learning.

### 5.3.2.1 Change in Professional Understanding

In common use, *understanding* refers to perceiving the meaning of something and is often used with reference to knowing and learning. In this study understanding encapsulates more than this. The word itself was widely used in interviews in the study. It was referred to by participants in the sense of being aware that they had learnt. The most common phrase used to describe understanding was *making sense*.

There is a holistic rather than purely cognitive sense to their notion of understanding that involves all aspects of being a professional. Participants described understanding that included sensory perception, bodily awareness, humour, intuition, imagination and emotion, as well as cognition. Phrases used include *I saw it differently, I have a gut feeling, I just know when movement's wrong, I learn so much from being hands on*. Thus professional understanding is described as cognitive, intuitive, bodily, practical and emotional.

Professional understanding refers to all the professional is and does as a particular professional, for example, an experienced speech pathologist working in a rural setting. Professional understanding includes this professional's way of perceiving situations as well as way of practicing. These aspects are not separate, as the way a professional approaches situations determines what she does and vice versa. Professional understanding draws together all aspects of being a particular professional and is integral to practicing as a professional. That is, without a certain professional understanding it would not be possible to function in daily practice.

While change can take many forms in professional experience, such as instigation of workplace changes, change in professional understanding is the crux of all the experiences of APL described by the participants. Only when change in professional understanding occurs is APL experienced. Professionals described their professional understanding as *second nature* or *commonsense*. When a change in understanding occurred through learning one participant described this as *having a new sense about it . . . rather than a common sense about it* (Kim).

In the descriptions of learning, participants included who they are as a professional and how they change through learning. They commented that the way they saw themselves (or understood themselves) as a professional changed, using phrases such as *I'm more realistic, I'm more confident, I'm more resilient*. Many descriptions highlight the embodied nature of learning as a professional, that is as much about who the professional is, as it is about what she knows. Sometimes this description was explicit: *My learning makes a change in my being, I become more aware of what I am* (Charlie). At other times it was implicit: *It really came home to me* was how Mary describes her change in understanding about a work situation, where the word "home" implies self.

The varied experiences of APL described by the participants changed the professionals' understanding in some way. APL involves a change in the way of thinking about self and work (who they are as professionals), the way of practicing (what they do as professionals), what they felt they know or their way of working with others. Professional understanding encapsulates all that a professional does and is, so that change in understanding alters some aspect of being a professional. But a professional is not an aggregate of parts, existing rather as a whole. All these aspects of professional understanding presuppose a prior, implicit understanding of being a professional in a particular way.

The participants were articulate about their own particular way of being a professional, although such a specific question was not asked. When discussing APL, they made comments such as *that's just who I am, I'm by nature a reflective sort of person, I like to keep everyone happy at work* or *I like challenges*. Although such observations could also refer to their way of being more generally, these comments were made as part of their descriptions of learning *as a professional*. Thus professional understanding encapsulates all that a professional embodies and expresses through being a professional in everyday practice. Through learning, there is some change in the professionals' understanding of being a professional.

### 5.3.2.2  Learning Transitions

It is implicit in the nature of change that there is a transition from a previous condition to a different one. APL involves transitional situations where a professional's understanding changes, often over an extended period of time. The participants were aware of learning taking place in those situations, either at the time, on subsequent reflection or years later. Sometimes this change is apparently small, as Nerida described in the beginning of this book: *I saw him and his abilities in a different way after that*. At other times the change seems far-reaching. For example, Kim said, referring to a change in her way of understanding her practice: *It was wonderful. It was just like I'd opened a door and the situation was different then*. Together these transitions in understanding constitute the experience of APL.

Although it occasionally appeared that there was a single transition point, an "ah ha" experience, further discussion always revealed a series of transition periods leading to a learning situation, as well as following it. Transition periods are part of the texture of the professional's life-world, so that changes are understood in the context of the person's current understanding of being a professional. In Nerida's experience of learning mentioned above, her prior knowledge of the client and of what communication entails enabled her to learn from that brief exchange. Such interconnection of experiences is explained in detail in constituent 3.

A change in understanding implies a prior understanding. The professionals bring a prior understanding to professional situations based on their previous experiences and way of being a professional. For example, many therapists describe learning new techniques but they approach such learning situations with a sense of what the technique is and its potential relevance; otherwise they would not be able to make sense of their further investigations.

In the descriptions of APL this prior understanding was sufficient to engage interest, but insufficient for the requirements of the situation. All the participants spoke about uncertainty or not knowing what to do as part of learning, using phrases such as *we didn't have a clue* or *I felt unprepared*. Prior understanding ranged from a feeling of not knowing to wanting to know more, for example: *It was intriguing, I was curious*. This prior understanding is not always experienced as a conscious awareness on the part of the professional. At times it is only through change that prior understanding can be identified. For example, *I now know what to do* implies I previously did not know. Change from an insufficient prior understanding to a new or different understanding is interpreted by participants as learning.

### 5.3.2.3 Varying Types of Transitions

As stated, there is considerable variation in the type of changes in understanding that occur in different learning transitions, yet all are interpreted as APL. Three types of transitions where professional understanding changed are described in the structure of APL: type 1 describes learning involving "knowing what to do," type 2 describes learning through "thinking about what to do" and type 3 describes learning that involves "questioning what is done". Each is described below.

During the interviews a number of participants articulated how they had learnt but not realised it at the time. Learning through making and monitoring an on-the-spot judgement was a common description. It is described as *doing it and seeing if it works* or *trial and error*. A professional does something, sees the result and modifies what she is doing immediately. This can be described as a type one transition (knowing what to do) where thought and action are inseparable. The professional is aware of what she is doing and the situation makes sufficient sense to modify and move on, yet she does not describe a process of deliberation, just a straightforward *I tried it and saw if it worked*. This is also described as *making a professional judgment*. It is a part of what the participants describe as *everyday learning*, which they value highly:

> *I think people miscredit the experience of just being in there and doing it. They don't realize how much you actually get from that. You develop a bit of a feel for things, after years you can short cut a bit because you know where things are heading or what things are more likely to work.* (Gerri)

All the participants also described learning involving type 2 transitions (thinking about what to do) as a conscious awareness of *thinking* to *make sense of situations*. Thinking is described in terms of *going inside my head, racking my brains, untying a few knots* or being able to *visualise what had happened*. All the professionals spoke about thinking and doing in these experiences as separate though related. Many participants value time to think or talk about a situation when they are uncertain, to try to understand or *work out what is happening* or *what is really going on*, so they can proceed. Type 2 transitions occur when the professional is engaged in a situation that is challenging or when something unexpected happens, for example, if what they are doing *doesn't work out as planned* and they *try to work out why*. This type of transition often, but not always, involves the use of problem-solving or clinical reasoning strategies.

Everyone said they thought about situations in this way, but they rarely used the term "reflection". When they did use this term it was usually in the sense of thinking about what to do. The outcome of reflection, described as *productive reflection*, is valued. Nerida explained her perception of reflection: *I don't know that I [reflect] as productively as I could. I think I do sometimes tend to spend too much time thinking about stuff rather than actually trying it and putting it into practice.* When asked for more details, she replied: *You can theorize about whether or not something's going to work but you can't actually know until you try it.*

Whereas all participants described instances of type 1 and 2 transitions, only six of them described type 3. It is included within this constituent, however, as a variant of change in understanding. Type 3 transitions involved not merely thinking about practical situations, but questioning assumptions underlying these situations. In other words, although in all cases of learning, professional understanding changes in some way, in type 3 transitions the professional consciously reflects on certain aspects of professional understanding. For example, Sam described learning that involved questioning her assumptions about being a professional, describing this as *Standing back and thinking – am I imposing my values, my ethics, my morals onto the [client] and do I have the right to do that.*

These six participants spoke about understanding of being a professional in a substantially altered way because of learning, as exemplified by Gina, below, describing *a whole new way of looking at everything*. All situations involved a challenge to the professional's understanding of being professional. Olivia described how she saw a serious misunderstanding in professional communication as being due to *our different assumptions*, and how she learnt to *re-evaluate my way of communicating [as a professional]*. All the professionals who described type 3 transitions as part of their learning were experienced therapists, but not all experienced therapists described learning that involved such challenges. Others may of course have questioned in this way but not mentioned it in the interviews. This type of transition alters the framework through which the professionals interpret and derive meaning from their practice.

The fact that both level 2 and 3 transitions take time to think was seen as a problem for the many professionals who are in the busy work situations outlined earlier. Those who expressed a desire for more time to think sometimes found it difficult to make time as they always have *higher priorities*. Some saw thinking as such a high priority that they made time even if it was outside work hours. The varied impact of such constraints on learning is detailed in constituent 4, openness.

### 5.3.2.4  Vignette: A Whole New Way of Looking at Everything

The following example illustrates the way that constituent 1 is an essential part of the experience of APL for one professional. An experienced therapist,[1] Gina, described

---

[1] I use the generic term therapist rather than occupational therapist, physiotherapist or speech pathologist and alter some details of practice to maintain anonymity.

how she learnt through attendance at a course a decade ago. Gina had worked for some time with the children who were used as case studies in the course and she had experienced some frustration with previous approaches to therapy with these children. Unlike many courses she had attended, during this one she experienced a significant change in her professional understanding (constituent 1):

> *It was like magic. Seeing the course leader work with a child we knew, how the child responded so quickly to her non intervention. We saw a better way to go. A whole new way of looking at everything, about how to get activity from a child. A real changeover in my thinking. It was immediate, it happened that day, it was huge.* (Gina)

Learning in this situation involved a significant challenge to the way that Gina and her colleagues understood their way of working. Gina was able to critically examine her previous assumptions and make changes in her way of practicing (an example of type 3 transition):

> *The course leader was direct. She told us the methods we were using were hopeless. Some people got defensive, some liked it. I was excited as the child was happy and I saw she was learning. I decided to try and use it almost immediately at work. She made sense, she was credible because we'd seen her work. I was challenged. I was trusting my gut instinct and what she said, but it was really flying across traditional therapy thinking.* (Gina)

Gina has learnt more about this approach since then, exploring it through ongoing active engagement in practice (constituent 2): *How did I get a grasp on what she was saying? From practical experience. I'm a very practical learner.* She continues to learn through day-to-day situations with clients in an iterative manner: *I did read what she wrote but I had to go over and over it, and then something would click with my practical observations.* As Gina works, observing her clients' reactions and making small changes to what she does, she describes interpreting what happens on the spot (type 1 transition): *There are certain illuminating experiences. Not every day, but then a run of them. I tend to respond intuitively to what I see.* In this way her experiences are interlinked (constituent 3).

Her learning also involves type 2 transitions, thinking about what is happening with clients through discussion with other staff and going back over books on the topic: *We've had lots of discussion about how we would put it into practice. Every time I read the books something else comes out. Once I've seen a practical situation, it makes sense. I take home books and plan – a lot of time spent thinking, problem solving.*

Over a number of years, Gina's understanding of being a professional has changed considerably through these experiences of learning. As she explained, with reference to her current professional understanding: *Now I have a clearer understanding, I have a more rounded holistic approach in general.*

This example demonstrates several aspects of constituent 1, how Gina's professional understanding changes through APL. Her understanding involves more than cognition, encompassing all she embodies through being a professional: her *gut instinct*, her *way of looking at things*. Through the experience of APL her prior understanding of her practice was demonstrated to be inadequate, and changed. This example also demonstrates all three types of transitions. Although she experienced a major transition, there are continuing *illuminating experiences* often interconnected *as a run*. Elements of constituents 2 and 3 can be seen as her understanding continues to evolve through ongoing engagement in practice and interconnection over time with others.

Thus understanding in this analysis is complex and multilayered. To reiterate, professional understanding is a broad, holistic concept referring to understanding of a specific professional situation at the same time as it refers to how someone understands themselves as a professional. All the different forms of professional understanding described in this constituent presuppose a certain understanding of being a professional. Change in professional understanding is the core constituent of the experience of learning as a professional, permeating the other three. These other constituents describe how professional understanding changes through APL.

### 5.3.3 *Learning Through Engagement in Professional Practice*

Constituent 2 describes how changes in professional understanding occur through engagement in practice. In all the learning experiences described by participants, including the example of Gina above, a change in understanding occurred whilst the professional was actively engaged in some aspect of professional practice. Specifically, learning occurs when they care about this aspect, perceive it as uncertain and a novel feature is revealed. There is wide variation within this constituent because of the diversity of learning situations and types of engagement described in the data. There is also variation in how uncertainty in professional practice is perceived.

#### 5.3.3.1  Active Engagement in Professional Practice

All the participants strongly expressed, in different ways, that being actively engaged is essential to the experience of learning as a professional. This is the most readily apparent constituent of the structure of APL. Although all the descriptions of learning involved work situations, active engagement in professional practice did not necessarily mean being located at work. Professional practice encompasses a broad range of activities related to being a professional. While at work, they may be working with clients or talking with colleagues. In some cases they describe being at PD workshops or weekend social events with people from work. Sometimes they are at home at night thinking about work, a commonly reported occurrence.

All the descriptions of learning involved the professional being actively involved in professional practice in some way, by thinking, talking, watching, writing or taking action, usually in combination over a period of time. Taking action varies from working with a client to going to a library to get information.

Situations where learning takes place are commonly related to an issue at work involving a client. It may be working out why a specific client has problems, or more broadly related to service delivery, such as learning to work with other staff in implementing a programme. Many comment that it is only through active engagement in practice, when they *do something* for themselves or *see something work* for themselves, that they feel they learn.

For example, Lisa had read about a therapeutic strategy but didn't understand it until she used it following a workshop. She said: *I flicked through the book a couple of times but it just didn't quite gel with me. It didn't really make much sense, I suppose because I hadn't seen anyone use it. I like to see it for myself.* Wim also described a workshop where she and experienced peers worked with clients together, noting the doing was enough: *because I had a bit of a background, it wasn't as important to discuss the whys, it's really seeing it in practice that's what we needed.*

Amongst less-experienced professionals there is often a problem becoming engaged. They felt they have a lot of theory but had trouble *putting it into practice.* Describing her first year of work, Nerida stated: *the more I knew, the less I could act, because I felt like I knew I didn't know enough, or I wasn't taking everything into consideration.* A significant learning experience in Nerida's first year of work involved working with a therapy student, as it reminded her that she knew more now than she had as a student, but was now less willing to act. She reflected on her current assumptions about having to know it all before acting and describes her changed understanding following the student's visit as follows:

> *It doesn't matter if I don't know everything to start with, as you can just try and learn as you go. Next time I had a client as soon as we worked out a focus, I made the resources and started support instead of dilly dallying for ages. It's good if you can take everything into consideration, but if you can't, then you can still give things a go, and if it doesn't work then you modify it instead of thinking you have to have it perfect to start with.* (Nerida)

### 5.3.3.2  Caring About Practice

The second important aspect of all the situations where professionals learnt is that they cared about the situation. There are a variety of ways that the participants describe how certain aspects of professional practice in which they are engaged *concern them* or *matter to them.* They all expressed a deep concern about their clients' well-being and valued their role in making a difference through helping or assisting them. Dom stated: *I really feel there are not too many jobs where you feel as though you have the opportunity to have an effect on the way that somebody else lives their life.* Nerida related what many professionals expressed: *what's the point of learning unless you can make a difference to clients?*

But *caring about* the situation extends beyond caring about the clients. As a few professionals noted: *We have to make therapy interesting to engage clients and likewise we only learn if we're interested* (Gina). Professionals described themselves while learning as *excited, curious* or *stimulated.* They say they *enjoy learning.* They sometimes expressed a passion for *finding a better way* through learning and describe learning as *active exploration.* Carl maintained that APL is about finding *creative new ways to practise, a fresh approach to stop [the client] getting bored as well as us, to spice things up for ourselves and them.*

Caring about aspects of professional practice included difficult as well as positive emotions. Some professionals consider they learnt a lot from situations that were challenging or even disturbing, but only where they *cared about* the situation or valued the potential outcome. Gerri reported how she learnt through the challenge of presenting to her peers. She cared about the impression her peers formed about her work and consequently about her. She described how her professional understanding changed not because her practice altered, but because her confidence in what she was already doing was enhanced.

> We had to video ourselves working with [a client] as a case presentation to our professional peers. It was all very confronting, exposing myself, that was very terrifying, but it was very helpful. And I've tended to find that the things that are the most confronting or the most difficult tend to be the ones that you learn the most. (Gerri)

This notion of caring about aspects of practice reinforces the essential nature of this sub-constituent in that it is not possible to make a professional learn, because APL involves active engagement in a situation that the professional cares about. The participants were explicit about the fact that they don't learn when they are not interested or they saw situations as irrelevant to them. Gina as well as many others described how she only learns from PD courses that are directly relevant to her practice: *I always forget the others, about half are useless.* Carl demonstrated the need to care about professional practice in APL. He described how he thinks it time he left the profession, as he has disengaged from his professional practice, and worried that he no longer fulfils his professional responsibility in continuing to learn.

### 5.3.3.3  Uncertainty in Learning

Another important feature of the experience of APL is that something was uncertain or unsatisfactory about situations where professionals learnt. Expressions were used such as *his movement was unusual* or *his behaviour didn't fit any pattern I knew.* Sometimes there was a perception that something about the situation needed to change. In situations involving miscommunication, for example, comments were made such as *we got to a point where we had to act* or *I just hit a brick wall.* These perceptions triggered the transition where learning is experienced.

The uncertain and ambiguous nature of everyday professional practice with multiple factors to be considered was seen as a problematic feature for many, but not all, of the participants. There was significant variation in the degree of comfort with uncertainty amongst professionals. Less-experienced therapists say they felt unprepared for this: *Practice isn't clear cut like at Uni.* Regardless of the professional's feelings about uncertainty in practice, uncertainty is an important feature of learning.

Uncertainty or not knowing was identified by all participants as one of the features of situations where they learnt. A common experience of learning involves working out what to do in uncertain situations, often with the help of others. Nola, for example, described how she learns with her team members:

*I guess with most of the [clients] here, they have lots of different issues so it's trying to pick apart and decide where to start. So there's been some where we've just had no idea. As a team, we've had to do an observational assessment and through trial and error – just work it out.* (Nola)

Uncertainty about situations is related to *not knowing*. Admitting to not knowing enables professionals to learn from what doesn't work and from others' experiences. Sam noted that professionals *have to be willing to admit they've made mistakes and be open to learn from them*. Being able to express not knowing and accept that it is *impossible to know everything* is dependent not only on the professional's self-confidence but also on the workplace culture in which she works, as is discussed in constituent 4. Not knowing is an important precursor to learning.

Regardless of the type of learning experience described, uncertainty is a feature of situations where learning takes place. Something was *different* or *unusual*, *unclear* or *confusing* or *needed changing* in situations where professionals learnt. Being engaged in and caring about these situations leads to learning. Through learning, a situation, as part of the experience of being a professional engaged in practice, is understood in a novel or different way.

### 5.3.3.4 Revealing the Novel

When participants learnt, they described something new being revealed or added as part of learning. In many cases participants described new *information*, in the form of something they read, heard or saw that they could draw on to help make sense of an uncertain situation. Participants usually expressed preferred ways of seeking information such as *I like to watch others and then try something, I get a lot from reading, talking to others helps me make sense* and *I learn so much from client feedback*. Thus the experiences of professionals are interconnected (constituent 3) through interaction with others whilst being engaged in learning.

Sometimes information is actively sought and brought back to a complex situation, whilst at other times it is remembered from a past situation. Information is never seen as all being available at one time, but is *accumulated over time*. Often information is described as *clues* about a situation that give the professional *ideas about what to do*. A number of participants described learning as *finding new ways of doing something*, to keep themselves *stimulated* and their clients interested: *I really like to look for things that are new, so I get quite excited when I find something* (Kathy). New ideas or information on their own are not sufficient for learning however. It is only when these relate to a situation that the professional cares about, is engaged in and sees as uncertain or unsatisfactory, that they lead to learning.

On occasion, the new occurrence is a shift in the professionals' understanding because of what a client or co-worker says or does that *enlightens* them or *illuminates* the experience. Sometimes a prior understanding about the situation is confirmed so that what changes is the professional's confidence about her own perspective, such as when Gerri presented to her peers. Sam commented that what she learnt from a workshop served to reconfirm what she had been thinking: *That it wasn't just me thinking this is really important, that I was on what I perceived philo-sophically to be the right track.* Indeed one therapist described learning as *becoming aware of something that I was previously unaware of* (Nerida).

In whatever way a novel feature is revealed, it precipitates a change in the professional's prior understanding of that aspect of professional practice. This change varied widely amongst the participants depending on the learning situation they described. It can range from a specific change in understanding how to use a technique (*I know how to do that now*) to a broad change in understanding practice (*I'm more holistic, I see the big picture when I treat*). It can range from an altered way of understanding a client (*I saw him in a different way*) to a new personal insight into who they are as a professional (*I really had to look at my assumptions about how I communicate as a professional*). No matter how diverse these changes are, they have in common that when professionals learn, their understanding of being a professional alters so that they understand and approach their practice differently.

### 5.3.3.5  Vignette: Putting the Pieces Together

Mary's experiences illustrate how APL occurs through engagement in practice, linking the sub-constituents of constituent 2. Mary, an experienced therapist, described a recent situation where she learnt through *working out what was happening* with a specific client, who presented as a challenging problem *that didn't fit any particular pattern I knew.* Mary had been working with this client for some time and tried different strategies but nothing seemed to work. She felt uncertain, explaining: *I didn't really know what's going on.* Mary values her ability as a logical problem solver and feels that *being able to work out what's going on is the essence of what I do as a professional.* She describes her learning:

> *Usually when you find a situation that doesn't quite fit the picture you try to expand. Okay, so it's not just the normal quality of movement there are other factors going on here. And you consider the many different conditions and the many different combinations that can occur, and there can still be ones like this [client] where they still don't quite fit with all of those pictures that you've built up in your mind.* (Mary)

In relation to this situation, Mary also described a course she'd done 2 years ago and how she kept going back to the course notes as she worked with different clients. Over time, through a combination of course information and experience with clients, her understanding about the situation with this client changed. Suddenly she saw the situation in a novel way, so that she knew what to do and where to go next. In addition, her understanding about the content of the course also changed, influencing the way she now approaches and acts with clients in other situations. She describes this transition experience as follows:

> *You thought you had an idea of what the course leader was actually talking about at the time, so you go back through, and then it's like revising, it's almost like going back over it again and going yes, now I do really understand what she was talking about. I have seen that now in what I have actually found lately. And suddenly that penny drops. I really have taken that knowledge on board, and I know that bit now. So, you're continually finding that the pieces are all fitting in and are falling into place.* (Mary)

Mary described being actively engaged in learning in situations where she feels uncertain as *putting the pieces together*, through multiple interconnected experiences over time. Moreover, she cares about being able to *really work out* what is happening in such uncertain situations as she values this way of being a professional. Mary described how through such experiences her professional understanding changes. She describes herself as a professional who is becoming *less rigid in my thinking, more open to new ideas with a more holistic and long term focus with clients.*

This example clarifies what makes a situation in professional practice one where a professional learns through engagement. It is not just working actively with a client that leads to learning, it is not just the gaining of new information from books or courses that leads to learning and it is not just caring about work that leads to learning. These are drawn together, changing a professional's understanding, through engagement in practice. Mary's descriptions also highlight that her learning involved interconnected experiences over time, as described in constituent 3.

## 5.3.4 Learning Through Interconnection Over Time

Constituent 3 describes how APL involves the interconnection of multiple experiences in a complex web of understanding. As stated, this constituent accounts for and integrates the social and temporal dimensions of APL. No participants described learning that was isolated to a single transition situation. In other words, the experience of APL is broader than specific learning situations and more than the mere accumulation of them. Professionals learnt with others over time in a dynamic, circuitous and iterative process creating a web of interconnected understanding.

Participants were clear that APL is *ongoing* and *continuous*, with many using the term *lifelong*. Those with extensive experiences spoke of continuing learning after retirement: *Learning is my way of operating. It's just something that I've probably done continuously over the last 20 years. It's a normal part of my life* (Mary). Another aspect of the continuing nature of PL is that there is *always more to know*, you can *never know it all*. Inexperienced professionals found this aspect overwhelming, whereas some others felt stimulated by the never-ending nature of APL and said that continuing to learn stopped them from feeling *bored* or *stagnant* in their work.

### 5.3.4.1 Circuitous and Iterative Web

Although learning *evolves* or *unfolds* over time, professionals did not describe this process as structured or linear. When Olivia was an undergraduate 3 years ago, she saw knowledge as more *precise* and *determined*. She now concludes that *learning isn't a straight path*. Neither is it a path that is easily followed in a prescribed manner, as Carl describes below:

> I think what I tend to do for professional development, I tend not to follow up things to the letter, I tend not to go back over my notes and it'll be little islands of information that I happen to retain and I think, well I can apply that in some way, but I cannot just do things as prescribed. (Carl)

Because of the interconnected nature of learning, professionals spoke of becoming aware how numerous situations can be viewed as connected in a web of significance. Charlie described learning as a journey where one thing led to another in a circuitous way, with learning in one area applicable to other areas. For example, he heard about a theory years ago and saw its applicability as a way of making sense of certain features of his practice. He described how, as his understanding changed, he saw it could help him make sense of other areas as well:

> *I read more about it just for fun, like a search for meaning through work as well as thinking well this is actually worth it. It was not until I began to study it I saw I could apply this everywhere – and it's like having a new religion, you know a thing that you saw the whole world through, a way of understanding the world.* (Charlie)

Professionals described APL as iterative as well as circuitous, saying: *I often revisit situations, I keep going back until it makes sense.* It is also described as circular. Gerri explains, *I've got to sort of loop right the way round and there actually is an end point if I can remember where I started.* In the vignettes above that summarise constituents 1 and 2, Mary and Gina described going backwards and forwards, from observing and working with clients to reading and discussing with colleagues, until they understood a situation.

Although circuitous and unstructured in many ways, continuity and perseverance over time were noted as important in APL to see what worked and learn from that. This is only possible where professionals care enough about the situation. Wim described how she learnt by working through a difficult situation she wanted to resolve: *I think it's the fact that I didn't run away the first time it all went wrong. But said, let's try this a different way.* As she stated: *learning is about perseverance and sticking to your guns and continuity in seeing what happens in the end.* It is often in hindsight, when learning is viewed as an entire process, that various parts of it made sense. The vignette of Olivia at the end of this constituent highlights this feature.

In these examples, the professional's understanding changed through a circuitous learning process that shifts backwards and forwards, as well as round and round, creating complex web-like interconnections of significance as understanding changes. Through this process the professional's understanding of specific situations as well as overall understanding of being a professional can change over time.

### 5.3.4.2 Imagination Draws Together

In this study, the professionals described using their imagination to draw on past experiences, integrate them with the present situation and anticipate and plan for future possibilities. Imagination is described here as a dialectic entwining of the past, present and future in professional practice. For example, Carl talked about a workshop where he learnt about a new therapeutic strategy he was interested in. He described his (present) perception at the workshop, saying: *this is something I imagine could work* (in the future), referring to clients with whom he'd had little success with (in the past).

Those who did not use the word imagination expressed this notion in other ways involving imagery. The concept of *images* was widely used by participants in their descriptions of learning. Many described bringing up *visual memories* of past experiences. Visual imagery was used to describe changing awareness during present situations: *it was illuminating, I could see it work.* Imagination was also used to anticipate *creative ways to work with clients in the future.* Thus the professional's imagination provided a link between engagement in situations referred to in constituent 2 and openness to possibilities in constituent 4.

Imagination includes planning what to do next with a client or work situation and thinking of creative ways in which to do it, drawing on memory and visualisation. For example, Gerri described how she and another professional tried to work out creative ways to obtain a particular response from a child: *You're continually using your imagination and problem solving. You know what you want to happen, but how are you going to get it to happen?* Together, they worked from past experience with the client, using their imagination to think up creative possibilities to try. She described how, because they can anticipate possible future results, they know when something works in the present, and thereby learn new ways to approach similar problems in the future.

Anticipation of possibilities is reliant on past experiences, although not limited to those of the individual professional, as experiences are shared through interaction. For example, Nola, a relatively new graduate, described how, despite her theoretical knowledge, she found it difficult *to know what to actually do* as a therapist. In particular, *being creative and doing new things with [clients] was where I struggled.* She drew on other professionals' past experience, by observing them in present situations and asking them for creative ideas to try in the future. Thus imagination allows sharing of experiences with others over time, linking the social and temporal components of this constituent. In other words, through interaction with others' experiences over time, understanding can be shared.

### 5.3.4.3 Dynamic Interaction with Others

In this study, participants stressed the social nature of APL, involving interaction with a wide range of peers, clients and their families. These interactions were highly valued and dynamic, incorporating multiple changing interplays between people over time. Even in solitary activities, such as reading, the professionals described relating what they read to professional practice, which is by nature a social activity. The importance of dialogue between people was stressed, not only spoken but also written, virtual (in cyberspace) and imaginary (remembered or anticipated).

Learning involved both *learning with others* and *learning about others* through a range of shared experiences. The nature of these interactions and the PL involved varied with the degree of understanding between people. Thus PL can result from situations such as collaborative team problem solving where understanding is shared as well as from situations involving misunderstanding and confrontational, interpersonal conflict. In describing the widely varying nature of interaction in APL, I focus first on the people involved, second on the nature of interactions where people learn and finally on the degree to which understanding is shared.

All participants stressed that they learn from others. Although experienced professionals can be helpful mentors in APL, participants also learnt from less-experienced professionals as well as from clients and their families. Client feedback was sometimes immediate, in that professionals gained a response to intervention and integrated that into their next action intuitively. Professionals also gain long-term feedback from clients as part of their learning about *what works*. In fact it was often from people (professionals or clients) who had a different perspective that participants learnt the most: *They just know different things and you learn from them and you see their perspective and that is really helpful* (Wim).

Networks or teams acted as valuable learning resources for most of the professionals, offering the opportunity to talk, question and share ideas. Many commented that they learn most at PD days from talking to others. Where supportive networks were not available, a few proactive professionals described establishing their own online.

Professionals learnt by sharing experiences with their peers through watching or talking with them. Nola described: *I would remember by looking and then I'd kind of visualize the situation again.* Wim had learnt the importance of *making better use of the ideas of other people, whereas I had felt a kind of pressure that all the solutions had to come from me.* Many participants expressed an opinion that whilst learning from others' work was acceptable initially, they shouldn't continue doing so as it exposed the embarrassing fact that they *didn't know*.

Two key issues about the nature of the interactions described are the degree of trust and the ability to question. These issues are related. Learning between peers usually involved giving and receiving of feedback. A number of participants clearly articulated the importance of a *sense of trust* between colleagues before candid feedback could be shared. Olivia mentioned the value of *people being comfortable with one another, knowing that you haven't got to present an image.* She later explained such trust in more detail: *It's really about learning to feel comfortable expressing what you don't know.*

The texture of such learning interactions became clearer after I visited workplaces and network meetings. Questioning played an important role, as described in the observation of work in Chapter 1. I observed that it was in more relaxed environments where interactive questioning occurred. Most of the questioning between professionals involved questions such as *Why do you think that happened?* or *What will I do now?* There was little questioning of underlying assumptions described in peer learning. Many participants seemed uncomfortable with such challenges.

Some participants described a sense of *belonging* or *connection* when a cohesive team or network developed a sense of trust where open questioning was possible. Gerri reported that learning within her interdisciplinary team involved trust and the development of a shared perspective through valuing others' perspectives:

*The people on the team are not very defensive professionally. I know it takes a little while whenever you're starting your job to sort of wriggle your way in and work out what your*

*boundaries are with the other professionals, so that you are not treading on toes and offend-*
*ing each other, and yet still feeling that you're able to practise the way that is appropriate.*
(Gerri)

Learning from those of a different profession, as described above, is possible when professional boundaries are flexible. Like others, Gerri noted how her understanding of being a professional changed through such interactions: *My value systems and my concepts of what's possible and appropriate have evolved massively over these last few years, because of the influences of the range of people on the team.* She added how through such learning experiences, she has *grown as a person.*

A crucial aspect of such interactive PL was learning about other people's perspectives. This was usually described as: *understanding others, learning to work with others* or *interpersonal skills.* It was described as not only one of the most important aspects of learning to be a professional, but one of the most valuable ways to learn as a professional. Many participants commented that their professional education did not adequately prepare them for understanding the perspectives of others.

Sometimes different perspectives can be confronting but for the few professionals who felt comfortable being challenged, these are seen as valuable learning opportunities. Sam described an interaction with another professional who had very different opinions on issues. This other professional was *very forthright in her opinions,* but Sam *respects her credibility to challenge* and actually seeks out such challenges because they help her to question her assumptions about her practice. Charlie agreed with this approach, noting that *other peoples' perspectives show up things that have become rituals and habits of what we do.*

Learning can occur through misunderstandings, even when these are problematic. For example, much of the therapeutic intervention planned by therapists is implemented by others. Often there is a difference in the way that intervention is understood or valued by different people. Participants commented that *people wouldn't follow through* with therapy programmes. Many participants described situations where they were frustrated by miscommunication. Despite feelings of exasperation, some commented that problematic workplace situations such as these can lead to profound PL experiences. Such learning stems invariably through clarifying a *mismatch in expectations, when people work from different assumptions* (Olivia). The professionals described a number of ways that their understanding of themselves and their practice changed through learning to work with others. Often such learning lead to more effective practice: *so it actually works and makes a difference.*

#### 5.3.4.4  Vignette: How Will I Do It Differently Next Time?

The sub-constituents of learning through interconnection are drawn together in the description of Olivia's experience of APL. By describing how she learnt through interaction with others over time, Olivia explains the interconnection of social and temporal aspects of APL in this constituent. She described drawing on her imagination to link what she and others experience in finding creative solutions to problems. In particular, in working with others with different perspectives, she examined and reframed her own assumptions about how she understands herself as a professional (constituent 1).

Olivia described learning through a situation involving miscommunication. She explained: *We're working with clients but also their carers and there can be a big difference between what could be done versus what the carers can actually do.* Because of conflict over this issue, Olivia re-examined her understanding about how she communicated as a professional. She changed by focusing on *building an alliance with the carers through reflecting a lot and trying to understand and see what are the different lives for these people.* She tried to see the perspectives of others in situations: *The carers have many other factors that they're coping with.* Through doing so, Olivia described reframing her expectations and the focus of her therapy to suit the circumstances: *Moving away from textbook approaches or big goals that could actuate if everyone was on board, instead taking it back down to tiny simple meaningful things that the carers can achieve.*

Olivia also spoke about other learning situations where as a team she and colleagues have worked through conflict, developing shared trust. She explains that: *There were people wanting to leave work and yet we've managed to come together. It's been their learning experience as well as mine.* She has learnt through these shared experiences with the team to deal with difficult organisational issues involving unstated expectations and miscommunication. Olivia explained how learning as a professional extends beyond learning about therapeutic interventions with clients: *It relates to any professional. It's not just the discipline specific stuff – that other interpersonal area of learning has been really big for me.*

Olivia explained that through her active engagement in these uncertain aspects of practice that she cares about (constituent 2), learning with and about others, her professional understanding has changed over time. She noted the iterative way in which she learnt about communication from previous experiences, for example:

> I've learnt that there is perhaps more of a process to communication, and working through that whole debriefing process and making sure that you're wrapping it up is important. Because where I have made mistakes is where I have not completed that process properly. My learning is about how am I going to deal with it, how am I going to do it differently next time? (Olivia)

For Olivia, interaction with others is crucial to learning as a professional. Through developing *shared understanding* and *relationships* with others, she is able to question both her assumptions and those of others. She explains that:

> The bottom line is we're all people and sometimes you're facing really tough issues whether its colleagues, managers, or day to day carers. So learning is not just to do with your core profession, although it's related to it, but such a large part is also just learning as a person (Olivia)

Like a number of other professionals, however, Olivia was worried that through a focus on people instead of techniques she has moved away from *being a real therapist.* Through continuing to learn as a professional, Olivia described a change in her understanding of being a professional to one who is *more open* to different possibilities: *That's what learning is for me. Understanding that there's not just that one way but it's a big broad area with many branches.* The way in which the experience of APL can be described as open is described below.

## 5.3.5  Learning as Circumscribed Openness to Possibilities

Constituent 4, openness, describes how APL is a process that is open to possibilities due to the very nature of the other three constituents. Thus the professional's active engagement in the complexities of practice, through an interconnected web of experiences with others over time, opens a broad range of possibilities that shape changes in understanding.

This sense of openness in the learning experiences described by participants makes APL different from most undergraduate learning in which participants described processes, situations and outcomes as contained. Yet this openness is not infinite but is experienced by participants as circumscribed by boundaries, some more explicit and overt than others. These boundaries shape the experience of learning, sometimes constraining it, at other times offering opportunities. Tensions exist between the possibilities of openness and the circumscription of many contexts that are resolved by the professionals in different ways. Because this tension reflects a multifaceted interplay between each professional and her working context, its resolution is complex and varied.

### 5.3.5.1  Openness to Possibilities

Openness to possibilities in APL is a sub-constituent with two interrelated features. As alluded to in constituent 3, APL involves an open-ended process with no clear beginning or predetermined outcome. Because of this, professionals described the need to develop an open attitude to cope with the inherent uncertainty of learning. I describe first the open process, followed by the way professionals deal with this openness.

Being web-like and open ended, APL is not structured in any well-defined or step-by-step way. Neither was learning described as neat and self-contained, but often messy and always interconnected. It was often difficult to identify a starting point. Some professionals commented that they *didn't set out to learn* about a particular area and that the process of learning is sometimes *serendipitous* once the professional is engaged in it. An initial spark that engages the professional can often be identified in hindsight, as Dom described: *I get a really interesting child or I have an idea of an approach that might work and follow that lead. It's amazing how your interest in a particular area appears to attract clients with those sorts of issues.* Dom explained how as an interest develops, the professional notices or is more attuned to similar issues.

The open-ended nature of APL raises the question of how the professionals know they have learnt. Many professionals described being unaware of learning something, until they thought about the situation at a later time. In many cases this awareness arose through comparison with others' experiences. For example, Lisa described how working with a student helped her *realise how so much that you do becomes second nature and how much you learn without realizing it.* In most cases no real endpoint is identified in learning, with APL described as never-ending by many. *When I first graduated I thought I'll learn a bit more and then I'll be on top of things and I realize now you never are* (Kathy). That there is always more to know was described as *frustrating* by some and *stimulating* by others.

Although the experience of APL is generally unstructured, logical stepwise processes were followed by many professionals as part of their learning. Clinical reasoning guidelines were described as useful for providing some structure for problem solving, especially for new graduates. However, even when following these processes learning does not always proceed as planned. Many possibilities are encountered, often involving unintended outcomes and learning through *trial and error*.

That APL is uncertain and inherently open as an ongoing process means professionals require an openness or flexibility of attitude to continue to learn. As Kim noted, learning involves understanding possibilities rather than certainties: *understanding what might happen if you do such and such.* An open attitude allows for different possibilities of change in understanding. Mary encapsulated this open attitude well:

> *I think you do come out from university as a therapist, a little bit rigid in your thinking. But time and working with many different people, does allow you to realise that there are many different ways of solving the same problem. You have to be open to new ideas and other people's perspectives.* (Mary)

All the professionals concurred about the need to develop an open attitude, regardless of the extent of their experience. There was significant variation in how comfortable they felt about this openness. Through APL, many professionals learn there are different ways to approach situations and they develop an eclectic perspective that is adaptable to the client and circumstances. Yet for some professionals, coping with uncertainty in their practice and in learning was challenging. Being in uncertain situations where they don't know or cannot control the outcome was described by some as *unnerving* and led to them feeling *inadequate* as professionals. Thus there is a tension for some between accepting the need to be more flexible and open, yet feeling *uncomfortable* about it.

Some professionals, such as Sam, are comfortable with uncertainty. She described how, if a professional is open to being led by the client, they can learn a lot. It was about *being confident enough to say, no I'm not in charge of this and I will allow a kid to guide me.* She argued that *therapists sometimes try to make the kids fit the rule instead of really looking at the skills of the kids and learning from them.* Letting the client's needs direct therapy intervention may be easier said than done. Some therapists, despite agreeing with this approach, found it uncomfortable as it led them to question their role as a professional. Kim described this ambivalence:

*You come in as a therapist with education and ideals and ideas of therapy and maybe undeserved confidence. It's sometimes easier to be a competent therapist than being led by the family. It unnerves you a little bit. You're not sure where your place is.* (Kim)

This attitude of openness is also what allows professionals to access their imagination and creativity in learning situations as mentioned in constituent 3. It allows professionals to see links between ideas and approaches that may be useful in very different situations: *You see a new perspective and that lightens up previous difficult or complex situations and opens up new vistas. So you stick your head out a bit further* (Charlie).

### 5.3.5.2 Opportunities and Constraints of Professional Context

The possibilities of APL, or how far a professional could *stick their head out*, are not limitless but are contained within the boundaries of the professional's working context. These include features of the local work environment, the structure of the employing organisation and expectations of the wider professional community. Some of these features were discussed earlier in the professional life-world section. These features circumscribe the openness inherent in APL. Although all participants described ways in which their learning experiences were shaped by these boundaries, the same feature can act to enhance learning opportunities for one professional yet constrain learning for another. Participants described four features of the professional context that have a particular impact on learning: staffing, workload, organisational culture and professional expectations. Although they are interrelated, I deal with them one at a time.

As noted in constituent 3, the participants learnt from a range of different people. In most instances, the local staffing situation offers many opportunities for APL through such interactions, depending on the nature of these interactions. Some professionals described their local peer group as *open and sharing, not just caring about their own profession* (Wim). Other groups were different. Kathy described working in one situation where *nobody discussed clinical issues openly.* She described how difficult it was to learn in that situation as no one felt comfortable asking for help about uncertain situations.

Many professionals referred to the sometimes intangible atmosphere within a work group that affects interactions and hence learning. Referring to the situation in the previous vignette, Olivia said: *It's the unsaid, it's the feel, things that aren't spoken, the environment affects you.* She discussed how the working atmosphere, described by her as *the energy at work,* changed as team issues were resolved, allowing more open communication.

With respect to workload, all the professionals lived busy working lives yet not everyone saw this as a problem with respect to learning. The perception varies with the degree of autonomy professionals have in structuring their days. Where time was a constraint on learning, it was a lack of time to think that was the issue. For example, Mary described herself as feeling very stressed with an increasingly high workload, leaving *little time to think.* She felt that work was *very demanding of my mental capacity. You can have so much happening that you can completely drain yourself and your capacity to plan or think.*

Many others described only having time to think about work situations at home and a number found that home and work boundaries were increasingly blurred. Sally exemplified this issue, describing how she *always struggles with time* at work:

> *I'd like to be able to stay... and just have my time, sitting at my desk, going inside my head where I get all my ideas. Where I've always wanted to be, quiet by myself and I don't get that time. [At work] there's people around and I don't learn enough in the busy environment. I can't switch off and I need it. I take my notes home and I sit at the desk at home and I go inside my head and just think about it.* (Sally)

As described in constituent 2 (engagement), time to think is important for APL, but there was no evidence from the data that questioning assumptions requires additional time. In fact one participant who did challenge assumptions stated that the constraint of time factors depends on your perceptions:

> *There are barriers to everything if you want to consider them as barriers. I mean you find ways around them if you're motivated. You can hide behind those things and say there's not enough time, or I've got too much paper work to do. It's partly in the way that you prioritise things, whether you prioritise your own professional development highly enough, but it's something that's very important to me.* (Dom)

Only professionals from the two large government organisations noted that the organisational culture impacted on the possibilities for PL. A culture of regulation and control was highlighted by those participants but the impact on individual professional's learning varied. Organisational culture was not mentioned by the three professionals from smaller agencies, but small numbers make it impossible to draw conclusions from this.

One aspect of organisational regulation is the time required for administrative paperwork that participants complained leaves limited time available for other professional pursuits including learning. Part of this complaint was about the requirement to use organisational jargon relating to strategic outcomes in reports: *We've got to relate everything to them and coming from a therapy background and training, that's not the way you think. It's just a word game trying to justify what we're doing. But really, I live with it* (Sally). Like Sally, most professionals found pragmatic and sometimes imaginative strategies to cope with this constraint.

Some were more strident about the lack of autonomy that organisational control allowed. Paula argued that too much structure imposed from above resulted in a lack of space to be creative, limiting her learning: *You need to have all of those things that creativity needs which is space and confidence and support to take risks. We're not given the space to be creative.* It was only those professionals who spoke about questioning assumptions who mentioned the link between autonomy and creativity.

An organisational issue of greater concern for the participants was alignment between organisational values and the values of the professionals. Many professionals from the large organisations described discord between the focus of the organisation and their own focus on *making a difference* to the lives of their clients. With respect to learning, they described feeling unsupported by the organisational culture, but mostly learnt to deal with this by being *pragmatic, realistic* and *adaptable* with respect to what is and is not feasible: *I try not to let the environment get me down too much. I'm able to see where I can make a difference and where I can't* (Nerida).

Finally, as mentioned earlier there are widely shared and clearly articulated professional expectations with respect to continuing learning. All participants said they accepted these expectations. As Sally explained: *It's an obligation, we're expected to keep up-to-date and I think that's part of what you take on when you take on being a professional person.* Being a professional person implies being part of a professional community. Many professionals' descriptions of learning invoked comparison against the yardsticks of professional expectations, leading to feelings of inclusion or exclusion.

When professional networks worked well, a sense of shared understanding was expressed as being a valuable support for APL: *Your own profession understands where you're coming from. We share the same language* (Nerida). It helps professionals confirm that what they are doing fits in with what others are doing and is supported by them: *Knowing that everybody else is doing it gives me confidence* (Paula). But comparison with professional expectations led some therapists to conclude that they were *not a real therapist* because they did not fit the norm. For example, some professionals felt excluded by the very language that others shared. Gina has tried for years to use everyday language in her work with children and families and now finds the use of professional jargon intimidating, commenting that: *other therapists come out with all the proper words.*

All the professionals spoke about the value of what they called *everyday learning* through their engagement in practice with others, as described in the previous constituents. Many expressed a concern, however, that this learning was not valued or supported by their professional associations, universities and workplaces. Gerri described the development of intuition that she and many of the other professionals stated was an important part of everyday PL: *You develop that intuitive aspect, getting a feel for things. I've got that innate knowing what to do, but I know that they'd gnash their teeth at the university if I said this.*

Although she feels her intuitive knowing is important, Gerri doesn't feel her profession values it, focusing instead on analytical evaluation of evidence on which to base practice: *Generally as a profession I feel that innate knowing has been devalued which has probably made me feel or wonder how well I perform as professional.* Kim described an increasing focus on more formal PD courses: *I felt maybe earlier on that the learning was much more exciting. It was much more an adventure, whereas now it is much more an expectation and it's much harder to do and it's much more expensive.*

Many issues about the context for learning raised in this section are not widely or openly discussed within the professional community, unless professionals work in supportive environments with colleagues who they trust enough to be open with. These issues, such as admitting to not knowing or using intuition and imagination in making judgements, are a feature of APL as described by the participants but are often hidden in the public rhetoric about PD. Thus there is a dissonance between what the professionals valued in APL and what they perceived to be valued by sectors of the workplace and professional community.

### 5.3.5.3   Resolution of Tensions

While the professional context offers opportunities for APL, there are a number of tensions between the openness of APL and constraints of context outlined in the previous section. Professionals described the need to develop a sensitive grasp of the nuances of their working context, its possibilities and constraints, as part of learning to be a professional. The way each professional resolves these tensions shapes her learning. Thus, although all the APL experiences described share the same structure that has been detailed throughout this section, each professional's learning has a unique quality.

Tensions vary around two aspects of APL: the professional's attitude towards the inherent openness and uncertainty of APL, and the mix of opportunities and constraints afforded by the varying contexts in which the professionals worked. Although all participants described ways in which their learning was shaped by these tensions, they used different approaches and strategies to resolve them. Thus the experience of APL is a continual interplay between the professional (including her experience, attitudes and professional understanding) and the various situations in which she practices (with the uncertainty and challenges, opportunities and constraints, social settings and organisational structures therein). The constituent of openness surrounds and infuses the entire experience of learning as a professional. Thus resolution of tensions, as a sub-constituent, also refers to tensions in this overall experience, although they are particularly apparent in this fourth constituent.

Participants identified the need to find a realistic balance between adopting an open, flexible attitude to APL and dealing with the constraints of their professional context. How each participant finds this balance depends on her level of comfort with uncertainty and challenge, the level of autonomy and support her context affords and whether she accepts or questions the context. This balance shapes her way of learning. Gerri reached the following resolution about balancing her way of learning and professional expectations:

> *With therapy there's always that thing about excellence. We always aim for excellence. I think the profession expects it, and personally as I get older I've learned to live with the fact that it's okay if I'm not the best therapist in the world, so long as I do a thorough and fair job with people that I see.* (Gerri)

Some professionals spoke about putting on a professional persona when they are not comfortable with this balance: *If you're feeling there are barriers to being open, in a way you still put that professional cloak on. You don't want to seem dumb or an idiot or you're not doing it well enough* (Olivia).

One of the professionals who questions assumptions as part of her learning, and whose professional understanding changed significantly as a consequence, reinforces this notion of needing to feel comfortable in order to be open. Sam felt some of her colleagues hid behind professional personas and were unwilling to be open about changing their perspective. She explained: *they don't feel comfortable enough to be challenged so they put up all the barriers so they don't encourage people to question.*

Lisa described putting up such barriers in order to appear confident: *You have to come across in a way that fools people into thinking you really know what you're talking about.* She described her professional persona as *a big act a lot of the time. You might be feeling really doubtful about what you're suggesting but you've got nothing else so you just make that suggestion and do it confidently.*

#### 5.3.5.4 Vignette: The Theoretical Framework Doesn't Match Reality

The following example from Sam draws together the sub-constituents of openness. It illustrates one way of resolving tensions between the way she views the possibilities of openness in APL and the way she deals with the varying opportunities and constraints of her working context. It describes her way of learning.

Sam is an experienced and well-respected professional who described herself as: *proactive in my own learning.* For her, APL is about: *constantly challenging myself and seeking out information. I'm really willing to learn from others.* She viewed challenge as a productive way of learning and seeks to question the status quo when she feels there could be a better way of working.

She sometimes had difficulty finding others who were as comfortable as she is with challenge and whom she respects as being credible. Being proactive, she has developed an international online network to find such people. Sam describes learning as being reciprocal and open: *We challenge each other. It's not a closed book approach. It's okay well I can see your point but I don't do that because* .... Her online community enabled *a much more productive discussion on issues than just taking a textbook off the shelf.*

Sam is passionately engaged in professional practice where she learns in an interconnected way: *For me it's about putting knowledge or skills you might have into a really realistic practical thing that's going to work, that is meaningful. It may not be puristic but it's not a puristic world out there.* She described past experiences where she had tried to make therapy more effective by gaining insight into the lives of her clients. By doing so, she saw a different perspective on her clients' carers:

> *They were really trying to do an impossible job with no training and lack of respect for therapists who they sort of saw as glorified Queens (laugh) who would strut in and always be late and often create more havoc than actually anything constructive. (Sam)*

Sam learnt about dealing with contextual constraints, such as *how much funding influences practice. Many of the changes I sought didn't occur until there were changes in disability funding.* In addition, these experiences led her to question the difference between the backgrounds and life experiences of many young therapists and those of the clients. She was concerned that there was little insight into this difference or awareness of the contextual factors that impact on therapy:

> *There is no concept of the family dynamics and the other priorities that might be more important at that point in time, and maybe not a lot of insight into the stress levels and*

*anxiety of parenting and also the difference between graduates and the socio-economic status of many of the parents.* (Sam)

Although Sam is confident and experienced, and often supported others in their learning, she stated that she consciously avoided using the expert mode. She felt learning was *always mutual. I guess I've always been willing to learn from others and be able to say I don't know, and underlying that I basically respect other team members.*

Whilst Sam proactively used the opportunities for learning within her working context, like other participants who questioned assumptions, she is critical of what she sees as a lack of support for the reality of professional practice and APL:

*Professional associations are out of touch. A lot of what they are doing is irrelevant. I find university is fairly unrealistic, distant from what it's actually like at the coal face. At work issues out in the field are not understood. The theoretical framework of how it should be and what you should do doesn't match the reality and therapists feel unsupported as a result.* (Sam)

Sam felt that new graduates were not encouraged to question assumptions and were unprepared in many ways to cope with real practice. She claimed that *there should be more challenging of the philosophy underlying therapy.* Sam was planning to leave her current position, stating that frustration about being undervalued and unsupported was a factor in her decision:

*There is little awareness in the organisation of what I do and that's pretty unrewarding. There is also no acknowledgement through the system for going the extra yard or the personal compromises that you make to do that.*

Thus Sam describes a tension between being open to learn, constantly questioning her professional understanding though engagement and interconnection in practice, and what she sees as the lack of support for this openness from her professional context. She deals with this tension in the proactive way described. She chose to move to another organisation where she felt the environment was more supportive of open and inquiring learning.

Sam prided herself on the congruence between her beliefs and her actions as a professional, that is, she acts on her beliefs in an authentic manner: *I like to think my credibility is that I do what I say I do.* Her way of learning is congruent with her understanding of herself as a professional who is authentic. Moreover, her way of learning is an expression of who she is as a professional.

## 5.3.6 Summary of the Structure of APL

Throughout this section the four constituents of APL, understanding, engagement, interconnection and openness, have been described using concrete examples of participants' lived experiences. The vignettes illustrate the way in which the constituents are intertwined and the varied and complex manner in which they are expressed through each professional's experiences.

As one example of this interdependence, I reiterate the nature of uncertainty in APL. The open-ended nature of APL (constituent 4) means that uncertainty is a feature of the overall experience of continuing to learn as a professional. It is also a feature of specific situations where professionals learn, where uncertainty is related to not knowing (constituent 2). In constituent 3, uncertainty is related to the complexity of the interconnected web of experiences that is APL. As noted in constituent 3, feeling comfortable about uncertainty or saying you don't know requires an atmosphere of trust in a supportive workplace. Feeling comfortable with uncertainty enables assumptions to be questioned in learning (constituent 1). This example of uncertainty as a quality woven through the constituents highlights the holographic nature of a phenomenological structure. Each constituent describes a slightly different perspective on the whole experience of APL.

Finally, for the purposes of clarification, it is useful to reflect on what APL is not, calling upon the phenomenological construct of imaginative variation, referred to in Chapter 4. Thus, no participant described learning without a change in understanding about some aspect of being a professional, whether the change was simple or far-reaching. Neither did any participant describe learning when she was disengaged from practice nor did not care about the situation in which she was involved. Instead, participants described many cases where they did not learn because of disinterest or disengagement.

No participant described an experience of APL taking place in isolation as a single unconnected situation. Past experiences and future possibilities were always brought into play. No participant described learning without reference to interaction with other people, whether supportive or problematic. Similarly no APL experiences were described as a controlled process with predetermined outcomes, separate from the constraints of the working context. Finally, all APL experiences included the constituents and sub-constituents described in this section, interwoven into a whole. These four constituents are essential to the experience of APL for these participants.

## 5.4  Learning as Part of Being a Professional

So far in Chapter 5, the life-world of the health professionals in this study has been sketched, with an overview of situations where the professionals learnt. The phenomenological analysis of APL described a common structure that also illustrated the unique quality of each professional's learning. The data corpus is evaluated in this section from a broad perspective that considers what part APL plays in the experience of being a professional.

The interviews revealed more than the experience of APL. They also allowed glimpses into professional experience in general. In addition, personal issues or overall philosophy of life were disclosed, although not directly sought. The data revealed that APL is indeed part of the experience of being a professional, through rich descriptions of various aspects of professional being. Throughout the phenomenological analysis, APL experiences are foregrounded whilst the more general aspects of professional experience are maintained as background. In this section, I

**Table 5.2**  Sources of variation in participants' experiences of APL

---

*Variation in understanding oneself as a professional:*
- The degree of self-awareness and insight the professional has about herself as a professional and as a learner.
- The differing conceptions of learning held by the professional.
- The ability to question one's own and other's assumptions about learning, professional practice and the world.
- The degree of comfort the professional feels in dealing with uncertainty in learning and professional practice.
- The ability to be proactive in finding learning opportunities that suit the professional's way of learning.

*Variation in understanding in interaction with colleagues:*
- The perception of trust between colleagues at work.
- The ability to learn from others and be open to another's perspective.
- The way the professional compares herself to other professionals.
- The perceived degree of support from others at work.
- The degree of comfort the professional feels in being questioned by others.

*Variation in understanding the professional context of practice:*
- The perception of autonomy available in organisation of the professional's work and learning.
- The perception of time pressures and the value placed on time for thinking.
- The degree of adaptability to the nuances of the environment and how pragmatic the professional is about what can and can't be changed at work.
- The degree to which the professional questions her working milieu.
- The feeling of dissonance between what the professional values in APL and what is perceived to be valued by the workplace and profession.
- The degree of comfort the professional feels in speaking out about her experience and what she values about work.

---

draw on evidence from these background features in interviews, observations and documents to provide a more comprehensive understanding of the variation in APL in relation to the wider scope of professional experience.

Whilst undertaking the analysis, comments not directly relevant to the developing structure were placed into column 6 (see Chapter 4), for example, comparisons between professionals dealing with the same dilemmas in different ways. Examining these comments in the light of the data corpus enabled the construction of a table of possible sources of variation in experiences of learning. As summarised in Table 5.2, learning is shaped by variation in understanding of being a professional, ranging from understanding oneself as a learner to understanding colleagues and context of practice. These sources of variation are mentioned throughout the previous section, but are drawn together in this table. Variations in these aspects of professional being shape each professional's "way of learning".

These sources of variation relate to the tensions described in the experience of APL, for example, to varying degrees of comfort with uncertainty, openness to being challenged or questioning of contextual issues. The way in which tensions in APL are resolved shapes the professional's way of learning, as noted in the vignette about Sam's experience. Way of learning does not refer to what is commonly expressed as learning styles or ways of gaining information. Although each professional expressed preferences for ways of accessing information, these varied with circumstances with different strategies used in different contexts. Way of learning refers to the idiosyncratic quality that permeates each professional's experience of APL. Examining this idiosyncratic quality highlights how APL is shaped by different ways of being a professional.

Whilst it was not the aim of this research to identify qualitatively different ways of being a professional, stark differences were apparent from the data. Only cautious statements are made, but some account of how these differences shape learning experiences is necessary in understanding APL. Participants drew themselves and who they were as professionals into the interview. They expressed their understanding of themselves as professionals in many ways. Paula makes the point, for example, that there are aspects of being a professional that are core features of who she is, not just her way of acting out a professional persona: *I've always loved children and I take that into my job. I mean I can leave work behind, but that love of children is just me; that's not me just doing my job, that is actually just me.* Loving children is integral to Paula's way of being a health professional.

Moreover, the way a professional experiences APL is an expression of who she is as a professional. The four vignettes in the previous section illustrate the variation in ways of being a professional that shapes each participant's learning. In these vignettes, the focus was on the shared nature of the experience of APL. In the following descriptions, the focus is on the idiosyncratic quality of each of these professionals' learning as an expression of her way of being a professional.

Gina described how a learning experience significantly changed her way of being a professional. As the vignette (Section 5.3.2.4) describes, she was willing to rethink her assumptions about her practice when she saw *a whole new way of looking at my practice.* Gina's description highlights her flexibility as a professional, noting that as a professional you have to be *open to hear different opinions and not get locked into one mode.* She is open to making changes in her practice if she sees it makes sense and makes a difference for her clients. She trusts her intuition in learning about new areas although she wonders if she is no longer *a real therapist* because of her flexibility. She values that learning involves: *moving on, that there's something else new to try.* Gina's way of learning as a professional has a focus on flexibility by being open to new ideas as part of an interesting journey.

Mary described herself throughout the interview as a professional who is a competent problem solver. She likes to see the big picture, stepping back to evaluate situations. Her learning reflects this. As the vignette (Section 5.3.3.5) describes, she highlights the holistic viewing of a situation in her experience of learning. She actively seeks to collect all relevant information and reflect on problems. Mary places a high value on clinical reasoning processes to understand problems, so she knows what to do and can develop practical strategies to resolve them: *I value developing the skills to be able to assess – being able to really work out what's going on.* Mary describes this ability as *the essence of what I do as a professional.* Mary's way of learning as a professional highlights the value she places on logical problem solving.

Olivia described herself as a professional who seeks to find meaning from her work. She highlights her search for meaning in life, both personal and professional. As described in Section 5.3.4.4, relationships at work, communication and shared understanding are a vital part of her way of being a professional: *To me it comes back to the style of person you are and I'm a person that likes to keep harmony and balance.* For Olivia, *the key thing about my professional learning has been learning about myself and the way I communicate with others.* As she explains, *first and foremost I'm not really a therapist I'm a person.* She describes how she has developed her self-awareness through critical reflection on her own and others' assumptions. Olivia's way of learning as a professional highlights personal growth.

Sam described herself as a professional who has a strong sense of social justice, is proactive and happy to challenge the status quo if she believes something can be improved for her clients: *I certainly don't just accept situations.* When she has sought to make changes in the past she has sometimes *had to stand my ground.* She explains: *I've always been a fairly individual person who values creativity and lateral thinking.* As the vignette in Section 5.3.5.4 describes, Sam values acting on her beliefs in an authentic way and is happy to challenge the assumptions underlying those beliefs. Being authentic is the basis of her experience of APL. She finds being challenged an important part of her learning as *it makes me rethink about my practice.* She proactively seeks situations and other people who she can learn from in this way. Sam's way of learning as a professional invariably involves standing up for what she believes, yet inviting challenge about those beliefs.

As these examples demonstrate, the way participants describe learning reveals some of their assumptions about themselves, knowledge, professional practice and the world. The varying ways of being a professional expressed in these descriptions flavour the experiences of learning. In this study, each professional's experience of APL has an idiosyncratic quality that is an expression of who she is as a professional. Because APL involves change in professional understanding, learning also shapes each professional's way of being. Thus APL has an important ontological dimension: APL is as much about *who* a professional *is* as it is about *what* a professional *knows*.

# Part IV
# Integration

In Part IV, problematic issues are raised from the empirical findings of this research presented in the previous part. These issues are related to challenges for professionals learning in the contemporary working context. I do not claim to resolve such issues, but propose an argument that aims to shed some light on the original purpose for this research, namely, to understand why PD practices remain substantially unaltered and in what way support for APL can be improved.

A climate of regulation in professional practice is likely to continue, according to any realistic appraisal of the current system. Uncertainty and complexity will always be an implicit feature of learning and practice for professionals. Tensions in professional experience between a search for certainty and the inevitability of uncertainty, described in Chapter 2, will remain. What can realistically be done to support professionals to learn in this context and how can insights from research into the experience of professionals suggest possible future directions?

In this book, I argue for a paradigm shift in the conceptualisation of PD. It is not sufficient to move from a focus on development to learning, although this is important. The main argument of Part IV is that there is dissonance between the reality of the professionals' experiences of learning, described in Chapter 5, and the contemporary rhetoric of stakeholders' expectations about PD, discussed in Chapter 2. This dissonance is largely hidden from public discourse, being mainly voiced between professionals in supportive environments. The hidden nature of this dissonance is one possible reason for the lack of significant change in PD practices, in that few professionals publicly question PD practices or the current context for learning.

In articulating this argument, Chapter 6, "Rhetoric Versus Reality" questions the current professional context for learning, investigating this claim of dissonance and other problematic issues relating to PD. Chapter 7, "Authenticity in Professional Life", discusses the ontological implications of APL and how the dissonance between rhetoric and reality is often internalised as an individual issue rather than externalised as a shared professional concern. In Chapter 8, "Finding a Way Forward", suggestions about a culture of inquiry, from Chapter 6, and support for reflexive authenticity, from Chapter 7, are integrated within possible guidelines and models of support for APL.

This part integrates the description of the experience of APL with other empirical research and phenomenological philosophy, in arguing for reshaping of traditional PD practices through a fundamental shift in assumptions about how professionals learn and how they can be supported as they learn.

# Chapter 6
# Rhetoric Versus Reality

Besides enhancing understanding about the experience of APL, this research reveals concerns about the current focus of PD. As described in Section III, APL is shaped through continuing interplay between who the professional is and the opportunities for and constraints on learning within her professional context. To support learning, opportunities need to be enhanced and problematic issues addressed. This chapter questions the current professional context for learning, whilst being cognizant that the impact of context on learning varies with each professional.

The problematic nature of dissonance, between professionals' experiences of learning and rhetoric from the workplace and professional associations about developing professionals, is clarified in this chapter. Differences between the experience of APL and rhetoric about PD reflect different assumptions about the nature of learning. Within the epistemological focus of PD discourse, the ontological dimension of APL and the impact of context tend to be overlooked.

The implications of dissonance are described by examining empirical evidence. As dissonance is largely hidden, many related issues are not openly discussed amongst professionals. These issues, related to questioning of assumptions, dealing with uncertainty, imagining others' perspectives and voicing what is valued about learning, are raised. The chapter concludes with a discussion of how the hidden nature of dissonance with respect to learning is reflective of a wider context of professional dissonance, impacting especially on those working in the caring professions.

## 6.1 Dealing with Dissonance

Before dealing with dissonance between the described experiences of APL and official rhetoric about PD, the credibility of this research needs to be raised. As with most phenomenological research, participant numbers are low and specific details are context bound to this cohort. Justification for making broader statements about APL is drawn from the nature of phenomenological research and from continuing research with other professionals. As described in Chapters 3 and 4, phenomenology is focused on expressing essential commonalities across diverse experiences, rather than individual experiences. Ongoing research with other professional groups continues to validate the phenomenological structure described in Chapter 5. Other empirical research, described in Chapter 2, confirms many claims made about the nature of learning and concerns of context.

This research confirms that these professionals perceive problems in their working context with respect to learning. They feel work pressures have intensified, limiting time to think, although they deal with this issue in different ways. Most comment negatively on the working culture of regulation and control. The way that many participants described coping with this culture involves acceptance of the need to *play the game*. Overall, these professionals experienced conflict between the everyday uncertainty of dealing with human beings and the quest for certainty expected from their workplaces.

Given the research about PL from Chapter 2, some of the findings of this study are not surprising. For example, active engagement (in constituent 2) and interaction with others (in constituent 3) are widely recognised as important in undergraduate and workplace learning (e.g. Barnett & Coate, 2005; Beckett & Hager, 2002). This study empirically confirms these features specifically for the continuing learning of professionals. In addition, through the relationship of engagement with uncertainty (in constituent 2) and linking of social interaction with temporal aspects of learning (in constituent 3), the nature of engagement and interaction in APL is clarified. However, as other researchers note (e.g. Coffield, 2000; Groundwater-Smith & Mockler, 2009), even such widely acknowledged features of active engagement and interaction with others in PL are not highlighted in discussions about PD responsibilities and "implementation" of PD programmes.

Constituents 1 and 4 extend what is known about learning as a professional. Change in understanding through learning has been demonstrated by other researchers. In many studies, the epistemological perspective of understanding as "making sense" of knowledge is highlighted, although Elizabeth Beaty and colleagues identify change "as a person" (Beaty, Dall'Alba, & Marton, 1997). The ontological dimension of professional understanding is highlighted in constituent 1 in this study, reinforcing the research of Ron Barnett (2004) and Gloria Dall'Alba (2009) into the notion of professional being. The contextualised nature of learning in constituent 4 also resonates with established research on workplace learning, detailed in Chapter 2. However, the foregrounding of tensions between the open yet circumscribed nature of APL makes a further contribution to understanding learning within the current professional working context.

The phenomenological analysis illustrates the inherent richness of APL when examined as a holistic experience rather than as a collection of factors. As demonstrated, APL is experienced as a change in understanding through active engagement in practice in an interconnected and open way, rather than as a passive, isolated, contained development of a professional through receipt of knowledge. That is, the experience of continuing to learn is not simple, singular, straightforward or standardised but is complex, diverse, multifaceted and idiosyncratic.

These findings reveal that the experience of learning for participants is not congruent with the rhetoric of learning providers. Although these professionals take their responsibility to be accountable seriously, the learning experiences they value are ones where they grow as people and professionals rather than simply keep up to date. They value learning as exciting and stimulating although they know they must adhere to certain professional requirements.

These findings raise questions of dissonance. Within traditional PD discourse, learning is still primarily viewed in epistemological terms as change in professional practice knowledge, with the professional viewed as deficient and in need of developing. Whilst recognising the importance of knowing, in this study the ontological dimension of APL is highlighted, so that who the professional is shapes and directs what and how the professional knows, through interplay between the professional and her context. In much PD, the ontological dimension of learning and constraints of context are not usually accounted for. Although research into workplace learning has increasingly highlighted the interplay between identity and context, this nexus is still not enacted in most PD programmes.

As noted in Chapter 2, the main focus of PD is on the implementation and outcome of activities, rather than on the learning that does or does not occur. The rhetoric of PD highlights the professional's responsibilities, with PD linked to the registration of professionals, monitoring of accountability, supervision of standards and promotion of evidence-based practice. Thus PD focuses on performative features of learning that can be regulated and assumes knowledge is a commodity that can be controlled. Susan Rodrigues (2005, p. 2) comments wryly, with respect to the measurement of PD of teachers for performative purposes, that "simply measuring one's height has never told us what makes that person grow". Although professionals need to be accountable and quality of practice is important, traditional means of PD provision may not achieve these ends (Coffield, 2007). As this study reveals, the participants were enthusiastic learners who took their professional responsibilities seriously, but considered that their continuing learning was richer and more complex than this narrow PD interpretation.

In addition, continuing to learn as a professional in practice is different from other types of PL experiences. For example, APL, as open ended, differs from higher education programmes (undergraduate or postgraduate) with their focus on assessable, measurable outcomes leading towards a specific goal. Yet much PD implicitly shares the assumptions of most higher education programmes that learning can be predetermined. Moreover, APL differs from organisational training in workplaces for the purpose of policy implementation and change management initiatives. In many cases, such training is termed learning by the organisations. Although professionals' practice may alter in response to organisational imperatives, the experience may not be seen as learning by professionals, as my research demonstrates. Whilst professionals will usually be involved in organisational training and may undertake postgraduate or continuing education, these experiences are not synonymous with learning, although such experiences may contribute to APL. The fact that APL differs from undergraduate education, formal continuing education or workplace training is not widely acknowledged in the literature, although the participants in this research are aware of these differences.

The participants dealt with the dissonance *between* the reality of their learning experiences and professional expectations in varying ways, just as they resolved tensions *within* the experience of APL in varying ways. Some participants learnt in their own authentic way, discounting official rhetoric as irrelevant. Others felt uncomfortable about the dissonance, seeing it as an individual problem and indicative of their failure to live up to the rhetoric of the "ideal" health professional, although they too continued to learn in their own authentic way. Interestingly, regardless of how comfortable they were with dissonance, all participants in this study describe how they were "different" in some way, from their image of a *real* or *ideal* therapist. Those comfortable with this difference felt that voicing the reality of their professional experience made them mavericks. Others felt they were impostors, not quite *good enough* although they worked hard keeping up to date. The participants' feeling of difference varied between these two extremes.

Because dissonance is not widely discussed amongst peers, nor acknowledged by stakeholders in PD, most participants assumed their way of learning was different from the norm. There was little awareness that their experience is a shared reality. Research that highlights the value of informal learning or learning from experience is not available to most professionals in the workplace, other than those in education. Thus the key feature of the dissonance was its largely hidden quality. Although happy to voice concerns in situations where they do not feel vulnerable, most of the cohort studied were hesitant to speak publicly about their learning experiences. This is despite widespread covert concerns about the disparity between what happens in professional practice and official expectations of stakeholders. Consequently, the dissonance was internalised by most participants as an issue about who they were as professionals, rather than externalised as a public professional concern.

As detailed in the structure of APL, all participants described a similar reality about how they learn in practice, which differs from the rhetoric about what is expected and valued as PD by professional organisations, workplaces and universities. This empirical confirmation of dissonance provides one answer to the problem raised in the beginning of this book, about the lack of change in PD despite decades of relevant research, suggesting better ways to support learning. The nature of PD may not have changed significantly because few professionals publicly question its limitations. The internalisation of dissonance as a private issue may underlie this lack of public questioning by health professionals, and others in the caring professions, about performative features of the workplace that constrain learning. The next section addresses four problematic features of the findings that reveal more about how dissonance is dealt with by professionals.

## 6.2   Problematic Issues in APL

Many shared realities of APL experiences are unvoiced in public discourse. These include, but are not limited to: not knowing, uncertainty, using imagination and intuition, or feeling different from the ideal therapist. There was limited evidence from this study that participants critically questioned assumptions: about their own thinking, other people's perspectives, the nature of practice or the status quo in the workplace. Thus there was a lack of open discussion about the doubt and uncertainty inherent in APL and a hesitancy to openly question professional expectations and assumptions about what is important in learning. Current professional culture has a focus on supervision of standards rather than support for learning. Participants perceived that stakeholders, including supervisors, did not value everyday learning experiences.

In Part III, the experience of APL is described, based on the empirical data. This chapter highlights what is absent from these descriptions, yet stressed as valuable by other empirical research into learning. In phenomenological descriptions, absences as well as presences may contribute to understanding of a phenomenon (Sokolowski, 2000). Four paradoxical issues from the findings are addressed in this section. These centre on the following: the importance of thinking in APL, but the limited evidence that assumptions were questioned when thinking; the primacy of action in APL, but discomfort with uncertainty inherent in learning through active exploration; the value of communication and imagination in APL, with evidence that difficulty was experienced in imagining others' perspectives; and a shared awareness of dissonance between the experience of APL and expectations of PD, but a hesitancy to voice this publicly and raise possibilities for change. These issues are discussed under the headings of questioning assumptions, engaging with uncertainty, imagining conversations and voicing what is valued.

### 6.2.1 Questioning Assumptions

Although thinking is mentioned as part of learning by all the participants, they described little questioning of assumptions. There are many assumptions that can be questioned in a profitable manner in learning as a professional. Examples include assumptions about self and communication with others, the purposes of and ways of undertaking practice, the workplace and professional status quo and philosophical questions of meaning and knowing in professional life. There was little evidence that participants in this study engaged in critical reflection, despite years of research supporting the value of critical reflection in PL (see Chapter 2).

In constituent 1, three types of transition are described, where professional understanding changed through learning (see Table 5.1 in Chapter 5). All participants described the first two transitions, *knowing what to do* and *thinking about what to do*. It is not surprising that knowing and thinking form a part of APL. However, in contrast to much of the rhetoric about knowing and thinking in PD, the participants descriptions of *knowing what to do* and *thinking about what* to do reflected a sense of knowledge as embedded in and integral to, rather than separate from, their everyday professional experience. In this aspect, my research supports Gloria Dall'Alba and Robyn Barnacle's (2007) critique of higher education, where they argue that learning should involve integration of "ways of knowing, acting and being" within shared professional practices.

Although thinking was stressed, reflection was not mentioned widely by the participants; and when it was, reflection was usually spoken of in terms of *thinking what to do*. That is, reflection was generally to do with construction of practice in the form of practical problem solving, rather than its deconstruction through challenging assumptions (Day, 1993). My study confirms others which have identified that reflection in professional practice is usually for practical or analytical purposes and is unlikely to be critical (Brockbank, McGill, & Beech, 2002; Ng & Tan, 2009; van Manen, 1977). This is not to devalue such construction of practice through thinking. Clinical reasoning, as one way of structuring thinking in professional problem solving, is crucial to professional practice in health. The problem may be that the focus of reflection in professional undergraduate education is often an analytical prescribed process, with little questioning or challenging of assumptions or context (Boud & Walker, 1998). Moreover, many students learn to play the reflective assignment game, "producing" reflective content for assessment (Macfarlane & Gourlay, 2009).

What is conspicuously absent in most of the data in my study, therefore, is evidence of critical reflection involving questioning of assumptions. The third type of transition in learning, *questioning what is done*, was mentioned by only six participants. Most of these questioned some assumptions underlying their practice, but only Sam questioned assumptions about her taken-for-granted understanding of being a professional. A need has been established for health professionals, and other professionals, to develop a greater awareness and questioning of the philosophical underpinnings of their practices, "reflecting not only *in* or *on* but also *about* practice" (Abrandt Dahlgren, Richardson, & Kalman, 2004, p. 15).

If reflection, or thinking, is to illuminate present understandings and question assumptions, then it must involve some distance from the task, argue Jörgen Sandberg and Gloria Dall'Alba (2006). They point to the need to step back from practice or engage in dialogue with others to gain sufficient distance. Donald Schön (1983, p. 283) also mentions the "circle of self-limiting reflection" and how the input of others is necessary to highlight assumptions. Thus research findings concur that reflective practices crucial for learning involve interactive dialogic questioning (Clouder, 2000; Dall'Alba & Sandberg, 2006; Gardner, 2009). Yet my findings concur with others that dialogic reflective practices rarely occur in work environments, nor does workplace culture typically promote critical reflection.

The importance of questioning for learning is that questioning opens possibilities. Hans-Georg Gadamer (1965/1979, p. 338) observes that, "questions always bring out the undetermined possibilities". In my study, Nerida spoke of how she learnt about dealing with the different assumptions of other people at work when she took time to talk to them about a range of issues, asking questions and listening carefully to the answers. She said:

> *Sometimes you find that you have to sit and talk to somebody about a whole lot of things and you'll get the information you want, not when you ask the direct question, but it'll come out later. So I'm better at listening, and maybe even a little bit better at finally trying to find the real meaning behind things, instead of just taking things at face value.*

That is, questioning can be both active and receptive. It involves actively asking, whilst listening with openness to the possibilities of different meanings. It involves both dialogue and thought. Martin Heidegger (1959/1966) distinguishes between thought as deliberation on facts, such as problem solving, and reflective thinking. He describes the latter as not only thinking to make sense of something but also at the same time gaining a calmness that allows access to "a distant view that opens" (Heidegger, 1954/1977, p. 181). Such a calm awareness has been described as mindfulness (Hyland, 2009). This calm thinking is reminiscent of Sally's plea for *quiet time to go inside my head* that she couldn't find whilst work was busy and noisy. In fact Heidegger (1959/1966, p. 44) comments, as do current researchers, about how space and time for reflective thinking are limited by the busyness of everyday professional life:

> Let us not fool ourselves. All of us, including those who think professionally … are often enough thought-poor; we are all far too easily thought-less. Thoughtlessness is an uncanny visitor who comes and goes everywhere in today's world. For nowadays we take in everything in the quickest and cheapest way, only to forget it just as quickly.

For Heidegger, reflective or questioning thinking is a path: a direction rather than a destination. He states that "questioning builds a way" (1954/1993, p. 311). Barnacle (2001, p. 11) describes Heidegger's assertion that such thought is never complete, by referring to the "in-between nature" of thought. Such thinking in learning is reflected by the notion of APL as open ended.

I suggest the term "mindful inquiry" to describe a form of thinking involving questioning that some participants in my research used. Drawing on Heidegger, mindful inquiry can be both active and receptive. It is active in the sense of raising and questioning taken-for-granted assumptions. It is receptive in the sense of openness to possibilities, as a journey without a specific ending. Both require some distance from everyday practice yet are grounded in that practice. Neither appears to be encouraged in current working contexts. Both may involve not only periods of stillness but also interaction and dialogue with other people. It would be a mistake to see them as opposites. They are not separate forms of thinking but variations of the one.

The lack of questioning of assumptions or mindful inquiry amongst many participants in this study may have multiple antecedents. Time constraints in a busy practice could be one. However, even when some professionals did not feel pressured by time, reflection was not always seen as important. As Lisa described: *I suppose I don't see it as a big priority to timetable time for reflection.* The workplaces described in the study did not adequately support a culture of inquiry through open dialogue. Also, questioning assumptions means opening one's self to doubt and uncertainty, a potentially vulnerable situation in contemporary workplaces. One aspect of APL that needs questioning is the assumption that certainty can ever be attained in professional practice within the human sciences.

## 6.2.2 Engaging with Uncertainty

Uncertainty is revealed as an essential feature of APL in the findings. Participants highlight the primacy of action in learning, whilst expressing discomfort about the uncertainty that arose when actively experimenting with possible actions in practice. There are three important aspects of uncertainty in APL discussed in this section. Uncertainty is acknowledged as a feature of APL linked to not knowing, which allows openness to possibilities such as mindful inquiry. The realisation that practice will always be uncertain because of the ambiguities of human nature is also highlighted here. Finally, the positive value of uncertainty in learning as a source of creativity, innovation and stimulation is raised.

The notion of uncertainty has been frequently referred to within the context of the changing world of work and education. It is a problematic notion, not only with respect to the difficulties purported to be linked to it but also because it is conceptualised in different ways by researchers. There are three main foci of rhetoric about uncertainty in research literature: describing its "impact" on culture and organisations (e.g. Handy, 1996), finding ways to "manage" it (e.g. Kramer, 2004) and trying to "understand" it (e.g. Molloy, 2004). Increasing uncertainty has been described as a determining feature of our current "mode two" society and a driver of the need for collaborative, applied interdisciplinary research (Nowotny, Scott, & Gibbons, 2001). Yet life has never been certain; it is merely the expectation of modernity that features of life can be made certain.

Since Werner Heisenberg's "uncertainty principle" was proposed in the 1920s, uncertainty has been accepted as a feature of scientific investigation requiring management and control (Grbich, 1999, p. 20). From this scientific perspective, uncertainty is linked to notions of control, evidence, reliability and risk. These are notions that are also implicit in the moves towards certainty exemplified by increasing professional regulation with a focus on evidence-based practice. Yet a scientific perspective is only one way of understanding the world. In the 1950s, Heidegger (1954/1993) critiqued a technological or scientific perspective that assumes the world can be controlled by man and made increasingly certain. He also commented on the fear of error within the scientific perspective that feeds a constant "element of distrust" (Heidegger, 1950, p. 87). The search for certainty in the contemporary workplace, and focus on supervision and regulation of professionals to control risk and error, also implies an element of distrust of professionals. Underlying increasing regulation of PD are issues of power and trust (Coffield, 2007; Easterby-Smith, Crossan, & Nicolini, 2000).

In contrast with the risk control of a scientific perspective, a humanities perspective views uncertainty as necessary for creativity: a powerful source of generative and productive energy (Garner, 2008). It has also been proposed as vital to a productive life: as a motivator for questioning and change and as an antidote to boredom and inertia (Molloy, 2004). Some of the research participants mentioned this aspect of uncertainty in learning. Recognition has been made of the artistry and creativity of professional practice, by researchers since Schön, with acknowledgement that professional decisions always involve degrees of uncertainty and risk (Andresen & Fredericks, 2001; Fish, 1998; Schmid, 2004; Titchen & Higgs, 2001). Such recognition of the uncertainty of practice highlights the need to draw on a broader concept of evidence than scientifically controlled trials in making professional judgements (Hasnain-Wynia, 2006; Stwine & Abrandt Dahlgren, 2004). Current moves towards this broader concept of evidence are reflected in a change in terminology from evidence-based to evidence-informed practice in some areas (Cordingley, 2008; Pollard, 2002). In what could be seen as an early critique of evidence-based practice, Heidegger (1966/1993, p. 449) describes the "incessant frenzy of rationalization" in scientific perspectives as sometimes "irrational", stating that "it is uneducated not to have an eye for when it is necessary to look for proof and when this is not necessary".

In research about learning, the value of uncertainty is highlighted as essential for transformative learning (Brookfield, 1987; Mezirow, 1990). Learning, for example, can transform a professional's way of being (Dall'Alba, 2005). In higher education, Barnett (2000) describes preparing students to cope with uncertainty, outlining two forms of uncertainty related to the current "supercomplexity" of the world. One form is related to information overload from the vast volume of "pertinent evidence" available; the other form is more personal, related to the constant challenges people face to their assumptions, in the face of an "unknown" future (2004, p. 250). He talks of the need for "mode three" knowledge to deal with uncertainty, described as "knowing-in-and-with-uncertainty" (2004, p. 251). Whilst concurring with the need to alter the higher education curriculum to embrace uncertainty, the need to define new modes of knowledge seems redundant. Perhaps the capability for being-in-uncertainty is a more useful formulation.

Fundamental to the different ways of thinking about uncertainty described above is that uncertainty implies not being certain, thereby assuming a certainty/uncertainty dichotomy. Mats Alvesson (2004) talks of ambiguity rather than uncertainty, arguing that ambiguity is the feature of work environments that should be acknowledged. Ambiguity is distinct from uncertainty as "ambiguity . . . cannot be clarified just by gathering more facts" (p. 48). Thus Alvesson highlights the ambiguity of reality referred to by many phenomenologists. As Maurice Merleau-Ponty (1964, p. 41) says: "One is always ambiguous when one tries to understand others. What is ambiguous is the human condition". Ambiguity is perhaps a more apt term than uncertainty when describing human experience, as certainty is never possible.

But the participants of this study did not speak of ambiguity; indeed they did not use the word uncertainty. They frequently referred to "certainty" and their lack of it in situations. Most expressed what I have described as uncertainty in terms of *not knowing what to do* in situations that are *not cut and dried*. I use the term uncertainty to capture their search for certainty, achieved by gathering more facts. Other researchers discuss the uncertainty of practice, where professionals are called upon to consider multiple and sometimes contradictory factors, including policy directives, research evidence and client perspectives (Mullavey-O'Byrne & West, 2001). Kathryn Denhardt (1991) highlighted workplace issues that are resonant with the dilemmas described in Chapter 2 between professionalism and the demands of managerialism and consumerism (see Freidson, 2001). Denhardt describes situations where professionals were required to be responsive to both superiors and clients, despite conflicting demands; or to increase efficiency and minimise costs yet maintain a high-quality service. Many dilemmas at work may not be clear-cut, often requiring a choice between "right and right" (Badaracco, 1997).

In other words, the quest for certainty of practice in any human services profession is, and has always been, elusive, involving dealing with human beings whose very nature is ambiguous. Within the health professions, there is a call from some researchers for an acceptance of this: for practitioners to learn to "sit with uncertainty" (Charles, 2001, p. 68). Besides sitting with uncertainty, though, there is a need to examine how professionals act with uncertainty, as they do when they learn. There is a possible paradox in APL between the decisiveness implied in taking action and the uncertainty arising from that action. Such uncertainty could prompt mindful inquiry.

The importance of uncertainty in APL is linked to not knowing. As an undergraduate, not knowing is expected and higher education involves demonstrating through assessment that the student has learnt. Following graduation, requiring evidence of learning can be counter-productive, but this expectation is continually implied within a performativity agenda that requires demonstrations of competence and production of measurable outcomes. Kim described the anxiety that not knowing engenders when demonstration of knowledge was expected as a practicing professional: *I remember how anxious I was because I didn't know what the outcomes of processes would be.* All professionals feel uncertainty, but the degree of comfort with uncertainty varies.

As participants highlighted, being able to say you don't know or are uncertain is important in APL. Yet there are many situations where professionals feel uncomfortable about not knowing and hide behind *a professional cloak.* I have drawn from Stephen Brookfield's (1995, p. 229) term "impostership", where he describes a similar feeling of being the only professional who doesn't know enough. The high value that is currently placed on evidence from sources other than experience may lead professionals to doubt knowledge from their own experiences. This can be exacerbated by feelings of guilt about not keeping up to date, because of the strong moral commitment that most professionals have to practice. Schön (1983, p. 69) claims that, because of a mismatch between the realities of practice and the technical rational focus of professional education, "uncertainty is a threat; its admission is a sign of weakness". A strong imperative exists to foreground uncertainty in both practice and learning. Brookfield (p. 247) describes the importance of speaking out about the experience of impostership and by doing so, breaking the "conspiracy of silence".

How is a transition made from not knowing to knowing more through learning? Crucial to APL is the notion of *caring about practice* as the catalyst allowing *active engagement with uncertainty* to reveal something *novel* (see constituent 2 in Table 5.1). In examining the role of intuition in learning, Inna Semetsky (2004) refers to John Dewey's "leap" (p. 443) and Nell Noddings "bridge" (p. 435) to describe this learning transition. Semetsky describes the need for an affective state of "desire" as well as open receptivity in order to make the leap. That is, you have to care in order to engage with uncertainty.

Acknowledging publicly that uncertainty is a positive feature of APL and ambiguity is inherent in the human condition is crucial for professionals learning to adapt in changing circumstances. Being able to ask questions is linked to "the knowledge of not knowing" (Gadamer, 1965/1979, p. 326). As other researchers also claim, acceptance of uncertainty, tolerance for ambiguity, and a capacity to question and reframe understandings are important when learning in today's context of change (Abrandt Dahlgren et al., 2004; Helsing, 2007; A. Jones, 2007).

Finally, uncertainty in learning implies dynamic interchange between the known and the unknown, like a dialogue or conversation. Etienne Wenger (1998, p. 41) describes learning as a social practice, "straddling the known and the unknown in a subtle dance of self". In a compelling fictional account of an engineer describing uncertainty of practice in the field, Kate Grenville (1999) writes: "The solution to one problem created another [so that] it was an exchange, backwards and forwards. Some men thought of it as a war, but to him it was like a conversation" (p. 63). This description aptly illustrates the difference between conceiving uncertainty and ambiguity in practice as a source of interest and creative inspiration, rather than something to be controlled and avoided. There are many forms of creative conversations in APL, most clearly expressed within the constituent of interconnection.

### 6.2.3 *Imagining Conversations*

A substantial amount of research has confirmed the social nature of learning, as indicated in Chapter 2. In relation to PL, researchers have investigated the role of mentors and networks (Devos, 2004; Gibson & Heartfield, 2005; McCormack, Gore, & Thomas, 2006) and the value of working with professionals from other disciplines (Barr, 2003; E. Hall, 2005; Reeves, Freeth, McCrorie, & Perry, 2002). Not unexpectedly, my findings confirm the crucial importance in APL of talking, listening, watching and working with others. The findings demonstrate that where mentors, supervisors or peers are supportive in APL, it is the quality of the relationship, rather than a predetermined process, that is the crux of that support. Participants also reported that learning was a two-way dialogue, in that more-experienced colleagues can learn from less-experienced ones and vice versa. The role of dialogue in learning has been raised already with respect to questioning of assumptions.

Learning through interaction with people in constituent 3 involves not only learning *from them* but also learning how to *work with them*, especially those from other professions. Yet most participants reported feeling unprepared for common miscommunication issues in the workplace. Good communication was stressed as crucial by participants, but there were different views about what communication entailed. Although the development of communication skills is a common aim in professional education, these are often portrayed as "soft skills" to be tacked on after important knowledge is taught (Beckett & Hager, 2002, p. 28).

Participants noted that the development of communication skills in their undergraduate programmes focused on rapport with clients and negotiation of roles in teamwork. Yet some participants highlighted how learning to work with others involves more than the development of a set of communication skills. It involves openness to alternative points of view and the ability to see other people's perspectives. Participants who were open and questioning found they learnt a lot about themselves and their practice through such communication. Those who did not question referred to communication in practice in terms of *persuading others* in order to *sell their therapy program*. They seemed to have problems seeing the perspective of others, if it differed from their own.

Imagination is vital in seeing differing perspectives in learning. That is, imagination has a social role in APL. With respect to the role of empathetic communication in transformative learning, Mezirow (2000, p. 20) observes that:

> Imagination is central to understanding the unknown; it is the way we examine alternative interpretations of our experience by "trying on" another's point of view. The more reflective and open we are to the perspectives of others, the richer our imagination of alternative contexts for understanding will be.

The role of imagination in learning needs clarification. In interconnection, constituent 3 in the APL structure, imagination is mainly described in a temporal sense (see Table 5.2). That is, imagination refers to the way in which the professional draws together significant experiences from her past and the past of others, as future possibilities for the current situation. Imagination describes the ability to traverse time and space in the present. Cheryl Mattingly (1998, p. 155) uses a similar image in her analysis of professional practice of occupational therapists, referring to the ability of practitioners to "see backward" from a future imagined endpoint.

Imagination also refers to the creative way experiences are interconnected in APL. Creativity in professional practice (often referred to as artistry) is about finding innovative solutions to problems. A creative imagination is linked to the ability to remain open to possibilities and tolerate uncertainty, to see patterns and interconnections (Howkins, 2009). It is proposed as being the basis of innovative intellectual and scientific breakthroughs (Florida, 2002; Marginson, 2008). What most accounts of imagination stress is a creative rupture in habits that allows new ways of seeing the world (Steeves, 2004, p. 5).

Imagination has been identified as crucial for the ability to make judgements based on experience since Immanuel Kant's writings centuries ago (Beckett & Hager, 2003; Heath, 2003; Lohmar, 2005). An important aspect of making professional judgements is the ability to see something as something else through creative imagination (Schön, 1983, p. 185). Barnett (2004) also refers to the need for imagination to cope with uncertainties of the future. Despite such references, imagination receives little attention in studies on learning (Morley, 2005). James Morley describes imagination as a "confounding variable" in judgement that science sought to control through the experimental method. Moreover he highlights the importance of imagination in research into human experience, stating: "The power of imagination to transcend the giveness of existence in favour of its *possibilities* may actually define the human condition itself" (p. 117).

Those participants who could see another's perspective in APL used imagination. In the constituent of interconnection, then, imagination has a social as well as temporal function. Johnson (1987, p. 172) draws on phenomenology and cognitive science to argue the centrality of imagination in understanding and communication, describing imagination as embodied structures of understanding by which we make sense of the world (p. xiii). He proposes that structures of imagination are shared when we understand each other, and thus are integral to our ability to communicate.

The role of imagination in seeing the perspectives of others is not highlighted in the literature about learning from other people. Referring to Heidegger's work, Brian Elliott (2005, p. 153) claims that imagination is the very "materialization of social understanding", noting, however, that "just as language at once facilitates and restricts individual acts of discourse, imagination resists as much as conducts what the individual means to say". In other words, imagination offers possibilities for both shared understanding and misunderstanding, as the findings of my research illustrate.

Imaginative conversations in learning may enable understanding to be shared. In the workplace, genuine shared conversation can create a social space of understanding. Referring to Gadamer's conception of the "betweenness" of conversation, Bela Banathy and Patrick Jenlink (2005, p. ix) state that "genuine dialogue is a turning together in conversation, to create a social space – a betweenness – in which personal opinions and ideologies are suspended and wherein persons conjoin in community to search for new meaning and understanding". Genuine dialogue is valued by professionals in APL, but, as many researchers note, such dialogue may not be valued or supported as seen in the workplace (Brockbank et al., 2002; Dall'Alba & Sandberg, 1996).

### 6.2.4  Voicing What Is Valued

What is valued in APL? There was general agreement amongst participants of this study that they valued APL as a complex web of open-ended experiences that engaged their whole being. They valued that these experiences were interconnected with the experiences of others over time, especially in a climate of trust and support. As constituent 4 of APL (circumscribed openness) demonstrates, workplaces offer many opportunities for learning. As a site of conversation and interchange with others, of engagement with the realities and uncertainties of practice, workplaces are integral to the experience of APL. But such interaction and engagement are not always valued or supported by stakeholders, other than the professionals. Problems with the contemporary workplace as a site for APL, raised by others in Chapter 2, were confirmed by my research. Staff shortages, timetabling problems and time spent on what was perceived as administrative trivia were described as counter-productive for learning. The findings also suggested that participants felt their education did not adequately equip them to cope with workplace challenges.

Workplace challenges are discussed in this section by examining the professionals' perception of performative features of their working context, highlighting supervision of their learning and practice. As mentioned earlier in this chapter, there was general agreement from participants that work pressures have intensified. Perceptions of stress have certainly increased, as revealed most cogently in the second round of interviews. Research confirms this perception (Burchell, Ladipo, & Wilkinson, 2002; Dollard, Winefield, & Winefield, 2003; Mimura & Griffiths, 2003;

Williams, Pocock, & Skinner, 2008; Winefield, 2008). In time-pressured environments, the "drive to produce outputs [may] hurry the thinking time", suggests Elizabeth Smythe (2003, p. 55) in her critique of the contemporary university context. Certainly, few participants reported having any quiet time for thinking, except at home. In discussing learning from others at work, David Boud and Heather Middleton (2003, p. 201) suggested that constant change at work may hamper the development of stability required for trusting relationships in a group to develop. My findings concur with these authors. Participants were rushed, but coped by drawing on a fluid network of relationships in finding support for learning, not necessarily single mentors or stable long-term communities.

Despite concerns, however, there was general acceptance from the participants that such pressures are part of being a professional at work. All descriptions of APL experiences involved dealing with varying demands of the complex circumstances that constitute professional practice. In fact learning about the nuances of workplace politics, and how to negotiate systems to gain the best outcomes for clients, was stressed by all as crucial to learning to work as a professional. Boud and Middleton (2003, p. 199) also discuss how professionals at work learn to negotiate the political and bureaucratic processes as they learn to work with others. Like many other areas of learning, participants felt such workplace challenges should be raised as part of their professional preparation. Beverley Axford's (2005) research identifies similar problems for student teachers, engineers and nurses in their transition to work in Australia, highlighting the need for more realistic preparation.

Learning about the performative features of work was described by participants as learning to "play the game". Despite some concerns about playing the game, there was little critical questioning of the rules of the game, or the possibility of changing the rules, except by participants such as Sam. For example, supervision was discussed by participants as a synonym for support without questioning the taken-for-granted assumption of the need for supervision. As mentioned previously, the words supervision and support were used interchangeably in everyday discourse and in official documents gathered from the professional associations and workplaces. Yet the two concepts are very different. This lack of clarity between supervision and support is fraught with difficulties (T. Hall & Cox, 2009).

Participants recognised that new graduates needed supervision or more structured support. Those who graduated more recently described various ways in which they learnt from the support of others, highlighting the quality of the relationship and the feeling of trust as important factors in supporting learning. In a study of public sector workplace learning, Chris Hughes (2004) suggests there are problems with the assumption that supervisors will facilitate continuing learning of staff. He identifies potential conflicts of interest between the role of supervisors in facilitation of learning and surveillance of staff standards. Hughes (2002, p. 64) discusses the "burden of trust" in this relationship as asymmetrical, in that the employee needs to prove his trustworthiness by portraying himself as competent. He identifies an interesting conundrum in that the more autonomous workers are, the more they must prove their trustworthiness and the more difficult it may be for them to let down their guard in admitting what they don't know (p. 68).

My findings support Hughes' studies. Trust rather than trustworthiness was stressed as crucial in supportive relationships in APL. In a culture similar to that described by Hughes, the descriptions of many of my participants as hiding behind *a professional cloak* and not voicing what was valued are not surprising. In the network meetings I attended, there was more open discussion about uncertainties and letting down of professional guards when supervisors were absent. In the vignette that opens this thesis, Sally is concerned when asked to talk about her experiences in public, in that she tried several strategies before finding what worked with her clients. She felt she *couldn't talk about what not to do*, so she spoke about the literature instead. Although she learnt from giving the talk on the literature review, she also learnt from trial and error with her clients, but didn't feel comfortable voicing this aspect of her learning with her supervisor.

Support for learning involves a combination of trust and challenge. Within a supportive environment where uncertainty and doubt can be raised in open conversations, questions that challenge assumptions may be posed. Angie Titchen (2000) refers to a combination of challenge and support in her conceptual framework of "critical companionship" to assist experiential learning of colleagues through critical and reflective dialogue. Other research supports this combination. Michael Fullan (2001, p. 91) stresses the need for both "pressure and support" with respect to learning in times of change. Whilst questioning the use of pressure as a term, I concur with his explanation of the success of PL communities as related to the "seamless" combination of these elements.

Can openness be supervised? Can learning be controlled? Empirical evidence suggest not. There is a need for a culture of support and inquiry that values APL as it is experienced. The discourse of supervision needs to be replaced with one of support, where "stewardship" in guiding another may be exercised without a focus on control (Wadsworth, 2001, p. 421). This would involve the valuing of professionals and their practice, whilst challenging and questioning elements of that practice. In accepting and valuing PL as it is experienced, trust, support and agency could be highlighted instead of supervision, surveillance and control.

## 6.3  Wider Context of Professional Dissonance

The fact that participants dealt with dissonance in APL in different ways highlights the idiosyncratic nature of APL involving interplay between the professional's way of being and the professional culture. Questioning assumptions, acceptance of uncertainty and imagining other perspectives were not apparent in many descriptions of learning gathered in this study. Yet these features have been raised by current researchers and past philosophers as crucial to learning in changing circumstances. I suggest that the hesitancy of most participants to speak out about what is valued in APL is linked to discomfort with questioning and uncertainty within the current work culture and attendant difficulties seeing the possibility of change.

In concluding this chapter, two implications of dissonance are discussed. First, the claim is made that the dissonance with respect to learning is reflective of competing life-world discourses currently impacting on professional life. Second, the hidden nature of dissonance is linked not only to this professional context but also to how the participants understand being a professional, highlighting the ontological dimension of PL that is often neglected in traditional PD.

### 6.3.1  Competing Life-World Discourses

Dissonance between the reality of the experience of APL and the rhetoric of PD expectations can be seen as reflective of a wider dissonance in the current working culture for professionals, especially human service professionals. I have described tensions within the experience of APL between the openness of learning and circumscription of context (Chapter 5), dissonance between the reality of APL experiences and rhetoric about PD practices (Chapter 6) and the dilemmas raised for professionals by the inherent uncertainty of practice whilst working within a climate seeking the certainty of regulation (Chapter 2). All these ways of describing tensions reflect a wider dissonance between a technicist, economic rationalist perspective operating within contemporary working life and the ambiguity of the human condition that makes working in human services inherently uncertain.

For participants of this study, this wider dissonance was reflected in what was valued at work. Essentially a disconnection was perceived between what the professionals valued in their work and what they perceive was valued by their employers. That is, participants *could live with* and accept the need to *play the game*, with its outcomes focusing on demonstrating efficiency and accountability. What caused significant unease for these professionals was not feeling valued, so that what they value in their practice and learning appears to be discounted by the organisations for which they work. What the participants valued was clearly and universally stated. It is *making a difference* to the lives of their clients. They described how their work is meaningful for them on this basis. This meaning is linked to learning, as it determines which situations the professionals care about sufficiently to actively engage with in learning. They said: *what's the point in learning if it does not make a difference to what matters.* This is the nub of the problem in organisational training for the purposes of introducing policy changes. Unless professionals can see the relationship of proposed changes to what they value about work (in this case making a difference for clients), they are unlikely to fully engage in learning.

With respect to learning, participants described feeling unsupported by an organisational hierarchy that *shows no interest or realises the value of the work you do* (Olivia). Paula described how she perceived this lack of valuing of staff as a lack of support for learning. She states that her ability to *find creative solutions in difficult situations* with problems of staff shortages and increasing busyness is hampered by bureaucratic constraints. Although it is important to support staff in such situations, especially *the way they feel about their work*, Paula felt this wasn't happening. Stating that the participants' work was not valued raises the question of what is valued. It appears that fiscal efficiency rather than empathy with others and evidence of outcomes rather than making of meaning are valued.

In a critique of the contemporary context for teachers, Bronwyn Davies (2003) highlights the way that a culture of distrust and surveillance, where work is valued for its economic outputs rather than its meaning, leads teachers to question their value as professionals. The participants in my study emphasised that the lack of valuing of them and their work impacted them negatively, particularly in a climate where continual PD is stressed. The comments of some of my participants resonate with Davies' (2003, p. 95) statements below:

> The constant threat of external punitive surveillance potentially erodes the professional judgement of everyone.... The personal dynamic that is set up is potentially exhausting and debilitating, since it is likely that no one can experience themselves as "good enough" when the basis of assessment is externalised, constantly escalating, subject to change, and often at odds with the professional knowledge on which previous good practice was based.

Increasing standardisation of professional practice in the public health sector in Australia, with consequent constraints on professional autonomy, has been called "hyper-rationalisation" by sociologist John Germov (2005). Groundwater-Smith and Mockler (2009) highlight a similar context of standardisation in teachers' lives and the resulting negative impact on PL. In a climate of increasing litigation, regulation of workplaces is typically described as important for risk control. Ulrich Beck's (1992) recognition of the control of risk as a determining feature of society has been garnered in critiques about increasing control of society. The argument is made that control is increased to manage and order uncertainty and risk (Davies, 2003; Weil, 1999). Yet risk-aversion through regulation hampers the risk taking inherent in creating innovative possibilities for learning and practice (Coffield, 2007).

Whilst agreeing that the public need to be protected through some means of professional regulation, the degree of risk posed from well-educated professionals in caring professions is questionable. Despite the occasional instance of unethical behaviour brought to the attention of registration boards, there is no compelling evidence suggesting that public sector professionals would run amok if the closed fist of control and supervision were loosened in favour of more trust and support. The rhetoric of risk management is not only about safety and litigation but also about economic factors. Max van Manen (1977, p. 223) notes the translation of accountability into "countability" in such a climate, as reflected in Sam's lament that it was patently obvious she was *just a position number.*

There are two competing social discourses currently implicated in the professional life-world. They are related to what is valued in professional work as well as what is considered important and worthwhile in life in general. Such discourses are currently portrayed in both popular and academic literature. On the one hand, there is an economic rationalist discourse that values technical advances with outcomes that can be evaluated in an instrumental manner. I refer to this as the discourse of performativity. Within this discourse, people's knowledge is valued as a resource to be controlled, and learning is related to a search for certainty. From this perspective, life can be improved through progress and growth, involving a constant search for improved efficiency and better economic outcomes. Time is perceived as accelerating: people doing more, better and faster (Nowotny, 1994). This is the predominant discourse in society today, especially in the public world of work (Ball, 2003; Davies, 2005; Giddens, 2002).

At the same time, there are moves in society, mirrored in education and public discourse, that increasingly express a yearning for meaning, purpose, spirituality or wholeness in life. The importance of ethics, quality of life, relationships and social connections is stressed. This discourse is reflected by an interest in slowing the pace of life. From this perspective, life is perceived to improve through enhancing the well-being of individuals and society. Social scientist Clive Hamilton (2003) draws on Aristotle's notion of "eudaimonia", commonly interpreted as "human flourishing", to describe a worthwhile life for individuals and society, linked to well-being that includes meaningful work. I refer to these ideas as the discourse of meaning. Although the outlook within this discourse of meaning is disparate in comparison to the monolithic performative hegemony, a coherent framework is emerging (Armstrong, 2009; Eckersley, 2004; Sennett, 2006; Taylor, 2007). With respect to professionals in the caring professions in particular, arguments have been strongly made for a way of working as a professional that is related to a life of meaning and value for the professional and society (Aloni, 2008; Gardner, 2009; Groundwater-Smith & Mockler, 2009; Hostetler, Macintyre Latta, & Sarroub, 2007; Noddings, 2002; Sullivan, 1995; Tsivacou, 2005). The vignette of Olivia described this perspective clearly, although other participants referred in various ways to the importance of meaning derived from learning at work.

Philosopher Charles Guignon (2004) describes a tension between two similar "worldviews" as deeply opposed conceptions of what life is about. Although he uses different descriptors, he comments that many people experience a split between a performative-based outlook required in working life, with a focus on economic outcomes, and a meaning-based outlook in private life with a focus on social relationships (p. 79). In the former, processes are valued more than people; progress more than meaning. He raises problems with such dissonance similar to those discussed in this chapter. Stephen Ball (2003, p. 221) describes this "split" in teachers' working lives as "values schizophrenia".

The feeling of dissonance as a professional may reflect more than a dissonance between the reality of APL experiences and the rhetoric of PD expectations. Dissonance between meaningful lives as professionals and meeting performative professional expectations is, I suggest, an aspect of being a professional within a society where competing discourses exist: where professionals are expected to "set aside personal beliefs and commitments and live an existence of calculation" (Ball, 2003, p. 215). This issue is discussed in the following chapter.

### 6.3.2  The Hidden Nature of Dissonance

Why is dissonance in APL effectively hidden? The fact that there was little questioning of performative aspects of the workplace by participants could be related to the implicit nature of professional regulation mentioned in Chapter 2. Thus organisational processes are experienced as a given: taken for granted as "a set of rules and regulations that determine the truth and therefore what is said, who says what, and where" (Horsfall, Byrne-Armstrong, & Rothwell, 2001, p. 91). Drawing on Foucault, Debbie Horsfall and colleagues also argue that implicit power differentials at work are enacted through accepted discourse about work. Such power may not be coercive, but operates through "discourses and practices, which normalise, categorise, measure and generally regulate" (Usher, Bryant, & Johnston, 1997, p. 77). In linking power, meaning and identity, Michael Apple (1999, p. 173) notes that the discourse of institutional life normalises and disguises these power relationships.

In my research, an implicit power relationship is evident in the unquestioned need for professional supervision. No participants questioned the assumption that as professionals, of any age or level of experience, they needed to be supervised, although their private sector counterparts are not. Bronwyn Davies (2003, p. 93) argues that resistance in professional work is often "silenced or trivialised" because the established way of working is implicit and hence unquestionable.

Although trust is identified as important for workplace learning in this study and others (Coffield, 2007; English-Lueck, Darrah, & Saveri, 2002; Gilbert, 2005; Marginson, 2008), many institutions seem to work on the assumption people can't be trusted. Charles Handy (1996, p. 141) describes systematic surveillance of workers to prevent error as "audit mania". Davies (2003, p. 93) also critiques the surveillance of professional educators as endemic within rampant managerialism. In describing how trust is undermined, she notes that resources that could support professionals' work are redirected towards surveillance and auditing.

In questioning the connection between trust and accountability in professional work in the public and private sectors, philosopher Onora O'Neil (2002) argues against the micro-management involved in the increasingly downward spiral of audited accountability. She describes "relentless demands" on professionals that require them to record and report in detail on performance indicators devised for "ease of measurement". She maintains that the demands of accountability often obstruct and distort professionals' ability to conduct their "real work" of teaching or nursing, for example. Her argument is premised by the notion that risk can never be obviated by control measures, as there can never be total guarantees of others' performances. O'Neil concludes: "If we want greater accountability without damaging professional performance we need intelligent accountability," with increased self-regulation for professionals, paying "more attention to good governance and fewer fantasies about total control" (p. 5).

Inquiries into the public service have identified a culture of defensiveness and shifting of blame in certain circumstances when mistakes occurred. Instead of learning from errors, attempts were sometimes made to cover them up, thereby avoiding public scrutiny with attendant political fallout (A. J. Brown, Magendanz, & Leary, 2004; Preston, Sampford, & Connors, 2002). Victoria Marsick's (2006, p. 61) research also noted organisations who "punished" those who "took calculated risks" or made mistakes, rather than creating a safe environment where people could innovate, try out new ideas and learn from errors of judgement. A culture of defensiveness is an anathema for professional inquiry and open conversations about uncertainty. In such climates, expressions of doubt and not knowing will be hidden by many professionals.

The absence of challenge to the status quo in professional work environments, by professionals or other stakeholders, is alarming. As mentioned in Chapter 2, there is robust widespread critique of professional regulation in the literature related to the teaching profession (Apple, 2001; Ball, 2003; Davies, 2005; Groundwater-Smith & Mockler, 2009), but the voice of resistance elsewhere is a whisper expressed at the margins (e.g. C. A. Brown, Bannigan, & Gill, 2009; C. Jones, Ferguson, Lavalette, & Penketh, 2004; Trede, Higgs, Jones, & Edwards, 2003). The voice of resistance has to begin somewhere. It can begin with the voices of professionals about their workplace experience such as the critique raised in Sam's description.

The difference between the participants who saw constraints in learning as a problem with themselves (such as Sally) and those who questioned the system as the source of dissonance and subsequent tensions (such as Sam) is illuminating. Sam is the participant who stands out in that she raised all the questions highlighted in this chapter in her own critique of her profession (although other participants raised some of these questions). The impact of dissonance between rhetoric and reality in APL varies with each professional's way of being a professional as detailed in Chapter 5. Clarifying differences between participants' experiences of APL can allow insight into ways of supporting professionals to continue learning. These differences relate to the ontological dimension of APL and concept of authenticity.

In summary, Chapter 6 questions the current professional culture as problematic for APL. There is a need for more open dialogue in professional life, involving questioning and challenging of ideas within a professional and workplace culture of inquiry, trust and support. The professional interacts with and shapes her professional life-world; therefore, any discussion of support for APL needs to address the holistic nature of being-in-the-world as a professional. In addition to problems with context, lack of recognition of the ontological dimension of learning in PD is also important in explaining the hidden nature of dissonance. Chapter 7 discusses the ontological implications of learning as a professional, with respect to authenticity.

## References

Abrandt Dahlgren, M., Richardson, B., & Kalman, H. (2004). Redefining the reflective practitioner. In J. Higgs, B. Richardson, & M. Abrandt Dahlgren (Eds.), *Developing practice knowledge for health professionals* (pp. 15–33). Edinburgh; New York: Butterworth-Heinemann.

Aloni, N. (2008). Spinoza as educator: From eudaimonistic ethics to an empowering and liberating pedagogy. *Educational Philosophy and Theory, 40*(4), 531–544.

Alvesson, M. (2004). *Knowledge work and knowledge-intensive firms*. Oxford; New York: Oxford University Press.

Andresen, L., & Fredericks, I. (2001). Finding the fifth player: Artistry in professional practice. In J. Higgs & A. Titchen (Eds.), *Professional practice in health, education and the creative arts* (pp. 72–89). Oxford: Blackwell Science.

Apple, M. W. (1999). *Power, meaning, and identity: Essays in critical educational studies*. New York: P. Lang.

Apple, M. W. (2001). *Educating the "right" way: Markets, standards, God, and inequality.* New York; London: RoutledgeFalmer.

Armstrong, J. (2009). *In search of civilization: Remaking a tarnished idea.* London; New York: Allen Lane.

Axford, B. (2005). Entering professional practice in the new work order: A study of undergraduate students and their induction into professional work. *The Australian Educational Researcher, 32*(2), 87–104.

Badaracco, J. L. (1997). *Defining moments: When managers must choose between right and right.* Boston: Harvard Business School Press.

Ball, S. J. (2003). The teacher's soul and the terrors of performativity. *Journal of Education Policy, 18*(2), 215–228.

Banathy, B. H., & Jenlink, P. M. (Eds.). (2005). *Dialogue as a means of collective communication.* New York: Kluwer Academic/Plenum Publishers.

Barnacle, R. (2001). Phenomenology and wonder. In R. Barnacle (Ed.), *Phenomenology* (pp. 1–15). Melbourne, VIC: RMIT University Press.

Barnett, R. (2000). Supercomplexity and the curriculum. *Studies in Higher Education, 25*(3), 255–265.

Barnett, R. (2004). Learning for an unknown future. *Higher Education Research and Development, 23*(3), 247–260.

Barnett, R., & Coate, K. (2005). *Engaging the curriculum in higher education.* Maidenhead: Open University Press.

Barr, H. (2003). Practice-based interprofessional learning. *Journal of Interprofessional Care, 17*(1), 5–6.

Beaty, E., Dall'Alba, G., & Marton, F. (1997). The personal experience of learning in higher education: Changing views and enduring perspectives. In P. Sutherland (Ed.), *Adult learning: A reader*. London: Kogan Page.

Beck, U. (1992). *Risk society: Towards a new modernity.* London: Sage Publications.

Beckett, D., & Hager, P. J. (2002). *Life, work, and learning: Practice in postmodernity.* London; New York: Routledge.

Beckett, D., & Hager, P. (2003). Rejoinder: Learning from work: Can Kant do? *Educational Philosophy and Theory, 35*(1), 123–127.

Boud, D., & Middleton, H. (2003). Learning from others at work: Communities of practice and informal learning. *Journal of Workplace Learning, 15*(5), 194–202.

Boud, D., & Walker, D. (1998). Promoting reflection in professional courses: The challenge of context. *Studies in Higher Education, 23*(2), 191–206.

Brockbank, A., McGill, I., & Beech, N. (Eds.). (2002). *Reflective learning in practice.* Aldershot, England; Burlington, VT: Gower.

Brookfield, S. (1987). *Developing critical thinkers: Challenging adults to explore alternative ways of thinking and acting.* San Francisco: Jossey-Bass.

Brookfield, S. (1995). *Becoming a critically reflective teacher.* San Francisco: Jossey-Bass.

Brown, C. A., & Bannigan, K., & Gill, J. R. (2009). Questioning: A critical skill in postmodern health-care service delivery. *Australian Occupational Therapy Journal, 56,* 206–210.

Brown, A. J., Magendanz, D., & Leary, C. (2004). *Speaking up: Creating positive reporting climates in the Queensland public sector.* Retrieved May 5, 2006, from http://www.cmc.qld.gov.au/data/portal/00000005/content/21045001129616284299.pdf

Burchell, B. J., Ladipo, D., & Wilkinson, F. (Eds.). (2002). *Job insecurity and work intensification.* London: Routledge.

Charles, C. (2001). The meaning(s) of uncertainty in treatment decsion-making. In J. Higgs & A. Titchen (Eds.), *Professional practice in health, education and the creative arts* (pp. 62–71). Oxford: Blackwell Science.

Clouder, L. (2000). Reflective practice: Realising its potential. *Physiotherapy, 86*(10), 517–522.

Coffield, F. (Ed.). (2000). *Differing visions of a Learning Society: Research findings* (Vol. 1). Bristol: The Policy Press.

Coffield, F. (2007). *Running ever faster down the wrong road: An alternative future for Education and Skills*. London: Institute of Education, University of London.

Cordingley, P. (2008). Research and evidence-informed practice: Focusing on practice and practitioners. *Cambridge Journal of Education, 38*(1), 37–52.

Dall'Alba, G. (2005). Improving teaching: Enhancing ways of being university teachers. *Higher Education Research and Development, 24*(4), 361–372.

Dall'Alba, G. (2009). Learning professional ways of being: Ambiguities of becoming. *Educational Philosophy and Theory, 41*(1), 34–45.

Dall'Alba, G., & Barnacle, R. (2007). An ontological turn for higher education. *Studies in Higher Education, 32*(6), 679–691.

Dall'Alba, G., & Sandberg, J. (1996). Educating for competence in professional practice. *Instructional Science, 24*, 411–437.

Dall'Alba, G., & Sandberg, J. (2006). Unveiling professional development: A critical review of stage models. *Review of Educational Research, 76*(3), 383–412.

Davies, B. (2003). Death to critique and dissent? The politics and practices of new managerialism and of "evidence-based practice". *Gender and Education, 15*, 91–103.

Davies, B. (2005). The (im)possibility of intellectual work in neoliberal regimes. *Discourse: Studies in the Cultural Politics of Education, 26*(1), 1–14.

Day, C. (1993). Reflection: A necessary but not sufficient condition for professional development. *British Educational Research Journal, 19*(1), 83–92.

Denhardt, K. G. (1991). Ethics and fuzzy worlds. *Australian Journal of Public Administration, 50*(3), 274–278.

Devos, A. (2004). The project of self, the project of others: Mentoring, women and the fashioning of the academic subject. *Studies in Continuing Education, 26*(1), 67–80.

Dollard, M. F., Winefield, A. H., & Winefield, H. R. (2003). *Occupational stress in the service professions*. London; New York: Taylor & Francis.

Easterby-Smith, M., Crossan, M., & Nicolini, D. (2000). Organizational learning: Debates past, present and future. *Journal of Management Studies, 37*(6), 783–796.

Eckersley, R. (2004). A new world view struggles to emerge: Are we seeing the emergence of a new view of what makes life worth living? *The Futurist, 38*(5), 20–25.

Elliott, B. (2005). *Phenomenology and imagination in Husserl and Heidegger*. London: Routledge.

English-Lueck, J. A., Darrah, C. N., & Saveri, A. (2002). Trusting strangers: Work relationships in four high-tech communities. *Information, Communication and Society, 5*(1), 90–108.

Fish, D. (1998). *Appreciating practice in the caring professions: Refocusing professional development and practitioner research*. Oxford: Butterworth Heinemann.

Florida, R. L. (2002). *The rise of the creative class: And how it's transforming work, leisure, community and everyday life*. New York: Basic Books.

Freidson, E. (2001). *Professionalism: The third logic*. Chicago: University of Chicago Press.

Fullan, M. (2001). *The new meaning of educational change* (3rd ed.). New York; London: Teachers College Press; RoutledgeFarmer.

Gadamer, H. G. (1965/1979). *Truth and method* (2nd ed.). London: Sheed & Ward.

Gardner, F. (2009). Affirming values: Using critical reflection to explore meaning and professional practice. *Reflective Practice: International and Multidisciplinary Perspectives, 10*(2), 179–190.

Garner, H. (2008). *Creativity and uncertainty*. Available from http://www.communication.uts.edu.au/conferences/aawp/garner-lecture.pdf

Germov, J. (2005). Managerialism in the Australian public health sector: Towards the hyper-rationalisation of professional bureaucracies. *Sociology of Health and Illness, 27*(6), 738–758.

Gibson, T., & Heartfield, M. (2005). Mentoring for nurses in general practice: An Australian study. *Journal of Interprofessional Care, 19*(1), 50–62.

Giddens, A. (2002). *Runaway world: How globalisation is reshaping our lives* (2nd ed.). London: Profile.

Gilbert, T. (2005). Trust and managerialism: Exploring discourses of care. *Journal of Advanced Nursing, 52*(4), 454–463.

Grbich, C. (1999). *Qualitative research in health: An introduction*. St Leonards, NSW: Allen & Unwin.

Grenville, K. (1999). *The idea of perfection*. South Melbourne, VIC: Picador.

Groundwater-Smith, S., & Mockler, N. (2009). *Teacher professional learning in an age of compliance: Mind the gap*. Dordrecht: Springer.

Guignon, C. B. (2004). *On being authentic*. London; New York: Routledge.

Hall, E. (2005). "Joined-up working" between early years professionals and speech and language therapists: Moving beyond "normal" roles. *Journal of Interprofessional Care, 19*(1), 11–21.

Hall, T., & Cox, D. (2009). Clinical supervision: An appropriate term for physiotherapists? *Learning in Health and Social Care, 8*(4), 282–291.

Hamilton, C. (2003). *Growth fetish*. Crows Nest, NSW: Allen & Unwin.

Handy, C. B. (1996). *Beyond certainty: The changing worlds of organizations*. Boston: Harvard Business School Press.

Hasnain-Wynia, R. (2006). Is evidence-based medicine patient-centred and is patient-centred care evidence-based? [Editorial]. *Health Services Research, 41*(1), 1–8.

Heath, G. (2003). Connecting work practices with practical reason. *Educational Philosophy and Theory, 35*(1), 107–111.

Heidegger, M. (1950/2002). Hegel's concept of experience. In K. Haynes & J. Young (Eds.), *Off the beaten track* (pp. 86–156). Cambridge; New York: Cambridge University Press.

Heidegger, M. (1954/1977). Science and reflection. In W. Lovitt (Ed.), *The question concerning technology and other essays* (pp. 155–182). New York: Harper & Row.

Heidegger, M. (1954/1993). The question concerning technology. In D. F. Krell (Ed.), *Basic writings: Heidegger* (pp. 311–341). London: Routledge.

Heidegger, M. (1959/1966). *Discourse on thinking* (J. M. Anderson & E. H. Freund, Trans.). New York: Harper & Row.

Heidegger, M. (1966/1993). The end of philosophy and the task of thinking. In D. F. Krell (Ed.), *Basic writings: Heidegger* (pp. 428–449). London: Routledge.

Helsing, D. (2007). Style of knowing regarding uncertainties. *Curriculum Inquiry, 37*(1), 33–70.

Horsfall, D., Byrne-Armstrong, H., & Rothwell, R. (2001). Embodying knowledges: Challenging the theory/practice divide. In J. Higgs & A. Titchen (Eds.), *Professional practice in health, education and the creative arts* (pp. 90–102). Oxford: Blackwell Science.

Hostetler, K., Macintyre Latta, M. A., & Sarroub, L. K. (2007). Retrieving meaning in teacher education: The question of Being. *Journal of Teacher Education, 58*(3), 231.

Howkins, J. (2009). *Creative ecologies: Where thinking is a proper job*. Brisbane, QLD: University of Queensland Press.

Hughes, C. (2002). Issues in supervisory facilitation. *Studies in Continuing Education, 24*(1), 57–71.

Hughes, C. (2004). The supervisor's influence on workplace learning. *Studies in Continuing Education, 26*(2), 275–287.

Hyland, T. (2009). Mindfulness and the therapeutic function of education. *Journal of Philosophy of Education, 43*(1), 119–131.

Johnson, M. (1987). *The body in the mind: The bodily basis of meaning, imagination, and reason*. Chicago; London: University of Chicago Press.

Jones, A. (2007). Looking over our shoulders: Critical thinking and ontological insecurity in higher education. *London Review of Education, 5*(3), 209–222.

Jones, C., Ferguson, I., Lavalette, M., & Penketh, L. (2004). *Social work and social justice: A manifesto for a new engaged practice*. Retrieved September 14, 2009, from http://www.socialworkfuture.org/?page_id=50

Kramer, M. W. (2004). *Managing uncertainty in organizational communication*. Mahwah, NJ: Lawrence Erlbaum Associates.

Lohmar, D. (2005). On the function of weak phantasmata in perception: Phenomenological, psychological and neurological clues for the transcendental function of imagination in perception. *Phenomenology and the Cognitive Sciences, 4*(2), 155–167.

Macfarlane, B., & Gourlay, L. (2009). The reflection game: Enacting the penitent self. *Teaching in Higher Education, 14*(4), 455–459.

Marginson, S. (2008). Academic creativity under new public management: Foundations for an investigation. *Educational Theory, 58*(3), 269–287.

Marsick, V. J. (2006). Informal strategic learning in the workplace. In J. N. Streumer (Ed.), *Work-related learning* (pp. 51–69). Dortrecht: Springer.

Mattingly, C. (1998). *Healing dramas and clinical plots: The narrative structure of experience.* Cambridge; New York: Cambridge University Press.

McCormack, A., Gore, J., & Thomas, K. (2006). Early career teacher professional learning. *Asia-Pacific Journal of Teacher Education, 34*(1), 95–113.

Merleau-Ponty, M. (1964). The primacy of perception and its philosophical consequences. In J. M. Edie (Ed.), *The primacy of perception and other essays on phenomenological psychology, the philosophy of art, history, and politics* (pp. 12–42). Evanston, IL: Northwestern University Press.

Mezirow, J. (Ed.). (1990). *Fostering critical reflection in adulthood: A guide to transformative and emancipatory learning.* San Francisco: Jossey-Bass Publishers.

Mezirow, J. (Ed.). (2000). *Learning as transformation: Critical perspectives on a theory in progress.* San Francisco: Jossey-Bass.

Mimura, C., & Griffiths, P. (2003). The effectiveness of current approaches to workplace stress management in the nursing profession: An evidence based literature review. *Occupational and Environmental Medicine, 60,* 10–15.

Molloy, C. (2004). *Understanding uncertainty: A new dimension.* Ringwood, VIC: Brolga Publishing.

Morley, J. (2005). Introduction: Phenomenology of imagination. *Phenomenology and the Cognitive Sciences, 4*(2), 117–120.

Mullavey-O'Byrne, C., & West, S. (2001). Practising without certainty: Providing health care in an uncertain world. In J. Higgs & A. Titchen (Eds.), *Professional practice in health, education and the creative arts* (pp. 49–61). Oxford: Blackwell Science.

Ng, P. T., & Tan, C. (2009). Community of practice for teachers: Sensemaking or critical reflective learning? *Reflective Practice: International and Multidisciplinary Perspectives, 10*(1), 37–44.

Noddings, N. (2002). *Educating moral people: A caring alternative to character education.* New York: Teachers College Press.

Nowotny, H. (1994). *Time: Modern and postmodern experience.* Cambridge, UK; Cambridge, MA: Polity Press; Blackwell Publishers [distributor].

Nowotny, H., Scott, P., & Gibbons, M. (2001). *Re-thinking science: Knowledge and the public in an Age of Uncertainty.* Cambridge: Polity Press.

O'Neil, O. (2002). A question of trust: Called to account. *Lecture, 3,* from http://www.bbc.co.uk/radio4/reith2002/

Pollard, A. (2002). *Reflective teaching: Effective and evidence-informed professional practice.* London: Continuum.

Preston, N., Sampford, C. J. G., & Connors, C. (2002). *Encouraging ethics and challenging corruption: Reforming governance in public institutions.* Annandale, NSW: Federation Press.

Reeves, S., Freeth, D., McCrorie, P., & Perry, D. (2002). "It teaches you what to expect in future...": Interprofessional learning on a training ward for medical, nursing, occupational therapy and physiotherapy students. *Medical Education, 36*(4), 337–344.

Rodrigues, S. (Ed.). (2005). *International perspectives on teacher professional development: Changes influenced by politics, pedagogy and innovation.* New York: Nova Science Publishers.

Sandberg, J., & Dall'Alba, G. (2006). Re-framing competence development at work. In R. Gerber, G. Castleton, & H. Pillay (Eds.), *Improving workplace learning: Emerging international perspectives.* New York: Nova Publishers.

Schmid, T. (2004). Meanings of creativity within occupational therapy practice. *Australian Occupational Therapy Journal, 51*(2), 80–88.

Schön, D. A. (1983). *The reflective practitioner: How professionals think in action*. Aldershot, England: Arena.

Semetsky, I. (2004). The role of intuition in thinking and learning: Deleuze and the pragmatic legacy. *Educational Philosophy and Theory, 36*(4), 433–454.

Sennett, R. (2006). *The culture of the new capitalism*. New Haven, CT: Yale University Press.

Smythe, E. (2003). Preserving 'thinking' in the thesis experience. *Focus on Health Professional Education, 5*(1), 54–65.

Sokolowski, R. (2000). *Introduction to phenomenology*. Cambridge; New York: Cambridge University Press.

Steeves, J. B. (2004). *Imagining bodies: Merleau-Ponty's philosophy of imagination*. Pittsburgh, PA: Duquesne University Press.

Stwine, D., & Abrandt Dahlgren, M. (2004). Challenging evidence in evidence-based practice. In J. Higgs, B. Richardson, & M. Abrandt Dahlgren (Eds.), *Developing practice knowledge for health professionals* (pp. 147–164). Edinburgh; New York: Butterworth-Heinemann.

Sullivan, W. M. (1995). *Work and integrity: The crisis and promise of professionalism in America*. New York: HarperCollins.

Taylor, C. (2007). *A secular age*. Cambridge, MA: Belknap Press of Harvard University Press.

Titchen, A. (2000). *Professional craft knowledge in patient-centred nursing and the facilitation of its development*. Oxford: University of Oxford.

Titchen, A., & Higgs, J. (2001). Towards professional artistry and creativity in practice. In J. Higgs & A. Titchen (Eds.), *Professional practice in health, education and the creative arts* (pp. 273–290). Oxford: Blackwell Science.

Trede, F., Higgs, J., Jones, M., & Edwards, I. (2003). Emancipatory practice: A model for physiotherapy practice? *Focus on Health Professional Education, 5*(2), 1–13.

Tsivacou, I. (2005). Designing communities of ideas for the human well-being. In B. H. Banathy & P. M. Jenlink (Eds.), *Dialogue as a means of collective communication* (pp. 41–70). New York: Kluwer Academic/Plenum Publishers.

Usher, R., Bryant, I., & Johnston, R. (1997). *Adult education and the postmodern challenge: Learning beyond the limits*. London; New York: Routledge.

van Manen, M. (1977). Linking ways of knowing with ways of being practical. *Curriculum Inquiry, 6*(3), 205–228.

Wadsworth, Y. (2001). The mirror, the magnifying glass, the compass and the map: Facilitating participatory action research. In P. Reason & H. Bradbury (Eds.), *Handbook of action research: Participative inquiry and practice* (pp. 420–432). London: Sage Publications.

Weil, S. (1999). Re-creating universities for 'Beyond the stable state': From 'Dearingesque' systematic control to Post-Dearing systematic learning and inquiry. *Systems Research and Behavioral Science, 16*(2), 171–194.

Wenger, E. (1998). *Communities of practice: Learning, meaning, and identity*. Cambridge; New York: Cambridge University Press.

Williams, P., Pocock, B., & Skinner, N. (2008). "Clawing back time": Expansive working time and implications for work life outcomes in Australian workers. *Work Employment and Society, 22*(4), 737–748.

Winefield, A. H. (2008). *Job stress in university staff: An Australian research study*. Bowen Hills, QLD: Australian Academic Press.

# Chapter 7
# Authenticity in Professional Life

The way that a professional continues to learn is an expression of her way of being a professional, in dynamic interplay with her particular professional context. Conversely, learning shapes that way of being and, therefore, way of dealing with the context. Learning as a professional has an important ontological dimension: what and how a professional learns vary with who she is as a professional. Thus APL is an ontological as well as an epistemological concern: APL is as much about who the professional is and what she values, as it is about what the professional knows and how she acts. Although the professional referred to here is a health professional, claims about the ontological dimension of learning have relevance for other professions.

In this chapter, ontology is highlighted rather than epistemology (which is also important), as the usual conceptualisation and implementation of PD focuses on professional knowledge. Although lip service is given to recognition of professionals as individual people through flexible delivery of PD programmes, the notion of "being a professional" is rarely addressed. Evidence for ontological claims is examined as part of my argument for a shift in the way that continuing to learn as a professional is conceptualised. The ontological implications of understanding, engagement, interconnection and openness, as constituents of APL, are discussed.

Recognising the ontological dimension of APL not only helps in understanding the experience of learning but also has implications for supporting learning. Two examples, comparing how different ways of being a professional impact on learning, illustrate this contention, with respect to the notion of authenticity in learning and how learning in certain situations may transform professional being.

## 7.1 Ontological Claims

A valid criticism of this research could be that an ontological dimension of learning is assumed, because of the explicit phenomenological perspective taken in the research design. That is, because the experience of APL is conceptualised as involving the whole professional inextricably intertwined within a shared and meaningful professional life-world, APL is necessarily related to being a professional.

A. Webster-Wright, *Authentic Professional Learning*, Professional and Practice-based Learning 2, DOI 10.1007/978-90-481-3947-7_7, © Springer Science+Business Media B.V. 2010

Researching PD as a collection of factors that influence learning would not highlight ontology. This argument is circular, in a hermeneutic sense, in that the phenomenological perspective was chosen to address problems with the current focus on PD that led to this research. In other words, because of my implicit preunderstanding of problems in support for the learning of professionals, I found in phenomenology "what I was looking for" as an approach to examine learning.

Providing evidence for ontological claims in research is problematic. As explained in Chapter 3, under Heidegger's radical project, the primary task of ontology in investigating reality is to examine the meaning of "being", particularly of being human. Although investigation of "being" is "the most basic and the most concrete" of tasks, "being" remains a slippery though ancient concept (Heidegger, 1927/1962, p. 29). He explains:

> It is said that "Being" is the most universal and the emptiest of concepts. As such it resists every attempt at definition. Nor does this most universal and hence indefinable concept require any definition, for everyone uses it constantly and already understands what he means by it. (p. 21)

In claiming that ontological implications of APL are revealed through analysis of the empirical evidence in this study, two avenues are sought. The first is the claim of verisimilitude of the findings when presented to other professionals, both during this research and in continuing related research since. The evidence presented in Part III, particularly the claim that APL is as much about "who a professional is" as about "what a professional knows", appears to resonate with the experience of others, rather than appear as empty philosophical theorising. The second avenue is the examination of the findings in the light of the phenomenological ontology of Martin Heidegger, Maurice Merleau-Ponty and Hans-Georg Gadamer. Merleau-Ponty (1945/2002, p. viii) muses that readers interested in human experience may find, upon reading phenomenological philosophers such as Heidegger, not something new, but a "recogni[tion of] what they had been waiting for". This chapter demonstrates how concrete examples of APL experiences resonate with such philosophical investigations of human experience.

In his phenomenological analysis of being, Heidegger (1927/1962) begins with an ontological examination of what it means to be a human being, capable of enquiring into the nature of being. Similarly, this chapter examines what it means to be a professional who learns. Following Heidegger (see Chapter 3), I argue that most analyses of how professionals learn are ontic examinations of elements contributing to learning, such as professional behaviour, knowledge and skills. In contrast, this study includes an ontological examination of the experience of being a professional who learns, highlighting how various ways of being a professional shape learning. To begin, I examine how "being a professional" is understood in the related literature on learning.

### 7.1.1 What Does "Being a Professional" Mean?

This question is rarely asked in the professional literature. As discussed in Chapter 2, being a professional implies belonging to a certain profession, described in terms of membership of a professional group, such as doctors, engineers, teachers or architects. The boundaries of that group, typically determined by the possession of certain educational attributes and the undertaking of particular responsibilities, are regulated by registration boards and professional associations (Freidson, 1986).

Although additional attributes (such as interpersonal skills or professional artistry) are added to the notion of what a professional is, there is little evaluation of assumptions about what it means to be a professional in the literature. The question of who professionals are, as opposed to what they know or can do, receives little consideration. There is increasing interest in the notion of professional identity, subjectivity and agency, but, as argued in Chapter 2, a problem with much of this conceptualisation is that these professional notions are considered in contradistinction to context and practice: as related yet separate, rather than inextricably embedded. Certainly consideration of the complexity of the interrelationships between the individual professional and her practice is becoming more sophisticated (e.g. Billett, 2008a, 2008b). A phenomenological examination of professional being contributes a different perspective to these considerations.

The concept of "being" is addressed in some literature on the professions: principally in teaching, nursing and occupational therapy (Brook, 2009; Kleiman, 2008; Parse, 2004; Wilcock, 1999), occasionally in other health professions (J. Higgs & McAllister, 2005; Joy Higgs & Titchen, 2001), rarely in professions beyond those designated as "caring" (Sandberg & Pinnington, 2009). As educators, Robyn Ewing and David Smith (2001, p. 16) note: "It is impossible for us to separate out who we are from what we do. . ... Being is embedded in our practice of doing and, through the doing, as practitioners we continue to become who we are." Consideration of being is an important move away from a strongly epistemological focus in professional education, research into the professions and professional practice. Nevertheless, apart from those mentioned above, there is rarely an explicit consideration of what being actually means or the ontological and educational implications of the notion of professional being.

What is missing in most considerations of being a professional is the relationship between membership of a professional group and identification as a professional, through enactment of professional practice. It is in this relationship that the experience of learning described in this study is constituted. The interrelationship between learning, community, practice and the development of professional identity is given attention by Etienne Wenger (1998). He argues that learning involves the "formation of an identity", not in the sense of a conscious self-image, but in terms of being a member of a community of practice (p. 96). He asserts that "the experience of identity in practice is a way of being in the world" (p. 151).

Recently, a few researchers have drawn from Heidegger in arguing that higher education has an ontological dimension that is rarely addressed (Barnett, 2004; Dall'Alba & Barnacle, 2007; Peters, 2009; Thomson, 2004). Gloria Dall'Alba (2009) argues that professional education needs to address ways of becoming and being professionals, rather than focusing purely on teaching professional knowledge and skills. Drawing on the theme of "ontological education" implicit in much of Heidegger's work, Iain Thomson (2001) calls for an ontological shift in education, moving from a focus on gaining knowledge to developing insights into being human as the basis of all knowing.

Heidegger's phenomenological conception of being-in-the-world offers an insightful, cogent (albeit dense) ontological analysis that serves to clarify the findings of this study. In particular, he offers a way of thinking about different ways of being a professional in APL that privileges neither self (through professional identity) nor context (through membership of a professional group), instead their interrelationship is examined through the study of life-world experience. Following Heidegger, then, I contend that the essential aspect of being a professional is "being-in-the-professional-world".

## *7.1.2 Being-in-the-Professional-World*

As stated in Chapter 3, Heidegger's analysis of being-in-the-world constantly reinforces the holistic nature of being. Therefore humans are more than the sum of their parts. They are not only in an already existing world of activities: not only affected by and affecting others in the world. The profound nature of Heidegger's work is his conceptualisation of the interrelated totality of being human, through active involvement in everyday practice, underpinned by a temporal structure that gives the world, activities and self, significance and meaning.

Drawing on Heidegger, a professional is inseparable from the world of professional practice. To identify as a professional in a specific practice implies being within a shared and intersubjectively meaningful professional life-world. All the participants in this study considered themselves to be professionals. They spoke of themselves as belonging to a specific category of professional, a physiotherapist, for example. Thus, of primary importance here, each participant answered questions about learning from her particular (albeit shared) understanding of what it is to "be a…therapist".

As stated, the world with which people are concerned is a public world. Heidegger describes "being-with", as humans are always involved in some specific shared practices. They are socialised into culturally and historically formed roles so that they know what to do and how to be, for example, as therapists (Dreyfus, 1991, p. 163). As mentioned in Chapter 3, Heidegger's (1927/1962, p. 120) term "for-the-sake-of-which" describes how activities make sense to a person within a particular social role. A social role, such as being a therapist, has assumed norms that shape ways of being as "a self-interpretation that informs and orders all my activities" (Dreyfus, p. 95).

For example, Nerida described her use of a piece of equipment in her practice from her understanding of being a therapist, as just right for the purposes of a particular activity. She described not its physical characteristics, but its usefulness in the context of a specific learning situation, reflecting on the difficulties with its purchase, installation and safety guidelines. Nerida's involvement in this situation made sense to her in an integrated way because of her implicit understanding of being a professional therapist.

Crucial to Heidegger's analysis of being human is time. Heidegger (1927/1962, p. 39) claims that time provides "the horizon for all understanding of Being and for any way of interpreting it". He clarifies that this temporal nature of being allows a sense of self and of meaning in being-in-the-world (p. 41). It is the ability of a person to view her "whole life" at any moment, going forward as well as back in time and returning into the present, that gives her a sense of being a "unified self" (Elliott, 2005, p. 121; Inwood, 2000, p. 91). Even though experiences vary over time, a person has a sense of continuity of self, with a certain "selfsameness and steadiness" (Heidegger, p. 367). This temporal nature of being human allows a "range of possibilities for the future that lets past come alive and mean something to us" in the present (Guignon, 2004b, p. 128).

## 7.1.3 Ontological Dimensions of Learning

When taken as a whole, the experience of APL can be considered to have an onto-logical dimension. The claim, that who professionals *are* is as important as what they know in determining what and how they learn, has a commonsense appeal. In examining resonance between empirical data and phenomenological ontology, it can be seen that all four constituents of APL reflect this ontological dimension. The following section briefly indicates such resonance, as a way of clarifying the ontological claims of this study, as well as illustrating the potential of phenomeno-logical philosophy for gaining insight into the experience of professional practice in future research. I draw on Merleau-Ponty's and Gadamer's phenomenological ontology in addition to Heidegger's in this section. Although Heidegger's concep-tion of being-in-the-world implies the embodied nature of being and the interactions of being-with, these other philosophers offer a clearer insight, in my opinion, into the ontological dimension of certain aspects of APL.

### 7.1.3.1 Understanding of Being a Professional

Constituent one of the structure of APL, change in professional understand-ing, highlights the ontological nature of continuing to learn as a professional, as explained through Heidegger's ontological consideration of understanding. As stated in Chapter 3, understanding, as familiarity with the world, is essential to being human, enabling people to constantly make sense of the world and their involvement in it. Heidegger describes different forms and levels of understanding (Dreyfus, 1991). The most primordial, their "understanding of being", permeates all that human beings do and are in the world (Dreyfus, 2000; MacAvoy, 2001). All forms of understanding (of things, self, others or world) and ways of relating to the world (through thinking, valuing, acting or speaking) pre-suppose an understanding of being. Yet at the same time, understanding of being pervades and includes all forms of understanding and ways of relating to the world.

As the participants described in this study, understanding of "being a pro-fessional" is not a purely cognitive understanding about professional practice.

Understanding encapsulates all that a professional is and does, allowing a professional to cope with everyday practice. Thus, understanding of being a professional is essential to being-in-the-professional-world, practicing as a professional.

In the findings of this study are many examples of different forms of understanding. For example, professionals sometimes referred to learning by *trial and error* as knowing what to do. In *knowing what to do* they did not discuss specific cognitive processes, yet were not "thoughtless". Through an understanding of being a professional they were able to act, adapting if something did not proceed as they expected. Heidegger (Heidegger, 1975/1982, p. 163) describes such skilful everyday coping where environs, equipment and self become transparent. In this study it was often the therapist's hands and body that were transparent in that she was not consciously directing their action. If situations were unusual or something went wrong, she would talk of *thinking about what to do* and occasionally *questioning what was done*.

The understanding that changes through learning was not just related to understanding a particular situation or element of professional practice, although it certainly included those. Neither was understanding purely related to the present circumstances or past experiences, although it also included those. Underpinning all of these aspects of understanding was their understanding of being a professional that included all they embodied and expressed through their professional practice. This notion of understanding transcends distinction between action and thought as it allows, and is more basic, than both (Heidegger, 1975/1982, p. 276). Thus, understanding of being a professional underpins all interpretation, reflection, action or interaction as a professional. This is what changes through learning.

All understanding involves preunderstanding. That is, all understanding is grounded in something already understood. As Heidegger (1927/1962) explains, understanding involves not random knowledge, but our accumulated background experiences. Our past experience, including our cultural and professional socialisation, "goes ahead" of us to form our preunderstanding (p. 41). Because of her preunderstanding, a professional can notice if a client does not respond as expected, interpreting what happens as a problem requiring another course of action. The findings highlight that such prior understanding changes when learning occurs, so that an altered understanding is brought to the next situation. Understanding even allows people to be aware of when they do not understand something (p. 385). The participants describe not knowing or uncertainty in situations where they learn, but they need a certain understanding of being a professional to be aware of not knowing.

Drawing on Heidegger, then, understanding of being a professional permeates and shapes all that a professional is and does in their professional life. This understanding, that changes through learning, is embodied in practice, as described in constituent two.

### 7.1.3.2 Embodied Engagement in Practice

Understanding is embodied in the experiences of learning described in the study. The therapists' descriptions of learning used many phrases implying embodiment: *I feel, I sense, I see, my gut reaction.* Their change in understanding revolved around notions of active doing, which is why I grouped them under the headings of *knowing what to do, thinking about what to do* and *questioning what was done.* No analysis of learning as a professional could do these experiences justice without overt reference to their embodied nature. Our embodied experience in the world has an ontological dimension: an expression of being. As Merleau-Ponty (1945/2002, p. 231) describes: "I am my body ... and yet at the same time my body is ... a provisional sketch of my total being".

Learning through active engagement in professional practice appears self-evident. It is worth noting that the action involved in learning includes both thinking and doing in participants' accounts. Understanding as described above provides a theoretical account of the shared basis of thinking and doing that avoids a dichotomous relationship. It is not that thinking and doing are the same; they are clearly different, but cannot be separated in APL. Nor can they be separated in practice, and practice is prominent in all accounts of APL. Mary's comments, that she *really understands something* when she can *put it into practice,* resonate with Heidegger's account that understanding is revealed through everyday practice (Dreyfus, 1991, p. 184).

As mentioned in Chapter 3, Merleau-Ponty (1964) questions the privileged position of rationality, arguing that all rational and critical thought arise out of less-articulated forms of embodied experience. Thus the "body", for Merleau-Ponty, refers to the embodied origins of all understanding, thought or experience as inseparable from the world, rather than the body as a purely material substance. Others have drawn on Merleau-Ponty to highlight embodiment as integral to all human experiences (Cheville, 2005; Gallagher, 2005; Ihde, 2002). The embodied nature of professional understanding is described in my research by a focus on learning through engagement in professional practice. My findings support the research of Gloria Dall'Alba and Robyn Barnacle (2005, p. 725) who highlight the ontological nature of "embodied knowing" in higher education, explaining that "embodiment ... facilitates, rather than obstructs, knowing".

### 7.1.3.3 Expressing Shared Interconnection

As embodied beings-in-the-world, an essential constituent of any lived experience is being-with others. Constituent three highlights the social nature of APL through the interconnection of experiences with others over time. All interactions with others in learning involve embodied expressions, including speech. In fact, speech can be viewed as an expression of embodied understanding. Merleau-Ponty (1945/2002, p. 209) states that the speaker usually does not think while speaking as "his speech is his thought". Embodied understanding does not need to be shared through face-to-face interactions. For example, many of Sam's most important learning experiences were through interactions with her internet community. Sam did not gain random information from the internet. From her understanding of being a professional, which is particularly open to learning through challenging assumptions, she deliberately sought international colleagues to learn with. Her interaction with her virtual network is also an expression of her particular embodied understanding of being a professional.

Interactions between professionals in learning involve sharing experiences. As described in Chapter 3, Gadamer (1965/1979) illuminates the place of dialogic conversation in understanding others when experiences are shared. According to Gadamer, people have a horizon of understanding that defines what they can understand from their current perspective (p. 269). This horizon changes with experiences and interaction (and learning). When understanding is truly shared in communication, horizons merge (p. 273). Gadamer (p. 341) describes the ontological nature of true communication as changing our very being:

> To reach an understanding with one's partner in a dialogue is not merely a matter of total self-expression and the successful assertion of one's own point of view, but a transformation into a communion, in which we do not remain what we were.

This description is uncannily reminiscent of those participants whose own understanding was transformed through being able to imagine another's perspective in learning. For example, Olivia's descriptions in the vignette in Chapter 5, describe how her professional understanding changed through imagining the carer's point of view, allowing a shared understanding of what was possible in that situation.

### 7.1.3.4  Possibilities of Circumscribed Openness

As stated, understanding forms the basis of a person's ability to adapt to changing circumstances. Heidegger's concept of understanding is orientated towards possibilities (Elliott, 2005, p. 118). Drawing on Heidegger, Jörgen Sandberg (2001, p. 18) explains how "understanding constitutes not only our doing and being, but also our possibilities of doing and being something at all".

People's understanding of social situations and roles they take up in the world determine which possibilities they see as feasible in certain circumstances. Thus understanding is about "being ready in particular circumstances to respond appropriately to whatever might normally come along" (Dreyfus, 1991, p. 103). It is not just possible choices for any given concrete situation that Heidegger (1927/1962, p. 385) is referring to, rather he talks about understanding as being central to broader possibilities for being as "Dasein always knows understandingly what it is capable of". The possibilities for being are not limited to cognition, but concern who one is capable of being in particular situations. Choice is possible within this circumscription of possibilities, as I discuss in the following section with reference to Heidegger's notion of "authenticity".

The range of possibilities available allows "room for manoeuvre" with respect to feasible choices to make (Dreyfus, 1991, p. 186). Thus what it makes sense to do as a female speech pathologist working with clients with intellectual impairment is limited to certain horizons of possibility. Only certain possibilities present themselves to her as meaningful and doable within given circumstances. Depending on her previous background experiences, her current involvement, the significance of the current situation – that is, her current understanding of being a speech pathologist – she makes certain choices. Hubert Dreyfus (p. 188) describes this clearly: "What I am currently doing makes sense in terms of my self-interpretation. I am thus defined not by my current projects or goals, but by the possibility of being a [professional]".

In constituent four, the openness of APL towards possibilities is circumscribed by the professional's working context. Yet context is not separate from who the professional is. It is the professional's understanding of that context, as part of her understanding of being a professional in the professional world, that circumscribes the possibilities of learning. Thus what my participants described in everyday language is reflected in Heidegger's ontological analysis of experience.

### 7.1.3.5  Summary of Ontological Dimensions of APL

In summary, APL is ontological in that learning involves a change in understanding of being a professional, embodied and expressed through a particular way of being a professional in practice, which allows certain possibilities to appear meaningful and doable. This philosophical description clarifies the ontological nature of the concrete learning experiences described by the participants. Being-a-professional-in-the-professional-world involves a dynamic interplay between the professional and the world, where meaning is intersubjectively constructed through being with others over time. Professionals are socialised into this world through their education, ongoing expectations of professional associations and everyday practice with others. A sense of self as a professional is constructed over time through these interactions, so that habitual structures of meaning develop as a particular way of becoming a professional.

It is not just who a professional is that matters in APL, in the sense that they express learning in idiosyncratic ways related to their way of being a professional. In supporting APL, it is also important that both professionals and other stakeholders have a better awareness of what it means to be a professional, in the current professional world. The value of viewing the ontological dimension of APL through a phenomenological lens, as described above, is that an ontological perspective on being does not privilege the self over the world, but highlights their chiasmic interrelationship. Such an ontological analysis of the findings is not only reflective of the reality of the experience of APL but also allows insight into the professional context as dealt with in Chapter 6 and the way that different ways of being a professional shape learning, as dealt with below.

Two issues, authenticity and transformation, are examined in the following two sections. Different participants' experiences of learning are compared, illustrating the usefulness of a phenomenological ontological analysis of the findings. The experiences of Sally and Nerida, who begin this thesis, are compared with those of Sam and Gina from Part III to describe ways of dealing with dissonance in APL and ways that APL and professional being shape each other.

## 7.2  Authenticity in Professional Learning

All the participants felt they were in some way different from an "ideal" or "real" therapist, as described in Chapter 6. The terms "mavericks" and "impostors" are used to describe how comfortable therapists were with this difference. The way that dissonance between experiences and expectations in APL is dealt with by Sam and Sally is discussed below by contrasting their different ways of being a professional. By doing so, the notion of authenticity is raised.

### 7.2.1  Mavericks and Impostors

Sam's experience depicts a way of learning in terms of being authentic as a professional. She saw the dissonance between her experiences and the official professional expectations as a problem with the current professional culture. In contrast, Sally expressed a way of learning that reflects her feelings of not "good enough" as she compares herself with the established rhetoric about PD responsibilities. It is this comfort or discomfort in different ways of dealing with dissonance in learning that highlights the notion of authenticity, as explained below.

#### 7.2.1.1  Vignette: I'm Never Sure if What I'm Learning Is the Truth

Sally is an experienced professional who likes to know she has done things to the best of her ability, but in interviews and conversations she constantly referred to feeling as though she could always do better. She *loves learning* and sees it as a *professional responsibility, an essential part of being a professional.* For Sally, learning is equivalent to studying in many ways, and she called herself a *continual student.* She described learning as *putting it all logically into my brain so I can give it out to others.* Learning for Sally is about certainty and facts, and she feels uncomfortable with the uncertainty of professional knowledge:

> Studying therapy sometimes frustrates me because the picture is not complete. I'm never sure if what I am learning is the truth or whether it will change in the next few years. I find that frustrating and often cannot get excited about new ideas in case they change.

Although she is recognised by others as competent and experienced, Sally compared herself negatively to her peers in many ways, feeling they were smarter and knew more: *I've always thought that other therapists seem to know heaps, so I'm constantly challenged that I'm not quite up to speed. I'm challenged when other people start talking about something I don't understand.*

Sally described feeling inadequate as a professional in many ways. For example, she commented that she didn't do enough professional reading, compared with her notion of the ideal therapist. Lack of time at work means she can only read professional articles at home, yet she saw this problem as personal, rather than a wider workplace issue. Sally's descriptions reflect a conception of learning as a search for immutable truths that she could study and know in her systematic, logical way. Her feelings of inadequacy seem to be related to a perceived failure to live up to her perception of an ideal therapist who keeps up to date with the research and knows most things.

### 7.2.1.2   Being an Authentic Professional

In contrast, Sam demonstrated being authentic as a professional, as described in her vignette and description of her way of being a professional in Part III. Authenticity, here, refers to being comfortable practicing, valuing and articulating a way of learning as congruent with a way of being a professional.

Sam spoke of acting in congruence with her values and beliefs both as a professional and as a learner. This is very different from Sally who expressed discomfort and inadequacy in the way that she learns, as well as her way of being a professional. Examples of other participants were given earlier, of hiding behind a professional persona or putting on a professional act. These examples indicate a lack of comfort with expressing a certain way of being a professional, or uncertainty about how to be, or who to be, as a professional.

This is not to imply that there is a "correct way" of learning or of being a professional. Part III highlights the idiosyncrasies permeating the shared structure of APL. It is the degree of comfort with expressing this unique quality that is the issue. Professionals such as Sally, Olivia and Gina demonstrated different ways of learning but, through the interviews, all expressed the feeling that by learning in their way they were inadequate, not being a real therapist. Yet all are enthusiastic and responsible about learning as professionals, describing a way of learning that expresses who they are as professionals. This sense of being different from a real therapist is mostly unspoken in professional practice, but internalised as an individual issue.

Sally and Sam differ markedly with respect to conceptions of learning, comfort with uncertainty, openness to being challenged and questioning of workplace constraints. Yet their experiences of learning revealed similarities, as expressed in the structure of APL in terms of changed understanding, engagement with practice, interconnected experiences and circumscribed openness. Their differences, rather than similarities, are highlighted in the vignettes chosen for this book. How comfortable they felt with their own way of learning and its dissonance with professional expectations was very different from each other.

In exploring how APL shapes and is shaped by professional ways of being, authenticity is examined. Referring to Sam, I argue that a sense of authenticity as a professional is necessary for questioning assumptions, dealing with uncertainty, having open conversations and voicing what is valued, all problematic issues in APL as discussed in Chapter 6. It is certainly necessary for resisting the status quo. Heidegger describes authenticity with respect to his analysis of the experience of being human. Although my analysis refers to the experience of learning as a professional, interesting parallels are apparent, as described in the following section.

## *7.2.2  Describing the Concept of Authenticity*

This section examines the social construction of the "ideal" therapist, by exploring authenticity in learning as a professional. I draw on Heidegger and interpretations of his work by others (Ferrara, 1998; Leland, 2001; Mulhall, 1996; Taylor, 1992; Thomson, 2004), in particular Charles Guignon's (2004a, 2004b) insightful analysis of being authentic in contemporary society.

The commonplace notion of authenticity is based on the concept of the self acting in congruence with one's own beliefs, separate from society. Recent years have seen a postmodern scepticism of the notion of an autonomous, cohesive self. In its place is a "polycentric, fluid, contextual" subject (Guignon, 2004b, p. 109). Such a perspective radically challenges the usual notion of authenticity, yet a postmodern sense of the self as a mere "placeholder" in a social context, without agency to act, has also been strongly criticised.

Heidegger's notion of authenticity offers a way of conceptualising a socially and dialogically constructed self, with agency to shape her own life; a person able to change perspectives, yet maintain a coherent sense of self. To explain, I begin with the social construction of self, moving through the impact of the professional world on "professional ways of being" (Dall'Alba, 2004) to the notion of authenticity as it relates to learning as a professional. Such authenticity is not a self-absorbed search for an inner self, but a social awareness of being a professional in the professional world, able to question values and expectations of that world and act in the interests of that world.

### 7.2.2.1  Social Construction of Self

Heidegger (1927/1962) acknowledges a self in his analysis of being-in-the-world, as something with unity and coherence over time, because of its embodied and temporal nature. He talks of self-awareness as "knowledge of the self" (p. 186), but never self-sufficiency, highlighting the social nature of "knowing oneself" as grounded in "being-with" others (p. 161). In other words, self-awareness involves awareness of what is usually taken for granted, that being enmeshed in the world interacting with others is integral to being human.

Such a conception of self stresses social interaction with others as fundamental to the development of identity (Ferrara, 1998, p. 13; Guignon, 2004b, p. 121). This also applies to the development of professional identity. For example, professionals form opinions through trying them out in the public arena. They stabilise their views over time about what is important to do or know in professional contexts through dialogue with others. Conversation is not only external, but includes self-talk as inner dialogue with real or imagined others, or interaction with texts, as described in this study.

A sense of self as a social and temporal unfolding explains the fluidity and capacity for change within one's self, and also allows for coherence and selfsameness over time as one's own story is shaped within the horizons of a sociocultural context (Guignon, 2004b, p. 126; Mattingly, 1998, p. 154). Participants in this study spoke of this experience of a professional self as having continuity, yet ability to change over time. Mary described herself as *becoming more holistic* professionally, yet it is always the same self she referred to. In discussing the social construction of professional identity in the workplace, Alvesson, 2004 (p. 194) proposes that stable self-identity, or "ontological security", is necessary for well-being in an uncertain working world. Yet being fluid and able to change is also important and is integral to learning.

Thus the professional self has coherence and continuity, yet is fluid and able to change. It is socially constructed through dialogue with others. Agency, or the ability to make choices within this social construction, has not yet been described in this section. Before doing so, the impact of the public professional world on the professional self is examined in more detail.

### 7.2.2.2  Public Professional World

As stated, possibilities for being are drawn from a shared world, with its tradition, customs and values. Possibilities for being a professional are drawn from a specific professional world (such as a speech pathologist working in Australia in 2005). Such shared domains are a "constellation of equipment, practices and concerns" (Dreyfus, 1991, p. 90). Once socialised or educated into a role, everyday practices are accepted as the norm and generally not questioned. These shared domains of practices are similar to those described by Thomas Kuhn (1962/1996) in his description of a "disciplinary matrix" (p. 182) of beliefs and practices shared by members of a professional community (p. 175).

It is through experiencing differences "in appearance, behaviour, lifestyle and opinion" from others in a particular shared world that a sense of self in relation to the shared world develops (Mulhall, 1996, p. 67). The participants of this study described such dialogic experiences through learning with others in the professional world, as they watched, talked with and imagined what others would say: *I learn by watching and talking with them, watching their responses to what I did (Nola).*

Heidegger (1927/1962) talks about the public world in terms of the "they", referring to an amorphous entity rather than a specific group of people. As he describes, absorption in the world of everyday activities usually involves "Being-lost in the publicness of the 'they'" (p. 220). Being part of the public world allows the development of shared norms of behaviour. The positive aspect of publicness allows the world to be intelligible, through shared meanings (Dreyfus, 1991, p. 155). Belonging to a professional community, for example, is important for the participants' sense of identity. New graduates especially spoke of *keeping up with what is new* so they could *join in professional conversations* and generally *fit in*.

The negative aspect of publicness is the "levelling" of conformity, leading to "suppression of all meaningful differences" especially in important matters (Dreyfus, 1991, p. 157). The basis of this conformity "gets obscured" so that certain ways of being are assumed as "familiar" and hence always the "right way" to act (Heidegger, 1927/1962, p. 165). Thus Heidegger refers to the "dictatorship of the 'they'" (p. 164). Gerri's description in this study illustrates this point. She talked about what other professionals, especially those in superior positions, would say about her *intuitive knowing what to do*, noting *they'd gnash their teeth* if they knew. Thus Gerri felt discomfort in expressing the realities of her experience of learning in public forums.

Heidegger (1927/1962) describes falling under the thrall of "tradition", where "tradition keeps [Dasein] from providing its own guidance, whether in inquiring or in choosing...When tradition thus becomes master, it does so in such a way that what it 'transmits'... becomes concealed" (p. 42). This concealing, described by Heidegger as "unobtrusive governance", usually goes unnoticed (Dreyfus, 2004, p. 2). Consequently a real problem with professional socialisation is the way it limits possibilities for acting, knowing, learning and particularly for questioning. However, although it is usually taken for granted, it is possible to illuminate and critique such governance.

There are two problems with professional socialisation with respect to APL. One is the negative self-concepts that many of the participants form in comparing themselves to the amorphous professional "they". The other problem is that because professional socialisation is invisible it is barely discussed, let alone questioned in professional forums. Yet without questioning or challenging there is no open debate and little change. As Gadamer (1965/1979, p. 326) reminds us: "To ask a question means to bring into the open".

In other words, people often don't take action to change situations, even if they become difficult, but because of "blinding" to possibilities resort to "mere *wishing*" and bury themselves in activities of the world (Heidegger, 1927/1962, p. 239). How does a professional break out of such conformity if merging with the normal way of doing things in particular roles in life is part of being human? It may appear to be contradictory to argue that the public social world inhibits authentically being oneself, but also shapes self-identity. To explain, I describe being authentic as a professional, drawing on Heidegger and Guignon.

### 7.2.2.3  Being Authentic

For Heidegger, being human can be authentic arising out of "one's own self" or inauthentic as belonging to the "they". Although he maintains that Dasein's everyday way of being (as absorbed in the world) is inauthentic, Heidegger does not denigrate it, but points to the possibility of an authentic existence as "a deepening of the self-understanding expressed in everydayness" (MacAvoy, 2001, p. 455).

Heidegger describes being lost in the public everyday world, keeping busy with constant activity, until an awareness or moment of insight about another way of being occurs. Although Heidegger gives an example of this insight relating to anxiety, there are other possible triggers to cause reflection on one's place in the world. A feeling of discomfort, "uncanniness" or "not-being-at-home" is one trigger (Heidegger, 1927/1962, p. 233). It was the relationship between Heidegger's "unsettling" way of being and the dissonance and discomfort participants expressed when comparing themselves to other "real" therapists that led me to explore authenticity. Taking up certain ways of behaving as a professional is often unconscious, but a level of discomfort may be a clue that one is acting in a way that feels inauthentic. Cheryl Mattingly (1998, p. 154) refers to such discomfort in her analysis of occupational therapy practice:

> [There is a] deeply disturbing relationship between trying to live lives which makes sense to us ... and finding our attempts interrupted by the world around us or, equally disconcerting, finding we need to revise our conceptions of what a good life should or could, realistically, be.

As Heidegger (1927/1962, p. 233) says, being absorbed with the "they" is akin to being "tranquilised". When a professional turns away from disquiet into busyness, "the 'not-at-home' gets 'dimmed down'" (p. 234). The following quote resonates with Sally's feelings about her busyness and lack of time at work (see transcript at the end of Chapter 4).

> Busily losing himself in the object of his concern, he loses his time in it too. ... But just as he who exists inauthentically is constantly losing time and never 'has' any, the temporality of authentic existence remains distinctive in that such existence, in its resoluteness, never loses time and 'always has time' (Heidegger, 1927/1962, p. 463).

Being authentic involves facing up to situations, through weighing up possibilities within an understanding of social responsibilities. Heidegger refers to such "resolute" authenticity as "tak(ing) a stand" with awareness of a situation and what is possible (Guignon, 2004a, p. 128). Weighing up a situation within the bigger picture allows people to determine ways of reacting to situations that are aligned with an understanding of what the person and their culture consider to be of value. Taking a stand involves following through insight about possibilities with concrete action, focusing on what is "truly worth pursuing" (Guignon, 2004a, p. 130).

The examples of Sam through this book illustrate taking a stand as a professional. Through a reflexive awareness of what she, her clients and her profession value, she has made choices to act and speak out on behalf of her clients. She questions her own values, and whose interests are being served by her professional practices. She also takes a stand against the conforming pressure of the professional "they" with respect to unrealistic expectations of PD as well as other features of professional life. I describe the authenticity she demonstrates as "reflexive authenticity", drawing from Alessandro Ferrara (1998), as a social and personal construct with a reflective and ethical component. As explained in Chapter 8, reflexive authenticity refers not to a self-indulgent reflection but to awareness of the fundamentally social nature of being a professional with public responsibilities. Such a way of being a professional resonates with the core promise of professionalism, to enhance the public good, as described at the end of Chapter 2 (Freidson, 2001; Sullivan, 1995).

There are references to being an authentic professional or authentic learning in the literature (Barnett, 2004; Cranton, 2006a; Joy Higgs & Titchen, 2001; Laursen, 2005; Manathunga, Smith, & Bath, 2004; Walker, 2001). These authors refer to authentic tasks in learning (as genuine and embedded in real life) or authenticity as a professional (through a congruence of beliefs and actions), or both. Whilst the concept of authenticity described in this section has similarities to aspects described in references above, the authors do not refer to the same context or theoretical framing as this book.

How does a professional in the constant everyday busyness of professional life express authenticity? Despite the conformity of everyday being to the sameness of the "they", Heidegger (1927/1962, p. 239) maintains there is always a choice to grasp one's own being by responding to situations differently, noting that potentiality for authentic being is never "extinguished" but merely concealed. He talks of a moment of vision that illuminates the world as the "clearing" of understanding. Such moments may occur within the calm space of mindful inquiry. Such moments of insight involve "a breaking up of the disguises with which Dasein bars its own way" (Heidegger, p. 167). This statement about disguises is prescient of the participants' talk of hiding the self behind professional masks or cloaks. Transformative moments in learning, when choices are made to examine assumptions behind such disguises, are discussed in the next section.

## 7.3 Transformation Through APL

In this study, different ways of being a professional are evident. Like ways of learning, ways of being a professional are both unique and shared. That is, participants share certain notions of what it means to be a therapist, acquired through socialisation in the shared professional life-world. Yet, as the examples demonstrate, their professional ways of being have a unique quality. The idiosyncratic quality in APL, related to different ways of professional being, is explored in this section through examination of change in learning.

### 7.3.1 Change Through APL Experiences

The changes that occur in APL in this study ranged from small shifts in understanding to profound transformations in ways of considering the world. Thus, after a particular experience, Nola understood herself as a therapist who was better at making splints, whereas Olivia's altered understanding of communication affected all areas of her life. In demonstrating different changes in understanding through learning, the experiences of Nerida and Gina are compared below.

The following vignette about Nerida has two purposes. The first is to illustrate how less experienced professionals in this study learnt to be professionals through learning to do what professionals do at work. The second purpose is to describe different types of change through APL, postulating reasons for such differences. In the vignette, Nerida describes learning as a relatively new graduate, and how cumulative changes in understanding shaped her way of being a professional over time. A dialectic between learning and being, as expressed in Heidegger's work, is illustrated by this section and in other examples through this book.

#### 7.3.1.1 Vignette: Learning to Do What a Professional Does

At the time of this study, Nerida had graduated 18 months previously, and since then had worked with a cohort of adult clients with disabilities. All the clients were residential in small group homes with their day-to-day care undertaken by support staff. For Nerida, the experience of learning as a professional was permeated with the feeling of being relatively inexperienced in a fairly isolated and challenging situation. She described having *so little knowledge* of this area when she began that she *really didn't know where to start* with a client when she got a referral.

Nerida initially tried to learn through intensive reading, but even after a year of working she still felt like she *wanted to bury myself in a mountain of books and just keep trying to learn.* Over time, Nerida felt she gained *more theoretical knowledge* as well as *practical experience*, but was *still learning how to put that knowledge into practice.* She would like to put more ideas into action instead of just thinking about them, noting: *You can theorize about whether or not something's going to work but you can't actually know until you try it.* When you do try something, she continued, *you can learn a lot from what goes wrong.*

Describing herself as an *idealist*, Nerida became a therapist because she wanted to contribute *positively to people's lives.* Currently, however, she finds her work *really challenging* and *a bit demoralizing* due to staffing problems and misunderstandings with support staff that result in her achieving less change for clients than she would like. She felt she was *not completely prepared* for working in that environment, but has learnt to cope to some extent by being more realistic about where she can and can't *make a difference, and trying not to get so bogged down worrying about the stuff that I really can't do all that much about.*

Nerida described her experience of learning as *cumulative*, occurring *over time*, from *lots of small situations*, such as the incident beginning this book. Many aspects of learning at work, which Nerida described as crucial to learning what to do as a professional, don't fall within the usual expectations of PD, such as learning about working with others with different perspectives, as well as learning to cope with challenging and uncertain situations.

For example, Nerida felt her communication skills have improved since she began working. She feels she is more *assertive* as well as being a *better listener.* Through talking with others at work, she has learnt more about hidden agendas underlying some practices at work and has been able to *find the real meaning behind things, instead of just taking things at face value.* This has helped her develop strategies to cope with some of the misunderstandings between herself and other staff that affected her practice. She summarised what she has learnt over her time at work as learning *to be more resilient*, as well as learning about herself. It could be said that, through learning at work, her way of being a professional is being constructed.

### 7.3.1.2 Way of Being a Professional

As described earlier, professional understanding changes through an ongoing dialectic as professionals continually re-orientate to changing circumstances. Professionals affect the life-world through activities and are affected by this shared world. Thus this notion of understanding of being a professional is fluid and malleable. Yet, as described in relation to authenticity, there is some sense of understanding of being one's self that remains constant. Understanding of being a professional, therefore, is malleable to change, whilst retaining a core continuity over time.

Understanding of being a professional is enacted and expressed through different ways of practicing as a professional. Through ongoing professional socialisation and everyday practice, as Nerida described, certain ways of understanding and acting as a professional become her way of being a professional. Drawing on Heidegger, Dall'Alba (2004, p. 680) describes how understanding constitutes a "professional way of being":

> Understanding is embedded within the dynamic, intersubjective flow that is practice. Accordingly, understanding of professional practice is enacted in and through practice. It constitutes, then, a professional way-of-being that is afforded meaning within the particular traditions of practice of which it forms a part.

In drawing from the findings of this study, my interpretation of Dall'Alba's professional way of being refers to a notion that is neither as transitory as just being able to respond to a specific context nor as fixed as an entrenched belief system. Rather, it is a way of relating to the world, which becomes part of the context of that world in an ongoing dialectic exchange, that has at its core a continuous sense of professional self. Thus, whilst having a core sense of being a certain type of professional, a professional way of being is malleable to changing circumstances, through experiences of learning.

Both Nerida's and Gina's professional way of being changed. In the vignette about Gina in Chapter 5, she describes a profound transformation in her way of being a professional through particular learning experiences. As with Nerida, Gina's professional understanding had changed in many ways over her professional life as she learnt, both constructing and shaping her way of being a therapist. However, in contrast to Nerida, the transitional situations Gina describes in the vignette involved a significant transformation in her entire way of being a therapist, so that she saw "everything" differently; her understanding of herself as a professional and her way of practicing were all profoundly transformed.

Some of the participants described similar transformative change. Two aspects are common to these descriptions of transformation. First, the professional actively questioned assumptions about being a therapist in a particular context. Second, the professional was involved with a workplace that supported open inquiry and reflexive thinking. Gina describes how questions, raised from her practice and a course she attended, challenged core notions of what she did and who she was as a therapist. She shared her doubts and questions with colleagues in an open and supportive environment. Nerida's workplace provided little collegial support and few opportunities to question her practice. Although both therapists described changes in professional understanding, Gina's changes were experienced as being transformative.

There are other differences between these two vignettes related to level of experience. Because of the small number of participants in this study, only tentative suggestions are made about such transformative situations, but findings from other research presented throughout the book allow firmer claims about the value of support and challenge in facilitating transformative learning.

## 7.3.2 Transformative Learning

Learning can transform being. This notion has been given consideration in the adult education literature, since a United Nations report into the future of education (Faure et al., 1972). Entitled "Learning to be", it proposed that education over a person's life should address the whole person, not just their mind, attending to the notion of what it means to be human (see also Dawson, 2003). More recent examples of transformative adult learning can be found in research (Cranton, 2006b; Leonard & Willis, 2008; Rehorick & Bentz, 2008; Willis, McKenzie, & Harris, 2009).

Jack Mezirow's (2000, p. 22) notion of transformative learning describes various phases, beginning with "a disorientating dilemma" and ending with "reintegration" of a different perspective into a person's life. These stages involve self-examination, questioning assumptions, recognition of feelings, looking at options and experimenting with them in particular situations. He describes different forms of transformative learning, ranging from those involving overt and recognisable processes of action learning to others more akin to a philosophical or psychoanalytical process (p. 23). Such learning can be facilitated, as he describes and I discuss in Chapter 8, in situations with a balance between support and trust in learning relationships, and questioning and challenging of assumptions underlying learning.

Change through APL in this study can be conceptualised in two ways, as change in understanding within a particular professional way of being (e.g. Nerida) and as transformation to a substantially different professional way of being (e.g. Gina). Dall'Alba and Sandberg (2006) refer to similar concepts of change. They comment that change in professional practice usually occurs within a particular way of understanding professional practice (reinforcement of practice) rather than involving a shift to a different way of understanding (renewal of practice).

Researchers have noted the difficulties of facilitating transformation of professional practice, often referred to in terms of a paradigm shift. As mentioned in Chapter 2, there has been a change in focus in therapy over the past decade, moving from "helping" patients to improve to "supporting" clients towards self-determination. Researchers have reflected on the difficulty of supporting therapists to make such transformations (Trede & Higgs, 2003). Transformation to a different way of being a professional requires significant change in professional understanding. Sandberg (2001, p. 22) notes that shifting to a different professional understanding requires interruption and challenge to the circular and reinforcing nature of previous understanding.

The need to move beyond constraints of habitual patterns of thought, through critically reflective practices that challenge assumptions, was raised in Chapter 2, as being necessary for transformative learning (e.g. Antonacopoulou, 2004; Brookfield, 2005; Cranton, 1997; Isopahkala-Bouret, 2008; Trede, Higgs, Jones, &

Edwards, 2003). Of course, as Christopher Day (1993, p. 88) points out, reflection is a "necessary but not sufficient condition" for such changes, continuing that "confrontation either by self or others must occur". Here confrontation could be construed as challenge. Ways in which a combination of challenge and support could facilitate transformative change in professional being, including the possibility of being authentic, are discussed in Chapter 8.

## 7.4  Values in Professional Life

In summary, APL is an ontological matter beyond its epistemological concerns. The argument in this chapter is that APL is integral to being a professional, constructing and shaping a professional way of being, and vice versa. Whilst drawing attention to ontological dimensions of APL, I am cognizant of its epistemological dimensions. Purely focusing on epistemology to gain insight into learning conceals the ontological foundations of learning found in differing professional ways of being. By considering what it means to be a professional and the dialectic between learning and being described in the idiosyncratic examples of learning in this chapter, I am not ignoring knowledge in professional learning. Instead, these examples draw attention to the way in which "who the professional is" shapes her learning and knowing: a matter that usually receives scant attention.

At the end of Chapter 2, as well as in this and the previous chapter, concerns about values have been raised. I have discussed tensions between what is valued by professionals and by their workplaces, and how competing life-world discourses place value on differing aspects of professional life. Axiology, the study of values, is not a primary concern of this book. It is the searching for, revealing and questioning of assumptions underpinning implicit values that are of significance in supporting APL. The need to question whose interests are served by acting in accordance with particular values is the axiological concern here, not the prescription of certain values as sometimes occurs in "value-driven" organisational enterprises (e.g. Alvesson & Sveningsson, 2008, p. 75).

Values permeate and shape our lives determining what we see as worthwhile in individual and community life (Dunn, 2006; Hart, 1971). Values are related to ethics, morals and notions of "the common good" in various ways. Although a matter of debate, this notion of common or public good is very different from that of good or best practice as articulated in the prescriptive quality assurance discourse (Coffield & Edward, 2009). Individual values such as freedom are inextricably linked to social values such as justice in an interconnected moral web (Prilleltensky & Prilleltensky, 2006, p. 54). The role of values in inquiry and the consideration that social well-being should guide judgements were central to Dewey's philosophy of learning (Hart, p. 38). For professionals, values shape how they make judgements and take action according to what they consider matters for their clients, their profession, organisations for which they work and also society.

The profundity of Heideggers' ontology is his examination of the essential nature of the question of being human. For Heidegger, ontological concerns are prior to those of epistemology or axiology (Geniusas, 2009, p. 69; Stenstad, 2006, p. 183). To reiterate it is our understanding of being that allows our actions in the world to have value and meaning. An ontological understanding of being a professional can inform epistemological understandings about professional knowledge and axiological understandings about values and ethics in learning to be a professional. In addition, awareness of the ontological dimensions of APL can lead to practical implications for supporting professionals as they learn.

There is a need for more public discourse about being a professional in the current context. Through such discussion, problematic issues within APL, as well as those wider than APL, such as the impact of competing life-world discourses, could be revealed as a shared rather than private concern. Such a move requires a culture of inquiry. There is also a need of support for a reflexive way of being a professional in the world with others, able to consider possibilities and take a stand about what matters. That is, there is a need for support for authenticity in professional life. Support for APL, which involves reflexive authenticity in a culture of inquiry, is discussed in Chapter 8.

# References

Alvesson, M. (2004). *Knowledge work and knowledge-intensive firms*. Oxford; New York: Oxford University Press.

Alvesson, M., & Sveningsson, S. (2008). *Changing organizational culture: Cultural change work in progress*. New York: Routledge.

Antonacopoulou, E. (2004). The dynamics of reflexive practice: The relationship between learning and changing. In M. Reynolds & R. Vince (Eds.), *Organizing reflection* (pp. 47–64). Hampshire; Burlington, VT: Ashgate.

Barnett, R. (2004). Learning for an unknown future. *Higher Education Research and Development, 23*(3), 247–260.

Billett, S. (2008a). Learning throughout working life: A relational interdependence between personal and social agency. *British Journal of Educational Studies, 56*(1), 39–58.

Billett, S. (2008b). Subjectivity, learning and work: Sources and legacies. *Vocations and Learning, 1*(2), 149–171.

Brook, A. (2009). The potentiality of authenticity in becoming a teacher. *Educational Philosophy and Theory, 41*(1), 46–59.

Brookfield, S. (2005). *The power of critical theory for adult learning and teaching*. Maidenhead: Open University Press.

Cheville, J. (2005). Confronting the problem of embodiment. *International Journal of Qualitative Studies in Education, 18*(1), 85–107.

Coffield, F., & Edward, S. (2009). Rolling out 'good', 'best' and 'excellent' practice. What next? Perfect practice? *British Educational Research Journal, 5*(3), 371–390.

Cranton, P. (Ed.). (1997). *Transformative learning in action: Insights from practice*. San Francisco: Jossey-Bass.

Cranton, P. (2006a). *Authenticity in teaching*. San Francisco: Jossey-Bass.

Cranton, P. (2006b). *Understanding and promoting transformative learning: A guide for educators of adults* (2nd ed.). San Francisco: Jossey-Bass.

Dall'Alba, G. (2004). Understanding professional practice: Investigations before and after an educational programme. *Studies in Higher Education, 29*(6), 679–692.

Dall'Alba, G. (2009). Learning professional ways of being: Ambiguities of becoming. *Educational Philosophy and Theory, 41*(1), 34–45.

Dall'Alba, G., & Barnacle, R. (2005). Embodied knowing in online environments. *Educational Philosophy and Theory, 37*(5), 719–744.

Dall'Alba, G., & Barnacle, R. (2007). An ontological turn for higher education. *Studies in Higher Education, 32*(6), 679–691.

Dall'Alba, G., & Sandberg, J. (2006). Unveiling professional development: A critical review of stage models. *Review of Educational Research, 76*(3), 383–412.

Dawson, J. (2003). Lifelong learning and T. S. Eliot's Four Quartets. *Studies in Continuing Education, 25*(1), 113–124.

Day, C. (1993). Reflection: A necessary but not sufficient condition for professional development. *British Educational Research Journal, 19*(1), 83–92.

Dreyfus, H. L. (1991). *Being-in-the-world: A commentary on Heidegger's Being and Time, Division I.* Cambridge, MA: MIT Press.

Dreyfus, H. L. (2000). Could anything be more intelligible than everyday intelligibility? Reinterpreting Division I of Being and Time in the light of Division II. *Appropriating Heidegger.* Retrieved February 12, 2005, from http://ist-socrates.berkeley.edu/~hdreyfus/rtf/Heidegger-Intelligibility_1099.rtf

Drefus, H. L. (2004). Being and Power: Heidegger and Foucalt. Retrieved February 7, 2009, from http://ist-socrates.berkeley.edu/~hdreyfus/html/paper_being.html

Dunn, R. (2006). *Values and the reflective point of view: On expressivism, self-knowledge and agency.* Aldershot; Burlington, VT: Ashgate.

Elliott, B. (2005). *Phenomenology and imagination in Husserl and Heidegger.* London: Routledge.

Ewing, R., & Smith, D. (2001). Doing, knowing, being and becoming: The nature of professional practice. In J. Higgs & A. Titchen (Eds.), *Professional practice in health, education and the creative arts* (pp. 16–28). Oxford: Blackwell Science.

Faure, E., Herrera, F., Kaddoura, A., Lopes, H., Petrovsky, A., Rahnema, M., et al. (1972). *Learning to be: The world of education today and tomorrow.* Paris: UNESCO.

Ferrara, A. (1998). *Reflective authenticity: Rethinking the project of modernity.* London; New York: Routledge.

Freidson, E. (1986). *Professional powers: A study of the institutionalization of formal knowledge.* Chicago: University of Chicago Press.

Freidson, E. (2001). *Professionalism: The third logic.* Chicago: University of Chicago Press.

Gadamer, H. G. (1965/1979). *Truth and method* (2nd ed.). London: Sheed & Ward.

Gallagher, S. (2005). *How the body shapes the mind.* Oxford; New York: Clarendon Press.

Geniusas, S. (2009). Ethics as a second philosophy, or the traces of the pre-ethical in Heidegger's Being and Time. *Santalka Filosofija, 17*(3), 62–69. Retrieved October 10, 2009, from http://www.coactivity.vgtu.lt/.../62-70_santalka_2009_3_geniusas.pdf

Guignon, C. B. (2004a). Becoming a self: The role of authenticity in Being and Time. In C. B. Guignon (Ed.), *The existentialists* (pp. 119–132). New York: Rowman & Littlefield Publishers.

Guignon, C. B. (2004b). *On being authentic.* London; New York: Routledge.

Hart, S. H. (1971). Axiology: Theory of values. *Philosophy and Phenomenological Research, 32*(1), 29–41.

Heidegger, M. (1927/1962). *Being and time* (J. Macquarrie & E. Robinson, Trans., 1st English ed.). London: SCM Press.

Heidegger, M. (1975/1982). *The basic problems of phenomenology* (A. Hofstadter, Trans.). Bloomington, IN: Indiana University Press.

Higgs, J., & McAllister, L. (2005). The lived experiences of clinical educators with implications for their preparation, support and professional development. *Learning in Health and Social Care, 4*(3), 156–171.

Higgs, J., & Titchen, A. (Eds.). (2001). *Professional practice in health, education and the creative arts.* Oxford: Blackwell Science.

Ihde, D. (2002). *Bodies in technology.* Minneapolis, MN: University of Minnesota Press.

Inwood, M. J. (2000). *Heidegger: A very short introduction.* Oxford; New York: Oxford University Press.

Isopahkala-Bouret, U. (2008). Transformative learning in managerial role transitions. *Studies in Continuing Education, 30*(1), 69–84.

Kleiman, S. (2008). *Human centered nursing: The foundation of quality care.* Philadelphia, PA: F. A. Davis.

Kuhn, T. S. (1962/1996). *The structure of scientific revolutions* (3rd ed.). Chicago: University of Chicago Press.

Laursen, P. F. (2005). The authentic teacher. In D. Beijaard, P. Meijer, G. Morine-Dershimer, & H. Tillema (Eds.), *Teacher professional development in changing conditions* (pp. 199–212). Dordrecht: Springer.

Leland, D. (2001). Conflictual culture and authenticity: Deepening Heidegger's account of the social. In N. J. Holland & P. Huntington (Eds.), *Feminist interpretations of Martin Heidegger* (pp. 109–127). University Park, PA: Pennsylvania State University Press.

Leonard, T., & Willis, P. (Eds.). (2008). *Pedagogies of the imagination mythopoetic curriculum in educational practice.* Netherlands: Springer.

MacAvoy, L. (2001). Overturning Cartesianism and the hermeneutics of suspicion: Rethinking Dreyfus on Heidegger. *Inquiry, 44,* 455–480.

Manathunga, C., Smith, C., & Bath, D. (2004). Developing and evaluating authentic integration between research and coursework in professional doctorate programs. *Teaching in Higher Education, 9*(2), 235–246.

Mattingly, C. (1998). *Healing dramas and clinical plots: The narrative structure of experience.* Cambridge; New York: Cambridge University Press.

Merleau-Ponty, M. (1945/2002). *Phenomenology of perception.* London; New York: Routledge Classics.

Merleau-Ponty, M. (1964). The primacy of perception and its philosophical consequences. In J. M. Edie (Ed.), *The primacy of perception and other essays on phenomenological psychology, the philosophy of art, history, and politics* (pp. 12–42). Evanston, IL: Northwestern University Press.

Mezirow, J. (Ed.). (2000). *Learning as transformation: Critical perspectives on a theory in progress.* San Francisco: Jossey-Bass.

Mulhall, S. (1996). *Routledge philosophy guidebook to Heidegger and Being and time.* London; New York: Routledge.

Parse, R. (2004). Teaching-learning process: A human becoming teaching-learning model. *Nursing Science Quarterly, 17*(1), 33–35.

Peters, M. (2009). Heidegger, phenomenology, education. *Educational Philosophy and Theory, 41*(1), 1–6.

Prilleltensky, I., & Prilleltensky, O. (2006). *Promoting well-being: Linking personal and community change , organizational.* Hoboken, NJ: John Wiley.

Rehorick, D. A., & Bentz, V. M. (Eds.). (2008). *Transformative phenomenology: Changing ourselves and professional practice. Lifeworlds, and professional practice.* Lanham, MD: Lexington Books.

Sandberg, J. (2001). Understanding the basis for competence development. In C. Velde (Ed.), *International perspectives on competence in the workplace* (pp. 9–25). Dordrecht: Kluwer Academic Press.

Sandberg, J., & Pinnington, A. H. (2009). Professional competence as ways of being: An existential ontological perspective. *Journal of Management Studies, 46*(7), 1138–1170.

Stenstad, G. (2006). *Transformations: Thinking after Heidegger.* Madison, WS: University of Wisconsin Press.

Sullivan, W. M. (1995). *Work and integrity: The crisis and promise of professionalism in America.* New York: HarperCollins.

Taylor, C. (1992). *The ethics of authenticity.* Cambridge, MA: Harvard University Press.

Thomson, I. (2001). Heidegger on ontological education, or: How we become what we are. *Inquiry, 44*(3), 243–268.

Thomson, I. (2004). Heidegger's perfectionist philosophy of education in Being and Time. *Continental Philosophy Review*, *37*, 439–467.

Trede, F., & Higgs, J. (2003). Reframing the clinician's role in collaborative clinical decision making: Re-thinking practice knowledge and the notion of clinician-patient relationships. *Learning in Health and Social Care*, *2*(2), 66–73.

Trede, F., Higgs, J., Jones, M., & Edwards, I. (2003). Emancipatory practice: A model for physiotherapy practice? *Focus on Health Professional Education*, *5*(2), 1–13.

Walker, M. (Ed.). (2001). *Reconstructing professionalism in university teaching: Teachers and learners in action*. Philadelphia, PA: Open University.

Wenger, E. (1998). *Communities of practice: Learning, meaning, and identity*. Cambridge; New York: Cambridge University Press.

Wilcock, A. A. (1999). Reflections on doing, being and becoming. *Australian Occupational Therapy Journal*, *46*, 1–11.

Willis, P., McKenzie, S., & Harris, R. (Eds.). (2009). *Rethinking work and learning: Adult and vocational education for social sustainability*. Netherlands: Springer.

# Chapter 8
# Finding a Way Forward

"Authentic Professional Learning" is the term I have used to represent the lived experience of continuing to learn as a professional. This term distinguishes the realities of the experience of PL from the rhetoric about PD expectations, whilst raising the notion of authenticity with respect to dealing with dissonance between the two. This chapter outlines a framework based on this notion of APL, proposing constructive possibilities for supporting professionals as they learn in the current context.

The professionals investigated in this book valued learning, especially within a climate of respect and trust. Their descriptions of APL revealed a complex, multifaceted mix of diverse, intersubjective experiences. The openness and apparent synchronicity of these experiences make it appear that APL is an amorphous part of professional life that cannot be planned. Although APL cannot be controlled, in that you cannot make another person learn, APL can be supported, particularly when there is acknowledgement of its shared essential nature and idiosyncratic qualities.

Chapter 8 integrates research findings from Chapter 5 with arguments from Chapters 6 and 7 about contextual and ontological implications of this research. Recognition of the ontological dimension of APL, in concert with awareness of taken-for-granted features of contemporary professional culture, can suggest a way forward. Considerations in enabling APL are outlined, with diverse, flexible professional learning pathways proposed, drawing on existing models and resources.

As suggested already, one reason for the continuation of traditional PD, despite decades of research about how professionals learn, can be traced to an absence of critical questioning by professionals in contexts that suppress dissent. Another reason for lack of change is one of practicality. How do we devise ways of support that are congruent with the open-ended and idiosyncratic way in which professionals learn, whilst respecting the diversity and complexity of such experiences? Suggestions made in this chapter remain a work in progress in collaboration with other researchers and professionals.

Reshaping traditional PD delivery towards support for APL requires more than a procedural move whereby PD groups are replaced by networks: cultural change would be involved. Changes would be required for workplaces to foster genuine inquiry and for professionals to openly question assumptions about habitual practices. In challenging and reconceptualising PD, a move could be made from a deficit model of delivering knowledge and skills towards a strengths model of supporting capable, independent professional inquiry into practice. Such inquiry has potential value for making a difference in areas that matter for professionals, clients, organisations and society.

## 8.1  Scaffolding Authentic Professional Learning

Two key issues have been discussed with respect to the findings of this research. The first is the problematic nature of current workplace and professional cultures, with a focus on supervision of standards rather than support for APL, where performance rather than understanding in learning is privileged. The second concerns the importance of supporting professionals to feel comfortable learning in their own authentic way, yet challenging them to reflect on and question their practice. These two issues are opposite poles of the same dilemma. That is, how to move forward in a realistic way, that respects and values professionals' ability to direct their own learning, whilst remaining cognizant of the realities of the current context. Issues raised here are recognised as broader than learning, being symptomatic of dilemmas involved in being a professional within the current working milieu.

A balance is not only possible but also desirable. In critiquing teacher PD, Susan Rodriques (2005, p. 8) suggests the need to "walk a fine line between trying to demonstrate accountability and impact, without loss of agency and inquiry". A way of supporting APL needs to be found that is cognizant of the requirements of the contemporary context for evidence and outcomes and sensitive to the need for proposals to be cost and time neutral in today's economic environment. In proposing directions, I draw on examples given by participants in the research, especially those who questioned themselves and their practice.

There are many possible ways in which professionals can be supported to continue learning in an authentic manner. It would be a retrograde step to recommend a particular form of support, equivalent to the "one size fits all' approach critiqued in arguments against the standards and quality agendas (Groundwater-Smith & Mockler, 2009). Learning will always be diverse, a chiasmic relationship between the professionals and their social, cultural and physical contexts. Guiding principles for change are suggested in this section under the headings of awareness as a resource, learning relationships, challenging support, critical capability, intelligent accountability and learning ecologies.

Scaffolding is a metaphor used to describe ways of structuring learning experiences, originally referring to children's learning, and adopted to describe support for workplace learning (e.g. Billett, 2001). As a verb, scaffolding refers to supporting, shaping and sustaining an emerging construction. It is a particularly useful metaphor to describe the guidelines suggested in this section, as they merely provide a conceptual language and framework as a way of venturing meaningfully towards supporting, shaping and sustaining changes to PD. As such the suggestions do not seek to prescribe ways of learning, but propose forms of self-directed inquiry, with professionals free to map their own path within the constraints provided by the constantly changing and uncertain landscape of everyday professional practice.

## 8.1.1 Awareness as a Resource

Although sociocultural transformation is complex, positive change does occur. All change begins with awareness of situations and imaginative ideas about future possibilities. In discussing educational change, Michael Apple (2001, p. 229) describes hope as a resource for supporting the possibility of transformation towards a better society. I think of awareness as the antecedent of hope.

The first step in supporting professionals as they learn is to highlight the shared nature of APL. It is important to publicly recognise the experience of continuing to learn as complex and multifaceted: involving change in professional understanding through actively engaging in professional practice with others, building an open web of interconnected experiences. There needs to be shared awareness of the diverse ways in which learning is experienced: that learning is not just about attending PD courses and keeping up to date with policy documents or research journals. Recognition of the idiosyncratic quality of APL is vital, with acknowledgement that a professional's way of learning is an expression of her way of being. Recognition of the shared reality of APL is based on awareness of professional experience as holistic, with learning involving the whole person. Being a professional could be recognised as a continuous process of becoming within an ambiguous life-world (Dall'Alba, 2009). Professional knowledge could be recognised as uncertain, and knowing as an open, ongoing inquiry.

I have mentioned Brookfield's (1995, p. 229) notion of the "impostor" syndrome, where professionals feel they don't know everything and fear being "found out". Brookfield describes a tendency in this situation for professionals to blame themselves when they don't know what to do, so they are less willing to ask for help. Evidence of impostorship was certainly found in many of the participants' descriptions of learning in my research. Brookfield (2000, p. 66) stresses the vital importance of making this phenomenon public knowledge rather than hidden doubt, arguing that "once impostorship is named as an everyday experience it loses much of its power". Brookfield (1995, p. 247) criticises the culture of silence, secrecy and individualism within the teaching profession. This critique can also be considered a valid criticism of the professional culture in therapy and many other professions.

For example, there is considerable critique currently about what is perceived as pressure towards mute compliance in academic culture (Davies, 2005; Jones, 2007; Rowland, 2006; Sparkes, 2007). Robert Holden (2009) refers to "a habit of silence" amongst academics, which conceals their deeply held values when they step into the public arena. Compliance in professional cultures leads professionals to hide values and concerns behind a professional persona, fearing that to voice them would be considered unprofessional. Susan Groundwater-Smith and Nicole Mockler (2009) argue, with respect to teacher PL, that it takes courage to speak out about moral concerns. Trust, "the bedrock of professional collegiality", is essential for sharing concerns, as such sharing is risky, exposing professionals' inner values (p. 31). They note that "authentic professional learning takes courage" (p. 40).

In a climate of respect and trust, open dialogue that questions assumptions and ways of acting and knowing can also be shared. Support for APL involves acceptance of the uncertainty of not knowing, as crucial to being open to learn. There would be an awareness of the shared dissonance that currently exists between the experiences of learning and professional expectations. In such a climate dissonance could be voiced, questioned and resisted. It is important that there is not only awareness of current experiences but also conversations about possibilities for change, to a culture where professionals feel valued and inquiry is supported. It is important when highlighting "what is" not to neglect "what might be" (Apple, 2000, p. 250).

Breaking habits of silence with respect to PD requires public dissemination and discussion about experiences of learning, at policy, management and practitioner levels of an organisation. In addition to publication of academic research, there is a need for stories of experiences to be shared between practitioners. Whilst academic discourse has its place, shared awareness of APL involves recognition of daily realities using everyday voices, as described in Part III. For change to be enacted, professionals need to be able to imagine practical changes are possible. Professionals need to be able to "picture them[selves] in action in daily situations", in different ways (Apple, p. 252). A climate of respect and trust within which to share experiences highlights the central importance of relationships to APL. If shared awareness is the start of change, relationships provide the crucial catalyst for sustainable change in support for learning.

## 8.1.2  Learning Relationships

As APL is a social phenomenon, learning relationships are central to a framework of support for APL. Relationships that supported learning in this research involved a fluid mix of interactions. I use the word relationships rather than communities, groups, networks or mentors, as interactions that support learning take many forms. Relationships could involve, for example, one person reading texts, a group of friends, the staff at an entire work site or a virtual online network. David Boud and colleagues (Boud, Cohen, & Sampson, 2001) describe peer learning relationships as networks: a concept more akin to the fluid web of learning relationships described in my study than that of communities. Such relationships need to be nurtured rather than imposed on professionals. That is, it is important that professionals have a sense of ownership and choice about developing learning relationships, so they can remain fluid, varying to suit changing needs.

Numerous articles discuss the value of different forms of relationships for learning. Although widely supported in the literature, some researchers have critiqued the unproblematic way in which new vehicles for developing relationships to support learning, such as communities of practice or mentor programmes, may be enthusiastically adopted without consideration of issues of power, coercion or trust (e.g. Burgh & Yorshansky, 2009; Fenwick, 2008a; Manathunga, 2007; Wood, 2007). There are also potential problems in artificially creating learning relationships or in colonising existing learning relationships that have developed organically at work.

As evidenced in my research and that of others, it is the quality of the relationship rather than the form of such collaborations that is important. The key feature of such relationships is mutual trust, where professionals can express doubt or uncertainty, excitement or passion about their learning or practice, without fear of being devalued or belittled. They can be "who they are" as professionals without needing to hide that reality. Successful learning relationships also enable responsibilities to be shared. In arguing for support for APL, I am not overlooking the crucial responsibilities that are part of being a professional. Participants in this study were aware of their responsibilities to clients, peers and the general community. When professionals are supported and valued, the importance of, and difficulties in fulfilling, responsibilities can also be discussed. When experiences are shared in supportive relationships, open dialogue and questioning of even basic assumptions can be entertained. Through authentic learning relationships, dissonance can be made public, idiosyncrasies accepted and possibilities explored. Such relationships allow a "place of possibility" (Gillespie, 2005).

Dialogue is at the heart of relationships that are generative of ideas and productive for learning. Referring to empirical research into teacher PL, Andrew Metcalfe and Ann Game (2008) demonstrated that "genuine" dialogue occurred when professionals shifted from defensive positions towards reciprocal openness to possibilities, through mutual respect of differences. Such relationships are "symbiotic and co-productive", yet reciprocity does not "flatten out differences" between peers (Boud & Lee, 2005, p. 511). Gerri's learning with the members of her multidisciplinary team offers a good example (Section 5.3.4.3), where the ability to see one another's perspectives was developed through non-defensive flexibility in professional boundaries. Ioanna Tsivacou (2005) describes relationships within a professional community that allow mutual encouragement and discovery of shared meanings. Such relationships "create in the heart of instrumentality and technical rationality an area devoted to human understanding" (p. 65).

Valuing learning relationships appears to be a "motherhood" statement, as no stakeholder in PD would argue against the value of relationships in learning. Yet the current working context may not nurture such relationships. As participants demonstrated in this research, important ways of developing relationships seem not to be encouraged or valued at work. Relationships develop over time, through working and sharing thoughts together. In particular, some flexibility and autonomy in organising work allows opportunities for the development and maintenance of relationships. In the name of efficiency, lunch breaks were often staggered or staff with similar interests worked on different days to prevent unproductive overlap of services. Heavy workloads, in particular, often stymied opportunities to talk. Yet relationships form the heart of support for APL.

## 8.1.3  Challenging Support

Learning relationships in this framework for APL are not only about support but also involve challenge and questioning of assumptions. The combination of challenge and support has been highlighted in variations on the notion of "critical friendship", with respect to learning through reflection on critical incidents, action learning sets and transformative learning (e.g. McGill & Beaty, 2001; Mezirow, 1990; Tripp, 1993). This notion of critical friends has been problematised as a possible contradiction in terms with respect to a tension in purpose between challenge and support (Swaffield & MacBeath, 2005). Drawing on Aristotle's distinctions, Paul Gibbs and Panayiotis Angelides (2008, p. 219) examine three types of critical relationships (friend, companion and acquaintance) with respect to variations in the continuity, equality and trust in the relationship. They note that all three may be useful for different purposes in supporting professional inquiry.

In an empirical study, Angie Titchen (2000, p. 111) uses the term "critical companionship" as a metaphor for the facilitation of experiential learning of nurses at work. She describes a nurse facilitator using a combination of "high challenge" with "high support" enabling a "critical dialogue" to be shared (p. 123). The learning relationship involves the use of open, challenging questions to support the nurse's reflection, allowing her to critically examine assumptions and explore other perspectives. The relationship is highly supportive involving "being with" the other, empathetic listening and humour. This description is similar to Sam's discussion of her support of other professionals' learning in her role as an experienced therapist. Like Titchen, Sam does not support from the position of expert, but asks questions, probes and critically evaluates situations in a productive way that does not belittle others' perspectives.

> I tell them "I value what you're saying. I'm not the expert" and I talk the issues through, and also say "I'm learning from you as well". I hate the specialist expert mode. I can't function like that. Also underlying that I basically respect other team members, my knowledge basis is only as valid as the last client I saw, and I guess I find humour helps. If it doesn't go well, humour can defuse the situation.

In the formative period of professional work, a formal facilitator, such as a mentor, provides valuable support that may challenge assumptions. This role is often undertaken by a supervisor. As mentioned, despite a need to maintain standards, facilitation of learning and supervision are potentially conflicting purposes (Hughes, 2004). Once power or lack of trust enters a learning relationship, the openness required for questioning may dissipate. Titchen's (2000) facilitation through critical companionship is described as constructive and empowering for the professional concerned. In a similarly constructive manner, Yolanda Wadsworth (2001), as leader of an action research group, describes different ways of providing guidance to suit different participants and stages of the process. All of these ways were based not on supervision but on "stewardship without control" (p. 420).

In addition to the role of more experienced professionals, supportive challenge is also possible between peers. As described in my study and supported by other research, a professional learns not only from those with more experience but also from those with different experiences, even from new graduates (Fuller & Unwin, 2004). Professionals can learn from working together informally as well as from more structured peer review (Harris, Farrell, Bell, Devlin, & James, 2009). In any peer relationship that challenges as well as supports, reciprocity is important.

The value of challenging support in learning is the possibilities it opens for transformation (E. W. Taylor, 2008). In relation to APL, it is apparent that some changes in understanding involve profound transformations in a professional's way of being. In my research, these changes occurred in situations where professionals questioned or challenged their practice as part of learning. Learning facilitators may be charged with challenging professionals to transform their way of practicing, as part of a change management process, in response to changing societal or professional expectations. For example, a shift has occurred in teaching from teacher as instructor to teacher as facilitator; in therapy a shift is under way from therapist as expert to therapist as guide. All challenge needs to start with support for the professional's current way of being. Yet this is not a frequent occurrence, according to the participants' descriptions and observations of their work environments in this research.

In addition, to move to a different way of professional being, the professional has to care about change and see it as relevant to what matters, which in this study was making a difference to the lives of clients. In other words, learning that involves a challenge to change requires a sense of agency and ownership, and the change needs to hold meaning and value for participants (Alvesson & Sveningsson, 2008; Fullan, 2007). As Sam said, referring to challenges to change through learning: *You only invest your personal commitment if you're part of that decision making process.*

### 8.1.4 Critical Capability

The development of professionals has been compared to third world community development, in critiquing the way that processes are imposed on those deemed deficient, thereby devaluing and undermining local context-sensitive knowledge (McWilliam, 2002). Another way of considering this comparison would be to draw on innovative, successful models of community development in reshaping PD. For example, in common with community development programmes, central policy implementation has been found to be ineffective in producing sustainable change in PD programmes in health and education. Working in a flexible way with local communities, building on grassroots initiatives, has proved to be more successful in changing these practices (e.g. Meads, Jones, Harrison, Forman, & Turner, 2009; Oakes & Rogers, 2007). Increasingly, effective community development processes focus on building the capacity or capability of local communities for self-determination.

In discussing support for learning, it is worth noting differences between capacity and capability. Although one may talk of organisational capacity, the term "human capacity", as used in organisational learning, reinforces the notion of a person as a container to be filled. Although the development of people's capability can be considered in the same instrumental manner, the functional capability model of community development, devised by economist Amartya Sen (1992, 1999), is broader. The notions of freedom, agency and well-being are interlinked in Sen's (1992, p. 56) approach, with capability representing a person's freedom to achieve well-being. Freedom requires agency to make "genuine" choices from amongst a range of "doings and beings," acting in a direction that, for that person, makes life "worthwhile" (Sen, 1999, p. 44). By agency, Sen refers to a person's ability to make informed choices to pursue goals that person "has reason to value" (1992, p. 5). Sen's perspective stresses self-determination as directly conducive to well-being.

There is increasing interest in this notion of capability development for students in education (e.g. Hinchcliffe & Terzi, 2009). Melanie Walker (2006, p. 27) has framed Sen's approach with relevance for higher education pedagogy, with capability encompassing what people are "actually free to be and do", rather than a narrow conception of their attributes, such as knowledge, competence or performance. She maintains that the capability approach "offers a compelling counterweight to neo-liberal human capital interpretations and practices of higher education as only for economic productivity and employment" (p. 42). Recently, Walker (2009a) has proposed a theoretical "alliance" between Sen's capability framework and critical pedagogy, describing both approaches as concerned with "human flourishing". She argues from this alliance for the interrelated development of students' agency and well-being, whilst working towards social justice and change that enhances the public good. Simon Marginson (2008, p. 287) has also drawn from Sen's model with respect to academic agency, in arguing for the value of "self-determining academic freedom" to support innovative advances in knowledge. He draws on Sen's notion of freedom as power in arguing that the managerial ethos of the current university constrains creativity.

Walker's "critical capability" model has potential for supporting and sustaining APL, in moving from fixing deficits in professionals to working to enhance their strengths in a way that supports open inquiry about the direction and purpose of change. The aim of fostering students' agentic and critical capabilities in higher education is that these will be enacted and strengthened through professional life, not abandoned for performative goals once immersed in the frenetic activity of work. If agency is the ability to exert control over one's own life and act in directions one has reason to value, what relationship would critical capability have to professional practice? Being able to make informed choices and critically evaluate those choices is central to the development of independent professional judgement, a key objective of undergraduate professional education (Boud, 2007, p. 19). What if the primary aim of PD was to continue to enhance ways of being a professional, capable of independent, nuanced professional judgement in complex and uncertain situations? How would that alter the way support for PD is organised?

## 8.1.5 Intelligent Accountability

Sen highlights two complimentary facets of capability: freedom and accountability. He maintains that freedom, as the power to act, "makes us accountable for what we do" (Sen, 2009, p. 19). Researchers have argued that the neo-liberal context achieves its ends by devolving responsibility for accountability, making subjects self-governing within narrow guidelines, in subversive ways that actually constrain agency (Ball, 2003; Davies, 2005; Marginson, 2008). The difference with self-determination within Sen's capability approach is the emphasis on rights as well as responsibilities. The cornerstone of such capability is the freedom to choose to act in the direction one has reason to value (or care about). The tension between accountability enforced through regulation, on the one hand, and freedom for agentic self-determination, on the other, can be related to a professional's capability for judgement. As described in Chapter 6 with reference to professional autonomy and trust, Onora O'Neil (2002) calls for "intelligent accountability" that respects professional judgement, rather than tightly prescribed accountability. Rather than being oppositional, both accountancy and agency are implicated in the freedom and power to take charge of one's own professional direction through self-directed learning. Indeed, in discussing the development of judgement, Paul Hager and John Halliday (2006, p. 232) describe the wise practitioner as having the ability and "disposition to go on developing and learning in a world of contingency and happenstance".

As accountability and quality measures become more standardised, Frank Coffield's (2007, p. 19) research identified that professionals found "more creative ways of coping", adapting policy so it aligned with their professional values and clients' needs. In my research, participants described learning to develop such nuanced professional judgements. In some cases, to do so meant bending the organisation's rules to achieve outcomes that the practitioner considered were in the clients' best interests. In calling for enhanced professional autonomy, Coffield talks about the need to support mature self-regulation, where professionals are given the "space and resources" needed to improve their practice (p. 39). He also refers to O'Neil's notion of intelligent accountability, an idea that needs urgent consideration. Debate about intelligent accountability must include ideas about how to support professional capability for making judgements that are nuanced, critical – and even wise.

Wisdom has been considered as the zenith of professional judgement, whereby knowledge and skill are enacted through artistry and intuition, with vision and consideration for morality and humanity (Benner, Hooper-Kyriakidis, & Stannard, 1999; Gibbs, 2007; Higgs & Titchen, 2001a; McKenna, Rooney, & Liesch, 2006). This notion of wisdom in professional judgement finds some resonance with Hager and Halliday's (2006) theorisation of the value of informal learning in developing nuanced contextually appropriate judgements. They highlight a moral dimension to wise judgement in "weigh[ing] up the risks" of various approaches and taking appropriate action (p. 232). Groundwater-Smith and Mockler (2009, p. 137) relate the notion of professional wisdom to the ability of teachers to act with "moral authority and agency" in the interests of individual students as well as towards broader social well-being, even if this means bending organisational rules. In contradistinction to the standards and quality agendas, they highlight both the responsibility and the right of teachers to act in this way.

Philosopher Martha Nussbaum has worked with Sen (1993) in proposing conditions that support human well-being and enhance quality of life for communities. Nussbaum (2000) developed ten universal human capabilities. Of these, Walker (2009a, p. 14) focused on "practical reason", which she defines as a central critical capability for students in higher education. Both Nussbaum's (2000, p. 79) original and Walker's (2009a, p. 14) "thickened" version of practical reason bear a relationship to Aristotle's notion of "phronesis" or "practical wisdom". Aristotle's practical wisdom has been drawn on as an appropriate philosophical basis for considering wise professional judgement (Rowley & Gibbs, 2008, p. 357). In considering support for the development and maintenance of professional judgement in working life, a starting point could be an adaptation of Walker's key critical capability, with its reference to critical judgement with awareness of social responsibility. As a future project worth researching, I propose that a key professional capability framed around a broad sense of wise professional judgement could be nurtured in support for APL. Such a capability, that supported the professional's freedom of choice within the context of her social obligations, could form the basis of "intelligent accountability".

## 8.1.6  Learning Ecologies

The broad context in which learning takes place is the final consideration in scaffolding APL. Capabilities and relationships can only develop within sociocultural systems, as "human well-beings cannot flourish in isolation" (Prilleltensky & Prilleltensky, 2006, p. 62). As discussed in Chapter 2, systems theories have become more sophisticated in describing support for learning in complex social organisations. Tara Fenwick (2008b) considers the development of practice-based systemic perspectives to be one of the most influential current trends in research into workplace learning. In a move away from the cybernetic basis of many organisational systems, a better way of envisaging social systems may be to think of them as organic ecologies.

From an ecological perspective, systems are viewed in a holistic manner with a diversity of organisms or components interconnected to each other, to different levels of organising structures and to the system or environment as a whole. Ecosystems are inherently complex, an inseparable, interdependent web of relationships in a state of flux, with change and adaptation continually occurring (Capra, 1996; Howkins, 2009). Considering learning within a sociocultural ecosystem is consistent with arguing for a holistic perspective in examining and supporting APL, rather than an atomistic focus on component factors and activities in PD. There are many other relevant means of conceptualising learning within complex interconnected systems, from a consideration of levels of influence on behaviour or sociocultural zones (Bronfenbrenner, 1979; Vygotsky, 1978) to various activity theories (Chaiklin, 2001; Engeström, 2001).

The value of an ecological perspective in considering scaffolding change in learning is in the generation of new ideas to support this change. A key issue in ecological considerations is that of sustainability, in terms of maintenance of the health and resilience of an ecosystem. Sustainability is supported by working within the system, observing and supporting healthy interactions and integration, and mitigating against influences that are destructive for parts or the entire ecosystem

(Norberg & Cumming, 2008). The need to work within the current context, to modify and adapt it for APL, with consideration for the needs of all stakeholders, was mentioned at the end of Chapter 2. An ecological perspective offers a way of conceptualising such a task. Instead of attempting to tightly control complex educational systems in the United Kingdom, for example, Susan Weil (1999, p. 171) argues:

> Innovation, development and partnership can only come from systemic learning and inquiry from 'within the mess'. Working with, rather than controlling, this epistemological diversity and richness could lead to the visualisation and enactment of alternative epistemological and ethical positions by government, employers and academics... that could enhance the capacity of society to work with and learn from challenges.

Local diversity is valued in ecological systems as integral to maintaining sustainability. In scaffolding APL, an ecological perspective runs counter to a standardised approach to delivering PD. In learning contexts, relationships, practice, history and meanings will always be different, so that support for learning should necessarily be flexible and diverse. In considering the value of diversity and sustainability, other researchers have drawn explicitly on an ecological framework. They have examined, for example, multiple interactions between stakeholders in the learning and skills sector (Coffield et al., 2008, p. 155), collaborations between researchers in learning to teach (Wideen, Mayer-Smith, & Moon, 1998) and development of environments that support creativity and innovation (Howkins, 2009).

With reference to the homogenisation of professional identity in a performative context, Ian Stronbach and colleagues (Stronach, Corbin, McNamara, Stark, & Warne, 2002, p. 121) use an ecological metaphor in an interesting way, arguing for a move from an "economy of performance" to "ecologies of practice". They compare the professional context as a performance economy, in terms of standardised, rigid mechanisms of control, to professional practice as ecological, in terms of being an organic, changing, ambiguous web of experiences. In ways paralleling the research in this book, they highlight inherent tensions between these positions that cause professionals to feel split between wanting to do meaningful work and the performative expectations of contemporary practice contexts (p. 118).

As another example of how an ecological perspective extends thinking about issues in learning, the role of outcome measures could be considered. Stronach and colleagues (2002, p. 131) maintain that "professionalism cannot thrive on performance indicators". I agree with their assertion, when such indicators measure aspects of performance that are readily measurable, rather than those that nurture growth of professionals and professionalism (see also Ball, 2003; O'Neil, 2002). In maintaining ecological health and integrity, measurements of integrator indicators are used to signal disturbance or disequilibrium indicating potential problems in an ecosystem (Hodge, 1997). Learning indicators could possibly be developed in a similar way to indicate satisfaction, engagement or concerns, of professionals and clients, not with the aim of measuring performance, but to gauge well-being or resilience of the social learning system (see Diener & Suh, 1997). Complex notions such as capabilities could even be mapped. For example, Walker (2009b) is under-taking empirical research investigating considerations of "public good" professional capabilities, to develop a usable capability "index".

In summary, this first part of Chapter 8 has offered considerations about scaf-folding changes in support for APL. Within such a loose conceptual matrix, diverse suites of opportunities could be offered to professionals in various inter-connected ways. The ecological framework of diversity and flexibility envisaged here requires shared awareness of the complexity and uncertainty of practice and learning, challenge offered from within trusting learning relationships and nurtur-ing of independent professional capability for judgement, as integral to intelligent accountability.

Concepts such as capability and ecology are not new, being underpinned by sub-stantial theoretical and empirical bases. Their application to professional practice and learning is relatively recent. The notion of holistic intertwining of people with their lived world, integral to the phenomenological perspective underpinning this book, is consistent with an ecological approach. Indeed, an eco-phenomenological literature is emerging (Thomson, 2004b). Caution needs to be exercised in remem-bering that the notion of ecosystems is a biological metaphor, rather than an explicit model, for considering complexity and diversity in social systems. Similarly, community capability development is clearly different in many ways from the development of professionals. Metaphors may confuse as readily as they illu-minate (Reydon & Scholz, 2009, p. 435). The possibilities of critical capability development in supporting intelligent accountability and ecological interconnect-edness in supporting sustainable practices in APL need to be scrutinised empir-ically. Although they could be criticised as idealistic, they offer possibilities for change.

Any successful change would require a philosophical challenge to ingrained assumptions about learning, as transfer of information, and to habitual practices of delivering expert solutions for solving practice problems. Cultural change would be required to foster independent inquiry as the norm for professional practice and development. Cultural change in organisations is "not so damn easy", however (Alvesson & Sveningsson, 2008, p. 99).

## 8.2   Creating Cultural Change

The possibilities of creating and sustaining a change to a culture that supports APL are considered in this section. Any culture is shaped through the actions and relationships of the participants of that culture in interaction with its struc-tures. From an ecological perspective there are multiple ways that change could occur. Here I consider two levers for change. A learning culture can be shaped by a top-down approach, whereby systemic changes occur through leadership from above, that encourage open inquiry. To some extent the small agency in which Gina worked can be considered to have features of a "culture of inquiry". A learning culture could be created through the efforts of individuals or groups in a bottom-up approach. Through her "reflexive authenticity", for example, Sam managed to create a culture of inquiry in her immediate environment. Both possible changes stem from awareness and valuing of the experience of APL and involve learning relationships that support as well as question assumptions about practice. Ideally both would reinforce each other, but either could help scaffold APL for those involved.

## 8.2.1  Culture of Inquiry

The terms, learning culture or culture of inquiry, are used widely but are very context specific (e.g. J. S. Brown, 1989; Groundwater-Smith & Mockler, 2009; P. Hodkinson, Biesta, & James, 2007; Ward & McCormack, 2000). Within the context of APL, a learning culture is one that values learning as experienced, supports practice inquiry through open dialogue with others and welcomes possibilities for positive change, even when these involve taking educated risks to try out innovative ideas (Marsick, 2006). It is a culture where learning is not provided but enabled; where the focus moves beyond building professionals' capacities to supporting the growth of capable professionals directing inquiry into their own practices. It can also be described as an "expansive" learning environment (Hodkinson & Hodkinson, 2005). Such a culture can build on positive features of a particular context, such as existing relationships as opportunities to learn. It would be safe to voice dissent and to challenge negative features by making common professional experiences public, such as doubt or impostorship.

A culture of inquiry requires an explicit systematic basis that values questioning through open discussions and debate, with support for questioning embedded in the processes and structures of the organisation (Rowland, 2006; Smith-Maddox, 1999). In many organisations, there are risks involved in trying out new practices. Even carefully designed changes in practice may take several iterations to be successful. If performance is constantly monitored in a culture that does not value professional inquiry, making such changes can be risky and brave. As described in Chapter 6, some organisational cultures effectively "punish" such attempts (Marsick, 2006). A culture of inquiry should not be confused with the ubiquitous claims of many organisations to be a "learning organisation". Such claims, made in mission statements using organisational jargon, describe aligning employees' learning with strategic goals. A culture of inquiry is quite different, but is not a theoretical flight of the imagination. Current working examples exist (e.g. Reid, 2004).

Referring to the practice of teachers in Australia, Alan Reid argues that most educational systems do not operate to support inquiry in practice. Instead, he claims that the structures, systems and processes of public sector organisations often mitigate a culture of inquiry (Reid & O'Donoghue, 2004). Other researchers, including myself, support these claims (Coffield, 2007; Groundwater-Smith & Mockler, 2009; Marginson, 2008; Sandholtz & Scribner, 2006). Reid (2004) describes a public sector initiative aiming to institutionalise a system-wide culture that builds policy around the work-based inquiries of its practitioners. He stresses, as this book has,

the importance of nurturing trust at all levels of the system if inquiry is to be genuine. In arguing for more trust of professionals as part of "intelligent" rather than
prescribed accountability, O'Neil (2002) calls for "good governance" rather than
procedural audits in seeking quality assurance. The notion of governance is widely
used in community development, with good governance described as locally based,
participatory, equitable and transparent (United Nations, 2009).

### 8.2.1.1  Celebration of Practice

Before questioning practice, an appreciation of what works well in practice is useful.
In a culture of inquiry, there is a need to celebrate positive aspects of practice and
value diversity of these aspects. The valuing of professionals and their practice,
whilst challenging and questioning elements of that practice, is discussed within
an appreciative inquiry paradigm (Cooperrider & Whitney, 2005; Fish, 1998). As a
philosophical basis for supporting change, the focus of appreciative inquiry is the
exploration of what is working well, rather than a focus on problematic areas.

Participants in my study described learning as stimulating and exciting.
Novel ideas and ways of understanding experience are revealed through learning
(Montuori, 2008). Professionals need to be engaged with their practice to learn
and the stimulation of the novel maintains that engagement. Besides voicing problems about learning in a public forum, therefore, there needs to be a celebration of
the commitment and enthusiasm most professionals bring to their practice and an
understanding that making of meaning is integral to the experience of learning.

One of the participants, Dom, described passion as integral to being a therapist, exhorting new graduates *to be innovative and creative and progressive and
even confrontational – be anything but bland.* As mentioned in Chapter 4, as professionals participated in this research voluntarily, they may have been particularly
enthusiastic about learning or had particular concerns about learning. Through my
involvement with professionals in the past, however, I am aware that most are deeply
committed to making a difference to the lives of others and of growing as individuals through this purpose. Certainly passion and enthusiasm need to be nurtured as
necessary for a culture of inquiry (Fullan, 1997).

Professionals in human service industries usually demonstrate a valuing of and
caring for their clients. Valuing and caring about their own practice is also important.
Sharing stories of professional practice is a way of celebrating that practice and an
entry point for inquiry into practice (e.g. Cranton, 2008; Johnson & Golombek,
2002; Mason, 2004; Mattingly, 1998). Recognition of the primacy of practice and
ways that practice and research can inform each other can lead to more practitioner-
based research. As Dom asserts:

> *Don't think the universities are the cutting edge. Clinical practice is at the coalface, that's
> the cutting edge, that's where we're mucking about with different treatment ideas. The uni-
> versities find evidence for what we're doing but the inspiration for that comes from clinical
> practice. That's how I really feel, that I do solve a million and one clinical problems every
> day.*

## 8.2.1.2  Creative Dissent

From the support offered through valuing and celebrating practice, creative dissent may arise. A culture of inquiry not only allows but also values creative dissent as a way of improving practice outcomes for both clients and professionals. That is, dissent in a culture of inquiry should be directed towards a meaningful purpose (e.g. Sullivan & Rosin, 2008). In arguing for a politics of resistance in education, Henry Giroux (2003, p. 5) stresses the need for "a language of critique and possibility that is as self-critical as it is socially responsible". Creative new ideas and possibilities in critical inquiry are then based on an appreciation of what matters to participants of that culture. In caring professions, such as teaching, critical dissent includes recognition of social responsibilities, social sustainability and, usually, a notion of social justice (Blackmore, 1999; V. A. Brown, Grootjans, Ritchie, Townsend, & Verrinda, 2005; Groundwater-Smith & Mockler, 2009).

As consensus about "what matters" is unlikely, ideas suggested through creative dissent may be unwanted or even seen as inflammatory. Deborah Britzman and Don Dippo (2000) suggest that the future of a profession may lie in its ability to ask difficult questions of itself and be open to deal with such "awful thoughts". For a profession to grow dynamically in response to social change, a culture of inquiry that enables APL is vital. Difficult questions about why certain practices are undertaken, whose needs are met by such practices and whether there is a better way of practicing can be debated. Such a debate could highlight notions of meaning and value rather than be dominated by economic efficiency.

Apple (1999, p. 173) describes the importance of critical dissent in generating agency for change. As discussed, there is little public dissent or resistance about the status quo in the health professions, although there are some exceptions. Franziska Trede and colleagues (Trede, Higgs, Jones, & Edwards, 2003), for example, suggest a model of emancipatory practice for physiotherapists akin to the culture of inquiry described here. They articulate the transformation of practice that could occur through questioning of, and critical reflection on, assumptions and taken-for-granted practices, with benefits for both professionals and clients.

A problem for participants of my research was that in all the public sector organisations where they worked (including health, education, communities, disability, families or aged care), they were a minority group. The power of therapists and other minority professions to create cultural change in organisations may be limited unless they form alliances (Williams, 2009). Another issue in creating change is the gendered nature of therapy as a profession, in common with professions such as nursing and teaching. The values that are important to these practitioners, such as caring about clients and making a difference, may be undervalued partly because of their traditional conceptualisation as feminine qualities (Noddings, 1992, p. xiii). The notion of caring as an important framework for considering practice in such professions is worthy of further research (Kleiman, 2008; Noddings, 2002; Phillips, 2007).

In a culture of inquiry, both celebration of practice and creative dissent would support APL. Enthusiasm for and resistance to various aspects of practice are necessary for change. Both are powerful emotions that need to be reconciled to provide the "energy for change" (Fullan, 1997, p. 223).

## 8.2.2  Reflexive Authenticity

Whilst system-wide change is the norm in organisations currently, a change to an inquiry-based culture is not. Although the support of an entire organisation for a culture of inquiry would be the ideal, even without systemic change, a culture of inquiry could be built within a profession, a department or a group of practitioners who engage in reflexive authenticity. Through the agency of individuals, workplace cultures can be transformed (Billett & Somerville, 2004).

As described in Chapter 7, with respect to Sam, reflexive authenticity is both a personal and social construct, with a reflective and moral component. It refers to a professional valuing her way of learning as an expression of her way of being, whilst being open to critically questioning that way of being and of practicing. Such authenticity implies practicing with a social and moral awareness of the responsibilities of being a professional. Reflexive authenticity involves a commitment to engage with others in practice in an open, imaginative and critical way. It involves critical reflection through questioning of assumptions, with awareness of the wider social, cultural and political implications of practice and of what matters for clients in different contexts. The reflexive authenticity I describe is a personal undertaking, as it entails personal integrity and responsibility, but it also has a social dimension through a sense of belonging to the wider social context that makes being authentic possible (Guignon, 2004b, p. 163).

Reflexive authenticity is needed to "stand back" from practice: accepting uncertainty and openly questioning practice. Reflexive authenticity is needed to "stand up" for what matters in the professional life-world: seeing other perspectives and voicing what is valued. It could form the basis of an emancipatory and transformative model of practice, allowing meaningful growth as a professional, intelligent accountability, advocacy for making a difference in clients' lives and contributing to the dynamic development of a profession.

### 8.2.2.1  Standing Back

The value of critical reflection for transformative learning, the dearth of evidence of critical reflection amongst participants in my research and possible reasons for this absence have been discussed. Change towards a culture that supports APL involves challenging professionals to critically reflect, through thoughtful questions grounded in everyday interactions. Standing back to gain distance from everyday practice is required, to allow insights into taken-for-granted features of practice and enable the development of a capability for making wise professional judgements.

In describing "standing back", it is worth entertaining the notion of "negative capability" described by the poet John Keats, as the ability to remain "in uncertainties, mysteries, doubts, without any irritable reaching after fact and reason" (Gittings

& Mee, 2002, p. 41). Negative capability can be conceived of as a state of mindful openness. It is reminiscent of the calmness of Heidegger's reflective thinking (see Chapter 6), which allows possible receptivity to the call of authentic Dasein (see Chapter 7). The ability to reflect, without immediately seeking the reconciliation of tensions or closure of solutions, may support wise judgement that is also authentic.

Reflexive authenticity involves self-understanding, as there is a need to be aware of values and assumptions before they can be critically examined (Brookfield, 1995; Mezirow, 2000). Referring to reflexivity in research, Mats Alvesson and Kaj Sköldberg (2000, p. 84) note that "every understanding ... contribu[tes] to a better *self*-understanding". As explained in Chapter 7, understanding self, or self-awareness, can also be considered as a social as well as personal construct. It involves recognition of the socially constructed basis of being a professional in the professional life-world, where much is controlled but little is certain.

As professionals become aware of themselves as learners, they may identify what they value and care about at work, what is valued by their clients and the privileged values of the professional and wider culture in which they are immersed (Crick & Wilson, 2005; Mackenzie, 2002). Shared awareness of different values can be developed through "genuine" dialogue. Reflexive authenticity, therefore, involves social dialogue that is receptive as well as active: that listens to understand as well as questions to inquire. Professionals with such awareness are then in a better position to discuss more openly and to critically reflect on values and practice.

### 8.2.2.2 Standing Up

Brookfield (1995, p. 217) stresses that for reflection to be described as critical, it should be directed towards action for meaningful change. Besides standing back to reflect on aspects of practice and learning, reflexive authenticity involves standing up for concerns once they have been pondered and discussed. This can be construed as taking a stand on what matters in professional life.

The concept of reflexive authenticity I have described earlier is not only awareness of self as a social being but also is linked to a concept of a meaningful life. The professionals in my research were passionate about making a difference to the lives of their clients. They described how the situations they cared about sufficiently to engage with and learn from were those related to this sense of a meaningful professional life. Many participants expressed a sense of purpose through their engagement in practice and noted that by learning about better ways of practicing they found meaning through everyday work.

Reflexive authenticity means becoming clear sighted and reflective about issues of importance that face professionals and their community, as well as taking a stand on such issues through action (Guignon, 2004b; Thomson, 2004a). Referring to Heidegger's concept of authenticity, Charles Guignon (2004a, p. 131) states:

> [This] concept of authenticity therefore provides the basis for making sense of the connectedness, continuity, and coherence of life. The integrity of a life ... is grounded ... in what we do in the world. Acting is a matter of resolutely drawing on the pool of possibilities opened by one's culture and remaining firm and whole-hearted in one's commitments....

An authentic life gains its meaning from the way the events and actions are focused on realizing something as a totality. In Heidegger's view, it is only by living in this way that one
can be an individual or a Self.

In a similar way, Alvesson and Sköldberg (2000, p. 82) describe authenticity as
"taking responsibility" for ourselves through moments of "clear-sightedness" that
enable "a realistic view of ourselves and our possibilities – neither underestimating
nor overestimating them". Reflective authenticity as a professional, then, involves
an embodied engaged agency with a view towards a purpose and meaning beyond
the self (C. Taylor, 1992).

Sam offers an example of reflexive authenticity as a professional. Her congruence
between her values and actions, her taking of professional responsibility to continually challenge what she knows and her standing up for issues of social justice in
relation to her clients are examples of authentic professional being. As such, reflexive authenticity involves awareness of social and professional responsibilities whilst
retaining personal and professional integrity. Sam described how through transformative experiences of APL she gained insight into such a professional way of being.
Other participants, even Sally, stand up when it matters, describing taking a stand
on behalf of clients. Silence over dissonance may not be an issue of confidence
per se, but confusion about what professionals are able to stand up for, within their
perceptions of what is possible in the public professional world.

Thus reflexive authenticity can be construed as the "social action of an authentic,
reflective self who founds (sic) its authenticity intersubjectively" (Tsivacou, 2005,
p. 45) Tsivacou is referring to communication in the modern workplace with reference to the notion of eudaimonia or shared well-being, described in Chapter 6
with respect to a life-world discourse of meaning. In arguing for cultural change in
organisations towards valuing both integrity and inquiry, Peter Senge (1990, p. 277)
describes two forms of openness: "participative openness", the freedom to speak out
about what matters, and "reflective openness", the valuing of questioning through
dialogue. His reference to these qualities of an organisational culture, not only mirrors but also would support reflexive authenticity of professionals in a way that
could enhance organisational as well as professional well-being.

## 8.2.3  Sustainable Change

Realisation of meaning in professional life is not a theoretical fantasy. There is a
growing discourse about the way that people find meaning in life and construct identities through everyday engagement in work (Gardner, 2009; Hostetler, Macintyre
Latta, & Sarroub, 2007; Iwama, 2004; Katz, Sutherland, & Earl, 2005; Palmer,
1998). Sabine Gurtler (2005) describes how such meaning relates to what matters in
a society, arguing that within the context of a worthwhile life, work can contribute
to the common good. The promise of professionalism as discussed in Chapter 2
(Freidson, 2001; Sullivan, 1995), may be possible if ways can be found to support
learning that are sustaining for professionals, whilst leading to sustainable changes
that enhance organisational and community well-being.

Developing sustainability of communities, organisations and ecosystems is one of the key challenges of the twenty first century (UNESCO, 2005). Sustainability generally refers to the ability of a system or development to meet short-term goals without compromising future long-term capacities (Norberg & Cumming, 2008). It is increasingly linked to the resilience and well-being of systems or communities and the components of those systems, including human beings (V. A. Brown et al., 2005). By referring to sustainability with respect to support for APL, I consider three particular issues. First, that change enacted through APL leads to positive outcomes for stakeholders in areas that matter to them. What matters for professionals, clients and organisations may differ, but change is only sustainable if there is some integration of these needs. Secondly, that any positive change is long-term and does not cease once an "intervention" is ended. Such outcomes will, and should, continue to be modified, but this is different from changes that are enacted "just for show" rather than because they mean something to participants. Thirdly, that change will take into account the need for resources of time, people's energies and material goods. In other words, although change may incur cost, that cost needs to be reasonable in terms of being integrated into everyday budgets.

Thus considerations of sustainability in support for learning include issues ranging from the well-being of professionals to fiscal needs of organisations. With respect to learning, sustainability has been described in terms of making decisions that consider the long-term future of the economy, ecology and equity of communities (UNESCO, 2005). Michael Fullan (2005, p. ix) describes organisational sustainability as "the capacity of a system to engage in the complexities of continuous improvement consistent with deep values of human purpose". He argues that sustainable change is not just about maintaining good programmes after implementation, not just pursuing continuous improvement with "relentless energy", but about "serious accountability and ownership". Fullan discusses "dynamic sustainability", noting that the idea of maintaining the momentum of change can be misleading. Change, like learning, is cyclic rather than linear. In other words, there will be bursts of energy and innovation followed by plateaus of observation, reflection and "bedding in". Expectations about the sustainability of change need to respect these cycles.

As mentioned, maintenance of diversity is crucial for sustainability of ecosystems. Sen (2006) maintains that valuing of human diversity and plurality of identity is crucial if our current global society is to thrive. Referring to diversity and resilience of social-ecological systems, Jon Norberg and colleagues (Norberg, Wilson, Walker, & Ostrom, 2008) describe two approaches for managers to support sustainable diversity. One is to promote local adaptations to introduced programmes. These can be shared if successful, but "too much sharing, however, such as nationally enforced 'blueprint solutions' or 'management fashions' ... may reduce regional diversity" (p. 71). The second approach involves actively working to minimise a focus on single solutions to problems to "avoid the trap of letting one solution dominate", even if it is a good solution (p. 71). Supporting multiple solutions enhances the resilience of systems in terms of the capacity to deal with future challenges. Although these approaches refer to social-ecological systems, the basic ideas for supporting local adaptations and multiple solutions to problems hold promise of applicability for sociocultural learning systems. For example, the field of social ecology is an emerging interdisciplinary field that focuses on investigating and changing complex social systems, dealing with interrelationships between people as well as economic parameters (Bookchin, 2003; V. A. Brown et al., 2005; Hill, 2005). Sustainable cultural change may be difficult, but it is possible.

## 8.3  Professional Learning Pathways

Beyond such theoretical positions about changing support for learning towards APL, the "gritty materialities" need to be considered, as ideas without plans for action are wasted (Apple, 2000; Fullan, 2007). In asking what support for APL would look like in practice, a clear answer is not available. It would look different in different situations and its basic constitution requires further research. Possible strategies that are relatively cost and time neutral are suggested below, based on the guidelines for scaffolding APL. The notion of scaffolding implies that support for changes will "fall away" as no longer required. This will only be possible if strategies of support are authentic and sustainable, relating to what really matters in professional lives in ways that can be sustained within contemporary organisations. Such a framework is congruent with, and supportive of, professional experiences described in this study, yet cognizant of the current needs of the workplace with respect to the demonstration of outcomes and accountability.

There are many existing models that can be adapted. It is important, however, that models suggested in this section are not just incorporated within the existing culture and PD framework. For example, Carl Rhodes and Hermine Scheeres (2004) critique organisational training masquerading as inquiry into values of employees. Whilst the aim of the programme was to explore cultural change in an organisation, the didactic and controlling methods of "developing" staff focused on alignment not exploration of values and to compliance rather than learning. Existing models or strategies could work within the guidelines proposed for APL. These involve shared awareness of everyday realities, with support for relationships and reflexivity, valuing of diversity and nurturing of independent capabilities, within a culture of inquiry and respect for intelligent accountability. In addition, it is important that models for supporting learning are not perceived as imposed from above in a didactic manner by experts, as yet another change that must be implemented.

### 8.3.1  Interconnected Matrix of Flexible Options

An interconnected, diverse range of opportunities and strategies that support learning could be offered, that respect professionals' agency and choice in how they go about learning (Goos, Hughes, & Webster-Wright, 2009). Using the term "pathways" deliberately evokes the notion of a learning journey, where "path" is related to established strategies and "way" foregrounds the individual's choices. Such pathways can be conceptualised as having horizontal and vertical trajectories in providing flexible approaches to support learning. The horizontal trajectory refers to a variety of opportunities, from informal learning (e.g. reflections or discussions on practice), through various forms of learning relationships (e.g. mentoring or networks), to more formal seminars and courses. The vertical trajectory refers to the way that the professional can be supported to map their own direction related to personal interest, professional needs and organisational goals. Professionals can direct their own APL pathway through this flexible matrix of opportunities whilst negotiating contextual constraints.

I have mentioned the need to find ways of balancing professional concerns and well-being with organisational requirements for impact and outcomes. At the end of Chapter 2, four threads of inquiry were identified that have influenced the development of PD practices: organisational training, continuing education, workplace learning and transformative learning. In changing to a different way of approaching PD, a mix of approaches offered within an APL framework may prove to be realistic. In my research, participants described learning from engagement in a variety of experiences, including workshops and courses, but in an interconnected, often unexpected and open way. For conceptual clarity, I discuss ideas in terms of the four strands mentioned, whereas ideally, hybrid forms would develop according to need, interest and the imaginations of those supporting learning in organisations.

For example, there is often a need in organisations to deliver information, such as new procedures, to large numbers in an expedient manner. Workshops or web-based dissemination may be useful, although care must be taken not to assume that such information leads to learning or changed practices, even if evaluation forms are positive. Continuing education courses, delivered in modules that can be credited and support career progression, are often popular with professionals as a way of exploring research and new ideas for practice. Even though these are assessed, unless the assessment supports enhanced professional judgement and continuing learning, sustainable changes in practice may not occur.

To be effective, both strategies would ideally be embedded within a workplace learning culture that explicitly values inquiry and supports relationships. Day-to-day workplace learning could involve support for a range of learning relationships: networks, mentors, internships, work shadowing, communities of practice or other groups developed around shared interests or concerns. Diverse pathways towards professional growth and career progression could be shared in work groups or more publicly through stories of practice and learning journeys available online. In addition, the possibility of transformation through learning may be approached through small APL support groups to discuss issues raised in this book in a trusting environment of people committed to professional inquiry and growth.

### 8.3.2 Authentic Professional Learning Groups

The phenomenological research in this book identified commonalties in diverse experiences of APL, described in terms of four interlinked constituents:

understanding, engagement, interconnection and openness. Issues of concern were also identified, to do with limited questioning of assumptions, difficulty seeing other perspectives, discomfort with uncertainty involved in practice and an unsettling feeling of disconnection between professional lives and organisational expectations that was dealt with in varying ways. Although change in understanding is the crux of the experience of APL, it is the notion of openness and associated issues of uncertainty and inquiry that offers an entry point into generative discussions about APL.

Drawing on these findings and research discussed in this book, I offer discussion prompts for an APL group, as one concrete example of a possible approach, which is being evaluated in current research with colleagues. Although support for organically evolved learning relationships and groups is vital, there may be a place for more structured support in initial scaffolding of APL changes in an organisation or professional group. The concepts introduced in such groups may not be readily accessible without skilled facilitation, or stewardship. In group conversations, ideas and issues about learning in the current climate could be shared, as participants did in this book, and strategies for future directions in supporting learning discussed. Such a group could involve a small workplace where a number of professionals are interested in engaging in practice renewal. It could involve a group of professionals charged with supporting the learning of others in an organisation. It could involve a group of professionals who have moved to management positions and are interested in fostering innovative policy directions and cultural change. Insight into one's own experiences of professional growth, in concert with research into learning as appropriate, can form a strong basis for considering support for the growth of others.

To discuss such ideas openly, a consensus would need to be developed initially about purpose, confidentiality, mutual respect and commitment to open shared inquiry. Sharing experiences of practice, learning and change would form a starting point, with later discussion of issues such as awareness, uncertainty, diversity, inquiry, creativity, meaning, values and action. The importance of relationships in professional life could be discussed, drawing on participants' experiences. The question of what sort of relationships support authentic learning can be raised and discussion of how they can be strengthened. Notions of doubt, uncertainty or not knowing can be explored through concrete situations where participants describe such feelings in professional life. Open questions about situations where participants felt challenged or uncomfortable, where there was miscommunication or conflict, can be explored. What happened in such situations? What was learnt? Underlying assumptions could be identified from these discussions: assumptions about self, clients, practice or knowledge. For example, is knowledge as used in practice certain? Are there certain truths and what knowledge is conditional?

At some early stage, the notion of what matters to the participants in professional life is explored through considering what each professional feels passionate about. Are there similarities or differences in the way the participants find meaning in their professional lives? What do they care about? How do these areas relate to their professional responsibilities? What are the assumptions behind such values? In what ways can work contribute to wider goals such as social justice or sustainability? In exploring the type of difference people want to make as professionals, the way that continuing to learn might contribute to making a difference can be explored. The current working culture for different professionals is discussed, including features that support or hinder APL.

Finally, participants would be asked to map a way forward for supporting learning and practice, in terms of an individual project or group action to continue support or advocate for change. The planning would be dependent not only on the issue that the professional is concerned about but also on what is feasible within the working situation. For example, a first project could focus on developing a particular learning relationship through exploring a relatively minor concern or could involve a more ambitious project developing a participative action research group. Plans would vary with different workplace structures, cultures and leadership styles and could be incorporated into existing learning support mechanisms. Ways of progressing in the future would be outlined, from finding information sources to developing critical friendships, including the possibility of continuing to meet as a group without facilitation. In such groups, strength can be developed through shared diversity: freedom through shared responsibility. Sharing could allow patterns to be seen as imaginative ideas are shared. Dissonance could be voiced and meaning valued.

These questions and ideas suggested for support groups could also be embedded in training workshops, continuing education courses and the diverse matrices of workplace learning opportunities, in an organisation that values inquiry and the satisfaction of their staff. For example, PD sessions could be organised around responses to questions about what areas of practice professionals feel passionate about, are uncertain about, are curious about or have problems with. Many of these ideas are in place in communities and workplaces within innovative models of support or leadership. For example, Walker (2001) discusses the establishment of a small group within a university, actively learning and changing their teaching practices, drawing on experiences from their professional and personal lives as resources. She and her colleagues discuss how through such a process of learning they construct a professional life of meaning and an "authentic professional self" (p. 29). She talks of the openness of the process as "welcoming complexity" and being "one way to prise open . . . claims to certainty" in practice (p. 35). Similarly, in an APL framework, professionals can articulate and value their own authentic way of learning and of being a professional, whilst questioning their underlying assumptions.

### 8.3.3  Existing Models for Supporting Learning

Six established models that could be drawn upon in creating an action plan through APL groups or other forms of support for learning are: action learning, action research, critical incidents, appreciative inquiry, inquiry-based learning and interdisciplinary professionalism. Many combinations and permutations are possible. Although devised with slightly different foci, all the models can be grounded in everyday work. They are congruent with the way professionals learn, yet able to be cognizant of professional expectations. They acknowledge uncertainty, yet have a structure. They support a questioning awareness of possibility and choice. They involve action leading to change, yet build in reflection. They support individual involvement and direction, yet may involve broader interdisciplinary exchange. Most are iterative, participative and collaborative. Each will only be briefly sketched, as detailed references are widely available.

Action learning, in particular, is uncannily similar to many of the participants' descriptions of learning in this study, where some action was trialled in practice, outcomes noticed and further change undertaken. Action learning usually involves a group, but could involve a single professional engaging actively with a professional issue that she cares about and wants to learn more about. The suggested APL support groups are essentially action learning groups. They work effectively when members meet regularly to share progress, questions and ideas. As mentioned in Chapter 2, interest in action learning is growing in professional and academic communities as a means of supporting PD (Cowan, 2006; Dilworth & Willis, 2003; McGill & Brockbank, 2004; J. O'Neil & Marsick, 2007).

Action research is also well documented (Gustavsen, 2008; Kemmis, 1995; Reason & Bradbury, 2001; Walker, 2001; Whitehead & McNiff, 2006). As mentioned in Chapter 2, action research is a participatory form of research with a particular focus on group learning leading to community or systemic change (Hyland & Noffke, 2005; Mattsson & Kemmis, 2007). Although it is established as a research methodology that pursues action and research outcomes at the same time, in its simplest form it can be viewed as authentic problem solving using a systematic process. It is also particularly applicable to practitioner research. Erica McWilliam (2004, p. 118) critiques and promotes practitioner research, referring to both formal and informal action-based research. In her evaluation of its strengths and weaknesses, she notes that it can achieve both PD and political action.

Another model for supporting practitioners' learning, used within teaching practice especially, is based on David Tripp's (1993) notion of critical incidents. This model draws on incidents from everyday practice that are analysed in terms of practitioners' assumptions and interpretations. The meaning of incidents in practice is determined not only by their context but also by the professional's "interpretation of the significance of an event" (p. 8). Tripp stresses that the professional interpretations teachers make "come more from their understanding of the situation and who they are than from any set of teaching procedures that they may follow" (p. 142). To examine such situations and learn from them, he outlines a process of searching for wider meanings, through asking significant questions, such as: "Why did this occur?"; "What is it an example of?"; "Where do I go from here?" (p. 27). This process is a means of examining habits of mind and practice, exposing implicit values and assumptions. The process can be supported by the use of reflective journals, a critical friend or a collaborative group.

Alternatively, a process involving appreciation of what currently works in practice could be used. The appreciative inquiry model has been mentioned as a way of celebrating practice and could be a useful process within an APL framework because of this aspect. Appreciative inquiry is described as a group inquiry that focuses on enhancing what is working well, as a way of investigating and changing problems in practice (Cooperrider & Whitney, 2005). Problematic issues are addressed, but in a generative rather than critical manner that involves imaginative discovery and exploration of ideals (p. 34). Della Fish (1998) takes a slightly different perspective within this appreciative paradigm, highlighting the concept of professional artistry in appreciating and inquiring about professional practice in a creative yet critical manner (see also Higgs & Titchen, 2001b).

Inquiry-based learning is a term that is sometimes used to frame a philosophical stance to PD that includes a variety of innovative ways of supporting professionals as they learn through practice (Groundwater-Smith & Mockler, 2009) and sometimes used to describe a specifically planned approach to continuing education (Cleverly, 2003). Interest is particularly strong in health professions such as nursing, in moving from problem-based learning to a more open approach with possibilities for workplace inquiry (Feletti, 1993). The starting point for inquiry is a question about practice rather than a problem with practice. As a way of fostering inquiry as a continuing process, this approach can support emancipatory goals, with possible transformation of participants' perspectives through shared challenging of taken-for-granted practices (Cleverly, p. 27).

Finally, a recent approach to interdisciplinary professionalism is mentioned. It is not a model as such but a report by William Sullivan and Matthew Rosin (2008) on an inaugural Carnegie seminar series, bringing together faculty and students from different professions with those in arts and science courses. The focus is on the development of professional judgement, as practical reasoning, to educate students for professional lives of "significance", engagement and responsibility. Reflection and critique are stressed, not as intellectual exercises, but as ways of deliberating on "possibilities for a life well lived, including their responsibility to contribute to the life of their times". They continue to describe how "practical reason grounds… critical rationality in human purposes [and] values embodied responsibility as the resourceful blending of critical intelligence with moral commitment" (p. xvi). The educational aim of ethically based practical reason is similar to Walker's critical capability approach but draws on different conceptual frameworks and practical strategies. The Carnegie seminars resonate with notions of intelligent accountability and the promise of professionalism, in supporting professionals to become more than competent practitioners: able to make a difference in a way that matters for society. There may be ways of adapting these objectives and interdisciplinary approach, within other models suggested above in supporting APL.

## *8.3.4  Existing Resources for Supporting Learning*

The value of adapting one of the suggested models as a means of structuring an APL project is that a systematic process could be established, being more acceptable to current organisations than conceptual guidelines alone. Outcomes could be described, as signposts marking a journey rather than predetermined, fixed destinations. In addition, the valuing, support, discussion and questioning arising from such processes would produce intangible outcomes beyond those formally identified. Electronic portfolios may be developed with interactive mechanisms to map what matters to the professional for learning, in ways that could demonstrate inquiry, reflections, associations, artefacts and changes in practice as outcomes of learning. Learning journals may be a useful way of structuring or recording thinking or questioning (Bolton, 2001; Moon, 1999). As learning groups have been established to read research articles, they could also be established to share reflective journals.

The adaptation of existing mechanisms within professional associations and workplaces is desirable. For example, many professionals are involved with PD through professional associations. In addition to maintaining standards, professional associations have a mandate to support continuing learning. They are well placed to move towards a framework of APL, instead of being limited to traditional PD. Courses offered through associations could support ongoing inquiry instead of providing isolated presentations. Stories of professional practice could be shared in newsletters as they currently are, but with more stories highlighting unvoiced concerns of professional lives. In this electronic era, electronic magazines or blogs may reach more people.

In workplaces, there are already avenues through which exchange of experiences can occur. Most workplaces have PD days and formal or informal networks in place that could provide opportunities for discussions about practice and learning. To some extent sharing already occurs, as participants explained. However, the focus is generally on clients, through the valued medium of case studies. Professional concerns, such as doubt, uncertainty or learning from mistakes, are only shared between trusted friends. It is possible that APL groups could be offered through video links to enable engagement of rural practitioners within their local communities. Instead of the "train the trainer" focus of the past decade, there could be a change to an "enable the enabler" focus.

There is no need for APL groups, other learning relationships or projects that arise from them, to take more time than current PD activities. The traditional PD industry already consumes significant amounts of time, energy, money and physical resources. By building on existing networks and resources, support for APL could be relatively cost and time neutral, once established. Although it is possible that APL projects could contribute to performance appraisal, care would need to be taken that learning rather than performance was a focus, grounded in real issues of concern from practice, as well as appreciation of organisational commitments.

## 8.4  Moving Forward

Two directions are necessary in scaffolding APL, to change organisational culture and to support individual professionals; the two are interdependent. That is, working cultures will change if more professionals act in authentic ways, reflectively inquiring into their practices and sharing and voicing concerns; yet there is a need for a change in cultures to enable valuing and support for APL as experienced, with processes that explicitly reward innovative and open inquiry. In authentic inquiry, there is a fine line between demonstrating intelligent accountability in learning and retaining agency or ownership of that learning. Support for APL needs to involve learners in the choice of strategies and processes used.

Stakeholders cannot control, regulate, force or coerce a professional into learning. However, they can support, facilitate and provide an environment that enables APL. We need awareness of possibilities for change. An awareness of the ambiguities of being human, uncertainties of learning and constraints of professional socialisation and context can lead to inquiry that has potential to transform professional understanding. From a basis of respect and trust, it may be possible to challenge professionals to question themselves, their habits, their clients' needs and the context: to consider other alternatives in revitalising their practice.

A framework for scaffolding APL not only supports professionals to learn in their own authentic ways but also supports them to consider who they might become as professionals: professionals who continue to learn to develop reflective, nuanced and critical judgement, with consideration of issues of morality and humanity within their professional ways of being. That is, a framework of APL supports not only professional *being* but also *becoming*. It allows the possibility of authenticity in professional life in ways that can make a difference to organisations and to society.

# References

Alvesson, M., & Sköldberg, K. (2000). *Reflexive methodology: New vistas for qualitative research.* London; Thousand Oaks, CA: Sage Publications.

Alvesson, M., & Sveningsson, S. (2008). *Changing organizational culture: Cultural change work in progress.* London: Routledge.

Apple, M. W. (1999). *Power, meaning, and identity: Essays in critical educational studies.* New York: P. Lang.

Apple, M. W. (2000). Can critical pedagogies interrupt rightist policies? *Educational Theory, 50*(2), 229–254.

Apple, M. W. (2001). *Educating the "right" way: Markets, standards, god, and inequality.* New York; London: RoutledgeFalmer.

Ball, S. J. (2003). The teacher's soul and the terrors of performativity. *Journal of Education Policy, 18*(2), 215–228.

Benner, P., Hooper-Kyriakidis, P. L., & Stannard, D. (1999). *Clinical wisdom and interventions in critical care: A thinking-in-action approach.* Philadelphia, PA: Saunders.

Billett, S. (2001). *Learning in the workplace: Strategies for effective practice.* Crows Nest, NSW: Allen & Unwin.

Billett, S., & Somerville, M. (2004). Transformations at work: Identity and learning. *Studies in Continuing Education, 26*(2), 309–326.

Blackmore, J. (1999). *Framing the issues for educational re-design, learning networks and professional activism.* Hawthorn, VIC: Australian Council for Educational Administration.

Bolton, G. (2001). *Reflective practice: Writing and professional development.* London; Thousand Oaks, CA: Paul Chapman; Sage.

Bookchin, M. (2003). An overview of the roots of social ecology. *Harbinger.* Retrieved July 9, 2006, from http://www.social-ecology.org/author/murray-bookchin/

Boud, D. (2007). Reframing assessment as if learning were important. In D. Boud & N. Falchikov (Eds.), *Rethinking assessment in higher education: Learning for the longer term* (pp. 14–25). London; New York: Routledge.

Boud, D., Cohen, R., & Sampson, J. (Eds.). (2001). *Peer learning in higher education: Learning from and with each other.* London: Kogan Page.

Boud, D., & Lee, A. (2005). "Peer learning" as pedagogic discourse for research education. *Studies in Higher Education, 30*(5), 501–516.

Britzman, D. P., & Dippo, D. (2000). On the future of awful thoughts in teacher education. *Teaching Education, 11*(1), 31–37.

Bronfenbrenner, U. (1979). *The ecology of human development: Experiments by nature and design.* Cambridge, MA: Harvard University Press.

Brookfield, S. (1995). *Becoming a critically reflective teacher.* San Francisco: Jossey-Bass.

Brookfield, S. (2000). Clinical reasoning and generic thinking skills. In J. Higgs & M. A. Jones (Eds.), *Clinical reasoning in the health professions* (pp. 62–67). Oxford; Boston: Butterworth-Heinemann.

Brown, J. S. (1989). Situated cognition and the culture of learning. *Educational Researcher, 18*(1), 32–42.

Brown, V. A., Grootjans, J., Ritchie, J. E., Townsend, M., & Verrinda, G. (Eds.). (2005). *Sustainability and health: Supporting global ecological integrity in public health.* Crows Nest, NSW: Allen & Unwin.

Burgh, G., & Yorshansky, M. (2009). Communities of inquiry: Politics, power and group dynamics. *Educational Philosophy and Theory,* 1–17.

Capra, F. (1996). *The web of life: a new scientific understanding of living systems.* New York: Anchor Books.

Chaiklin, S. (2001). *The theory and practice of cultural-historical psychology.* Aarhus: Aarhus University Press.

Cleverly, D. (2003). *Implementing inquiry-based learning in nursing.* New York: Routledge.

Coffield, F. (2007). *Running ever faster down the wrong road: An alternative future for education and skills.* London: Institute of Education, University of London.

Coffield, F., Edward, S., Finlay, I., Hodgson, A., Spours, K., & Steer, R. (2008). *Improving learning, skills and inclusion: The impact of policy on post-compulsory education.* London; New York: Routledge.

Cooperrider, D. L., & Whitney, D. K. (2005). *Appreciative inquiry: a positive revolution in change.* San Francisco: Berrett-Koehler.

Cowan, J. (2006). *On becoming an innovative university teacher: Reflection in action* (2nd ed.). Buckingham; New York: Society for Research into Higher Education & Open University Press.

Cranton, P. (2008). The resilience of the soul. In T. Leonard & P. Willis (Eds.), *Pedagogies of the imagination: Mythopoetic curriculum in educational practice* (pp. 125–136). Netherlands: Springer.

Crick, R. D., & Wilson, K. (2005). Being a learner: A virtue for the 21st century. *British Journal of Educational Studies, 53*(3), 359–374.

Dall'Alba, G. (2009). Learning professional ways of being: Ambiguities of becoming. *Educational Philosophy and Theory, 41*(1), 34–45.

Davies, B. (2005). The (im)possibility of intellectual work in neoliberal regimes. *Discourse: Studies in the Cultural Politics of Education, 26*(1), 1–14.

Diener, E., & Suh, E. (1997). Measuring quality of life: Economic, social, and subjective indicators. *Social Indicators Research, 40,* 189–216.

Dilworth, R. L., & Willis, V. J. (2003). *Action learning: Images and pathways.* Malabar, FL: Krieger Publishing Co.

Engeström, Y. (2001). Expansive learning at work: Toward an activity theoretical reconceptualization. *Journal of Education and Work, 14*(1), 133–156.

Feletti, G. (1993). Inquiry-based and problem-based learning: How similar are these approaches to nursing and medical education. *Higher Education Research and Development, 12*(2), 143–156.

Fenwick, T. (2008a). Understanding relations of individual collective learning in work: A review of research. *Management Learning, 39*(3), 227–243.

Fenwick, T. (2008b). Workplace learning: Emerging trends and new perspectives. In S. B. Merriam (Ed.), *Third update on adult learning theory* (pp. 17–26). San Francisco: Jossey-Bass.

Fish, D. (1998). *Appreciating practice in the caring professions: Refocusing professional development and practitioner research.* Oxford: Butterworth Heinemann.

Freidson, E. (2001). *Professionalism: The third logic.* Chicago: University of Chicago Press.

Fullan, M. (1997). Emotion and hope: Constructive concepts for complex times. In A. Hargreaves (Ed.), *Rethinking educational change with heart and mind* (pp. 216–233). Alexandria, VA: Association for Supervision and Curriculum Development.

Fullan, M. (2005). *Leadership & sustainability: System thinkers in action.* Thousand Oaks, CA: Corwin Press.

Fullan, M. (2007). *The new meaning of educational change* (4th ed.). New York: Teachers College Press.

Fuller, A., & Unwin, L. (2004). Young people as teachers and learners in the workplace: Challenging the novice-expert dichotomy. *International Journal of Training and Development, 8*(1), 32–42.

Gardner, F. (2009). Affirming values: Using critical reflection to explore meaning and professional practice. *Reflective Practice: International and Multidisciplinary Perspectives, 10*(2), 179–190.

Gibbs, P. (2007). Practical wisdom and the workplace researcher. *London Review of Education, 5*(3), 223–235.

Gibbs, P., & Angelides, P. (2008). Understanding friendship between critical friends. *Improving Schools, 11*(3), 213–225.

Gillespie, M. (2005). Student-teacher connection: A place of possibility. *Journal of Advanced Nursing, 52*(2), 211–219.

Giroux, H. (2003). Public pedagogy and the politics of resistance: Notes on a critical theory of educational struggle. *Educational Philosophy and Theory, 33*(1), 5–16.

Gittings, R., & Mee, J. (Eds.). (2002). *Selected letters: John Keats.* Oxford; New York: Oxford University Press.

Goos, M., Hughes, C., & Webster-Wright, A. (2009). *Building capacity for assessment leadership via professional development and mentoring of course coordinators.* Australian Learning and Teaching Council Report, University of Queensland.

Groundwater-Smith, S., & Mockler, N. (2009). *Teacher professional learning in an age of compliance: Mind the gap.* Dordrecht: Springer.

Guignon, C. B. (2004a). Becoming a self: The role of authenticity in being and time. In C. B. Guignon (Ed.), *The existentialists* (pp. 119–132). New York: Rowman & Littlefield Publishers.

Guignon, C. B. (2004b). *On being authentic.* London; New York: Routledge.

Gurtler, S. (2005). The ethical dimension of work: A feminist perspective. *Hypatia, 20*(2), 119–135.

Gustavsen, B. (2008). Action research, practical challenges and the formation of theory. *Action Research, 6*(4), 421–437.

Hager, P., & Halliday, J. (2006). *Recovering informal learning: Wisdom, judgement and community.* Dordrecht: Springer.

Harris, K.-L., Farrell, K., Bell, M., Devlin, M., & James, R. (2009). *Peer review of teaching in Australian Higher Education.* Retrieved October 12, 2009, from http://www.altc.edu.au/resource-peer-review-of-teaching-melbourne-2009

Higgs, J., & Titchen, A. (2001a). Framing professional practice: Knowing and doing in context. In J. Higgs & A. Titchen (Eds.), *Professional practice in health, education and the creative arts* (pp. 3–15). Oxford: Blackwell Science.

Higgs, J., & Titchen, A. (2001b). Professional practice: Walking alone with others. In J. Higgs & A. Titchen (Eds.), *Professional practice in health, education and the creative arts* (pp. 267–272). Oxford: Blackwell Science.

Hill, S. B. (2005). Social ecology as a framework for understanding and working with social capital and sustainability in rural communities. In A. Dale & J. Onyx (Eds.), *A dynamic balance: Social capital and sustainable community development* (pp. 48–68). Vancouver: UBC Press.

Hinchcliffe, G., & Terzi, L. (2009). Introduction to the special issue: Capabilities and education. *Studies in Philosophy of Education, 28*(5), 387–390.

Hodge, T. (1997). Towards a conceptual framework for assessing progress towards sustainability. *Social Indicators Research, 40*, 5–98.

Hodkinson, P., Biesta, G., & James, D. (2007). Understanding learning cultures. *Educational Review, 59*(4), 415–427.

Hodkinson, H., & Hodkinson, P. (2005). Improving schoolteachers' workplace learning. *Research Papers in Education, 20*(2), 109–131.

Holden, R. (2009). The public university's unbearable defiance of being. *Educational Philosophy and Theory, 41*(5), 575–591.

Hostetler, K., Macintyre Latta, M. A., & Sarroub, L. K. (2007). Retrieving meaning in teacher education: The question of being. *Journal of Teacher Education, 58*(3), 231.

Howkins, J. (2009). *Creative ecologies: Where thinking is a proper job*. Brisbane, QLD: University of Queensland Press.

Hughes, C. (2004). The supervisor's influence on workplace learning. *Studies in Continuing Education, 26*(2), 275–287.

Hyland, N. E., & Noffke, S. E. (2005). Understanding diversity through social and community inquiry. *Journal of Teacher Education, 56*(4), 367–381.

Iwama, M. (2004). Meaning and inclusion: Revisiting culture in occupational therapy. *Australian Occupational Therapy Journal, 51*(1), 1–2.

Johnson, K. E., & Golombek, P. R. (2002). *Teachers' narrative inquiry as professional development*. New York: Cambridge University Press.

Jones, A. (2007). Looking over our shoulders: Critical thinking and ontological insecurity in higher education. *London Review of Education, 5*(3), 209–222.

Katz, S., Sutherland, S., & Earl, L. (2005). Toward an evaluation habit of mind: Mapping the journey. *Teachers College Record, 107*(10), 2326–2350.

Kemmis, S. (1995). *Action research and communicative action: Changing teaching practices and the organisation of educational work*. Murdoch, WA: National Professional Developement Program, Murdoch University.

Kleiman, S. (2008). *Human centered nursing: The foundation of quality care*. Philadelphia, PA: F. A. Davis.

Mackenzie, C. (2002). Critical reflection, self-knowledge, and the emotions. *Philosophical Explorations, 5*(3), 186–206.

Manathunga, C. (2007). Supervision as mentoring: The role of power and boundary crossing. *Studies in Continuing Education, 29*(2), 207–221.

Marginson, S. (2008). Academic creativity under new public management: Foundations for an investigation. *Educational Theory, 58*(3), 269–287.

Marsick, V. J. (2006). Informal strategic learning in the workplace. In J. N. Streumer (Ed.), *Work-related learning* (pp. 51–69). Dortrecht: Springer.

Mason, J. (2004). Personal narratives, relational selves: Residential histories in the living and telling. *The Sociological Review, 52*(2), 162–179.

Mattingly, C. (1998). *Healing dramas and clinical plots: The narrative structure of experience*. Cambridge; New York: Cambridge University Press.

Mattsson, M., & Kemmis, S. (2007). Praxis-related research: Serving two masters. *Pedagogy, Culture and Society, 15*(2), 185–214.

McGill, I., & Beaty, L. (2001). *Action learning: A guide for professional, management & educational development* (2nd ed.). London: Kogan Page.

McGill, I., & Brockbank, A. (2004). *The action learning handbook: Powerful techniques for education, professional development and training*. London; New York: RoutledgeFalmer.

McKenna, B., Rooney, D., & Liesch, P. (2006). Beyond knowledge to wisdom in international business strategy. *Prometheus, 24*(3), 283–300.

McWilliam, E. (2002). Against professional development. *Educational Philosophy and Theory, 34*(3), 289–299.

McWilliam, E. (2004). W(h)ither practitioner research. *The Australian Educational Researcher*, *31*(2), 113–126.

Meads, G., Jones, I., Harrison, R., Forman, D., & Turner, W. (2009). How to sustain interprofessional learning and practice: Messages for higher education and health and social care management. *Journal of Education and Work*, *22*(1), 67–79.

Metcalfe, A., & Game, A. (2008). Significance and dialogue in learning and teaching. *Educational Theory*, *58*(3), 343–356.

Mezirow, J. (Ed.). (1990). *Fostering critical reflection in adulthood: a guide to transformative and emancipatory learning*. San Francisco: Jossey-Bass Publishers.

Mezirow, J. (Ed.). (2000). *Learning as transformation: Critical perspectives on a theory in progress*. San Francisco: Jossey-Bass.

Montuori, A. (2008). The joy of inquiry. *Journal of Transformative Education*, *6*(1), 8–26.

Moon, J. A. (1999). *Learning journals: a handbook for academics, students and professional development*. London: Kogan Page.

Noddings, N. (1992). *The challenge to care in schools: An alternative approach to education*. New York: Teachers College Press.

Noddings, N. (2002). *Educating moral people: a caring alternative to character education*. New York: Teachers College Press.

Norberg, J., & Cumming, G. S. (Eds.). (2008). *Complexity theory for a sustainable future*. New York: Columbia University Press.

Norberg, J., Wilson, J., Walker, B., & Ostrom, E. (2008). Diversity and resilience of social-ecological systems. In J. Norberg & G. S. Cumming (Eds.), *Complexity theory for a sustainable future* (pp. 46–79). New York: Columbia University Press.

Nussbaum, M. C. (2000). *Women and human development: The capabilities approach*. Cambridge, MA; New York: Cambridge University Press.

Nussbaum, M. C., & Sen, A. K. (Eds.). (1993). *The quality of life*. Oxford: Clarendon Press; New York: Oxford University Press.

Oakes, J., & Rogers, J. (2007). Radical change through radical means: Learning power. *Journal of Educational Change*, *8*, 193–206.

O'Neil, O. (2002). A question of trust: Called to account. *Lecture 3*, from http://www.bbc.co.uk/radio4/reith2002/

O'Neil, J., & Marsick, V. J. (2007). *Understanding action learning*. New York: American Management Association.

Palmer, P. J. (1998). *The courage to teach: Exploring the inner landscape of a teacher's life*. San Francisco: Jossey-Bass.

Phillips, J. (2007). *Care*. Cambridge, MA: Polity.

Prilleltensky, I., & Prilleltensky, O. (2006). *Promoting well-being: Linking personal, organizational and community change*. Hoboken, NJ: Wiley.

Reason, P., & Bradbury, H. (Eds.). (2001). *Handbook of action research: Participative inquiry and practice*. London; Thousand Oaks, CA: Sage Publications.

Reid, A. (2004). *Towards a culture of inquiry in DECS*. Retrieved May 5, 2006, from http://www.decs.sa.gov.au/corporate/files/links/OP_01.pdf

Reid, A., & O'Donoghue, M. (2004). Revisiting enquiry-based teacher education in neo-liberal times. *Teaching and Teacher Education*, *20*(6), 559–570.

Reydon, T. A., & Scholz, M. (2009). Why organizational ecology is not a darwinian research program. *Philosophy of the Social Sciences*, *39*(3), 408–439.

Rhodes, C., & Scheeres, H. (2004). Developing people in organizations: Working (on) identity. *Studies in Continuing Education*, *26*(2), 175–193.

Rodrigues, S. (Ed.). (2005). *International perspectives on teacher professional development: Changes influenced by politics, pedagogy and innovation*. New York: Nova Science.

Rowland, S. (2006). *The enquiring university: Compliance and contestation in higher education*. Maidenhead; New York: Open University Press; Society for Research into Higher Education.

Rowley, J., & Gibbs, P. (2008). From learning organization to practically wise organization. *Learning Organization, 15*(5), 356–372.

Sandholtz, J. H., & Scribner, S. P. (2006). The paradox of administrative control in fostering teacher professional development. *Teaching and Teacher Education, 22,* 1104–1117.

Sen, A. K. (1992). *Inequality reexamined.* New York: Russell Sage Foundation; Oxford: Clarendon Press.

Sen, A. K. (1999). *Commodities and capabilities.* Delhi; New York: Oxford University Press.

Sen, A. K. (2006). *Identity and violence: The illusion of destiny.* London: Penguin.

Sen, A. K. (2009). *The idea of justice.* London; New York: Allen Lane/Penguin Books.

Senge, P. M. (1990). *The fifth discipline: The art and practice of the learning organization.* New York: Doubleday; Currency.

Smith-Maddox, R. (1999). An inquiry-based reform effort: Creating the conditions for reculturing and restructuring schools. *The Urban Review, 31*(3), 283–304.

Sparkes, A. C. (2007). Embodiment, academics, and the audit culture: A story seeking consideration. *Qualitative Research, 7*(4), 521–550.

Stronach, I., Corbin, B., McNamara, O., Stark, S., & Warne, T. (2002). Towards an uncertain politics of professionalism: Teacher and nurse identities in flux. *Journal of Education Policy, 17*(1), 109–138.

Sullivan, W. M. (1995). *Work and integrity: The crisis and promise of professionalism in America.* New York: HarperCollins.

Sullivan, W. M., & Rosin, M. S. (2008). *A new agenda for higher education: Shaping a life of the mind for practice.* San Francisco: Jossey-Bass; Carnegie Foundation for the Advancement of Teaching.

Swaffield, S., & MacBeath, J. (2005). School self evaluation and the role of a critical friend. *Cambridge Journal of Education, 35*(2), 239–252.

Taylor, C. (1992). *The ethics of authenticity.* Cambridge, MA: Harvard University Press.

Taylor, E. W. (2008). Transformative learning theory. In S. B. Merriam (Ed.), *Third update on adult learning theory* (pp. 5–15). San Francisco: Jossey-Bass.

Thomson, I. (2004a). Heidegger's perfectionist philosophy of education in being and time. *Continental Philosophy Review, 37,* 439–467.

Thomson, I. (2004b). Ontology and ethics at the intersection of phenomenology and environmental philosophy. *Inquiry, 47*(4), 380–412.

Titchen, A. (2000). *Professional craft knowledge in patient-centred nursing and the facilitation of its development.* Oxford: University of Oxford.

Trede, F., Higgs, J., Jones, M., & Edwards, I. (2003). Emancipatory practice: A model for physiotherapy practice? *Focus on Health Professional Education, 5*(2), 1–13.

Tripp, D. (1993). *Critical incidents in teaching: Developing professional judgement.* London; New York: Routledge.

Tsivacou, I. (2005). Designing communities of ideas for the human well-being. In B. H. Banathy & P. M. Jenlink (Eds.), *Dialogue as a means of collective communication* (pp. 41–70). New York: Kluwer Academic/Plenum Publishers.

UNESCO. (2005). Education for sustainable development in action. *United Nations Decade of Education for Sustainable Development (2005–2014).* Retrieved September 12, 2008, from http://cms01.unesco.org/en/esd/publications/

United Nations. (2009). What is good governance? *Economic and Social Commission for Asia and the Pacific.* Retrieved September 20, 2009, from http://www.unescap.org/pdd/prs/ProjectActivities/Ongoing/gg/governance.asp

Vygotsky, L. S. (1978). *Mind in society: The development of higher psychological processes.* Cambridge, MA: Harvard University Press.

Wadsworth, Y. (2001). The mirror, the magnifying glass, the compass and the map: Facilitating participatory action research. In P. Reason & H. Bradbury (Eds.), *Handbook of action research: Participative inquiry and practice* (pp. 420–432). London: Sage Publications.

Walker, M. (Ed.). (2001). *Reconstructing professionalism in university teaching: Teachers and learners in action.* Philadelphia, PA: Open University.

Walker, M. (2006). *Higher education pedagogies: a capabilities approach*. England: Open University Press.

Walker, M. (2009a). Critical capability pedagogies and university education. *Educational Philosophy and Theory, 41*, 1–20.

Walker, M. (2009b). *Development discourses: Higher education and poverty reduction in South Africa*. Retrieved November 12, 2009, from http://www.nottingham.ac.uk/EducationResearchProjects/DevelopmentDiscourses/PapersandResources.aspx

Ward, C., & McCormack, B. (2000). Creating an adult learning culture through practice development. *Nurse Education Today, 20*(4), 259–266.

Weil, S. (1999). Re-creating universities for 'beyond the stable state': from 'dearingesque' systematic control to post-dearing systematic learning and inquiry. *Systems Research and Behavioral Science, 16*(2), 171–194.

Whitehead, J., & McNiff, J. (2006). *Action research living theory*. London; Thousand Oaks, CA: Sage Publications.

Wideen, M., Mayer-Smith, J., & Moon, B. (1998). A critical analysis of the research on learning to teach: Case for an ecological perspective on inquiry. *Review of Educational Research, 68*(2), 130–178.

Williams, L. (2009). Jostling for position: a sociology of allied health. In J. Germov (Ed.), *Second opinion: An introduction to health sociology* (pp. 452–475). Melbourne: Oxford University Press.

Wood, D. (2007). Teachers' learning communities: Catalyst for change or a new infrastructure for the status quo? *Teachers College Record, 109*(3), 699.

# Part V
# Conclusion

In describing and interpreting the findings of this research, I have attempted a productive discussion that does not claim to provide answers. As I gather the threads of the book together I hesitate in drawing firm conclusions. The tidiness of conclusions implies certainty. Yet, as argued, interpretation of research involves but one particular way of looking at evidence and any analysis of human experience involves ambiguity. Although phenomenology, as a philosophy and methodological approach, values rigour in analysis of the experiences of human beings, phenomenology also holds that ambiguity is inherent to being human.

In a sense my dilemma is reflective of a tension between performativity and meaning in research, similar to that described in professional practice in Part IV. There is the need to balance the performative goal of producing demonstrable and pertinent research findings using rigorous processes and the aim of speaking out on behalf of the professionals who lent me their voices. I follow academic conventions by attempting to provide a balanced view of what the data reveal about professional life and learning, whilst being acutely aware that this book only touches the surface of these embodied, felt, lived experiences. I know, as do professionals who spoke to me during the research and since, of some workplace situations that are more unsettling than I can do justice to in this book. Such difficulties emerge through the findings, but only in pastel hues, yet their influence more dramatically colours daily working life than this text implies.

Tensions and difficulties are part of any life, however, and most professionals have considerable intellectual, emotional and practical resources to draw upon as they negotiate reasonable pathways in dealing with dilemmas. I hope that the joys and satisfaction of life as a practicing professional are also revealed in this book. They certainly are part of being a professional, especially the privilege of contributing to society through making a difference to people's lives.

Chapter 9 begins by summarising the main arguments of the book, revisiting the original research intent in the light of the findings. The limitations and strengths of this approach to investigating professional learning are considered. Contributions philosophy can make to empirical research are discussed, in relation to this book. The importance of challenging the status quo and imagining different possibilities are highlighted in summarising ways forward, making practical and theoretical contributions towards a change in PD. Proposals for supporting learning, in ways that are authentic and sustainable, are summarised, in addition to more nebulous possibilities that may be addressed in future research. Chapter 9 concludes as the book began, with the voice of a practising professional.

# Chapter 9
# Making a Difference

To meet the global challenges of an uncertain future, continuing learning by all professionals, from academics and teachers, to engineers and social workers, is vital. The ability of skilled and innovative professionals to solve increasingly complex and diverse problems underpins productivity, sustainability and well-being in society. Through their practice and continued learning, professionals have a responsibility – and a privilege – to make a difference by contributing to priority areas of global concern: the development of innovative technology and infrastructure, environmental and social sustainability, and the well-being of individuals and communities.

As this book highlights, although extensive resources have been poured into the PD industry, much traditional PD is ineffective in inspiring significant change, sometimes alienating professionals rather than supporting their learning. Essentially 30 years of research has shown that professionals (and other adults) learn best when they work collaboratively over time, on problems that are genuinely important to them and related to their areas of professional interest. Creative inquiry involves professionals drawing on their own and others' experiences of what did and didn't work. They seek and incorporate new ideas through reflection or from research, when they see the relevance of them and are free to find their own ways of incorporating such changes into their practices.

There is acknowledgement in research of the need for self-directed learning, supported in ways that take into account the diversity and humanity of professionals as people, yet traditional PD is still delivered across a range of professions. The dominant discourse in PD centres on ensuring accountability and maintaining standards through performative measures. Increasingly, meeting these standards requires professionals to accrue PD points to remain registered. Despite lip service given to other means, didactic workshops with little follow-up or group support remain the predominant mode of acquiring points. In the name of efficiency, valuable research about learning is overlooked or discounted in the search for standardised, easily distributed and scalable programmes to produce learning outcomes. Although being scalable, in terms of widening the influence and impact of an approach, is a laudable goal, this is often attempted through a one size fits all solution, rather than one that is adaptable to suit local needs. Standardised solutions may stifle innovation, denying professionals freedom to creatively enhance their practice (Coffield, 2007).

As research quoted in the book highlights, innovative approaches to supporting PL are being enacted, particularly in teaching and parts of the health professions. Exciting stories of creative practices are difficult to hear, however, amongst the incessant drone about meeting PD standards. The research underpinning this book demonstrated a disconnect between the realities of professional life and the rhetoric about PD. Continuing learning was demonstrated to be an essentially self-directed activity that cannot be mandated but can be supported. The notion of "Authentic Professional Learning", developed in this book to describe learning as lived, provides an alternative way to understand continuing learning and develop authentic and sustainable strategies to support professionals as they learn.

## 9.1  Revisiting the Research

In Chapter 1, the genesis of the book in my own professional experiences and those of my colleagues and the subsequently reflexive, collaborative nature of this research were mentioned. In exploring the continuation of traditional PD, despite decades of educational research suggesting possibilities for change, the research underpinning this book aimed to understand more about how professionals learn, in order to improve support for that learning.

### 9.1.1  Exploration of the Field

In Chapter 2, diverse fields of research inquiry were explored to map the development of professions, and growing interest in the continuing learning of professionals, over past decades. By mapping development of practices, against changing social and professional contexts, in combination with evolving research into learning, the way that assumptions about PD came to be entrenched was investigated. Tensions in the contemporary working climate were identified: between regulatory control measures aiming for certainty in standards and the inherent uncertainty and growing complexity of professional practice in rapidly changing circumstances. In exploring changes, in practice, research and contexts, the socio-historic roots of this tension were considered.

Since the 1980s, researchers have queried the appropriateness of didactic approaches to PD, arguing for the value of self-regulated PL (Houle, 1980). This argument grew stronger through the 1990s with conventional wisdom about learning, as transfer of information into practitioners' minds, being challenged by research. Such research stressed the embodied, constructed and contextualised nature of learning. Research highlighting the largely informal and incidental nature of learning through practice at work has grown to a crescendo through the past decade. Despite changed understandings about learning in research, support for learning in professional practice remains mired in delivery of information updates (Wilson, 2000). Programmes of PD are often more flexible and practice related, but little has changed about the assumptions underpinning their delivery to professionals, who are implicitly deemed deficient, regardless of the depth of their experience or wisdom.

Through this same period, newer professions (such as therapies and social work) were establishing their educational credentials and credibility. To achieve these ends, through the 1970s and the 1980s, these professions were keen to embrace a rigorous and knowledge-based preparatory education, a scientific technicist discourse, and later on, an evidence-based framework of practice. Continuing education and PD reflected these priorities. Realisation began to dawn in some areas of the professional literature in the 1990s, that essentials from the "messy swamp" of practice had been somewhat devalued in this move, such as empathy with people or creativity in practice. Yet the voice of reasoned concern, that perhaps the pendulum towards prescribed, measurable standards had swung too far, was generally subsumed under the rising tide of a performative, managerialist control of workplace practices over the past decade.

As Chapter 2 illustrated, recent research critiques PD and aspects of the workplace as a context for learning (e.g. Penuel, Fishman, Yamaguchi, & Gallagher, 2007). Research into innovative models of support for PL is also growing. Nevertheless, traditional PD, grounded in the past search for credibility and reinforced by the performative present, continues to be the default approach in most professions. My research had a particular focus on practitioners' perspectives about learning and related workplace issues. Through exploring professionals' experiences of learning, I also sought to investigate if and how dilemmas highlighted in other research affected professionals' everyday working lives.

Chapter 3 described how phenomenology was used to research the lived experience of continuing to learn as a professional, in a holistic way that sought understanding from within the diversity and complexity of those experiences. This research demonstrated a fundamentally different conceptual framework for investigating learning as embedded within professional life. The phenomenological methodology used sought credibility as well as evocation of experience, using criteria of rigour, reflexivity and relevance as described in Chapter 4.

## 9.1.2 Key Findings of the Research

The two key findings of this empirical phenomenological research are the description of the essential structure of the experience of APL and the associated dissonance between this experience and expectations about PD. In examining this experience and associated dissonance, both the context for learning and ontological dimensions of learning are highlighted. In critiquing the assumptions and practice of PD, I argue throughout this book for a shift in the conceptualisation of, and support for, learning: from continually developing professionals to supporting authentic learning as an integral part of professional practice.

This book began with examples highlighting the complexity and diversity of continuing to learn. In Chapter 5, texture and depth were given to these adjectives, through describing the multifaceted phenomenological structure of APL, with vignettes highlighting the idiosyncratic way in which each professional experiences learning. The phenomenological analysis was integrated with other research and philosophical reflections to examine problematic features in professionals' working contexts in Chapter 6. How professionals learn to deal with workplace issues depends on their way of being a professional. Chapter 7 examined professional being, including the notion of authenticity and what being authentic might mean in professional life.

The descriptions of continuing to learn included a diverse range of experiences. Participants detailed many interrelated situations where they learnt: from attending a planned course to a seemingly inconsequential incident at work; from working with a client to participating in an online network; from undertaking a practice that failed to imaginative ideas gleaned from beyond work; from tea-room chats to thinking about work in the car on the way home. Both thinking and doing are involved in APL; both understanding and uncertainty are features of APL. Although diverse experiences are involved, continuing to learn is experienced in a holistic interconnected way rather than as differentiated and well-defined elements. Throughout this book I caution against categorisation of different aspects of experience, as potentially useful for analysis, but misleading if taken for granted as representing experience.

From the phenomenological analysis, four constituents were identified as essential for the experience to be described as APL. The four constituents (understanding, engagement, interconnection and openness) and their thirteen sub-constituents are interrelated in a holographic manner as the structure of the experience of APL (see Table 5.1, Chapter 5). Change in professional understanding is the core constituent. Active engagement in practice and interconnection with others over time describe in a chiasmic manner how such change in understanding occurs. The change in understanding in APL opens up many possibilities that are circumscribed by the professional's context. Insight is developed into the experience of APL through close examination of these constituents. Although described separately below, the inherently interrelated nature of these four constituents is demonstrated through vignettes in Chapter 5.

Understanding in APL is always more than cognitive, being embodied and expressed by participants through ways of being a professional in practice. The nature of the change in understanding, the crux of APL, varied from changes in the way that certain situations were approached to transformative changes to a different way of being a professional. Changes involved three types of learning transitions, with few participants describing the third type "questioning what is done". Despite a focus in the literature on the value of questioning assumptions through critical reflection, this research found that these professionals rarely did so, limiting reflection to analytical thinking and practical planning. Contextual and ontological reasons for this apparent absence were suggested in Part IV.

There are a wide variety of ways of engaging in different aspects of practice in APL. For participants, engagement was active, in areas that mattered to the professionals but they felt uncertain about. Participants were clear that what mattered to them as professionals was feeling they were making a difference in some way, to clients, and often, to society. Learning involved novelty, either from integration of new information or from transitions that triggered new ways of looking. Learning was often seen as an enjoyable way of renewing professional practice. Although uncertainty was revealed as integral to learning and creativity, its existence caused concern for many participants, who held a hidden misgiving that they were the only ones who couldn't establish certainty in their practice.

Temporal and social dimensions are revealed in interconnection in APL, whereby learning involves a complex web of experiences with others over time. Learning is circular and iterative rather than a linear means-end project. Interconnection in APL involved imagination, mentioned in various ways by all participants, but perceived to be undervalued by organisations. Imagination was integral to seeing creative possibilities for action as well as in communicating well with others. Some participants had difficulty imagining the perspective of other professionals or clients. For those uncomfortable with uncertainty, the safety of seeing one perspective aligned with the certainty related in seeking the one "best" way of practice. These participants recognised uncertainty in their practice, but thought its continuation was a failure on their part as a professional. Many commented on being unprepared by their education for practice uncertainties.

Because APL involves change in understanding through engagement in practice in an interconnected web of experience, APL is inherently open to a range of possible outcomes. Yet this openness is not infinite, but is circumscribed and shaped by contextual opportunities and constraints, in both overt and obscure ways. Although the participants were enthusiastic about learning, they described tensions within the experience of APL, particularly between the openness and uncertainty of learning and the circumscription and regulation of context. Resolution of tensions varied with each person's way of being a professional, so that each professional's learning had an idiosyncratic quality. Openness infuses the other constituents in APL and sharply highlights differences between APL experiences and PD expectations.

As learning is revealed as an expression of each professional's way of being, I argue that continuing to learn as a professional is an ontological as well as epistemological concern. Each professional's way of learning is an expression of her particular way of being a professional and shapes and is shaped by that way of being, in continual interplay with the professional context. The experience of learning as a professional, therefore, has a common shared structure but is expressed differently by individuals. Moreover, it is hypothesised that learning experiences help construct a professional way of being in the early years of practice.

### 9.1.3 Continuation of Traditional PD

This study empirically supports the proposition that continuing to learn is part of the lived experience of being a professional. Insight is provided into the nature of the experience of APL as complex, diverse, idiosyncratic and multifaceted. Much of the rhetoric and practice in continuing professional education, development or training is not consistent with the reality of continuing to learn as a professional. Although there may be a need for continuing education to introduce research findings to practitioners, or staff training to introduce changes in organisational direction, these interventions should not be confused with learning. Learning may, or may not, occur through such activities, in combination with other experiences.

Problematic features of the current professional context, with a focus on supervision of standards rather than support for learning, were examined with respect to dissonance. Participants did describe tensions at work between external regulation and control and the uncertainty and complexity of professional practice. I argue in Chapter 6 that tensions revealed in the experience of APL, and the overall dissonance between reality and rhetoric in learning, reflect wider concerns involved in being a professional in the current context, within competing life-world discourses of performativity and meaning. However, despite reporting increases in work intensity and stress, there was limited public dissent from professionals about work. Most of the cohort studied were reticent to express their concerns in public forums, despite widespread recognition of the disparity between what happens in professional practice and official expectations.

Therefore, although dissonance between reality and rhetoric in learning appears to be a common professional experience, it is largely hidden from official view. Dissonance was often internalised as a private individual issue, rather than externalised publicly as a shared professional concern. For allied health professionals, this privatisation of dissonance may underlie the lack of public questioning of performative features of the workplace that constrain both learning and practice. As the current focus of PD is rarely questioned overtly, there is little discussion about possibilities for change. The hidden nature of dissonance in a culture where questioning and dissent is not encouraged and professionals may feel their work is undervalued means that some professionals are uncomfortable with their way of learning and of being a professional. Examination of the ontological dimensions of learning allowed the notion of authenticity to be considered with respect to different ways of dealing with dissonance, raising issues of identity and values in professional life.

Questions about the lack of significant change in PD practices were a stimulus for this research. Reasons for the continuation of the status quo in PD in many professions have been hypothesised from the findings. I argue that the underlying assumptions of PD contribute to the lack of change in PD practices. Because of the epistemological framing of PD, on change in professional knowledge through developing the professional, PD overlooks implications of both ontology and context for learning. In this study there was a lack of overt discussion about doubt and uncertainty in professional practice and little public questioning of official expectations and assumptions about learning. If professionals don't voice concerns about dissonance between their experiences and others' expectations, dissonance becomes a personal, private problem. The contemporary working culture reinforces this status quo because the performative and regulatory focus, on supervision and control rather than support and trust, resists public dissent. That is, the assumptions of PD in interaction with the current professional context form a double-edged sword, resisting change in both the private and public arenas.

### 9.1.4 Finding What I Was Looking for

As mentioned, a criticism of using a phenomenological perspective in this research is that I found what I was looking for. Such a criticism is valid. Assumptions about the holistic nature of experience, the socially constructed nature of reality and the inter-subjective construction of meaning shaped the study's design and the way findings were interpreted. Any way of looking at a research problem necessarily precludes other ways of seeing the same problem. A strong case could be made for taking a different perspective of this same study, for example a critical discourse analysis or a gender-based analysis, which would highlight different aspects of the same experiences and situations, with different subsequent findings.

The research underpinning this book focuses on a group of health professionals. Although interpretative research aims to understand specific situations and cannot be abstracted to universal claims, the findings of phenomenology may be applicable more widely (van Manen, 1997). From this research, the essential structure of APL, based on commonality across diverse descriptions of learning, and critique of traditional PD and the current working context for PL may be pertinent to other professions. Whilst further research is needed (and continues) to validate these findings with other professionals, the experiences described and issues raised resonate with research reported elsewhere about other professions (e.g. Groundwater-Smith & Mockler, 2009). These issues play out in different ways for different professionals, workplace groups and organisations.

In the research I describe most participants as enthusiastic and responsible learners. As the participants were volunteers, the study may be skewed towards those interested in learning, although one participant openly expressed growing disinterest. General enthusiasm and a sense of responsibility about learning do resonate with my past involvement with professionals and with those professionals who gave feedback on the findings. I also claim there are problematic issues in the context for learning, yet only those with particular concerns may have volunteered. However, other research drawn on in Part IV make similar claims about the working context.

As detailed in Chapter 4, the fact that I was a health professional with experiences similar to some participants had positive and negative implications for this research. I was aware of issues of relevance for the participants and my involvement allowed candid dialogue. However, such empathy involved shared assumptions with participants that may have limited my probing, despite concerted attempts at reflexivity. My arguments in this book represent attempts to substantiate what seem plausible and worthwhile interpretations of the participants' experiences, in the light of established research. Whilst accepting the possibility of alternative interpretations, I aim to represent rather than "mis-represent" the reality of their experiences (see Garrick, 2000). No matter how rigorous the research, holistic investigation of lived experience will never "prove" any hypothesis. I can only hope to further our understanding of the experience of learning as a professional.

## 9.2  Philosophy and Practice

In this book, phenomenological research is used to investigate stories of experiences from the life-world. Findings are integrated with empirical research from interdisciplinary areas of inquiry, examined in the light of philosophical theories. Philosophical writings are often considered dense and their arguments obtuse, with little apparent relevance for professional practice. I contend that philosophy has much to offer investigations into problems of practice. In contrast to the (qualified) certainty of empirical research, the value of philosophy can be found in its absolute uncertainty. As Bertrand Russell (1912/1998, p. 91) maintained:

> While diminishing our feeling of certainty as to what things are, [philosophy] greatly increases our knowledge as to what they may be; it removes the somewhat arrogant dogmatism of those who have never travelled into the region of liberating doubt, and it keeps alive our sense of wonder by showing familiar things in an unfamiliar aspect. . ... Philosophy is to be studied, not for the sake of any definite answers to its questions since no definite answers can, as a rule, be known to be true, but rather for the sake of the questions themselves; because these questions enlarge our conception of what is possible, enrich our intellectual imagination and diminish the dogmatic assurance which closes the mind against speculation.

Both uncertainty and the questions and possibilities that arise from the ability to be in uncertainty reverberate in issues discussed throughout this book. Philosophical theories are helpful in holding open such uncertainties, questions and possibilities in research, whilst offering ideas as starting points for taking practical action towards change. A combination of empirical findings with theoretical interpretation extends research beyond what either can achieve alone. Educational researcher, David Silverman (2005, p. 107), claims: "Without theory, research is impossibly narrow. Without research, theory is mere armchair contemplation". I have drawn extensively on phenomenological philosophy, but also drew on other philosophers such as John Dewey, Martha Nussbaum and Charles Taylor as appropriate.

### 9.2.1  Contributions of Phenomenological Philosophy

To research learning in a holistic way, describing findings without falling back into the atomism of categories, is a difficult task. Research can never adequately capture experience as lived, nor can language liberate the insights claimed by the researcher. I have found not only the theoretical perspective but also the language of phenomenology to be useful in this attempt. Phenomenology is concerned with questions that arise from life. As demonstrated in Chapters 3 and 7, the phenomenological philosophy drawn on from Martin Heidegger, Maurice Merleau-Ponty, Hans-Georg Gadamer and Jean-Paul Sartre resonates with lived professional experience in many ways, allowing insights into the nature of, and dilemmas in, professional practice.

Of particular value in this research has been Heidegger's ontological analysis of being-in-the-world and interpretations and extensions of his work by others. Drawing on Heidegger's analysis of being human helped me interrogate the structure of experience of APL, raising questions in relation to the meaning of being-a-professional-in-the-professional-world. The usefulness of Heidegger's philosophy as a framework for studies of professional practice is the cogent manner in which he analyses human being, in a way that privileges neither person nor world, highlighting their interrelationship through the unity of lived experience. As discussed previously, ontological concerns prefigure epistemological and axiological concerns in Heidegger's phenomenological analysis. That is, our primordial understanding of "being-in-the-world" forms the basis for all our knowing and valuing, indeed for all our communicating, questioning or acting in that world. Such understanding also forms the basis for all our possibilities for being, including being authentic.

For Heidegger, then, authenticity arises from the ground of being-in-the-world. A call to authenticity can come by chance, for example, through a disorientating incident from "struggling" in communication with "the they", causing an individual to stop and think mindfully about values and concerns (Zickmund, 2007). Such an incident arose for Olivia. Dealing with miscommunication in her team led her to reassess what she stood for and her way of being a professional. Sometimes an active choice can be made, based on a reflexive awareness and questioning of assumptions underlying actions at work. Such resolute authenticity was demonstrated by Sam as her way of being a professional, which led her to take the actions of a "maverick" in standing up on behalf of her clients.

As I propose in Chapters 7 and 8, authenticity in professional life is constituted as a personal and social concern, with a reflexive and ethical awareness. Being authentic does not distance a professional from her practice in a self-reflective reverie, but allows authentic engagement with others in the world of practice. As Heidegger (1927/1962, p. 344) claims:

> Resoluteness, as *authentic Being-one's-Self*, does not detach Dasein from its world, nor does it isolate it so that it becomes a free-floating 'I'. . .. Only by authentically Being-their-Selves in resoluteness can people authentically be with one another.

Being authentic involves weighing up responsibilities and possibilities, to make judgements about what is worth pursuing and to take action. In making a reflexive choice to act, a professional's "authentic potentiality-for-Being" can be revealed from its "lostness" in the "they" (Heidegger, p. 312). Taking authentic action towards change does not necessarily infer physical action. For example, I have discussed the need to openly share stories of professional life and learning and the importance of questioning and resisting some current practices, if change towards support for APL is to be realised. "The term 'take action' ... must be taken so broadly that 'activity' will also embrace the passivity of resistance" notes Heidegger (p. 347).

Given the complexity of Heidegger's work, it could be argued that I have selected from his arguments only aspects that suit the purposes of this study. According to Hubert Dreyfus (2000) and Michael Inwood (2000), the authentic way to read and interpret Heidegger's works, or that of any philosopher, is not to follow blindly, but to use the work as a guide for thinking about real world issues. Heidegger (1963,

p. viii) talks about his aim of providing direction for independent reflection of his readers, on a path "which each must travel for himself".

## 9.2.2  What Matters in Professional and Public Life?

Reference is made through this book to what matters in professional life, what is worth pursuing and what is valued by professionals, organisations and the community. As discussed at the end of Chapter 7, exploring the diverse field of values, ethics and morals is a slippery and contested area of life and of research. Similarly, notions of valued ends worth pursuing, such as community well-being or social justice, are often loosely defined, yet sharply debated, in terms of "human flourishing" or the "public good". Despite this ambiguity in definition and delineation, philosopher Charles Taylor (2007, p. 16) argues that notions of valued ends shape our lives:

> Every person, and every society, lives with or by some conception(s) of what human flourishing is: what constitutes a fulfilled life? What makes life really worth living? What would we most admire people for? We can't help asking these and related questions in our lives. And our struggles to answer them define the views that we try to live by, or between which we hover. At another level, these views are codified, sometimes in philosophical theories, sometimes in moral codes, sometimes in religious practices and devotion. These and the various ill-formulated practices which people around us engage in constitute the resources that our society offers each one of us as we try to lead our lives.

Professionals in this research clearly state that learning is related to what they care about, value and see as worthwhile. Indeed implicit values underpin all professional judgements and actions. Paul Hager and John Halliday (2006, p. 249) end their book on informal learning, judgement and wisdom by stating, with reference to Dewey, that "how people want to live a life affects how they want to learn". Such a link between valued ways of living and ways of learning has also been made in this book. The way a professional values living her life, as an expression of her way of being, will affect her choices in practice. Recognition of this ontological link between professional life and learning highlights the importance of allowing for professional agency in making choices in directing learning. As discussed earlier, when denied freedom for some self-regulation, professionals still make choices to adapt rules according to what they hold as valuable and see as relevant to client needs (Coffield, 2007; Hoyle & Wallace, 2007). The problem with such covert actions is that rules and regulations that govern practice are not challenged or changed.

For example, contemporary philosophical consideration of values distinguishes between "the good", as a morally positive goal of our actions, and "the right" as a set of public norms that shapes our pursuit of the good (Joas, 2000, p. 166). Enhancement of client or community well-being, in the broad sense of the common good, is widely considered to be the ultimate goal for practitioners in the caring professions (Prilleltensky & Prilleltensky, 2006, p. 59). In the current working context, there can be tension between the good and the right in professionals' working lives, related to competing life-world discourses. This tension is described by Susan Groundwater-Smith and Nicole Mockler (2009) as the difference between "doing good", in attending to a moral purpose, and "being good" with respect to compliance with professional regulations. In discussing the importance of self-directed inquiry-based learning, they describe ethical dilemmas that teachers face in making choices between these often contradictory positions. Teachers may try to fulfil what they see as their ethical responsibility to act in the interests of their students, in the face of contradictory requirements that regulate their teaching. Groundwater-Smith and Mockler argue that "in the current age of compliance, rarely do they overlap" (p. 11).

Hager and Halliday (2006, p. 232) describe the wise practitioner as able to weigh up such conflicting possibilities and come to "a balanced view of what needs to be done". Their description resonates with the idea of "standing back", to reflect and question, and "standing up", to advocate or act, in my descriptions of reflexive authenticity in Chapters 7 and 8. I agree with their conclusion about the importance of a moral dimension underpinning judgement that is considered to be wise (p. 217). Analytical skill is not sufficient in wise professional judgement, nor is reflexivity. Is authenticity as I discuss in this book related to wise professional judgement? In returning to the voices of professionals in the research, I argue that a relationship exists. An ethical and moral platform underpins what they say they value, described in terms of making a positive contribution to clients' lives. It is in this light that I have considered the possibilities of authenticity in professional life. Taylor (1992) makes a similar link.

Authenticity is not granted an explicitly moral dimension in Heidegger's work. Heidegger's ontological philosophy is variously interpreted as preceding ethics (ante-ethical) or opposing ethics (anti-ethical). Describing evidence for both positions, Saulius Geniusas (2009, p. 69) argues that conflicting interpretations of Heidegger's work reflect an inherent tension in being moral as human beings, "torn between authentic motivations and inescapably inauthentic regulations". Heidegger's work has certainly been critiqued for its lack of consideration of moral dilemmas (Adorno, 1973; Ferrara, 1998; Irigaray, 1999; Rose, 1996; Wolin, 1993). As Hager and Halliday (2006, p. 232), and others, point out, although Heidegger was an insightful philosopher, he did not demonstrate wise judgement in making his own moral choices in life. In full awareness of Heidegger's focus on ontology rather than on axiology, recent authors have nevertheless drawn on his philosophy to provide an insightful guide for thinking about contemporary ethical and moral life-world issues (Guignon, 2004; Nicholson, 2009; Stenstad, 2006). I have also attempted to draw on his ontological analysis to throw light onto dilemmas within the professional life-world.

Values, with their moral and ethics subtexts, matter to human beings and are embedded in everyday life. Their impact on professional life is diverse. Despite caring about lives of clients, a range of other aspects of practice matter to professionals, from career progression to personal fulfilment. In addition, values may not have positive moral connotations but be related to ingrained prejudices. The important issue with respect to learning is that values, valued ends and assumptions underlying these need to be surfaced and queried amongst practitioners, asking questions such as: What is the purpose for this activity? Why do we do this? Whose interests are being served? Is there a better way? Supporting APL, as described in this book, can allow and facilitate such questions in a climate of inquiry and trust. Through questioning assumptions, "what matters" to professionals and to society, what is worth learning about and changing in practice and what is worth "standing up" for can be discussed.

## 9.3  Making a Difference by Supporting APL

The title of this book focuses on making a difference. Professionals in this research valued making a difference to the lives of their clients and valued learning they saw as relevant to this aim. The book's premise is that the continuing learning of professionals is valuable for society. I contend that by supporting APL in ways outlined in Chapter 8, it is possible to make a difference in areas that "matter" in professional and public life. Supporting the capability of professionals to inquire into their practices, in ways that are sustaining for them as individuals and lead to sustainable, worthwhile changes in practice has potential practical benefits in resolving issues of importance to society. Thus support for APL may lead to valuable outcomes that have an impact on many levels of society. Although critique of an outcomes focus has featured in this book, I recognise outcomes in professional practice as important markers and milestones reflecting change. It is the focus on predetermined outcomes, chosen for ease of measurement, that may have no meaningful connection to what matters in professional practice, that have been queried.

### 9.3.1  Making a Difference at Work

Sustainable cultural change is possible, although difficult, through working within whilst challenging aspects of that culture. But what type of conversations, proposals and actions would make a difference with respect to learning? In Chapter 8, possibilities for changing ways of sustaining professionals as they learn at work were raised, framed by discussions about building a culture of inquiry with support for reflexive authenticity of professionals. In an inquiry-based learning culture, diversity of opinion could be sought, questioning through open dialogue encouraged and the commitment and enthusiasm of professionals towards their practice valued. An inquiry-based culture allows challenging, and even dissenting, questions to be raised. Although problematic and disconcerting, questioning and resultant uncertainty offer opportunities for individual and collective professional growth and organisational resilience.

Such a culture could support professionals to actively inquire into areas they care about, are relevant to their current engagement in practice, interconnect with their past experience and those of others and allow them to use their imagination in a creative way. This is not to deny that professionals may need to find out about areas they do not currently care about or that they may need to respond to the imposition of systemic imperatives. My point is that the reality of APL described in this book means that professionals do not learn unless their professional understanding

changes. When enabling learning in areas that professionals are not currently interested or involved in, the starting point needs to be a connection with their current
experiences and what matters to them as professionals.

As argued, shared awareness of professional realities is a necessary first step in
encouraging constructive dialogue about change. In sharing stories of practice, it
is not just the important successes that are worth mentioning, but also the doubts
and dilemmas, including the question of what it means to be a professional, trying
to make a difference whilst working in the current context. Much of the discourse
that surrounds professional practice is out of touch with the realities of everyday
work, leading to professionals feeling torn between the professional personas they
present and who they are. Support for reflexive authenticity in an inquiry-based
culture would highlight the importance of reflection on social and moral issues, a
professional's responsibility to question assumptions and congruence between values and actions. Hager and Halliday (2006, p. 232) describe reflexivity as a possible
"antidote to paralysis" in making judgements. Reflexively "standing back" from
practice could perhaps allow groups of professionals to "stand up" to undertake
achievable changes together, instead of feeling powerless to influence their working
contexts.

Throughout this book I acknowledge the need to balance professional agency
and self-determination with professional accountability and responsibility in supporting APL. Central to Sartre's (1943/1989) adaptation of Heidegger's ontology
is the essential entwining of freedom and responsibility for choices. These are
also related in Amartya Sen's (1992, 2009) capability framework. Professional
freedom to take charge of one's own learning holds agency and accountability in
a contextual relationship. Connections between agency and accountability could
be considered, in a dialectic rather than oppositional manner, in discussions with
stakeholders. Consideration could be given to how support of professional capability for thoughtful judgement might shape "intelligent" rather than prescribed
accountability (O'Neil, 2002).

In Chapter 8, practical ways of scaffolding, supporting and sustaining APL were
discussed that build on professionals' strengths as capable individuals and respects
the meaning they draw from experiences, whilst encouraging "mindful inquiry". In
suggesting feasible proposals for change, a flexible matrix of opportunities could be
offered as PL pathways, shaped by guidelines that allow for diversity and encourage
adaptation as integral to sustainability. Regardless of specific strategies used, an
explicit focus could be made on shifting from control and compliance to a valuing
of creativity and innovation in finding ways of dealing with problems of practice.

Within this framework professionals could come together in supportive relationships, sharing stories of inquiry. Yet each individual, or small group, directs
action towards situations that have meaning for her (or them) within a specific
practice. Additional structure may be needed to support learning for newer professionals. However, such learning to be a professional could take place within the
professional world rather than separate from it in specific decontextualised induction programmes, as happens in many workplaces. It would mean a move from
supervision to stewardship, with acceptance, valuing and celebration of diversity in

professional ways of learning and of being. Such a learning culture would enable authentic professional growth and practice inquiry as a continuing professional journey of becoming (see Dall'Alba, 2009a; Higgs & Titchen, 2001).

### 9.3.2 Making a Difference Beyond Work

Professionals are more able to actively contribute to society when they maintain their own well-being. Through development of trust, mature self-regulation and intelligent accountability, the well-being of professionals and social sustainability of organisations could be enhanced. Enabling and supporting APL may enhance intervention with clients and invigorate a profession as a whole, with professionals who are open to other perspectives, able to question their practices and advocate for their clients. Through collaborations between professionals, employing organisations, professional associations and higher education, continuing research into professional practice may lead to innovative ways of dealing with problems in society.

There are recent inspirational arguments for innovative pedagogical changes in higher education towards educating the whole person, combining the development of critical and analytical abilities with a sense of moral purpose and social responsibility in contributing as citizens of the world (Dall'Alba, 2009b; Evans, 2009; Faust, 2009; Kezar, Chambers, & Burkhardt, 2005; Sullivan & Rosin, 2008; Walker, 2006). Empirical research undertaken by Melanie Walker (2009) and colleagues is developing such arguments into feasible propositions for change in professional education of different professions, from lawyers to social workers, with the aim of having a potential impact on poverty reduction.

Such worthwhile educational goals need to be accompanied by changes in the way that professionals are supported to continue learning, once they have graduated and are in the workplace. Not only would such a move reinforce admirable goals of higher education, but it could make the promise of professionalism, discussed in Chapter 2, a more achievable proposition (see Freidson, 2001; Sullivan, 1995). In sustaining outcomes of undergraduate education, it is important that the capabilities to be developed in undergraduates are reflected in the actions of academics and working professionals who guide, teach and provide role models for students of the vagaries and virtues of professional life. That is, if the continuing learning of academics and other practicing professionals is directed towards similar aims, these professionals could continue to develop their capabilities to make nuanced, ethical – even wise – professional judgements, thereby facilitating the same process in the following generation.

Collaboration between research into the education of professionals and research into their continuing workplace learning can be a fruitful area for exchange. Drawing on research from this book, for example, practitioners generally felt unprepared for the decisions of practice. A useful way to make connections between education and practice in undergraduate courses can be through work-based learning (Boud & Solomon, 2001). Community-based service learning is another way that

groups of practitioners, in collaboration with universities, can work with communities on issues of social concern (Hyland & Meacham, 2004; Madden, 2000; Oakes,
Rogers, & Lipton, 2006). Such collaborations can reinforce the need for discussions
between students, practitioners and educators about the realities of practice, within
a rigorous critique of the assumption of certainty in the human sciences. The need
to stand back from practice and pose questions as a continuing process of inquiry
needs to be reinforced throughout professional education.

In this changing world where innovation and creativity are becoming increasingly valued as a way of resolving complex societal problems, more interdisciplinary and inter-professional approaches to researching and supporting professional practice and learning are required (Klein, 2001). In a debate on interdisciplinarity, Steve Fuller (2003) describes academic disciplines as "holding patterns
of inquiry". A similar comment could be made about professional "silos" (Margalit
et al., 2009). A breadth of vision across disciplinary and professional boundaries
is useful in making interconnections between different perspectives. In viewing the
perspective of other disciplines, harmony is not always sought. As with any genuine
dialogue, different ways of dealing with issues can be respected whilst queried. New
ways of considering learning may arise from such a "cacophony" of harmony and
dissonance between perspectives (Gherardi & Nicolini, 2002).

## 9.4  Understanding Authentic Professional Learning

To investigate the lived experience of learning as a professional rather than an aggregate of factors in developing the professional leads to a different understanding of
continuing learning. By grasping experience as "a whole that does not reduce itself
to the sum of the parts" Merleau-Ponty (1968, p. 205) argues against breaking experience down into components. In most discussions about PD the manifestly multiple
aspects of learning are separated, although often acknowledged as linked. For too
long, we have talked and undertaken research into PD as if such separation reflects
the reality of learning as a practicing professional. Conceptualising APL in a holistic way as an expression of a way of being-a-professional-in-the-professional-world
allows new insights into problems with, and support for, learning.

Despite the value of professional knowledge and skills to organisations and to
society, it must be remembered that professionals are human beings, not resources.
Their learning reflects their being. Integral to how professionals practice and learn
to change is their idiosyncratic way of being professional, encompassing all they
are, what they value, know and can do. Learning that leads to sustainable change
involves understanding, caring about and meaning making. Through continuing
to inquire, professionals may find meaning and satisfaction as well as produce
outcomes for society. They may even develop their "*authentic* potential-for-being-
a-whole" (Heidegger, 1927/1962, p. 348).

Dilemmas in professional working lives often revolve around what I describe
as competing life-world discourses. Tensions between performativity and meaning,
instrumental ends and humanistic concerns, regulation and innovation, or standards

and ethics have been referred to through this book. Although tensions between these discourses are increasingly referred to in philosophy, social theory, empirical research and popular literature, thinking in oppositional dichotomous terms does not advance the situation in any productive way. The world needs instrumental ends: buildings built, sick people operated on, complex software developed. But we also need to honour the humanity of professional "being". Certainly, the impact of underlying tensions on professional life needs to be discussed. However, a productive way forward in dealing with dilemmas may require different ways of thinking.

A dialectic consideration of tensions proposes relationships between apparently opposing elements by considering them as part of a whole, in which these relationships continuously change and influence each other. Examples of such thinking include the western hermeneutic circle or eastern notions of the Tao. I have attempted to bring a dialectic consideration to tensions in professional life and learning such as accountability and agency. Ian Stronbach and colleagues (Stronach, Corbin, McNamara, Stark, & Warne, 2002, p. 130) in referring to similar irresolvable tensions in professional life suggest the need to develop more nuanced ways of considering performance from within the wholeness of practice, by developing, for example, a new "narrative ethics" of professionalism.

The rich and varied manner in which professionals continue to learn cannot be denied, standardised or controlled. Instead, in acknowledging and valuing learning as lived by professionals, we may develop insights and innovative approaches to support such learning in a way that is productive and beneficial for the professionals and meets the needs of society. To change support for the continuing growth of professionals and renewal of their practices, assumptions underpinning traditional PD need to be explicitly challenged, drawing on research investigating what it means to be a professional, learning and working in contemporary society. Professionals need to be encouraged to speak out and share their everyday realities, and their perspective must be valued. In working together, professionals, managers, researchers and policy makers can devise ways of practice that meet local needs with an eye to making a difference in terms of the wider public good.

It is time to progress from situations where professionals may feel undervalued or unsupported in facing dilemmas in working life that result in stress, uneasiness or dissatisfaction (Ball, 2003; Dollard, Winefield, & Winefield, 2003; Faragher, Cass, & Cooper, 2005; Williams, Pocock, & Skinner, 2008). As discussed in Chapter 2, the first decade of the new millennium has brought tumultuous change to many sectors of society. Taylor (2007, p. 473) examines changes during the past half century, since what he calls the "hinge moment" of the late 1960s. He notes the move towards individual ego development and unsustainable economic growth since then, focusing on changes in the "understandings of human life, agency, and the good which both encourage this new... individuation, and also make us morally uneasy about it" (p. 474). Taylor argues that what has emerged is a "real" value shift in the west in the last half of the twentieth century, leading to a current collective awareness of global issues, respect for ideals of fairness and a continued press for concerns of social justice (p. 484).

We must be able to imagine possibilities for change to occur. Sartre (1940/2004) describes imagination as crucial to the freedom to act. That is, imagination not only opens up possibilities but also suggests action. Yet there is always a tension between possibility and reality regarding what is feasible. Many suggestions in this book could be viewed as idealistic. The argument might be made that if we can't make professionals learn, then how could we ever make them reflective, capable, wise, ethical or innovative. The obvious answer is that we cannot. We need to begin from empirical research into practice. Both evidence and experience indicate that the vast majority of professionals are capable, intelligent and conscientious, rather than misanthropic charlatans who cannot be trusted. Certainly, there are issues to be addressed in supporting increased reflexivity and inquiry in professional life. I have repeatedly stressed that change is not easy. It is possible, however, that with support professionals can rise to meet such challenges, if they see some relevant purpose in change. In describing "vocabularies of hope" as "openness to the future" James Ludema (Ludema, Wilmot, & Srivastva, 1997, p. 1034) and colleagues note that hope does not deal with situations that "'have no place' but in situations that 'have no place as yet,' but could acquire one".

My challenge has been to present an alternative to the current professional and educational discourse that speaks from the heart of lived experience, through the rigour of established research approaches, drawing on philosophical notions resonant with that experience. The book has aimed to make a contribution to research and practice in the area of continuing learning, adding to an ongoing dialogue about professional practice in contemporary contexts. Merleau-Ponty muses that phenomenological philosophy is characterised by "both a taste for evidence and a feeling for ambiguity" (Moran, 2000, p. 400). My intent for the book mirrors his statement. I set out to understand more about the continuing learning of professionals. Through this journey, I came to understand more about my own assumptions and values as a professional researcher. In addition, I hope I have given voice to what is often not said, except in staff tea-rooms between trusted colleagues. The book ends, as it began, with the voice of one of the participants, Gina, reflecting on her day at work. It serves as a reminder of the rich messy life of practicing professionals who continue to learn.

## 9.5 Reflections on the Day

### *9.5.1 In the Car*

It was chaos at home this morning. Mornings are always rushed, but it's harder with John away. It's not that I can't cope, but without his help little things fall through the cracks – like we ran out of milk before we'd all had cereal and Isabella left the house in tears because I didn't have time to find an explorer outfit. What did explorers wear anyway? Just wear some old clothes I told her, after reminding her that telling me the morning she needed them was too late. The general mood wasn't helped by her brothers teasing her in the car.

Once I'd dropped them off I could take a deep breath and clear my head to think about the day ahead. I remembered that the researcher was coming in today, but I forgot yesterday to change that meeting with the De Faza family. When we stopped for two changes of lights, I wrote a reminder note on my hand. It's amazing how much worse the traffic is when I'm just a little bit late leaving home.

I wonder what the researcher, I think her name was Ann something, wants from me. Maybe it's to check up on my PD points. I know the registration board said there were going to be random audits for PD plans –maybe that's it. She says she just wants to chat about how I learn. I don't think I've got very much of interest to talk about. What was the last workshop I went to? Maybe I'll get the journal out and put it on the desk to make it look as if I'm reading it. That should impress her.

Alright, now I've got half an hour before she gets here and the playgroup starts. Liz and I can get the equipment out as Penny's away today and anyway, not being a therapist, she sometimes misunderstands what we want to achieve and sets up the play area differently. As I walk into my building I notice yet again how run down it looks. I guess aesthetics are the least of the Department's worries.

## 9.5.2 At Lunch Time

Oh well the morning went OK. Why did I have to start the conversation with Ann by talking about having to get the insects out of the sandpit before the families came because the cover was torn. That made us look unprofessional. I wonder if there's a workplace health ruling about sandpits. Once I knew she had nothing to do with audits I could relax, but I don't know what she got out of being there all morning. It was just a standard day – some kids sick, some parents needing to talk about crises, some ideas I had about what to do with certain kids and what might work better. And that joke when we had the birthday cake at morning tea. That was very politically incorrect – it's just that sometimes to survive working with the everyday dramas of disability, humour seems to help. It holds us together.

I really enjoyed being interviewed. It seemed like luxury to take the time to think about my experience as a therapist, and she seemed really interested in my stories. It reminded me that I do love most of what I do at work. I really feel that most of the time I'm making some sort of difference to the lives of the kids and their families. I get a real kick out of the breakthroughs that happen and feel just as good if it happens with one of my colleagues. We're all in it together here. Sometimes it seems that I'm not being a real therapist when I focus on what the family says they need right now, but I know in my heart that some of the things I used to expect a family to do as a therapy programme for their child were totally unrealistic. I've learnt that through having kids of my own and juggling the parts of an everyday working life.

I'm glad the first appointment after lunch was cancelled. I had time to finally get to my email. At last there's a positive response about my request from my manager. She doesn't really understand what we do here and I think that makes her a bit defensive. Maybe there's is a change in the wind after all. When we were told by our last manager that the real job of a public servant was to protect the minister, I felt angry. It seemed wrong that despite the department stating so nicely in its coloured glossy folders that our priority is always to the kids, we sometimes have to waste so much time doing irrelevant admin. I suppose I got my shoulders set, so maybe I haven't given this new manager a fair go.

### 9.5.3 In the Car

Ah, the day is over, well the paid part of it anyway. In the individual sessions after lunch, it's always a good time to talk to parents and ask about what they want. It's a bit slower in the afternoons, but often not a good time for the kids as they're tired. I wanted to try out that new approach I heard about in the course last weekend, but little Sam was too distracted. Maybe next time. Oh no, I didn't finish that report, either! Even though I feel like I'm running as fast as I can, it seems I can never get everything done.

Anyway I can't dwell on that now, I'm running late to get Isabella from childcare and it's triple the cost after six. It's not fair on my own family if I take work home in my head. It creeps in during the night sometimes, though. A good idea pops up and I think where did that come from? Maybe it's the peace and quiet when I'm lying in bed in the dead of the night. I should have told Ann about that. . . . I mustn't forget to buy the milk.

## References

Adorno, T. W. (1973). *The jargon of authenticity* (K. Tarnowski & F. Will, Trans.). London: Routledge and Kegan Paul.

Ball, S. J. (2003). The teacher's soul and the terrors of performativity. *Journal of Education Policy, 18*(2), 215–228.

Boud, D., & Solomon, N. (Eds.). (2001). *Work-based learning: A new higher education?* Philadelphia, PA: Society for Research into Higher Education & Open University Press.

Coffield, F. (2007). *Running ever faster down the wrong road: An alternative future for Education and Skills.* London: Institute of Education, University of London.

Dall'Alba, G. (2009a). Learning professional ways of being: Ambiguities of becoming. *Educational Philosophy and Theory, 41*(1), 34–45.

Dall'Alba, G. (2009b). *Learning to be professionals.* Dortrecht: Springer.

Dollard, M. F., Winefield, A. H., & Winefield, H. R. (2003). *Occupational stress in the service professions.* London; New York: Taylor & Francis.

Dreyfus, H. L. (2000). Could anything be more intelligible than everyday intelligibility? Reinterpreting Division I of Being and Time in the light of Division II. *Appropriating Heidegger.* Retrieved February 12, 2005, from http://ist-socrates.berkeley.edu/~hdreyfus/html/papers.html

Evans, W. (2009). Iris Murdoch, liberal education and human flourishing. *Journal of Philosophy of Education, 43*(1), 75–84.

Faragher, E. B., Cass, M., & Cooper, C. L. (2005). The relationship between job satisfaction and health: A meta-analysis. *Occupational and Environmental Medicine, 62*, 105–112.

Faust, D. G. (2009). *President's address to Harvard University.* Retrieved November 12, 2009, from http://www.president.harvard.edu/speeches/faust/090924_openyear.php

Ferrara, A. (1998). *Reflective authenticity: Rethinking the project of modernity.* London; New York: Routledge.

Freidson, E. (2001). *Professionalism: The third logic.* Chicago: University of Chicago Press.

Fuller, S. (2003). *Interdisciplinarity: The loss of the heroic vision in the marketplace of ideas.* Retrieved August 2, 2005, from http://www.interdisciplines.org/interdisciplinarity/papers/3/version/original

Garrick, J. (2000). The construction of 'working knowledge' and (mis)interpretive research. In J. Garrick & C. Rhodes (Eds.), *Research and knowledge at work: Perspectives, case-studies and innovative strategies* (pp. 203–216). London; New York: Routledge.

Geniusas, S. (2009). Ethics as a second philosophy, or the traces of the pre-ethical in Heidegger's Being and Time. *Santalka Filosofija, 17*(3), 62–69. Retrieved October 10, 2009, from www.coactivity.vgtu.lt/.../62-70_santalka_2009_3_geniusas.pdf

Gherardi, S., & Nicolini, D. (2002). Learning in a constellation of interconnected practices: Canon or dissonance? *Journal of Management Studies, 39*(4), 419–437.

Groundwater-Smith, S., & Mockler, N. (2009). *Teacher professional learning in an age of compliance: Mind the gap.* Dordrecht: Springer.

Guignon, C. B. (2004). *On being authentic.* London; New York: Routledge.

Hager, P., & Halliday, J. (2006). *Recovering informal learning: Wisdom, judgement and community.* Dordrecht: Springer.

Heidegger, M. (1927/1962). *Being and time* (J. Macquarrie & E. Robinson, Trans., 1st English ed.). London: SCM Press.

Heidegger, M. (1963). Preface. In W. P. Richardson (Ed.), *Heidegger: Through phenomenology to thought* (pp. vii–xxii). The Hague: M. Nijhoff.

Higgs, J., & Titchen, A. (2001). Framing professional practice: Knowing and doing in context. In J. Higgs & A. Titchen (Eds.), *Professional practice in health, education and the creative arts* (pp. 3–15). Oxford: Blackwell Science.

Houle, C. O. (1980). *Continuing learning in the professions.* San Francisco: Jossey-Bass Publishers.

Hoyle, E., & Wallace, M. (2007). Educational reform: An ironic perspective. *Educational Management Administration Leadership, 35*(1), 9–25.

Hyland, N. E., & Meacham, S. (2004). Community knowledge-centred teacher education: A paradigm for socially just educational transformation. In J. L. Kincheloe, A. Bursztyn, & S. R. Steinberg (Eds.), *Teaching teachers: Building a quality school of urban education* (pp. 113–134). New York: Peter Lang.

Inwood, M. J. (2000). *Heidegger: A very short introduction.* Oxford; New York: Oxford University Press.

Irigaray, L. (1999). *The forgetting of air in Martin Heidegger.* London: Athlone.

Joas, H. (2000). *The genesis of values.* Cambridge: Polity Press.

Kezar, A. J., Chambers, T. C., & Burkhardt, J. (2005). *Higher education for the public good: Emerging voices from a national movement.* San Francisco: Jossey-Bass.

Klein, J. T. (2001). *Transdisciplinarity: Joint problem solving among science, technology, and society: An effective way for managing complexity.* Basel; Boston: Birkhäuser Verlag.

Ludema, J. D., Wilmot, T. B., & Srivastva, S (1997). Organizational hope: Reaffirming the constructive task of social and organizational inquiry. *Human Relations, 50*(8), 1015–1052.

Madden, S. J. (Ed.). (2000). *Service learning across the curriculum: Case applications in higher education.* Lanham, MD: University Press of America.

Margalit, R., Thompson, S., Visovsky, C., Geske, J., Collier, D., Birk, T., et al. (2009). From professional silos to interprofessional education: Campuswide focus on quality of care. *Quality Management in Health Care, 18*(3), 165–173.

Merleau-Ponty, M. (1968). The visible and the invisible (A. Lingis, Trans.). In C. Lefort (Ed.), *The visible and the invisible: Followed by working notes.* Evanston, IL: Northwestern University Press.

Moran, D. (2000). *Introduction to phenomenology.* London; New York: Routledge.

Nicholson, G. (2009). *Justifying our existence: An essay in applied phenomenology*. Toronto, ON: University of Toronto Press.

Oakes, J., Rogers, J., & Lipton, M. (2006). *Learning power: Organizing for education and justice*. New York: Teachers College Press.

O'Neil, O. (2002). A question of trust: Called to account. *Lecture 3*, from http://www.bbc.co.uk/radio4/reith2002/

Penuel, W. R., Fishman, B. J., Yamaguchi, R., & Gallagher, L. P. (2007). What makes professional development effective? Strategies that foster curriculum implementation. *American Educational Research Journal, 44*(4), 921–958.

Prilleltensky, I., & Prilleltensky, O. (2006). *Promoting well-being: Linking personal, organizational, and community change*. Hoboken, NJ: Wiley.

Rose, G. (1996). *Mourning becomes the law: Philosophy and representation*. Cambridge, MA; New York: Cambridge University Press.

Russell, B. (1912/1998). *The problems of philosophy* (2nd ed.). Oxford; New York: Oxford University Press.

Sartre, J. P. (1940/2004). *The imaginary: A phenomenological psychology of the imagination* (J. Webber, Trans.). London: Routledge.

Sartre, J. P. (1943/1989). *Being and nothingness: An essay on phenomenological ontology* (H. Barnes, Trans.). London: Routledge.

Sen, A. K. (1992). *Inequality reexamined*. New York: Russell Sage Foundation; Oxford: Clarendon Press.

Sen, A. K. (2009). *The idea of justice*. London; New York: Allen Lane/Penguin Books.

Silverman, D. (2005). *Doing qualitative research: A practical handbook* (2nd ed.). London: Sage Publications.

Stenstad, G. (2006). *Transformations: Thinking after Heidegger*. Madison, WS: University of Wisconsin Press.

Stronach, I., Corbin, B., McNamara, O., Stark, S., & Warne, T. (2002). Towards an uncertain politics of professionalism: Teacher and nurse identities in flux. *Journal of Education Policy, 17*(1), 109–138.

Sullivan, W. M. (1995). *Work and integrity: The crisis and promise of professionalism in America*. New York: HarperCollins.

Sullivan, W. M., & Rosin, M. S. (2008). *A new agenda for higher education: Shaping a life of the mind for practice*. San Francisco: Jossey-Bass; Carnegie Foundation for the Advancement of Teaching.

Taylor, C. (1992). *The ethics of authenticity*. Cambridge, MA: Harvard University Press.

Taylor, C. (2007). *A secular age*. Cambridge, MA: Belknap Press of Harvard University Press.

van Manen, M. (1997). *Researching lived experience: Human science for an action sensitive pedagogy* (2nd ed.). London; ON: Althouse Press; University of Western Ontario.

Walker, M. (2006). *Higher education pedagogies: A capabilities approach*. England: Open University Press.

Walker, M. (2009). *Development discourses: Higher Education and poverty reduction in South Africa*. Retrieved November 12, 2009, from http://www.nottingham.ac.uk/EducationResearchProjects/DevelopmentDiscourses/PapersandResources.aspx

Williams, P., Pocock, B., & Skinner, N. (2008). "Clawing back time": Expansive working time and implications for work life outcomes in Australian workers. *Work Employment and Society, 22*(4), 737–748.

Wilson, A. (2000). Professional practice in the modern world. In V. W. Mott & B. J. Daley (Eds.), *Charting a course for continuing professional education: Reframing professional practice* (Vol. 86, pp. 71–79). San Francisco: Jossey-Bass.

Wolin, R. (1993). *The Heidegger controversy: A critical reader*. Cambridge, MA: MIT Press.

Zickmund, S. (2007). Deliberation, phronesis, and authenticity: Heidegger's early conception of rhetoric. *Philosophy and Rhetoric, 40*(4), 406–415.

# Index

Lightning Source UK Ltd.
Milton Keynes UK
UKOW04n2119020514

231004UK00016B/312/P